Data-Driven Modeling

Scrivener Publishing
100 Cummings Center, Suite 541J
Beverly, MA 01915-6106

Publishers at Scrivener
Martin Scrivener (martin@scrivenerpublishing.com)
Phillip Carmical (pcarmical@scrivenerpublishing.com)

Data-Driven Modeling

Edited by

Arindam Mondal

and

Souvik Ganguli

Scrivener Publishing

WILEY

This edition first published 2026 by John Wiley & Sons, Inc., 111 River Street, Hoboken, NJ 07030, USA and Scrivener Publishing LLC, 100 Cummings Center, Suite 541J, Beverly, MA 01915, USA

For more information about Scrivener publications please visit www.scrivenerpublishing.com.

Wiley Global Headquarters
111 River Street, Hoboken, NJ 07030, USA

For details of our global editorial offices, customer services, and more information about Wiley products visit us at www.wiley.com.

The manufacturer's authorized representative according to the EU General Product Safety Regulation is Wiley-VCH GmbH, Boschstr. 12, 69469 Weinheim, Germany, e-mail: Product_Safety@wiley.com.

Library of Congress Cataloging-in-Publication Data

ISBN 9781394287895

Front cover images supplied by Pixabay.com
Cover design by Russell Richardson

Set in size of 11pt and Minion Pro by Manila Typesetting Company, Makati, Philippines

Printed in the USA

10 9 8 7 6 5 4 3 2 1

Contents

Preface

The rapid expansion of data generation across scientific, industrial, and social domains has redefined how systems are modeled, analysed, and controlled. Traditional modeling approaches, once reliant on fixed analytical formulations, are now being complemented—and often surpassed—by *data-driven models* that learn directly from empirical evidence. This evolution has not only revolutionized how we perceive complex systems but also how we optimize, predict, and control them in real-world environments.

The book *Data-Driven Modeling* brings together a diverse set of perspectives and methods to bridge the gap between theoretical modeling and data-centric intelligence. It is a collaborative work by researchers and practitioners committed to advancing the frontiers of intelligent, explainable, and adaptive systems. The chapters cover foundational theory, methodological innovations, and applied insights from multiple disciplines, forming a coherent narrative from fundamentals to advanced techniques.

Chapter 1, *Fundamentals of Data Analysis and Preprocessing* sets the stage by discussing the critical importance of data preparation—covering data cleaning, integration, transformation, reduction, and discretization—and their collective role in ensuring robust modeling outcomes. The chapter underscores that quality data is the cornerstone of meaningful analysis and reliable decision-making.

Chapter 2, *Advanced Data Control Methods for Data-Driven Modeling* introduces modern approaches to data governance, decentralized control, privacy preservation, and federated data architectures. It explores how data control and adaptive regulation form the backbone of reliable, secure, and scalable modeling in domains such as healthcare, finance, and smart grids.

Chapter 3 provides a lucid exposition on *Machine Learning Algorithms* for Data-Driven Modeling, highlighting supervised, unsupervised, and reinforcement learning paradigms and their applications in classification, clustering, and predictive analysis.

Chapter 4, *Neural Networks and Deep Learning in Data-Driven Modeling*, delves into advanced neural architectures, including CNNs, RNNs, GANs, and attention mechanisms. It emphasizes their role in solving complex problems such as image recognition, NLP, time-series forecasting, and anomaly detection.

Chapter 5 advances the discussion into *Time-Series Analysis* for predictive forecasting—introducing classical models such as ARIMA and state-space approaches, and emerging deep-learning-based methods for dynamic systems prediction.

Chapters 6 and 7 bring the theory into *Agricultural Applications*, demonstrating how ensemble learning (Random Forests, Gradient Boosting, XGBoost) and AI-enabled decision systems can revolutionize smart and sustainable farming, particularly for Solanaceae crops.

Chapter 8, *Dynamic Multitask Transfer Learning*, discusses adaptive feature sharing and continual learning frameworks—critical for evolving data ecosystems where model reuse and cross-domain generalization are essential.

Chapter 9 applies data-driven forecasting techniques such as ARIMA to the renewable energy domain, illustrating *Solar Power Generation Prediction* and the transformation of non-stationary data into actionable insights.

Chapter 10, *Prognosticating Plays*, explores a fascinating application of hybrid Artificial Neural Network–Fuzzy Inference Systems (ANFIS) in sports analytics for dynamic score prediction and strategic modeling.

Chapters 11 and 12 showcase the intersection of control theory and machine learning through *PID Controller Design and Data-Driven Recognition in Nonlinear Systems*, integrating gradient-based optimization and intelligent modeling.

Chapter 13, *Temporal Resilience Redux* concludes the book with deep learning applications for *short-term load forecasting* using bidirectional LSTM architectures—demonstrating how temporal networks capture dynamic dependencies for precise energy demand estimation.

Across these chapters, readers will find not only state-of-the-art methodologies but also conceptual clarity and practical guidance on how to implement data-driven paradigms in diverse sectors—from autonomous vehicles and industrial control to agriculture, finance, and renewable energy systems. The editors have consciously designed the book to transition smoothly from fundamental principles to complex, cross-disciplinary applications, reflecting the true continuum of data-driven research.

The editors envision *Data-Driven Modeling* as both an academic reference and a practical compendium for engineers, data scientists, and researchers aiming to bridge the divide between data collection and intelligent decision-making. It is our hope that this volume will inspire readers to approach data not merely as numbers, but as the language through which systems communicate their behavior—awaiting interpretation, understanding, and innovation.

Arindam Mondal
Souvik Ganguli
Editors

1

Fundamentals of Data Analysis and Preprocessing

Sudipta Hazra[1]* and Arindam Mondal[2]

[1]*MCKV Institute of Engineering, Howrah, West Bengal, India*
[2]*Dr. B. C. Roy Engineering College, Durgapur, West Bengal, India*

Abstract
The general structure for data curation was proposed in this chapter. It covers the many stages of preparation and preprocessing for data. Many other datasets can be fitted by the overall framework that is described. Raw data that have not been cleaned and curated are typically unsuitable for drawing accurate conclusions. Within the topic of data curation and preparation, the most widely used algorithms and strategies are covered in detail in this chapter. The methodology for data curation, imputation, feature extraction, correlation analysis, and real-world implementation of these algorithms is covered in this chapter's framework. We also offered methods that we have created based on our data processing skills. Lastly, we demonstrated with a real-world example how applying various imputation techniques affects support vector machine efficiency and performance. The chapter outlines a process for taking unstructured, unprocessed data and turning it into well-organized data that may be used with sophisticated machine learning algorithms or other advanced data analysis techniques.

Keywords: Data analysis, data preprocessing, data mining

1.1 Introduction

Research in a wide range of disciplines, including science, engineering, management, and process control, starts with data analysis (DA). Symbolic and numeric attributes are used to collect data about a certain topic.

**Corresponding author*: sudiptahazra.nitdgp@gmail.com

Arindam Mondal and Souvik Ganguli (eds.) Data-Driven Modeling, (1–22) © 2026 Scrivener Publishing LLC

These data come from a variety of sources, including sensors and people, all with varying levels of complexity and dependability. A deeper comprehension of the relevant phenomenon results from the analysis of these data. Therefore, the primary goal of any DA is to find information that may be applied to decision-making or problem-solving [1]. Problems with the data, though, might make this impossible. Most of the time, data errors are not detected until the DA phase appears. For instance, DA is carried out in the creation of knowledge-based systems in order to find and produce new facts for assembling a trustworthy and extensive facts base. Therefore, the data determine the dependability of the knowledge base's section created using DA techniques such as induction.

Numerous efforts are being fabricated to either develop an analysis tool or use commercially available solutions for DA. A few initiatives have disregarded the reality that real-world data often have issues and that preparing the data in some way is typically necessary before doing an effective analysis of the data. This means that data preparation features should be available in research or commercial tools so that they can be utilized either before to or throughout the real DA procedure. Data preparation may have multiple goals. Apart from addressing data issues such as tainted data and absent or irrelevant attributes in datasets, there is a chance that someone would also like to know more about the type of data or alter its structure (such as granularity levels) to make it more suitable for a more effective DA.

Authors draw a similar parallel between human information processing and data preprocessing (DP): "Think about the information processing mechanism used by humans" [2]. Through the sense organs, sensory signals are received and processed. The initial phases of analysis are carried out by low level computing structures, after which the data are sent to other processing structures. Events or concepts can be used to drive the processing system. Whereas conceptually driven processing is usually reverse of bottom-up, propelled by objectives, motives, and appropriate data into prospect, processing based on events usually works from the bottom up, looking for structures in which to integrate the input.

Numerous justifications have been offered for the function of and necessity for DP. When it comes to modeling, the desired information can be combined with variations in the data that result from modifications in progression or system circumstances, furthermore in the gathering and transfer of data. These impacts can be avoided in advance with appropriate DP, leading to more frugal models. Although they might not be more accurate predictors, these models should be more reliable [3]. Therefore, fewer phenomena would need to be represented as a result of data preparation, but estimating errors might potentially contribute to an increase in variance. When it comes to learning, data pretreatment would enable users to choose which ideas to learn, how to show the DA results, and how to represent the data in a way that makes them easier to understand and use in the real world.

Preprocessing is typically the primary action performed on any batch of data. DP takes a lot of time and is frequently semiautomated. Effective methods for automatic DP are crucial because the volume of data generated by contemporary process supervision and data collecting systems is increasing and necessitating greater data processing [4]. In this study, we want to address common data-related issues, strategies for resolving them, and the advantages of using these approaches for data pretreatment.

1.2 Data Preprocessing

DP is the act of merely transforming raw data into a form that can be understood. Real-world data are not always complete, consistent, noisy, or redundant. Data preparation comprises several steps that help to organize raw data into a logical format. The Figure 1.1 below illustrates the many stages of data preparation.

Data cleaning: Data cleansing is the process of locating incorrect and corrupt records in a record set or database table. Finding inconsistent, erroneous, incomplete, and irrelevant data is the main goal of the cleaning process, after which techniques are applied to either update or eliminate it.

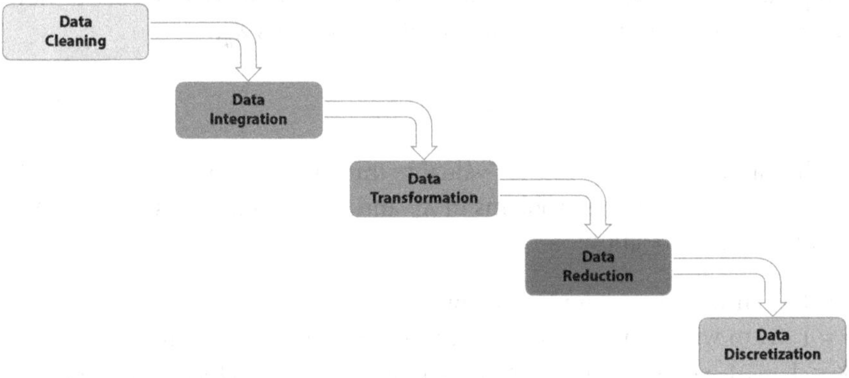

Figure 1.1 Steps in DP.

Data integration: The primary objectives of data integration are to unify data from many sources and show it in a coherent way. All disputes resulting from merging data with different representations are resolved. This process is crucial because of its many industrial and scientific applications. The importance of data integration increases with the amount and exponential growth of data.
Data transformation: In order to change raw data into a form that can be understood, data transformation is essential. It is made up of generalization, aggregation, and data normalization. Data normalization facilitates the organization of a database's tables and columns to reduce redundancy. This reduces the complexity and processing time. For a quicker overview, data aggregation aids in the creation of a concise summary. Another name for the process of generalizing data is rolling up data. It facilitates the generalization of data and builds assessment databases with various levels of summary.
Data reduction: The practice of organizing and simplifying digital information is known as data reduction. Most of the time, empirical and experimental methods are used to obtain these data. It entails breaking up massive volumes of data into more manageable and insightful pieces.
Data discretization: In situations where you want to classify a lot of numerical data using only nominal values, the idea of data discretization is crucial. The continuous data in this case are divided into discrete forms, and the nominal value is defined as the values of these discrete sets. In essence, it is the process of transferring continuous data properties with the least amount of information loss into a defined collection of intervals.

Everything done before the real DA process begins is known as data preparation. In essence, it is a transformation T that creates a set of new data vectors Y_{ij} from the raw real-world data vectors X_{ik}.

$$Y_{ij} = T\,(X_{ik}) \tag{1.1}$$

such that: (i) Y_{ij} preserves the "valuable information" in X_{ik}, (ii) Y_{ij} eliminates at least one of the problems in X_{ik} and (iii) Y_{ij} is more useful than X_{ik}.

In the above relation:

$i = 1, \ldots n$ where n = number of objects,
$j = 1, \ldots m$ where m = number of features after preprocessing,
$k = 1, \ldots l$ where l = number of attributes/features before preprocessing,
and in general, $m \neq l$.

Finding and presenting important facts, such as meaningful patterns in the data, are the aims of DA. Valuable information is knowledge that exists in the data. Four characteristics are defined for meaningful information [5]. These are legitimate, unique, possibly helpful, and finally intelligible. Data difficulties are circumstances that make it difficult to utilize any DA tool effectively or that could lead to outcomes that are not acceptable. Preprocessing data can be done for a number of reasons, including resolving issues with the data that might make it impossible to analyze it in any way, comprehending the character of the data and conducting a more insightful analysis, and deriving deeper insights from a particular set of data. The majority of applications requires more than one type of data preparation. Determining the kind of preprocessing for data is consequently an essential responsibility.

1.2.1 Issues with Data

The real-world data are seldom without issues. The easiest way to display these is in Figure 1.2, which is also covered below. Problems can vary greatly in nature and severity for a variety of causes, some of which are outside the control of human operators. Our worry is from how these issues affect the DA outcomes; our objective is to either identify or address data problems in advance of their impact or as they arise. Three categories of data difficulties can be distinguished: too little, fractured, and too much data. These will be covered in the following sections.

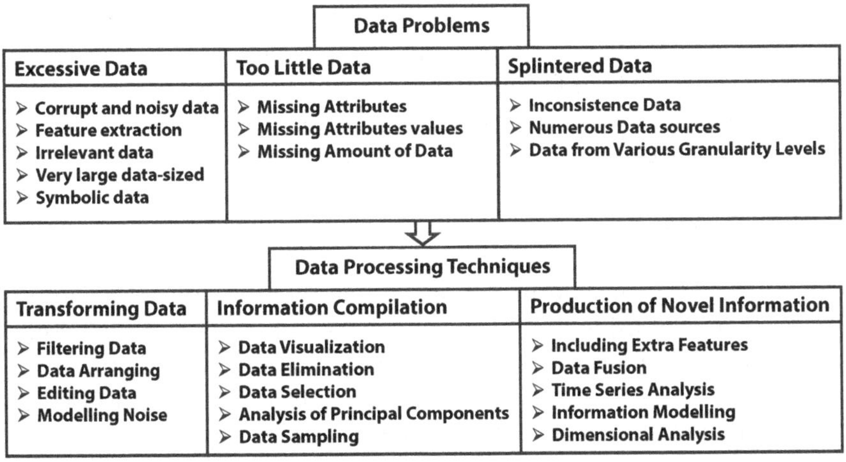

Figure 1.2 Data problems and DP steps.

1.2.1.1 Excessive Data

Corrupt and noisy data: Many of these causes may not have been known at the time of data assortment, but corrupt data can result from things such as poor data input, data transmission, or sensor failure. Several factors can be responsible for noise in the data:

- intrinsic factors, such as those of the systems or processes from which the data are gathered;
- data measurement or transmission faults.

Whatever the cause, noise and corruption in the data must be accurately detected, and appropriate solutions must be developed to address the issue. Generally speaking, data noise would reduce the features' capacity to forecast. Datasets can range from being totally noise-free to being slightly noisy, depending on the application. Conversely, datasets that appear noisy when viewed alone may be extremely prognostic and noise-free when visualized.

Feature extraction: Even though there may be hundreds of measurements in intricate online DA applications such as uses for pulp and paper, only a small number of events may actually be happening. Therefore, it is necessary to transfer the data from these measurements into descriptive descriptions of the event or events. Without the right tools for data pretreatment, this is a challenging task. In order to provide faster feature extraction and higher resolution in the future, preprocessing the data for correct interpretation is a form of feature extraction [6]. Numerical–symbolic interpretation, which maps numerical data from a process into meaningful labels, is an example of feature extraction. The boundary of the problem is established in reverse order from the label of interest, allowing feature extraction to be connected solely to the input needs necessary for producing the label.

Irrelevant data: Meaningful data must be extracted from massive data volumes for many DA applications. When humans are involved, they choose the pertinent information by concentrating on important details and occasionally using the remaining data simply to confirm or resolve uncertainties. Examples of situations where the ability to retrieve relevant information is essential from raw data are online expert systems used for DA [7]. Removing unnecessary data mostly serves to reduce the search space in DA. If superfluous data are removed and only the max pertinent aspects are used for DA, complexity may be greatly decreased. Because more training examples are required to attain a specified error rate, the effectiveness of a DA tool may be enhanced by reducing dimensionality (by removing unnecessary data).

Very large data sizes: Performing on-time DA may be hampered in many fields, including space (picture data, for example) and telecommunications (massive network operations), by the amount and rate of data production. Sometimes the amount of data exceeds the capacity of the DA tools and technology that are currently on the market. For instance, deciphering data from remote sensing devices necessitates costly, specialized computing equipment that can swiftly store and process vast volumes of data.

Symbolic data: Two forms of data are often available when data are organized for analysis:

- Numerical data, which come from measuring parameters that have a numerical representation. Numerical information might be continuous or discontinuous.
- Data that are categorical or symbolic that come from assessing system or process attributes.

DA with both numerical and emblematic parameters is a challenging undertaking that needs careful consideration during pretreatment of data and appropriate tool usage.

1.2.1.2 Too Little Data

Missing attribute: Examples of data issues include missing or insufficient attributes, which can make DA tasks more difficult, including learning, and make it more difficult for most DA systems to operate accurately. For instance, in the context of learning, these data deficiencies restrict accuracy on any stat-tools or algorithm used on the gathered data, regardless of the method's complexity or volume of data used. On the other hand, incorrect sensor measurements or issues with data conversion or transmission could cause the data to appear great at first glance but be out of range [8]. Out-of-range data can be filtered using data range tables and are accessible to the majority of factory management software systems.

A number of issues arise from missing or corrupted characteristics. The two examples that follow center on orientation as the method of DA:

Missing attributes in decision tree training result in unequal-length vectors. When comparing the information values of the two vectors that represent two qualities or testing the values of an attribute, this leads to a bias.

Dividing the data into training and testing sets is a common practice in DA applications. Even though the splitting procedure could be repeated multiple times, incomplete qualities could lead to an incorrect assessment of the outcome.

Missing attributes values: In this instance, several of the data records lack attributes values, making them incomplete. These data records cannot be removed because, even though there might not be enough data overall, the data record's remaining values may contain extremely valuable information. Usually, a record is deleted if more than 20% of its attribute data are missing.

Small amount of data: In this instance, the primary issue is that there are insufficient data overall to support all forms of DA, even though all data attributes are accessible. For instance, in order for most DA algorithms to be appropriately trained to classify future examples, they need to see about 100 examples of training data. If there are not enough examples provided, the concepts learned or rules created could not be reliable enough.

1.2.1.3 Splintered Data

Inconsistence data: When information is gathered from multiple sources, data compatibility becomes crucial. Sensing data must be combined with groupings of data because it contains a lot of language and symbolic properties. The incompatibility issues may arise from the human representation of the text or even from the data gathering process's use of natural language processing and understanding tools.

Numerous data sources: Data in large organizations may be dispersed across several departments and platforms. Majority of the time, several software systems are even used for data acquisition and maintenance. Throughout the company, there may be differences in the objective, scope, and caliber of data collecting.

Data from various granularity levels: There are real-world applications where data are sourced at multiple levels of granularity. Aerospace and semiconductor manufacturing are two examples. All phases of the semiconductor manufacturing process include the collection of data. These serve as metrics for every production unit. These stand for every measurement that needs to be taken on every wafer production unit. Data from specific locations on a wafer known as test sites may be used at a higher level. The purpose of gathering these data is to approximate the same qualities of every spot on a wafer. Wafer level and bin (batch) level are additional layers. When data are represented at the wafer level, they encompass the complete wafer, including raw wafer parameters and properties obtained after manufacture, including overall thickness [9]. The highest level at which the data indicate characteristics of a set of wafers in a container (bin) is called the bin level.

1.2.2 Setting Up for DA

There are still a few procedures that can be taken after data issues have been resolved and the data are ready before the actual DA begins. This group includes all steps done to comprehend the nature of the data and sophisticated methods used to carry out in-depth DA.

1.2.2.1 Recognizing the Types of Data

Once all issues with the data have been resolved, there are numerous reasons why knowing the nature of the data might be helpful:

The human brain is not capable of interpreting vast and complicated datasets or using the majority of DA tools correctly. For a better comprehension of the data, preparing it in some way is therefore helpful. Principal component analysis and data visualization are two examples.

The majority of DA tools have some restrictions based on the properties of the data. Therefore, being aware of these traits would be helpful for choosing and configuring the DA process. The percentage of missing attribute values across the whole data collection is one example.

1.2.2.2 Preparing Data for Detailed DA

Standard DA tools and methods offer ways to analyze data up to a degree that might not be adequate for every application. Additional support resources for data pretreatment are needed for in-depth DA, and they must be used correctly before the analysis can begin. Nonetheless, DA outcomes would be more significant if the data were changed to reflect trends rather than isolated incidents.

Additional methods of preprocessing data for in-depth analysis include (i) adding new features manually or automatically based on existing ones (which is similar to constructive induction), (ii) simulating data to create parameters not normally measured, (iii) fusing data gathered from multiple sources, and (iv) dimensional analysis.

1.3 Strategies for Preparing Data

Preprocessing data has several advantages. Neural network classifications allow for the removal of unnecessary data, which reduces confusion and speeds up learning because smaller datasets are used. Accuracy and result simplicity are frequently traded off in many applications, including neural networks [10]. The majority of real-world applications require some kind of data preprocessing. Nearly all inductive approach implementations necessitate the thoughtful deployment of data preparation techniques. The use of data preparation techniques is emphasized as a crucial component of any knowledge discovery from database projects [5].

We will first examine the definitions and prerequisites of data preparation techniques in order to set the stage for presenting an exhaustive list of these approaches. After that, we will give a framework for the methods now in use that have been documented in the literature. Every method could have a few advantages and disadvantages. Furthermore, in order to correctly use each of these strategies, one must also be cognizant of the underlying assumptions. Certain approaches, such as data sampling, aid in the selection of the most significant datasets, whereas others, such as principal component analysis and noise modeling, help with data compression and summarization. Examples of procedures connected to excessive data include data filtering and data removal, which discard data.

1.3.1 Transforming Data

The superiority and comprehensiveness of the data are the primary causes of the limits in data collecting and processing [11]. Erroneous input measurement or improper data feeding into a DA tool (such a classifier) can lead to a number of issues. Therefore, the main goal of DA is to locate these deficiencies and choose the appropriate approaches to address the issues.

1.3.1.1 Filtering Data

Broad data filtering is used. On one extreme of the range, data filtering addresses straightforward issues such as incorrect data. It handles noisy data at the other end. Data filtering serves as the foundation for many data preparation methods that eliminate unwanted data in the time–frequency domains. With the least amount of distortion to the pertinent signal features, the optimal filtering method should eliminate extraneous features.

The most popular filtering methods are (i) time domain filtering, which extracts the mean or median of the measured data within a predefined window; (ii) frequency domain filtering, which applies Fourier analysis to the data to remove high frequency contributions; and (iii) time–frequency domain filtering, which simultaneously applies time and frequency domain transformation to the measured data, allowing for the computationally efficient capture of a wide range of signal features. The fundamental premise of data filtering is that there is enough subject expertise available to prevent the loss of important information.

The most popular method is Kalman filtering, and conventional methods are described in Sorenson [12]. The utilization of Kalman filtering necessitates a thorough understanding of noise statistics, which may not be achievable in certain real-world scenarios. Furthermore, Kalman filtering assumes the system's linearity, the system noise's Gaussian distribution features, and the background noise of the observations from the outset [13].

1.3.1.2 Data Arranging

Applications that store data use data ordering most frequently. Putting the data in the right places (tables) for later retrieval and analysis is the major goal here. Usually, a conceptual data model is created initially. Relationships and entities are identified. The entities' attributes are listed, and the labels indicate the kinds of associations (1-1, 1-n, or n-1). The automatic preprocessing of patient data from electrocardiograms is an instance of data ordering [14]. Data ordering, which could coincide with data warehousing, necessitates a model of the system or process from which the data are obtained.

1.3.1.3 Editing Data

When preprocessing text or symbolic data types, data editing is used on data elements that are made up of one or more character strings that represent distinct information for a given characteristic. Examples include census-related data when information has been entered by staff members at a statistics center or by individuals who fill out questionnaires. Extensive topic knowledge is necessary for data editing because improper data editing might lead to data loss. Appropriate editing is also necessary for systems that use online text extraction to construct assertions for databases and natural language processing.

1.3.1.4 Modeling Noise

One of the most used techniques for noise modeling in data preprocessing is the Fourier transform. Traditional time localization is lost when using the Fourier transform to analyze data. For long-period signals, Fourier transform is hence suitable. For brief time frame, the Fourier transform can be used to improve time localization by limiting the transform length using a series of window functions. The lowest frequency often determines the size of the window.

For noise estimation, a number of adaptive techniques have been put forth. These techniques are divided into four categories: covariance matching, maximum likelihood, correlation, and Bayesian. The first two are computationally intensive and presuppose time-invariance of noise statistics. Through the autocorrelation methods, connecting these functions to the unknown parameters is obtained. In an effort to align the filter residuals with their theoretical covariance's, covariance matching techniques are used. Other types of noise smoothing and modeling are achieved by data compression, which involves removing low-frequency data components. Interpolation can be strengthened and improved by data compression, leading to better classifications on testing datasets [10]. Reducing the measuring time in tests such as diffraction might be possible by data smoothing, this is extremely dependent on the accuracy of the data [16]. The ability of noise modeling to assist with relevant data selection and appropriate threshold setting for data classifications is one of its most significant advantages.

1.3.2 Information Compilation

A system that inadvertently analyzes clean, sufficient data for a certain DA task might be conceptualized as a DA tool. When some internal parameters inside a DA tool are not properly established, DA is not effectively guided, or all data attributes are unknown, limited or partial results are obtained. In this section, we focus on interactive strategies that are applied to the data in order to enhance comprehending data and make better use of a particular DA tool. Another interesting idea to address the possible data scarcity issue in the building industry is transfer learning. The basic principle behind transfer learning, as seen in Figure 1.3, is to use the information gained from well-measured buildings to make the modeling process in poorly measured buildings easier.

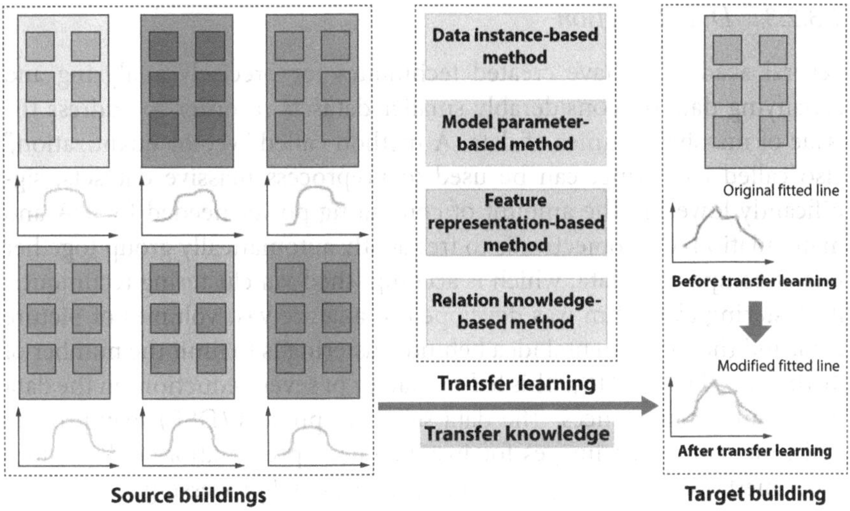

Figure 1.3 Operational DA for idea of transfer learning.

1.3.2.1 *Data Visualization*

Data visualization has gradually progressed from methods that imitate experimental procedures to more abstract representations of the data. This evolution has occurred for at least two causes. First, a lot of significant quantitative factors are difficult to measure directly [17]. Second, simplifying the display by isolating and drawing only the pertinent data features is necessary for accurate depiction of extremely varied data while also reducing visual clutter.

1.3.2.2 *Data Elimination*

Two goals can occasionally be accomplished through data elimination preprocessing:

- A significant reduction in the volume of data. Image DA is one example [18].
- A portion of the data is classified. Associating adjacent pixels in a picture is one example.

Using univariate limit checking techniques such as "absolute value check" is another way to eliminate data.

1.3.2.3 Data Selection

Several academics have created techniques for precisely analyzing and classifying data on considerably smaller datasets in order to address the issue of massive volumes of data. A method called "vector quantization," also called clustering, can be used to preprocess massive datasets, significantly lowering the amount of computing power needed for DA and manipulation. Our objective is to frequently automatically group together sets of comparable data, which is accomplished *via* clustering techniques. A clustering algorithm was developed to analyze vast volumes of picture data, and the fundamental idea behind clustering is to limit the number of distinct pixel values [18]. This led to a factor of seven reductions in the data in certain circumstances. The data selection process (DSP) may provide real-time subtracted images for instantaneous presentation and includes other methods of selecting relevant data for digital processing.

1.3.2.4 Analysis of Principal Components

Many studies have been conducted on the application of principal components [19]. The primary objective of principal component identification is to choose appropriate attributes for DA. Theoretically, choosing X basis vectors and extending these vectors' subspace are similar to choosing X characteristics (from Y). As a result, by locating the principal components, we can minimize the dimensionality of a database that contains a large number of interconnected variables while preserving the majority of the variation found within. This reduction is accomplished by converting to a new collection of highly uncorrelated variables known as principal components, which are arranged so that the first few maintain the majority of the variations seen in all of the original variables. Examining the linear relationship between independent variables in a collection of data attributes is necessary to identify major components. Use of primary components necessitates domain expertise, regardless of whether this is carried out automatically as part of the DA process or independently.

1.3.2.5 Data Sampling

Data sampling is especially important in situations where the DA algorithm requires a subset of the total data, such as when dividing the data for testing or training purposes or when assessing the algorithm's performance. The selection of appropriate samples is crucial in this case to achieve and maintain the optimal performance for the used algorithm. For instance, the training set, or tiny collection of correctly categorized patterns, is typically the only one available in neural network applications [20].

1.3.3 Production of Novel Information

The majority of DA applications entail finding solutions to issues that arise often in an organization's daily operations. Nonetheless, there are always objectives for in-depth DA even inside the same organization. In this instance, the objective is to invest more time and energy into conducting a thorough DA and finding every important piece of information that could be present in the data.

1.3.3.1 Including Extra Features

There are several situations where adding new features and the design of membership functions (fuzzy clustering) coincide, including constructive induction [21]. Deriving new features manually or automatically from the current features is the primary function of constructive induction. In a rule-based fuzzy system, membership functions are generated during the rule-based definition process, which is part of the DA process. Determining language variables is the first step in creating such a rule base [23]. In machine learning applications, methods for choosing appropriate linguistic variables for rule-based fuzzy systems have been proposed [22].

1.3.3.2 Data Fusion

A wide variety of sensors can be used to collect data about the surrounding environments. Examples include laser and ultrasonic range finders, as well as optical, thermal, proximity, and touch sensors. In these situations, various sensors have unique properties, work across a broad spectrum, and are built according to various physical principles. Nonetheless, the cooperative functioning of numerous sensors yields an abundance of data on the parameters being evaluated, enhancing the dependability and significance of the DA [24]. Only the adjustments that need to be made to certain measurements may be the cause of some of these data fusion strategies.

1.3.3.3 Time–Series Analysis

Compared to certain other approaches, such standard control charting techniques, the employment of time–series (TS) models, can be a more dependable method when the data show excessive variance or nonstationary behavior. Data from the majority of application domains contain variation. For instance, in industrial processes, this variance may result from the following factors: individual decisions or process plans, process environment, human operating procedures, and raw materials used in the process [25]. TS analysis in most process monitoring applications refers to the conversion of data into a static feature collection that depicts an operational view at a specific point in time. This is carried out in the data interpretation stage, when labels are given according to a discriminant that is related to the features that were extracted. TS analysis can also be used to restructure earthly data so that linked events with patterns across time are represented as a single record.

1.3.3.4 Information Modeling

The issue of unobtainable or immeasurable parameters in vast measurement spaces is addressed by data simulation. An illustration would be taking measurements of certain ambient environmental characteristics in a complicated manufacturing process that could be costly or difficult to measure. Because these parameters' impacts on the process are known, measuring and controlling them as needed might be justified. Data simulation and knowledge-driven constructive induction [26] build a new representation space using domain knowledge.

1.3.3.5 Dimensional Analysis

The main goals of dimensional analysis and the theory of similitude are to identify the relationships that must exist in order for data on processes or models to be collected to be used to make reliable predictions, as well as to identify the kind of relationship that exists between the features of the related physical phenomenon so that the most relevant data can be gathered and examined methodically. The foundation of dimensional analysis is the dimensions in which all relevant quantities associated with a phenomenon are stated. Dimensional analysis's primary benefit is that it produces qualitative associations as opposed to quantitative ones. Dimensional analysis can produce quantitative results and precise prediction equations when it is used in conjunction with experimentation and data collection.

1.4 Real-World Applications

Preprocessing and DA are important skills that are applied in a wide range of fields and applications. The following are some typical uses for which these methods are very important:

1.4.1 Machine Learning and Predictive Analytics

Preprocessing and DA are crucial phases in machine learning workflows. They include activities such as feature engineering (generating new features from preexisting data), data cleaning (removing duplicates, resolving missing values), and normalizing or scaling of data to get it ready for model training. Preprocessing ensures the data are properly organized and optimized for predictive modeling activities, whereas DA aids in finding patterns, trends, and linkages in datasets for predictive analytics.

1.4.2 Healthcare and Biomedical Research

Preprocessing and DA are utilized in the healthcare industry for tasks such as patient diagnosis, treatment planning, and medical research. Medical data from a variety of sources, such as wearable technology, medical imaging, and electronic health records, are cleaned and standardized using preprocessing procedures. Healthcare data can provide valuable insights into patient outcomes, treatment effectiveness, and disease risk factors. These insights can be gleaned through DA techniques including statistical analysis and machine learning.

1.4.3 Financial Analysis and Risk Management

Preprocessing and DA are used in finance for activities including risk assessment, financial modeling, and investment decision-making. Preprocessing methods are used to clean and standardize financial data, including market indices, economic indicators, and stock prices. Regression modeling and TS analysis are two DA techniques that are used to evaluate investment risks, predict future values, and spot trends in financial data.

1.4.4 Marketing and Customer Analytics

Preprocessing and DA are used in marketing for activities including market research, campaign optimization, and consumer segmentation.

Preprocessing methods are used to clean and modify marketing data, including purchase history, website interactions, and customer demographics. Techniques for DA, such as categorization and clustering, are useful for determining client categories, forecasting consumer behavior, and tailoring advertising campaigns.

1.4.5 Supply Chain Management and Logistics

Preprocessing and DA are used in supply chain management for activities including logistics planning, inventory optimization, and demand forecasting. Utilizing preprocessing methods allows for the integration and cleaning of data from many suppliers, manufacturers, and distributors. DA techniques that aid with supply chain DA include TS analysis and optimization modeling. These techniques help with efficiency analysis, cost reduction, and risk mitigation.

1.4.6 Environmental Monitoring and Sustainability

DA and preprocessing are utilized in environmental science and sustainability for activities including resource management, pollution monitoring, and climate modeling. Preprocessing methods are used to clean and standardize environmental data, including air quality indices, satellite photography, and meteorological measurements. Spatial analysis and machine learning are two examples of DA techniques that are used to examine environmental data in order to forecast environmental effects, comprehend ecosystem dynamics, and guide policy choices.

1.5 Conclusion

To sum up, the principles of DA and preprocessing are essential elements of almost all data-driven projects in a variety of disciplines and sectors. By means of diligent data handling and analysis, entities can extract significant insights, arrive at well-informed decisions, and stimulate innovation and enhancement. The capacity of DA to reveal links, patterns, and trends concealed in intricate datasets is what makes it so important [27]. Through the utilization of statistical methodologies, machine learning algorithms, and visualization approaches, analysts are able to derive actionable insights from unprocessed data, thus providing enterprises with a more profound comprehension of their markets, customers, and operations.

The insights obtained by DA and preprocessing enable organizations to make better decisions and generate positive outcomes, whether they are used for patient outcomes prediction in healthcare, financial trend forecasting in finance, or client segmentation in marketing [28]. Organizations may use data to solve complicated challenges, open up new opportunities, and promote sustainable growth in a world where data are becoming more and more important by embracing emerging technologies, building a strong data infrastructure, and developing analytical skills [15]. Fundamentals of preprocessing and DA are essentially the cornerstones of data-driven decision-making, enabling companies to convert unprocessed data into useful insights and effect significant change.

References

1. Hazra, S., Ghosal, S., Mondal, A., Dey, P., Forecasting of Rainfall in Sub-division of India Using Machine Learning. *5th Doctoral Symposium on Intelligence Enabled Research (DOSIER 2023)*, doi : 10.1007/978-981-97-2321-8-18.
2. Bobrow, D.G. and Norman, D.A., Some principles of Memory Schemata, in: *Representation and Understanding: Studies in Cognitive Science*, D.G. Bobrow and A. Collins (Eds.), pp. 138–140, Academic Press, New York, 1975.
3. Awujoola, O.J., Ogwueleka, F.N., Odion, P.O., Awujoola, A.E., Adelegan, O.R., Genomic data science systems of Prediction and prevention of pneumonia from chest X-ray images using a two-channel dual-stream convolutional neural network, in: *Data Science for Genomics*, pp. 217–228, 2023.
4. Chhillar, I. and Singh, A., Performance evaluation of machine learning techniques for breast cancer detection using WDBC dataset. *AIP Conf. Proc.*, 2919, 100006, 2024.
5. Fayyad, U., Piatetsky-Shapiro, G., Smyth, P., From Data Mining to Knowledge Discovery, in: *Advances in Knowledge Discovery and Data Mining*, U. Fayyad, *et al.* (Eds.), pp. 1–34, AAAI/MIT Press, Menlo Park, CA, 1996.
6. Davis, J.F., Bakshik, B., Kosanovich, K., Piovoso, M., Process Monitoring, Data Analysis and Data Interpretation. *Proceedings of the Intelligent Systems in Process Engineering Conference*, Snowmass, CO, pp. 1–12, 1995.
7. Bontrager, E., *et al.*, GAIT-ER-AID: An Expert System for Analysis of Gait with Automatic Intelligent Pre-processing of Data. *4th Annual Symposium on Computer Applications in MED CARE*, pp. 625–629, 1990.
8. Gon, A., Hazra, S., Chatterjee, S., Ghosh, A.K., Application of Machine Learning Algorithms for Automatic Detection of Risk in Heart Disease, in: *Cognitive Cardiac Rehabilitation Using IoT and AI Tools*, P. Bhowmick, S. Das, K. Mazumdar (Eds.), pp. 166–188, IGI Global, 2023, https://doi.org/10.4018/978-1-6684-7561-4.ch012.

9. Thirion, P., Direct Extraction of Boundaries from Computed Tomography Scans. *IEEE Trans. Med. Imaging*, 13, 2, 322–328, 1994.
10. McAulay, A.D. and Li, J., Wavelet Data Compression for Neural Network Preprocessing. *Signal Processing, Sensor Fusion and Target Recognition SPIE*, vol. 1699, pp. 356–365, 1992.
11. Cortes, C., Jackel, L.D., Chiang, W.P., Limits on Learning Machine Accuracy Imposed by Data Quality. *Proceedings of the First International Conference on Knowledge Discovery & Data Mining*, Montreal, Canada, pp. 57–62, 1995.
12. Sorenson, H.W., *Kalman Filtering: Theory and Application*, IEEE Press, New York, 1985.
13. Ohta, M., Uchinol, E., Nagano, O., A New State Estimation Method with Prefixed Algorithmic Form Matched to Effective Data Processing. *Acustica*, 77, 165–175, 1992.
14. Hazra, S., Chatterjee, S., Mondal, R., Naskar, A., Analysis and Comparison Study of Cardiovascular Risk Prediction using Machine Learning Approaches. *Proceedings of Algorithms for Intelligent Systems series/16171*, 2024.
15. Fan, C., Yan, D., Xiao, F., Li, A., An, J., Kang, X., Advanced data analytics for enhancing building performances: from data-driven to big datadriven approaches. *Build. Simul.*, 14, 3–24, 2021b, doi: 10.1007/s12273-020-0723-1.
16. Nikolayev, D. and Ullemeyer, K., A Note on Preprocessing of Diffraction Pole-density Data. *J. Appl. Crystallogr.*, 27, 517–520, 1994.
17. Hesselink, L., Research Issues in Vector and Tensor Field Visualization. *Proceedings of IEEE Workshop on Visualization and Machine Vision*, Seattle, WA, pp. 104–105, 1994.
18. Kelly, P.M. and White, J.W., Preprocessing Remotely-Sensed Data for Efficient Analysis and Classification. *Applications of Artificial Intelligence, Proceedings of SPIE-The International Society for Optical Engineering-1963*, Orlando, FL, pp. 24–30, 1993.
19. Duszak, Z. and Loczkodaj, W.W., Using Principal Component Transformation in Machine Learning. *Proceedings of International Conference on Systems Research, Informatics and Cybernetics*, Baden-Baden Germany, pp. 125–129, 1994.
20. Hazra, S., Pervasive Nature of AI in the Health Care Industry: High-Performance Medicine, 2024.
21. Weber, R., Fuzzy-ID3: A Class of Models for Automatic Knowledge Acquisition. *Proceedings of the 2nd International Conference on Fuzzy Logic and Neural Networks*, Tisuka, Japan, pp. 265–268, 1992.
22. Weiss, S.M. and Kulikowski, C.A., *Computer Systems That Learn*, Morgan Kaufmann Publishers, California, 1991.
23. Bezdek, J.C. and Pal, S.K., *Fuzzy Models for Pattern Recognition*, IEEE Press, New York, 1992.
24. Clark, J.J., *Data Fusion for Sensory Information Processing Systems*, Kluwer Academic Publishers, 1990.

25. Yarling, S.M., Time Series Modelling as an Approach to Automatic Feedback Control of Robotic Positioning Errors. *Proceedings of IEEE International Symposium on Electronics Manufacturing Technology*, pp. 443–449, 1993.
26. Hazra, S., Chatterjee, S., Mandal, A., Sarkar, M., Mandal, B.K., An Analysis of Duckworth-Lewis-Stern Method in the Context of Interrupted Limited over Cricket Matches, in: *Proceedings of International Conference on Data Analytics and Insights, ICDAI 2023*, ICDAI 2023. Lecture Notes in Networks and Systems, vol. 727, Springer, Singapore, 2023, https://doi.org/10.1007/978-981-99-3878-0_46.
27. Li, K., Sun, Y., Robinson, D., Ma, J., Ma, Z., A new strategy to benchmark and evaluate building electricity usage using multiple data mining technologies. *Sustain. Energy Technol. Assess.*, 40, 100770, 2020b, doi: 10.1016/j.seta.2020.100770.
28. Banerjee, S., Hazra, S., Kumar, B., Application of Big Data in Banking—A Predictive Analysis on Bank Loans, in: *Proceedings of 3rd International Conference on Mathematical Modeling and Computational Science*, ICMMCS 2023. Advances in Intelligent Systems and Computing, vol. 1450 Springer, Singapore, 2023, https://doi.org/10.1007/978-981-99-3611-3_40.

2

Advanced Data Control Methods for Data-Driven Modeling: Techniques, Challenges, and Future Directions

Aarushi Chatterjee[1] and Souvik Ganguli[2*]

[1]*Department of Electronics and Communication Engineering, Thapar Institute of Engineering and Technology, Patiala, Punjab, India*
[2]*Department of Electrical and Instrumentation Engineering, Thapar Institute of Engineering and Technology, Patiala, Punjab, India*

Abstract

This chapter explores advanced data control methods critical for ensuring the reliability, security, and scalability of data-driven modeling systems. As data continue to grow in volume, variety, and velocity, effective data control has become increasingly important across industries such as healthcare, finance, autonomous systems, and energy management. The chapter delves into key concepts such as centralized and decentralized data control, automated data governance, real-time data processing, and privacy-preserving technologies such as differential privacy and federated learning. In addition, it addresses emerging challenges such as scalability, data drift, and the need for real-time adaptive control. The role of cutting-edge technologies, including blockchain, edge computing, artificial intelligence–driven data control, and quantum cryptography, is explored as future solutions for managing the complexities of modern data environments. By implementing these techniques, organizations can ensure data integrity, privacy, and compliance while maintaining high-performance data-driven models. This chapter provides practical insights and case studies, offering a roadmap for mastering data control in evolving and increasingly distributed data ecosystems.

***Keywords*:** Data governance and control, real-time stream processing, blockchain for data integrity, adaptive and data-driven control, data drift

---

**Corresponding author*: souvik.ganguli@thapar.edu

Arindam Mondal and Souvik Ganguli (eds.) Data-Driven Modeling, (23–80) © 2026 Scrivener Publishing LLC

2.1 Introduction

In today's technology-driven world, as the generation of data increases in volumes generated by heterogeneous systems, sensors and devices are the new core values for research across lots of industries. Thus, due to the scale of data, it has led the pathway for the rise in data-driven architecture in modeling. This allows building a framework that is defined by the underlying patterns with dynamic decisions, while keeping in consideration of future predictions from the available datasets. The effectiveness of these models is directly proportional to the quality, integrity, and management of data for these models. The importance of data governance is still the basis for the success of the framework of model development, which can have loopholes even with the most advanced algorithms and result in inconsistent results [1].

Proper processing, management, and application of data on the basis of the specification of the models or systems are keys to data control, as they involve various methodologies. This includes other operations such as collecting data, verifying, processing, converting, and storing the data in check with access regulation and protection. Model development and its analysis are crucial while keeping the data safe, that is, protecting the data from corruption and unauthorized access [2].

Data-driven modeling is based on the control of data because the models directly learn from the data provided. It works on the principle "garbage in, garbage out" in order to quality control of input data used for training and validating models. Poor decision-making in these cases is very likely, as the data provided might be too noisy, incorrect, incomplete, inconsistent, or biased, which would have great consequences in fields such as healthcare, finance, autonomous systems, and energy management [3].

These issues sparked the significance of data governance and changes required with evolving patterns of contemporary data. The data now produced are influenced by streaming information, instant updates, and aggregation of data from multiple sources for which the traditional methods are insufficient. In order to include real-time data administration, decentralized architectures, and automated regulatory practices that address the intricacies and scale of modern data environments, new discipline needs to be introduced [4].

The next important factor in data-driven modeling is the data privacy and security. Strict regulations such as General Data Protection Regulation (GDPR) and the California Consumer Privacy Act (CCPA) are to be followed so as to have a grip on efficient control of data. Privacy breaches would attract heavy penalties and would also result in severe damage of reputation for the organization. The service industries that are entirely based on user data therefore require strong impenetrable framework and strong data governance [5].

This chapter highlights the importance of enabling the effectiveness of data-dependent models and the various data governance frameworks. It also includes the life cycle of data, right from the life cycle of data to the collection, preprocessing, deployment, and maintenance of the models. The interrelations between data management and model effectiveness are the basis for exploration of data governance, automated processing, and adaptive regulatory frameworks, which are shaping the future of data-centric systems [6].

In applications where decisions have to be made in real time, the importance of data control is critical. For example, in autonomous vehicles (AVs) or industrial control systems where the sensors provide a stream of continuous data, which can be impacted by environmental conditions, equipment failures, or network connectivity, disruptions would vary its functioning in the real world. In these cases, if the reliability and accuracy of the data are not verified, it can lead to catastrophic consequences. Thus, managing data becomes more crucial to be verified and observed constantly with immediate solutions, while ensuring the stability and optimizing its performance [7].

New methods such as federated learning, which are revolutionizing data governance in collaborative learning environments between decentralized systems during model training systems, are also discussed in this chapter. Allowing organizations to retain authority over their raw data while ensuring privacy and providing reduced bandwidth to updates on a global model. Blockchain technology unlocks new opportunities through immutable ledgers for ensuring data integrity in multiagent systems [8].

Finally, the chapter also provides an insight to the methods, techniques, and practices that would define modern data control approaches. During times of data drift and peak privacy concerns or changes in environments, the principles to design robust, efficient, scalable, well-performing, data-centric models are used by arm researchers and practitioners [9].

Consequently, the fundamental support for dependable data-driven modeling is managed by data. This ensures the data have superior quality, are safeguarded, and appropriately regulate the information received by the datasets. With the advancements in data management and expansion on the basis of quantity and intricacy, it ensures the efficacy in predictive modeling, decision-making processes, and system automation across various fields [10].

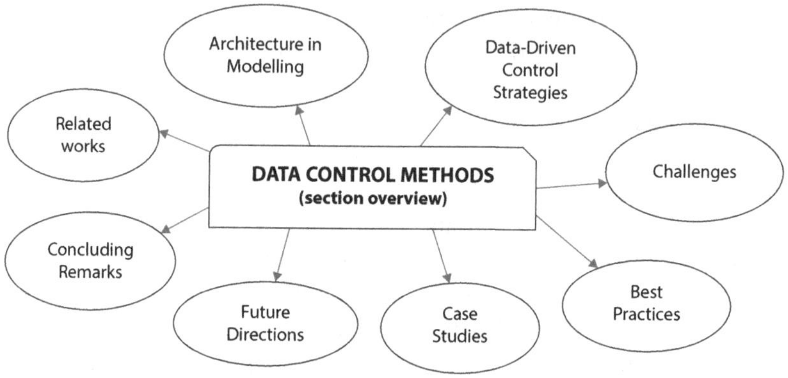

2.2 Related Works

Over the past few decades, the role of data control in data-driven modeling has evolved dramatically, shaped by advancements in database management, data mining, machine learning, and artificial intelligence (AI). Various studies have addressed the challenges of ensuring data quality, security, and scalability in the context of modern applications. This section provides an overview of the key literature, focusing on major contributions in the areas of data control for machine learning, big data systems, data governance, and privacy [11].

2.2.1 Data Quality and Preprocessing

The importance of data quality in predictive modeling has been extensively covered in the literature. Early works emphasized the critical role of data preprocessing in the machine learning pipeline. They highlighted techniques such as normalization, handling missing values, and outlier detection as foundational steps in ensuring the success of machine learning algorithms. More recent works have proposed automated data preprocessing frameworks, incorporating techniques such as automated feature selection and transformation to optimize data for machine learning models.

The concept of data cleaning has also been a significant focus pioneering the creation of a comprehensive taxonomy of data cleaning techniques, which include deduplication, data transformation, and integrity constraint enforcement. Their work laid the groundwork for many modern systems designed to handle large, messy datasets [12].

2.2.2 Data Governance and Control in Distributed Systems

With the rise of big data and distributed systems, data governance has gained increasing attention in academic and industry literature. The seminal work on data governance introduced the idea of treating data as an organizational asset, requiring policies and controls to manage its quality and use. The data governance framework has become industry standards for managing data across large enterprises, providing structured approaches to data stewardship, quality management, and compliance.

In distributed systems, studies on Google's Spanner on MapReduce have highlighted how large-scale data control mechanisms are implemented in cloud and distributed environments. These papers emphasize the need for scalability, fault tolerance, and automated data consistency checks to handle data streams and batch processes.

More recently, few researchers have also explored data governance in multicloud environments, highlighting the importance of unified governance tools for managing data across heterogeneous cloud platforms. Their work underscores the shift toward decentralized data control, where governance models are designed to operate across distributed and federated systems [13].

2.2.3 Data Privacy and Security

Data privacy has emerged as one of the most critical aspects of data control in light of regulations such as GDPR and CCPA. The literature on data privacy control methods, particularly in the context of machine learning and AI, is vast.

Differential privacy provides a mathematical framework to ensure the privacy of individual data points when aggregated into a larger dataset. This technique has become a cornerstone of privacy-preserving machine learning, allowing organizations to extract insights from sensitive data without exposing individual records. Extensions of this work on differential privacy in deep learning models provide practical tools for integrating privacy guarantees in data-driven models.

In the realm of data security, researchers have explored encryption techniques for secure data processing. Their work emphasizes the importance of maintaining data confidentiality while allowing for analytics through techniques such as homomorphic encryption, secure multiparty computation (SMPC), and privacy-preserving federated learning [14].

2.2.4 Model Predictive Control and Data-Driven Approaches

In control systems, the integration of data control techniques has been particularly prominent in model predictive control (MPC). The pioneering work highlighted how MPC can optimize control actions using data-driven models to predict future system behavior. Subsequent works extended these concepts, incorporating real-time data streams into control systems to enable adaptive control, where decisions are continuously refined based on incoming data.

Data-driven control strategies are also increasingly adopted in industrial applications. Recent works have also explored combining MPC with reinforcement learning (RL) techniques, allowing systems to learn optimal control policies from interaction with dynamic environments. This fusion of machine learning and control theory is driving innovations in autonomous systems, energy grids, and process control [15].

2.2.5 Data Drift and Adaptive Control

A persistent challenge in data-driven modeling is the issue of data drift, where the underlying statistical properties of the data change over time, leading to degradation in model performance. Few researchers have explored various techniques for handling concept drift in streaming data environments, introducing methods for online learning and adaptive model updating. Their work has informed numerous adaptive control systems, particularly in applications where data distribution is nonstationary.

Building on this, few researchers introduced frameworks for continual learning, enabling models to continuously adapt to new data while preserving knowledge from previous data. This work is particularly relevant in industries such as finance and healthcare, where data patterns evolve rapidly [16].

2.3 Data Control Architecture in Modeling

The pathway for data control architecture in modeling is dependent on how the given data are governed, compiled, processed, and utilized in its life cycle from its foundational stages to final refinements. The success of the architecture is defined if the data are reliable, accessible, and secure and support the robustness of the model generated from the given dataset. In this section, we focus on the essential aspects of data control architecture, that is, centralized and decentralized control, automated data governance, real-time data control and the emerging technologies in the field [17].

Table 2.1 Centralized and decentralized data control.

Centralized	Decentralized
Advantages	
Consistency	Scalability
Simplified Governance	Fault Tolerance
Efficiency	Reduced Latency
Disadvantages	
Scalability	Complex governance
Single point of failure	Data synchronization
Latency & Performance	Increased Security Risks

2.3.1 Centralized versus Decentralized Data Control

On the basis of how the data are stored or managed or its availability and usage across organizations or systems, the architecture of data control can be classified into two broad categories: centralized and decentralized. Both the classifications have their own applications, advantages, and disadvantages as illustrated in Table 2.1, thereby aligning the use of the system according to the system's need.

2.3.1.1 Centralized Data Control

The centralized data control architecture in modeling uses the data managed and governed from a single point of control, that is, by a centralized server or a database that allows a restrictive oversight, thus allowing an easier governance, and the process of data is streamlined.

Single-point management: In single-point management, the data flow, storage, and access permissions are all managed by a central repository. This flow of data helps in maintaining data security and uniformity in crucial structures and is used in financial institutions and healthcare facilities.

Advantages

i. **Consistency**: As the data are managed by a single-point system, the data are precise as the source is narrowed, thereby ensuring the legibility of the data as no data fragmentation across systems exists.

ii. **Simplified governance**: Because data fragmentation is omitted, and there is a single source, the access control, data usage, and data integrity are easier to enforce.

iii. **Efficiency**: Centralized systems with its consistency and simplified governance and monitoring help to streamline operations for real-time data access.

Challenges

i. **Scalability issues**: The single-point management system can fail to manage large-scale, geographically distributed datasets efficiently.

ii. **Single point of failure**: As the source is one point, any compromise or failure would lead to jeopardy of the entire central system.

iii. **Latency and performance**: The centralized systems can experience performance constraints in real-time applications as the volume of data from the incoming source increases.

Examples of centralized architectures

i. **Traditional database systems**: Relational databases such as MySQL or PostgreSQL have been used for business and research applications for a very long time as the backbone of centralized data control.

ii. **Cloud-based centralized systems**: Cloud services such as AWS S3 and Google Cloud Storage are used as centralized storage hubs that provide scalable and secure data management with centralized governance [18].

2.3.1.2 Decentralized Data Control

The decentralized data control in modeling the data is stored, managed, and governed across multiple nodes or systems, which is monitored separately in their respective nodes. This architecture is used in modern applications involving distributed systems such as edge computing and peer-to-peer networks, blockchain systems, and cloud-based distributed architectures.

Multiple points of control: In a decentralized system, each system has a degree of autonomy to some extent on its data with control and processing distributed across the entire network.

Advantages

i. **Scalability**: The scalability is not an issue in this system as the data are structurally divided into their respective nodes and can be managed and edited as per the need of the system.
ii. **Fault tolerance**: The risk of single-point failure is omitted in this system as any fails or compromise can be classified and worked on by looking up at that category.
iii. **Reduced latency**: The latency is significantly reduced in a decentralized system as the data control to nodes is geographically closer to users or devices, making it ideal for real-time applications such as AVs or industrial Internet of Things (IoT).

Challenges

i. **Complex governance**: The check-and-balance system needs to be rigorous in this system as the source is distributed, implying that each node may have different security, access, and governance standards.
ii. **Data synchronization**: As the data are decentralized, maintaining data consistency across all nodes can be difficult especially in systems with high volume of data intake or where nodes operate independently for extended periods.
iii. **Increased security risks**: The security risk is evident as there are multiple points of control, which may lead to introducing vulnerabilities at each and every node, leading to the need of more sophisticated security measures.

Examples of decentralized architectures

i. **Blockchain networks**: Systems such as Ethereum or Hyperledger use decentralized architectures for modeling in which the data are distributed across multiple nodes, with consensus mechanisms ensuring data integrity.

ii. **Federated learning systems**: In federated learning systems, the data remain decentralized across devices or edge servers, and models are trained locally without sharing raw data, only exchanging model updates [19].

2.3.2 Automated Data Governance

As the complexity and volume of the data amplify, the manual data governance methods appear to be futile and are no longer practical. This is where the automated data governance comes to existence as it involves the application of policies, rules, and algorithms on how the data are handled while their security and consistency are maintained across the organization or system [20]. The types of data governance are shown in Figure 2.1.

2.3.2.1 Metadata Management

Metadata basically explains the data provenance, its structure, and usage history. In automated data governance, effective metadata management is crucial as it provides the necessary elements to enforce governance policies and make decisions about data usage.

Automated metadata generation: With the increased use of AI and machine learning in systems to generate and update metadata, data flow automatically. This allows for real-time tracking and update of data lineage and usage, which is critical in systems where data are continuously updated.

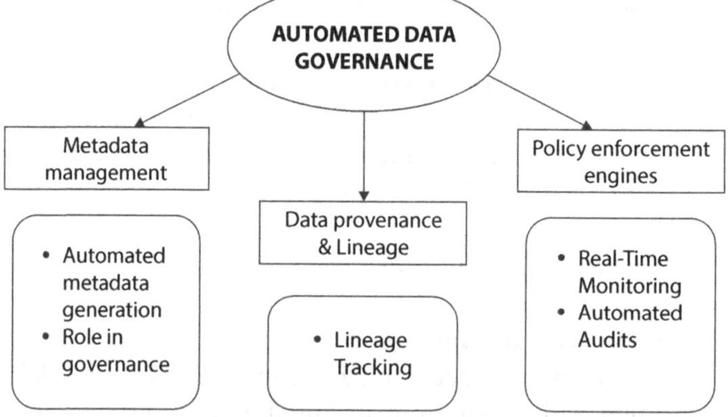

Figure 2.1 Types of automated data governance.

Role in governance: The definition of access control rules, a track of data transformations, and that only relevant data are used for specific modeling tasks are ensured, with the help of metadata. For instance, in managed systems such as healthcare or finance, metadata enables auditing of the owner of data, who, when, why, by ensuring to be in compliance with regulations such as GDPR and Health Insurance Portability and Accountability Act (HIPAA) [21].

2.3.2.2 Data Provenance and Lineage

Data provenance refers to the historical record of the data, that is, the origin of the data and how they were processed and have been used over time. It proves to play a vital role in establishing trust in data, ensuring that models are built on reliable data, and tracing the origins of errors or potential risks of plagiarism.

Lineage tracking: The lineage tracking systems are used as modern data control architecture as they follow data through every stage of its life cycle, that is, from ingestion, preprocessing, analysis, and storage. This method of tracking allows transparency and accountability in datasets, providing a deep insight into how datasets have evolved over the course of its lifetime and if the data are reliable and relevant for decision-making [22].

2.3.2.3 Policy Enforcement Engines

Policy enforcement engines are the automated branches having a set of governance rules and policies in real-time data, making sure that the data are handled in line with organizational standards and regulatory requirements.

Real-time monitoring: As the name suggests, these engines keep track of data pipelines in real time under the predefined policies (e.g., access control violations, data quality breaches). They have the ability to halt processes or flag issues when there is data compromise or the policies are breached.
Automated audits: In automated governance platforms, there is a continuous audit of data usage and access, which generates reports for internal governance bodies and external regulatory agencies [23].

2.3.3 Real-Time Data Control in Streaming and Dynamic Systems

Data control in streaming and dynamic systems, that is, real-time IoT systems or AVs, requires a revised strategy so that the real-time flow of data is processed well. Traditional processing architectures are incompetent in handling the real-time updates of these environments, thereby leaving a gap for development in specialized data control methods for consistent and smooth flow of the streaming data [24]. The classification of real-time data control is provided in Figure 2.2.

2.3.3.1 Windowing and Stream Processing

The streaming process involves the data to be processed in continuity so that a real-time control of data is established. This real-time data control is established by using the methodology of windowing. In windowing, the data provided are continuous, which are then divided into fixed-size or sliding windows for processing data easily and efficiently.

Sliding windows: Sliding windows process the incoming continuous real-time data while still keeping the considerations of past data within a given timeframe. This process plays a critical role in real-time decision-making in dynamic systems such as in finance for stock trading or in industrial monitoring for predictive maintenance.
Stream processing frameworks: The framework allows the platforms such as Apache Kafka, Flink, and Spark Streaming to implement robust mechanisms to ensure data consistency and reliability to the extent that it processes millions of data per second. These platforms are used to handle the high-velocity data streams, real-time analytics, monitoring, and control [25].

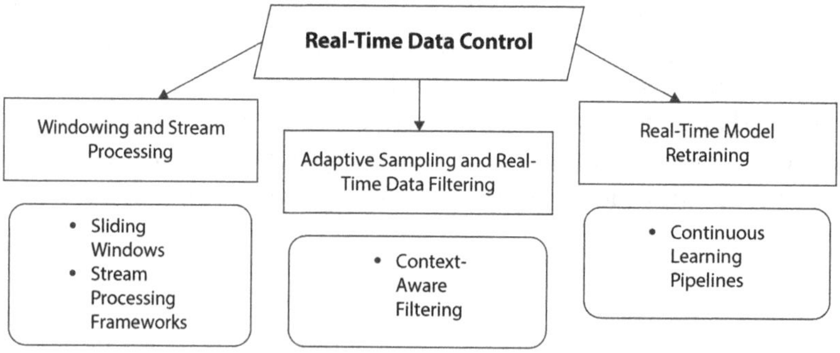

Figure 2.2 Classification of real-time data control.

2.3.3.2 *Adaptive Sampling and Real-Time Data Filtering*

The major challenge to be resolved in dynamic systems is when sheer volume of data is generated in real time and is required to be processed. Thus, adaptive sampling techniques help in adjusting the frequency and resolution of data collected based on the context and ensure that only the most relevant data are captured and processed.

Context-aware filtering: As the name suggests, this technique involves filtering of data in real time on the basis of the context of the data. The context can be important events or data patterns that are required to be prioritized. For instance, in an AV, the data received from sensors, that is, LiDAR cameras, are programmed to filter and focus only on objects within a range or velocity, which reduces the computational load while maintaining safety [26].

2.3.3.3 *Real-Time Model Retraining*

With the frequent updates in the dynamic environment, based on market trends, sensor data, and so on, model retraining plays an essential role in the success of these systems. This helps in maintaining the flow quality of data-driven model updated in real time and is an important component of data control architecture in these contexts.

Continuous learning pipelines: Pipelines are used to monitor the performance of models in production and trigger automated retraining in dynamic systems when there is data drift or environmental changes are updated in the data. This allows maintaining the accuracy and reliability of the data even when newer data are added to the dataset [27].

2.3.4 Emerging Trends in Data Control Architecture

In today's time with development in modern-day technology, the data control architecture is also rapidly developing by advancements in distributed systems, cloud computing, and edge computing. Two key trends stand out as game-changers in the future of data control: federated learning and blockchain-based data governance. The emerging trends in data control are highlighted in Figure 2.3.

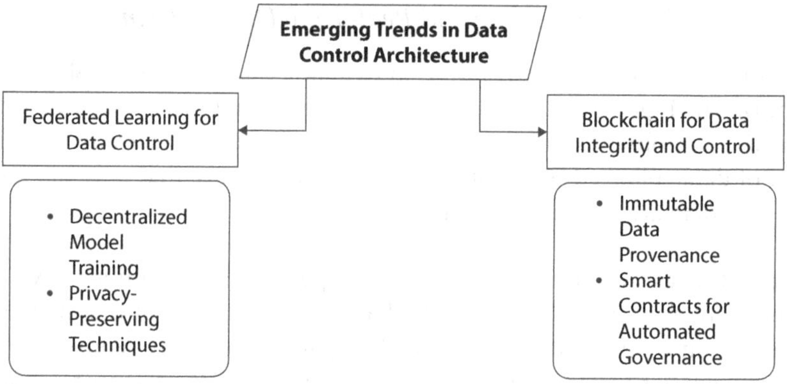

Figure 2.3 Emerging trends in data control.

2.3.4.1 Federated Learning for Data Control

In federated learning, multiple devices or edge servers are used by the learners or the users to train a model together on a network without sharing the raw data while ensuring data privacy and control. This technique has great importance to industries such as healthcare and finance, where data privacy is preeminent.

Decentralized model training: As the name suggests, in decentralized model training, the data remain decentralized at the source, and whenever there is an update, it is exchanged in the primary source, thus removing the need for central data storage, models are trained on a distributed network without any compromise, and safeguarding the user's intellectual properties.
Privacy-preserving techniques: To further enhance privacy, methods such as differential privacy or homomorphic encryption are integrated in federated learning systems, which ensure that all model updates are also not traceable to individual data points [28].

2.3.4.2 Blockchain for Data Integrity and Control

Blockchain technology introduces a fresh approach toward decentralized data control by providing a transparent and immutable ledger of data transactions across multiple parties.

Immutable data provenance: In this system, each and every transaction or modification to the data is recorded and stored in a tamper-resistant ledger, which allows provides robust data provenance and lineage tracking, ensuring that the integrity of data is never compromised.

Smart contracts for automated governance: Smart contacts help in automatic enforcement of data governance on the basis of the preset conditions in the blockchain system. This helps in increasing the efficiency in enforcing the policies in real-time data smoothly without manual oversight, thus streamlining governance in distributed data environments [29].

2.4 Advanced Techniques for Data Control

In order to meet the demands of real-time, dynamic, and distributed systems amid the evolving complexity and scale of the traditional methods, the data control methods fall short. Advancements in the data control technologies have led to solution of some of these problems, with a robust, scalable, and adaptive management of data. Technologies and concepts such as machine learning, control theory, real-time processing, and distributed computing when integrated in systems make the data enhanced with control over data flows and model development. This section explores the cutting-edge technologies for data control including data-driven control strategies, real-time control of streaming data, and methods for handling dynamic environments [30]. The major advanced techniques for data control are shown in Figure 2.4.

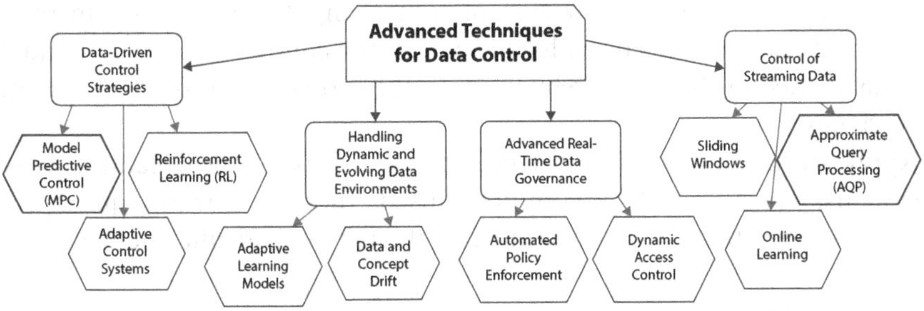

Figure 2.4 Advanced techniques for data control.

2.4.1 Data-Driven Control Strategies

Not only do modern applications involve the usage of data for informing decision-making, but also they are being used to control systems in dynamic systems. In many modern applications, data are used not only to inform decision-making but also to control systems in real time. When the approach relies on large-scale data, in order to adjust system behavior and optimize performance dynamically, it is known as data-driven control strategies. The analysis of historical and real-time data uses these strategies to make informed decisions about control actions, in predictive, reinforced, or adaptive environments.

2.4.1.1 Model Predictive Control

Among data-driven control strategies used in the industry, MPC is one of the most popularly used technique. This model predicts the future states of the system and also optimizes the control actions in the dynamic dataset. As the predictive accuracy of the model directly depends on the data, it directly becomes the most crucial element of the system, as it updates and refines the model.

Data for system identification: System identification is crucial for the working of MPC as it verifies data from the historical data, which is derived during the process, which is important as mentioned previously. Thus, its availability increases with the abundance in data, allowing room for continuous optimized updates, which are then reflected as changing system dynamics.
Real-time optimization: The data streamed by MPC are used to adjust the predictions and optimization of control inputs dynamically, in real-time applications. This provides a room for the controller to make manual adjustments on the fly, thereby limiting the errors and improving system efficiency.
Applications: In process control industries, such as chemical plants, energy systems, and AVs, MPC is commonly used. These industries require precise control actions in order to increase its stability and efficiency [31].

2.4.1.2 RL for Data-Driven Control

A machine learning technique in which the user on interaction with the environment learns to make decisions is known as RL. RL develops control policies that are used for the optimization of long-term rewards based on real-time feedback in the data-driven control.

Policy learning from data: In an RL system, an agent is in direct contact with a system that collects data from the results based on its action. This process of learning a data in order to learn a policy, that is, protocols that define if an action is in the best interest of that situation when used by an agent, is known as policy learning from data.
Model-free and model-based RL: When an agent adapts information directly from the interactions with the environment, it is a model-free RL, whereas when this interaction is between a model made by the agent and the model learns using the data of environment, its plan of action is done in model-based RL. The rise in the integration of both methods into control systems as the data are abundant and the environmental conditions are dynamic makes it an efficient method.
Applications: Complex systems such as robotics, autonomous systems, and energy management use RL-based data-driven control, as the environment dealt with is dynamic, and the traditional methods may not suffice [32].

2.4.1.3 *Adaptive Control Systems*

When the control systems adjust guidelines in real time to handle certain variables in the system, the adaptive controllers use data constantly, to refine control strategies based on observed system behavior.

Real-time parameter adjustment: Parameter adjustment includes the ability of the adaptive controllers over real-time data and its variables such as gains, time constants, and set points. Also, it ensures optimal performance even with the dynamics evolving in real time.
Applications: Adaptive control systems are used in aerospace, manufacturing, and energy systems where conditions may change rapidly, and preset control strategies may not be sufficient to ensure optimal performance [33].

2.4.2 Control of Streaming Data

The streaming data are continuous and are a real-time flow of information, which presents unique challenges due to its unbounded, high-velocity nature of data. The traditional control methods were focused toward processing static or batch-processed data and are not compatible for real-time applications requiring constant updates to data and model built on them. These challenges have been solved by efficient and scalable approach of control over streaming data systems by advanced technologies.

2.4.2.1 Sliding Windows and Stream Processing Frameworks

In real-time data environments, sliding windows and stream processing frameworks are critical for breaking continuous data streams into manageable chunks that can be processed and analyzed in real time.

Sliding windows: A sliding window divides the data stream into time- or event-based windows. Each window contains a subset of the most recent data points, allowing the system to update its models and control strategies based on the latest information.
Stream processing frameworks: Frameworks such as Apache Kafka, Flink, and Spark Streaming provide robust platforms for handling high-velocity data streams. These platforms support real-time data processing and analytics, enabling continuous monitoring and model updates in response to changes in the data stream.

Example use cases
AVs: Sliding windows can process sensor data in near real time to help a vehicle react to changing conditions on the road.
Financial trading systems: Stream processing is used to analyze financial data in real time to trigger automatic trading actions based on changing market conditions [34].

2.4.2.2 Approximate Query Processing

In environments with large-scale streaming data, exact queries may not always be feasible due to the volume of data and time constraints. Approximate query processing (AQP) offers a solution by sacrificing a small degree of accuracy to achieve much faster query response times.

Statistical sampling: AQP uses statistical sampling techniques to generate approximate answers to queries based on a subset of the data. This is particularly useful in time-sensitive applications where the need for speed outweighs the need for perfect accuracy.
Adaptive AQP: Some AQP systems are adaptive, continuously refining their estimates as more data become available, ensuring that the approximation improves over time.

Example use cases
Real-time analytics dashboards: AQP can be used in business intelligence tools to provide approximate, but actionable, insights from large data streams in real time.

Network monitoring: In large-scale network management, AQP helps in quickly identifying potential issues without processing every data packet in the system [35].

2.4.2.3 Online Learning for Streaming Data

In many real-time applications, models need to be updated continuously as new data arrive. Online learning algorithms provide a way to update models incrementally, rather than waiting for complete datasets to retrain the models.

Incremental model updates: Online learning algorithms update the model parameters as each new data point or small batch of data arrives, allowing the model to remain current with the latest information.
Handling concept drift: One of the key challenges in streaming data is concept drift, where the underlying patterns in the data change over time. Online learning systems are well-suited for handling concept drift because they can adapt their models to reflect these changes in real time.

Example use cases
Recommendation systems: Online learning is used in recommendation engines (e.g., for e-commerce) to adapt the model in real time based on user behavior and interactions.
Cybersecurity systems: Online learning algorithms are deployed in network security systems to detect and respond to evolving threats as they emerge in real-time data streams [36].

2.4.3 Handling Dynamic and Evolving Data Environments

In data-driven modeling, data environments are often dynamic, meaning that the data can change over time in unpredictable ways. These changes can be gradual, as in the case of data drift, or abrupt, as in the case of concept drift. Handling such dynamic environments requires advanced data control techniques that can continuously monitor and adjust the model to maintain optimal performance.

2.4.3.1 Adaptive Learning Models

Adaptive learning models are designed to adjust their parameters dynamically in response to changes in the underlying data patterns. These models are particularly useful in dynamic environments where static models may degrade over time.

Continuous retraining pipelines: Adaptive learning models are often integrated with continuous retraining pipelines that monitor the model's performance and trigger retraining whenever performance metrics fall below a certain threshold.
Real-time model evaluation: These systems perform continuous evaluation of the model's performance using metrics such as accuracy, precision, and recall, allowing them to detect and correct performance degradation due to changes in the data.

Example use cases
Predictive maintenance: Adaptive models are used to predict equipment failures based on sensor data. As the equipment ages, the model adjusts its parameters to reflect changing wear-and-tear patterns.
Smart energy grids: Adaptive learning models are used to optimize energy distribution in real time, adjusting to changing demand and supply conditions [37].

2.4.3.2 Handling Data Drift and Concept Drift

Data drift refers to changes in the statistical properties of the data over time, whereas concept drift refers to changes in the relationships between input and output variables in a model. Both phenomena can cause models to degrade if not addressed proactively.

Drift detection algorithms: Algorithms such as ADWIN (adaptive windowing) and Hoeffding trees are commonly used for detecting and responding to data drift. These algorithms monitor the data stream and trigger updates to the model whenever significant drift is detected.
Ensemble learning for drift: In some cases, ensemble methods are used to combine multiple models, each trained on different subsets of the data or time periods. When concept drift is detected, the ensemble can switch between models or combine them in new ways to maintain performance.

Example use cases
Fraud-detection systems: Concept drift is common in fraud detection, as fraudsters continuously evolve their tactics. Drift detection algorithms help ensure that models remain effective in identifying new types of fraud.
Financial forecasting: Data drift occurs frequently in financial markets as economic conditions change. Adaptive models help keep predictions accurate in these environments [38].

2.4.4 Advanced Real-Time Data Governance

In dynamic and streaming environments, ensuring data governance in real time requires advanced techniques that can apply governance rules as data are ingested, processed, and used. This is especially important for applications that involve sensitive data, such as financial transactions, healthcare systems, and autonomous systems.

2.4.4.1 Automated Policy Enforcement

In real-time environments, governance policies must be enforced automatically to ensure compliance with data privacy, security, and integrity standards. Automated policy enforcement engines continuously monitor data flows and apply governance rules as data are ingested and processed.

Real-time rule enforcement: These systems apply predefined governance rules in real time, ensuring that only authorized users can access sensitive data and that data are handled in compliance with regulations such as GDPR or HIPAA.
Automated auditing: Real-time auditing systems log every access and modification to the data, providing a continuous record that can be reviewed for compliance purposes [39].

2.4.4.2 Dynamic Access Control

In dynamic environments, data access control must also be dynamic, adjusting based on the context, user role, and data sensitivity. Dynamic access control systems use context-aware policies to determine who can access data and under what circumstances.

Context-aware access: Dynamic access control systems consider factors such as user location, time of access, and the sensitivity of the data to dynamically adjust access permissions.
Real-time access logs: These systems maintain real-time logs of all data access and use, providing detailed visibility into how data are being used across the system.

Example use cases
Healthcare systems: Dynamic access control is used in healthcare to ensure that only authorized personnel can access sensitive patient data, based on their role, location, and the current treatment context.

Financial systems: Financial institutions use dynamic access control to protect sensitive transaction data, ensuring that access is granted only to authorized individuals under appropriate conditions [40].

2.5 Challenges in Data Control for Modeling

With the complexities increasing day by day in modern data environments, data control in modeling has presented us with a plethora of challenges. The impact of these challenges is the accuracy, scalability, security, and reliability of data-driven models. The traditional methods of data governance and management prove to be ineffective with the increase in volumes of datasets and their dynamic nature, while being spread across various systems. In this section, we discuss the hurdles in the path of data control for modeling, which includes scalability issues, data and concept drifts, and real-time and collaborative data control. These challenges often affect the efficiency and accuracy of the models as they cascade effects on performance and reliability of models, which requires advanced technologies to mitigate their impact [41].

2.5.1 Scalability Issues

In data control for modeling, one of the major concerns is its scalability. In the wake of the rise in usage of IoT devices, social media, sensors, and transactional systems, it has led to an increase in volumes of the datasets. The management, processing, and control of these datasets at a large scale are the next hurdle toward scalability. Other concerns are the data storage limitations, which delay processing in real-time applications [42]. The challenges in data control are depicted in Figure 2.5.

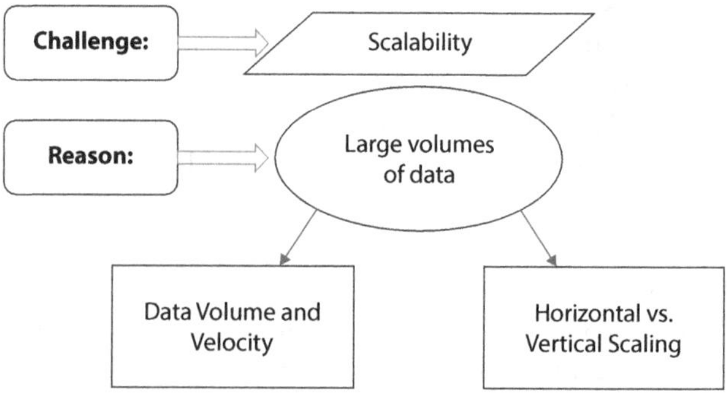

Figure 2.5 The challenges in data control.

2.5.1.1 Data Volume and Velocity

The traditional centralized data management systems are inefficient to deal with the vast amount of data generated in the dynamic environments with the rise of big data. The standard database systems that were at one point enough to support the datasets are now beyond the capacity due to the data velocity. Data velocity is the speed at which the data are generated, collected, and processed.

Storage issues: In order to have both reliable and cost-effective storage solutions to store and manage petabytes or even exabytes, the solution should be ensuring that the data's redundancy, security, and access control are well managed under the governance rules, which in huge volume is a challenge.
Processing bottlenecks: The systems in financial trading or AVs use real-time data processing systems in order to analyze data streams in microseconds. The minute delays in the data processing may hamper the systems' accuracy, which can be due to scalability issues and would lead to system failures [43].

2.5.1.2 Horizontal versus Vertical Scaling

Vertical scaling refers to enhancing the capacity of a single machine by adding more resources such as CPU or memory, while horizontal scaling involves adding multiple machines to distribute the workload across them. Horizontal scaling offers better long-term scalability solutions, but at the same time introduces concerns such as distributed consistency, fault tolerance, and load balancing in the data.

Distributed consistency: Methodologies such as CAP theorem, that is, consistency, availability, and partition tolerance, are used. This helps in highlighting trade-offs in decentralized systems, but maintaining consistent data in horizontally scaled system is still a challenge.
Data sharding: Some scalability issues can be resolved by the use of data sharding, that is, portioning datasets across various databases or machines. Even though breaking into shards is a better approach, maintaining its consistency across all shards and resharding with the increase in volume of data, the system architecture grows to be complex.

Example use cases
Streaming platforms: In order to maintain latency while streaming and ensuring scalability, as its part of the user experience in streaming platforms, this method allows platforms such as Netflix or YouTube to make sure that vast data from millions of users are protected simultaneously.
Smart cities: In real-time processing of the millions of data, from sensors across cities from the traffic management or energy grids, smart city applications pose immense scalability challenges [44].

2.5.2 Data Drift and Concept Drift

As the pattern of the data tends to change day by day, data and concept drift are general challenges to be dealt with in dynamic environments. This leads to degradation in the model performance, as the assumptions during training stage may or may not hold true now, leading to accuracy and precision of data being compromised. The detection of anomalies in the system due to these is a challenging task in data control. The process of data drift is reflected in Figure 2.6.

2.5.2.1 Types of Drift

Data drift: When over a period of time the input data change, their distribution structure due to seasonality, changes in market, behavioral shifts, or evolving sensor accuracy is known as data drift.
Concept drift: In concept drift, the change in relationship of input and output variables is involved. This can be explained with the example of a fraud-detection system where the system learns from the patterns and

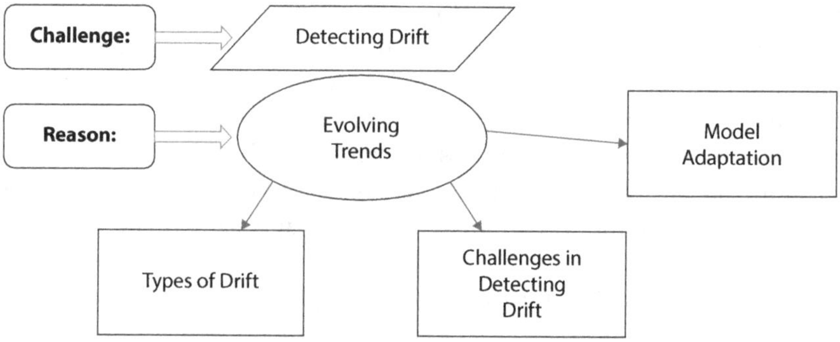

Figure 2.6 The process of data drift.

strategies used by fraudsters, which may evolve over time, but the previously learned patterns are now obsolete.
Covariate shift: When the relationship between input and output pattern remains the same, while the distribution of independent variables changes, it is known as a covariate shift [45].

2.5.2.2 Challenges in Detecting Drift

As the data distribution changes can be gradual or sudden, the anomaly detection for drift in data is not a piece of cake. The gradual shifts in data may not be identified as an anomaly as there is no sudden spike in behavioral shift of model, which could be recognized and will be prone to remaining unnoticed, while hampering the system's accuracy in the meantime. On the other hand, sudden spike in change and its error can be noticed, which would lead to an immediate issue in model.

Real-time detection: When dealing with large volumes of data or high-velocity streams, continuous monitoring of incoming real-time data is required to be done by systems to check for any anomalies in data as drifts.
False positives and negatives: The sensitivity of a detection system is crucial, as if too sensitive would lead to flagging of normal variations; that is, false positives or if the sensitivity is reduced, meaningful drifts can be ignored as well, that is, false negatives. Thus, finding the balance between sensitivity and robustness is the key to the successful drift detection [46].

2.5.2.3 Model Adaptation

Once the drift is detected in the model, the model is required to be modified and retrained with new appropriate data. This retraining process, on the basis of predefined criteria, is a resource-intensive process with systems that can dynamically adjust their parameters or trigger retraining program.

Incremental learning: As the new data are fed into the system without full retraining, it can be solved by incremental learning algorithms. The model is to be modified while retaining its historical and new data, which is a challenge.
Ensemble methods: As the data are distributed over systems or nodes, the ensemble of models in the multimodel system increases its complexity, and the data can be switched between models based on current data distribution.

Example use cases
Predictive maintenance: Data from sensors can drift due to equipment aging, environmental conditions, or sensor malfunctions. The industries are dependent on these systems for their failure predictions. Thus, failure in identification of drifts would lead to system collapse.
Financial forecasting: Building models that are accurate over a period of time is a challenging task due to data drift being a common error. This can be due to various reasons such as change in economic conditions, government policies, or market sentiment, in the financial markets [47].

2.5.3 Real-Time Data Control

In this robust world, models are required to receive and process data as quickly; it is generated and processed simultaneously. The accuracy of the system while processing the large amounts of data that need to be ingested, processed, and controlled is a major constraint in designing systems. The process of real-time data control is shown in Figure 2.7.

2.5.3.1 Latency Issues

A minor delay in data processing during real-time data interpretation can cause significant performance degradation or system failure, especially in fields such as AVs, industrial automation, or financial trading, where the data processed are crucial. In order to ensure that systems can make decisions, based on latest data without considerations and delays, low-latency data processing is essential.

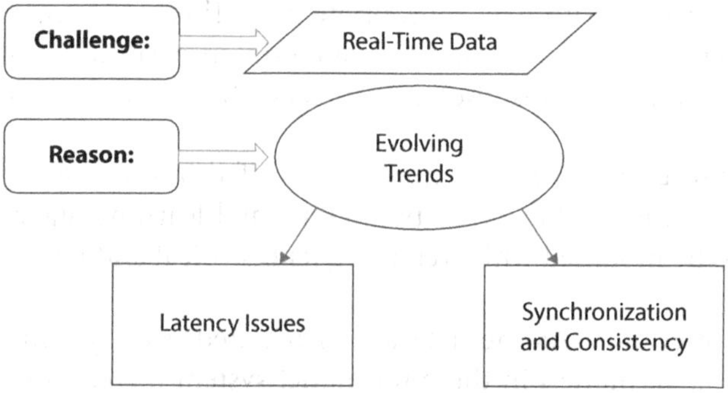

Figure 2.7 The process of real-time data control.

Data stream processing: Streaming frameworks such as Apache Kafka or Flink are enabled with real-time processing, whereas traditional processing techniques are of no use. Also, these frameworks have their limitations, as the real-time data processing requires significant infrastructure and configuration to handle high-throughput, low-latency data streams.
Edge computing: Latency can be reduced, and the real-time performance can be improved, if the data are closer to where it is being generated, while managing data control across both edge and centralized devices. This required balance adds a layer of complexity to the architecture [48].

2.5.3.2 *Synchronization and Consistency*

The synchronization and consistency across multiple systems or nodes are a challenge yet to be resolved. Data arrive at these nodes at various times, in different formats and differing levels of accuracy. Thus, there is a necessity to find a balance to increase the processing abilities accuracy.

Event time processing: As the name suggests, each data point is processed corresponding to the time it was generated and not when it was received. This is event time processing and helps in ensuring the consistency of dynamic environment.
Out-of-order data handling: In places where network delays are common, the data might be out of order. Thus, handling out-of-order data is complex, as it requires reordering and rearrangement of data to its correct sequence.

Example use cases
AVs: As the AVs are based on the predictions based of real-time data retrieved from the sensors for navigation, the accuracy of these data is crucial as it is in charge of critical decisions; if it fails, it would have potentially catastrophic consequences.
Real-time trading systems: Similar is the case in financial trading; the trades are based on the patterns formed by the data provided in real time, which allows to make choices for trade choices. If there is discrepancy in the data, this would lead to huge financial losses for the traders and lead to inconsistency [49].

2.5.4 Data Privacy and Security

The privacy and security of data are increasing with the complexity of data control systems. The reason is the distributed control system. In order to

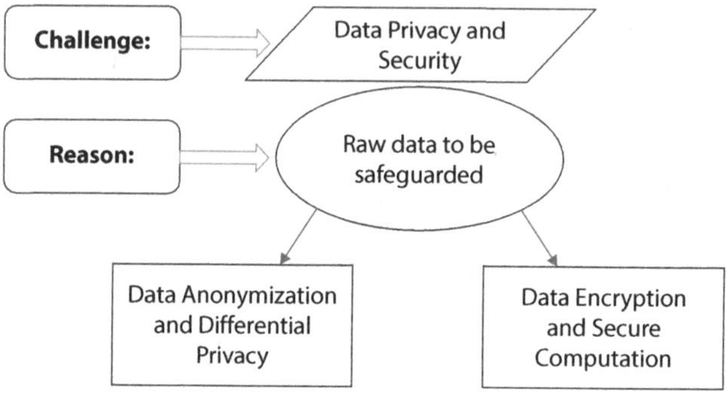

Figure 2.8 The issues of data privacy and security.

effectively manage the data on how data must be stored, processed, and protected, especially when dealing with sensitive or personal data, the regulatory frameworks such as GDPR and CCPA are imposed. The issues of data privacy and security are depicted in Figure 2.8.

2.5.4.1 Data Anonymization and Differential Privacy

Anonymization of data ensures the privacy of the data as the personally identifiable information is removed or masked. This allows to successfully hide the identification of the individual in the dataset. Even though it seems as a foolproof solution, still it has some loopholes, that is, in forms of reidentification attacks, which may lead to revealing the identities and are a topic of concern.

Differential privacy: Differential privacy provides a solution to the limitations posed by anonymization of data in an optimized and robust way. In this method, noise is added to the data or output of the model such that individual data points cannot be differentiated. Thus, the attacker would not be able to uncover the true identity of data. However, careful balance of data utility and privacy is still required.
Challenges in implementation: This method may be difficult in terms of integration into the system and reduce the accuracy of models. The balance for that right level of noise required to mask the detail is required while ensuring the model performance is not degraded is a significant challenge [50].

2.5.4.2 *Data Encryption and Secure Computation*

Advanced encryption protects data at rest and in transit while ensuring data security in distributed and cloud environments.

Homomorphic encryption: In this method, computations are allowed to be performed on encrypted data without the need to decrypt it, thereby providing a solution to privacy-preserving analytics. The disadvantage of homomorphic encryption is its being computationally expensive and difficult to scale, a major issue in dynamic systems.
SMPC: The inputs are kept private, while computation of functions among multiple devices is the working of SMPC. Thus, its best use case is for when data are shared and analyzed across different organizations, but the raw data are never revealed. However, SMPC also requires specialized protocols and is computationally intensive.

Example use cases
Healthcare systems: Research and analytics are critical in the healthcare sector while protecting patient data. This can be achieved using balanced data utility with privacy requirements.
Cloud-based systems: Cloud-based data control systems are used by organizations, as they can store and process data off-site. When dealing with sensitive data such as financial transactions or intellectual property, ensuring data encryption and security in cloud environments is a challenge [51].

2.5.5 Collaborative Data Control

With rise in use of multiple nodes, due to decentralized systems, collaboration among multiple teams, departments, or even organizations,

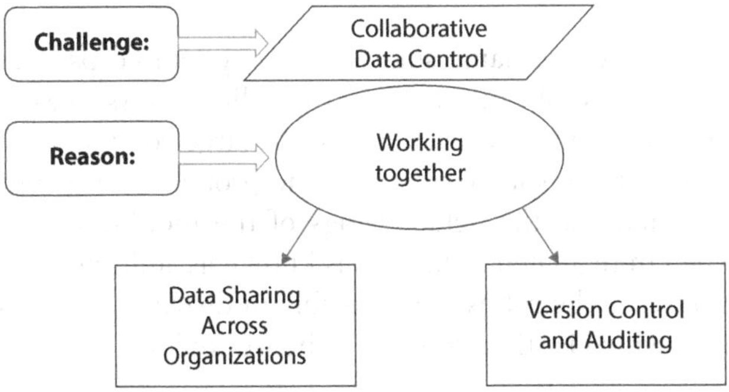

Figure 2.9 The process of collaborative data control.

the modeling projects in collaboration play a key role in contributing to the success of the model. The data when consistent, secure, and usable across different entities with its own set of policies, infrastructure, and governance standards are the basis of collaborative data control. The various aspects of collaborative data control are provided in Figure 2.9.

2.5.5.1 *Data Sharing Across Organizations*

Maintaining control over the data governance strategies is one of the major challenges faced by the system, when the data are shared across organizations or departments. Establishment of a unified data control framework is a difficult task as each organization has its own standards for data privacy, security, and quality.

Data federation: Without transferring the central location when data are shared, it is known as data federation techniques. In data federation, each party retains its power over its own piece of data even while maintaining shared analysis, ensuring consistency, and is in line with the governance policies.
Data sovereignty: Restricting how data can be shared across borders while ensuring it stays in line with data sovereignty is a crucial phase in many industries. Complying with these laws and ensuring data control is a challenge for multinational organizations [52].

2.5.5.2 *Version Control and Auditing*

It is essential to keep a track of changes of the data across all collaborators, in order to make sure that all are working with the same version of data. Consistency and traceability in dynamic environments are ensured by data versioning and auditing tools.

Data versioning: As the name suggests, this system keeps a track of the changes over a period of time enabling the collaborators to work with the recent updated versions. However, due to the large volumes of data across varied datasets, it is a resource-intensive and prone-to-error solution.
Auditing: Maintaining the detailed logs of the modification of data by whom or when in regulated industries is known as auditing. Auditing systems are required to be robust and scalable in distributed or cloud-based environments, which is still a concern to be worked on.

Example use cases
Cross-industry collaboration: Datasets are often shared among different industries or countries for research purposes. Thus, ensuring the access of the same data across all levels while respecting local privacy laws requires a more sophisticated approach.
Supply chain management: In order to share inventory, shipments, or production schedules in global supply chain, data consistency and control access are critical for smooth operation of the supply chain [53].

2.6 Best Practices for Data Control in Data-Driven Modeling

A comprehensive set of best practices accompanied by advanced techniques in data-driven modeling ensures effective data control. In order to ensure data quality, integrity, security, privacy, and scalability, these practices are used, but transparency and compliance with regulatory standards are to be kept into consideration. This section emphasizes the best practices available in data-driven modeling for data control, which involves methods such as data versioning and auditing, collaborative data control, metadata management, and automation in governance.

2.6.1 Data Versioning and Auditing

To maintain consistency, traceability, and accountability in data-driven modeling and collaborative control systems, the importance of data versioning and auditing is significant, as they work on the same datasets in which the data evolve over the input of data across the various systems. This helps in keeping track of all the changes made in the datasets over a period of time and tracing back to the origin. This allows the data to be more compatible and easier to proofread, maintaining compliance and reproducing results.

2.6.1.1 Data Versioning

The concept of data versioning is borrowed from software engineering, which involves version control systems such as Git track, which changes to code. In data versioning, the versions of data with changes over a period of time are kept in record. This allows the model to be trained on a specific

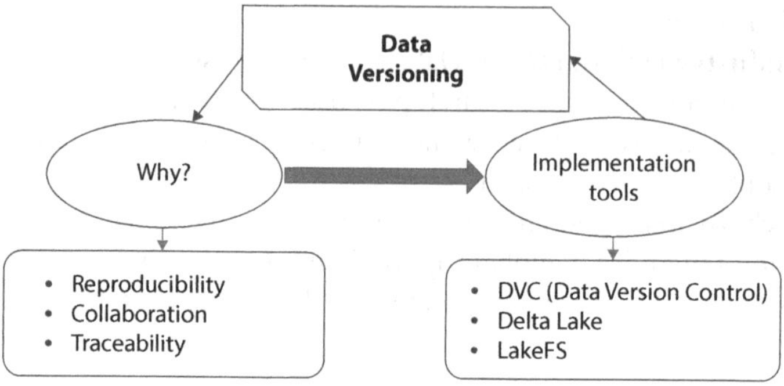

Figure 2.10 Data version control.

version as per the need of the system and can be traced back to a particular dataset version. The process of data version control (DVC) is shown in Figure 2.10.

Why versioning matters

Reproducibility: Using data versioning, users can retrace their steps of work with the exact versions of data required as per the need of model or the experiment required for research and production environments, thereby producing the warranted results.

Collaboration: In collaboration, as multiple users collaborate to work on the same dataset, there is a need to keep track of which version is being modified by each team in order to prevent inconsistencies or data drifts.

Traceability: Data versioning helps in tracing back any fault in data back to its origin source; therefore, in case of model efficiency deteriorating, the problem can be resolved sooner even if the changes were deliberate or an accident.

Implementation tools

DVC: DVC is integrated with Git to track both code and data changes and is designed for data science workflows.

Delta Lake: Delta Lake is a popular source that is built on Apache Spark and deals with big data control. It also helps to look after the different data versions used for model over a period of time and ensures atomicity, consistency, isolation, and durability; that is, ACID properties are followed.

LakeFS: LakeFS is similar to Delta lakes with version control such as Git to manage data, is used, and offers snapshots and branching for large datasets [54].

2.6.1.2 Auditing

When a detailed record of all modifications or changes on a dataset is included beginning from who accessed or modified the data to when and how is known as auditing. Auditing, which helps to maintain accountability in situations where sensitive data are managed or are in compliance to regulatory frameworks, is necessary. The various aspects of data auditing are provided in Figure 2.11.

Why auditing is important

Regulatory compliance: Organizations maintain detailed records of data and modifications to ensure accountability under regulations such as GDPR and HIPAA. An audit trail is reviewed during audits or investigations by organizations to meet the regulatory requirements.

Data security: Because auditing logs keep track of the modifications in the systems, this enables to check who accessed and altered the data, thereby identifying vulnerabilities and providing prompt response, in the event of data compromise.

Accountability: All data-related actions starting from modifications to alterations are kept in record in auditing, creating a transparent environment, which is established on the basis of accountability of the data.

Implementation tools

Apache atlas: Apache atlas is an open source that consists of comprehensive auditing capabilities, tracks data lineage and has an access across distributed environments, and is used to manage and govern data ecosystems.

AWS CloudTrail: The logging and monitoring of API calls on AWS environment help organizations on the basis of maintained detailed records of actions uploaded on cloud-based datasets [55].

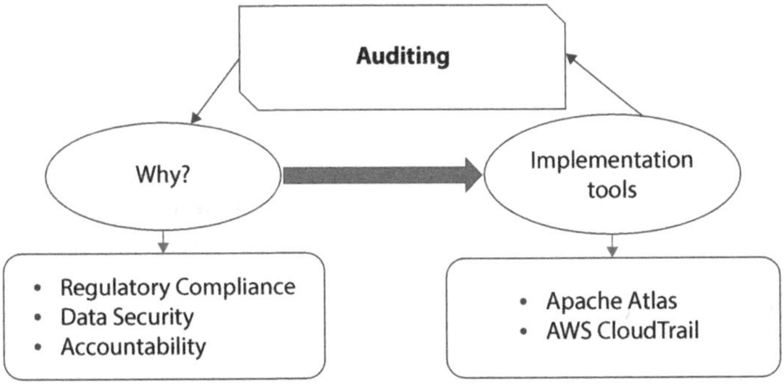

Figure 2.11 Data auditing.

2.6.2 Collaborative Data Control

With the rise in use of decentralized systems in data-driven modeling, collaboration is the key to bridge between the different departments involved in this system. It is necessary to ensure that the data are consistent, secure and traceable across different users while ensuring a smooth workflow in complex, dynamic multistakeholder projects.

2.6.2.1 Role-Based Access Control

All employees do not have the same importance in a company; as it depends on hierarchy, the same approach is applied to collaborative environments, and not all users have equal access to data. Thus, in a role-based approach on the basis of their role in the project, the data are provided to the respective user. This ensures to minimize the risk of data leak as unauthorized access or accidental data corruption would be difficult. The various aspects of role-based access control (RBAC) are provided in Figure 2.12.

How RBAC works

Role definition: On the basis of responsibilities of individuals or teams, role is defined. For example, engineers have full access to data, but analysts would have only read-only access of datasets only.

Granular permissions: When who can read, write, or modify is specified for a piece of data, the access control to each dataset type may also be varied and based on RBAC.

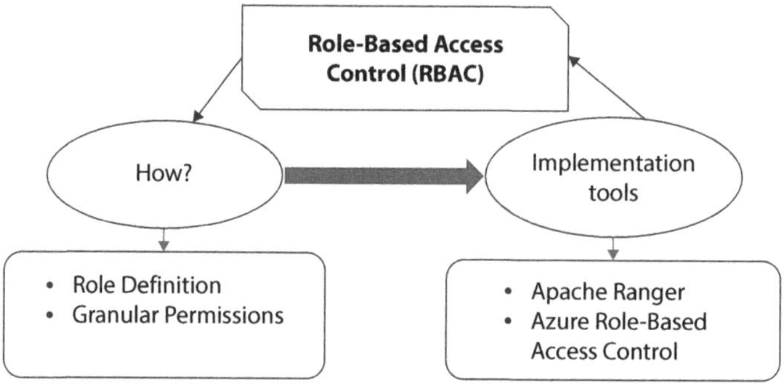

Figure 2.12 Role-based access control.

Implementation tools
Apache Ranger: RBAC policies for Hadoop-based data systems are on a comprehensive security-based approach, which ensures users to have access only to necessary data on the basis of their rules, and are done by Apache Ranger.
Azure RBAC: Granular permissions are offered to organizations by Azure RBAC for databases, storage, and analytics tools [56].

2.6.2.2 Data Sharing and Federation

When the data are distributed across different systems and across organizations or departments, it is a crucial step to ensure data control policies in collaborative environments. The process of data sharing is illustrated in Figure 2.13.

Federated data control: When organizations have full control their own data while participating in collaborative projects, it is known as federated data control. This ensures the in-house data are safeguarded and only the data required are shared for analysis purposes to other stakeholders and is practiced in industries such as healthcare or finance where data privacy of the users is important.
Data sharing agreements: Data sharing agreements are made to ensure that all the parties in the collaboration comply with the legal terms and regulatory requirements under their respective legislatures. The agreements should state the clauses clearly starting from data control responsibilities to access rights and governance policies.

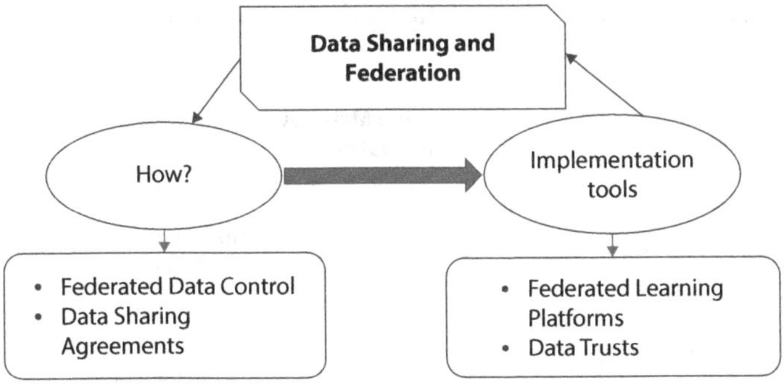

Figure 2.13 Data sharing.

Implementation tools

Federated learning platforms: Training models with the help of machine learning tools collaboratively across multiple locations without sharing the raw data can be done using the federated learning platforms such as Google's Tensor Flow.

Data trusts: A legal framework defined to maintain transparency and accountability of all parties for sharing and governing data in a collaborative environment is a data trust [57].

2.6.3 Metadata Management for Governance and Provenance

In order to ensure proper governance, tracking down data lineage, and maintaining the data integrity, metadata management plays a crucial role in the life cycle of the data. It provides us with the knowledge of the origin of the data, how they have been modified, and how they are in relation to the other datasets.

2.6.3.1 Automated Metadata Generation

When dealing with large volumes of complicated data, manual data management is labor-intensive and prone to errors. Thus, there is a need for automated metadata management tools. These tools help in tracking metadata at every stage of its life cycle, starting from collection to analysis, and are used by organizations. The entire process of automated metadata generation is depicted in Figure 2.14.

Why metadata matters

Data provenance: The origin and history of a dataset are accessible due to the metadata as it tracks all the data, so that when in time of need the data

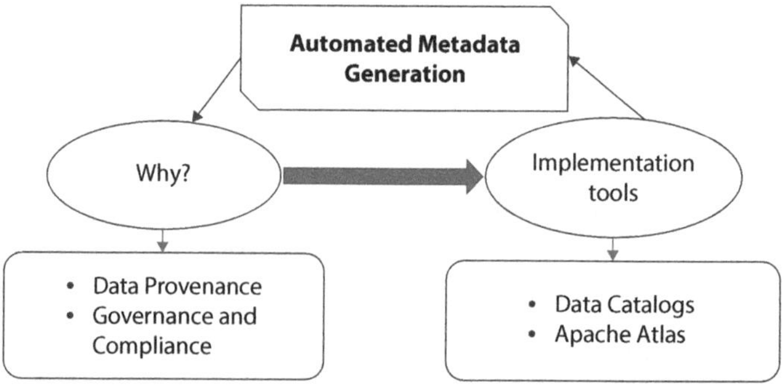

Figure 2.14 Automated metadata generation.

can be traced back to the specific versions and modifications. This helps in maintaining transparency and reproducibility of the results.
Governance and compliance: Because metadata has a track of who accessed and used the data to how the modifications were made, it helps in enforcing governance policies better and helps to meet the compliance requirements.

Implementation tools
Data catalogs: Automated metadata generation and management can now be done easily by using tools such as Alation, Collibra, and AWS Glue as they help in tracking data provenance and enforce governance policies.
Apache atlas: Apache atlas is also synonymous to automated metadata generation as it enables the organizations to track data lineage across all nodes [58].

2.6.3.2 Data Provenance and Lineage Tracking

Lineage tracking, from the literal meaning, helps to track the origin of the data or how they are modified, or where they have been applied, as this helps in ensuring trust and maintains a regulatory compliance. Lineage tracking asks and gives the solution to the following questions:

Where is the origin of the data?
What are the modifications applied to the data?
What are the models used to build the data?

The process of data provenance and lineage tracking is shown in Figure 2.15.

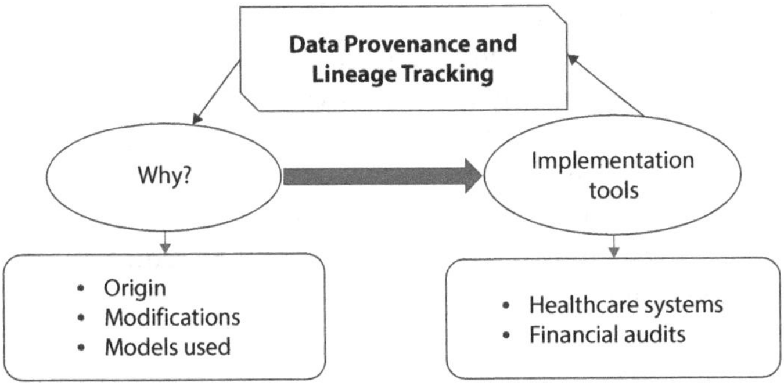

Figure 2.15 Data provenance and lineage tracking.

Data provenance frameworks: The organizations need to verify the integrity and quality of data at every step using the frameworks, which transforms and processes all the data at every step.

Example use cases
Healthcare systems: Ensuring patient privacy and data integrity is the most important factor in the healthcare industry, as the patient data are very sensitive and need to be handled carefully. Thus, analysis when run on these files, that is, data provenance, ensures the data can be traced back to the source.
Financial audits: In order to maintain transparency to ensure the financial models are accurate and based on verified data, data lineage tracking is followed [59].

2.6.4 Automation in Data Governance

Managing data manually in this technologically sound world seems to be impractical. Thus, data governance systems for large-scale systems are done in automation, and the governance rules and policies are applied across the whole data system. It is important to ensure that data governance is handled in compliance with regulatory frameworks and internal standards without the need of manual intervention.

2.6.4.1 Automated Policy Enforcement

When data governance policies are defined and enforced in a scalable and consistent manner by organizations, they are organized by automated policy enforcement systems. These regulations involve access control, data retention, compliance with privacy regulations, and security requirements.

Why automate governance?
Scalability: Traditional methods struggle to keep up with the large volumes of datasets generated in dynamic environments. Thus, managing the speed while keeping its consistency and accuracy automation helps in scaling governance practices.
Consistency: Governance policies should match across all organizations and models as decided by the organization, so as to reduce the likelihood of errors or oversight.

Implementation tools
Data governance platforms: Automated governance frameworks are offered by tools such as Collibra and Informatica, which ensure that policy enforcements are consistent and the burden on data managers is reduced across the organization ecosystem.
Automated data retention systems: Maintaining data retention and deletion in compliance to regulatory requirements by predefined policies is the working of automated data retention systems [60].

2.6.4.2 Automated Compliance Monitoring

Data privacy and security regulations are a key concern in data-driven modeling systems. The data usage and access are monitored continuously in order to ensure that the modifications comply with relevant laws and regulations, under automated compliance monitoring systems. The purpose and the implementation of automated compliance monitoring are provided in Figure 2.16.

Real-time auditing and monitoring: Because all the data are tracked in real time by the systems, flagging an anomaly in real time in compliance of regulations and policies is done by real-time auditing and monitoring systems. For example, unauthorized override on a system containing sensitive data or violations of data privacy laws is notified to the organizations for immediate response by these systems.
Reporting and alerts: Detailed reports on usage and compliance of data usage can be generated in order to help the organizations for the regulatory audits or legal inquiries using automated compliance systems. If any of the above is violated, the systems would alert data governance teams, allowing for quick response.

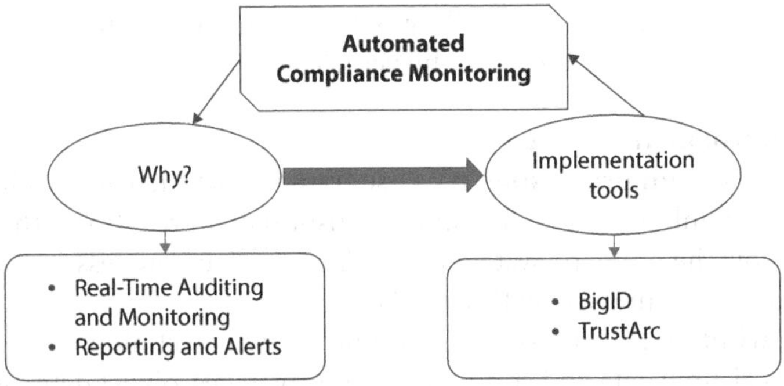

Figure 2.16 Automated compliance monitoring.

Implementation tools
BigID: BigID provides automated data discovery, classification, and compliance monitoring for regulations such as GDPR and CCPA, as a data intelligence platform.
TrustArc: Tracking data processing activities and management of regulatory compliance solutions for privacy management and enabling organizations are done by TrustArc [61].

2.7 Case Studies in Data Control Methods

In this section, we examine real-world case studies where data control methods have been successfully implemented to overcome complex challenges in data-driven modeling. These case studies highlight the application of advanced data control techniques such as real-time data processing, data governance, privacy-preserving technologies, and collaborative data sharing. By exploring the specific methodologies and technologies used in these scenarios, we gain a deeper understanding of how effective data control methods can drive innovation and solve real-world problems.

2.7.1 Real-Time Data Control in AVs

Industry context: AVs represent one of the most complex real-time systems in existence. AVs must process vast amounts of sensor data in real time to navigate roads, avoid obstacles, and make split-second decisions. This requires highly efficient data control methods that ensure the data are timely, accurate, and secure.
Problem: The AV ecosystem relies on multiple types of sensors, such as cameras, LiDAR, radar, and ultrasonic sensors, to gather environmental data. The challenge lies in processing these data streams in real time while ensuring data consistency, handling out-of-order events, and maintaining low-latency responses to ensure the vehicle's safety.

Data control methods used
Real-time stream processing: AVs use frameworks such as Apache Kafka or Apache Flink to process streaming sensor data in real time. These platforms allow the onboard system of the AV to collect, process, and react to sensor data continuously without delays.
Sliding windows: In AV systems, sliding window techniques are used to handle real-time data and compute moving averages, object detection, and tracking metrics. By applying sliding windows to the data, the vehicle's

control system can detect obstacles and adjust speed in response to rapidly changing environments.

Event time processing: AVs need to ensure that events (e.g., detecting an obstacle) are processed based on the time they occur rather than the time they are received. Event-time processing ensures that out-of-order sensor data are reordered and processed correctly, thus preventing potentially dangerous delays in decision-making.

Edge computing for data control: To reduce latency, many AV systems rely on edge computing. Instead of sending all data to the cloud for processing, edge devices process data locally on the vehicle, ensuring immediate responses to critical events such as pedestrian detection or collision avoidance.

Outcome: The implementation of real-time data control methods has significantly enhanced the reliability and safety of AVs. By leveraging edge computing and real-time stream processing, AVs can respond to environmental changes within milliseconds, ensuring safe and efficient navigation in complex driving environments [62].

2.7.2 Data Governance and Privacy in Healthcare

Industry context: The healthcare industry generates vast amounts of sensitive data, including patient records, diagnostic information, and clinical trial data. Managing and controlling these data while maintaining privacy and regulatory compliance are a significant challenge, especially in the face of regulations such as the GDPR and HIPAA.

Problem: A major hospital network in the United States needed to integrate data from multiple departments and facilities while maintaining strict compliance with HIPAA. The data involved patient health records (protected health information), and unauthorized access or misuse of these data could result in severe legal and financial consequences. Additionally, the hospital wanted to leverage these data for research and predictive modeling without compromising patient privacy.

Data control methods used

Automated data governance: The hospital implemented an automated data governance platform, Collibra, to manage access controls, data lineage, and compliance rules across its data ecosystem. This platform allowed the hospital to define and enforce RBACs, ensuring that only authorized personnel could access sensitive health data.

Differential privacy: To enable research without exposing patient identities, the hospital applied differential privacy to its datasets. Differential privacy introduced controlled noise into the data, preventing researchers from identifying individual patients while still allowing for valuable analysis.

Data lineage and provenance: The hospital implemented data lineage tracking to ensure full transparency over data usage. By tracking how data were collected, processed, and shared, the hospital could ensure compliance with privacy regulations and easily identify any unauthorized access to patient data.

Data encryption: All sensitive data were encrypted at rest and in transit using Advanced Encryption Standard, ensuring that even if the data were intercepted, it would be unreadable without the appropriate decryption keys. This helped the hospital mitigate the risks of data breaches.

Outcome: The hospital successfully integrated its data from multiple departments while maintaining full compliance with HIPAA regulations. By implementing differential privacy and automated governance, the hospital was able to protect patient identities and utilize its data for research purposes, resulting in more effective predictive models for patient care without compromising privacy. Moreover, the auditability provided by the data lineage system ensured that the hospital could quickly respond to any data security incidents or regulatory inquiries [63].

2.7.3 Collaborative Data Sharing in Financial Services

Industry context: In the financial services industry, collaboration between banks, insurance companies, and fintech startups is becoming increasingly common. These organizations often need to share large volumes of transactional data for purposes such as fraud detection, risk assessment, and market analysis. However, data sharing across organizations presents significant challenges in terms of data control, especially with regard to maintaining data security, privacy, and compliance with financial regulations such as Gramm-Leach-Bliley Act and Payment Card Industry Data Security Standard.

Problem: A consortium of banks wanted to collaborate on a shared fraud-detection system that leveraged data from all member institutions. However, each bank needed to maintain control over its own data and ensure compliance with financial privacy laws. The banks were also concerned about data sovereignty, as their operations spanned multiple countries with differing regulations.

Data control methods used

Federated learning for collaborative data control: Instead of sharing raw data, the banks implemented a federated learning system, where each institution trained a local machine learning model on its own data. The model parameters (but not the data itself) were then shared with a central server, where the parameters were aggregated into a global model. This approach allowed the banks to collaborate on building a shared fraud detection model without exposing sensitive customer data.

Data encryption and secure communication: The consortium used homomorphic encryption to ensure that even the model parameters exchanged between banks and the central server were encrypted. This meant that banks could collaborate on the model without revealing any proprietary information or sensitive customer data, even during the model training process.

RBAC: To ensure that only authorized personnel had access to certain aspects of the data or model, the banks implemented RBAC policies. Each organization controlled who could access specific datasets and who could contribute to the federated learning process.

Data sovereignty and local compliance: The consortium used geofencing techniques to ensure that data never left the country of origin, in compliance with data sovereignty laws. Each bank's data were stored and processed locally, ensuring that the collaboration remained compliant with each country's financial data regulations.

Outcome: The consortium successfully developed a collaborative fraud detection model without violating data privacy or sovereignty laws. By using federated learning, encryption, and RBAC, the banks were able to protect their proprietary data while benefiting from a more comprehensive and accurate fraud-detection system. The system was able to detect patterns of fraudulent behavior across the entire consortium's dataset, resulting in improved detection rates and reduced financial losses due to fraud [64].

2.7.4 Data Control in Smart Energy Grids

Industry context: Smart energy grids are dynamic, real-time systems that rely on vast amounts of data from sensors, meters, and power stations to balance energy supply and demand. These grids require effective data control methods to ensure that energy distribution is optimized while maintaining system reliability and preventing blackouts. The data involved are often distributed across different geographic regions, making it essential to manage data control in a decentralized and scalable manner.

Problem: A national energy provider needed to modernize its energy grid by incorporating real-time data from smart meters, sensors, and substations. The challenge was to process and control these data in real time to optimize energy distribution, reduce waste, and respond to demand fluctuations. Additionally, the provider needed to ensure data security and prevent unauthorized access to the energy grid's operational data, which could pose a significant security threat.

Data control methods used

Decentralized data control with edge computing: The energy provider implemented a decentralized data control system using edge computing. Data from smart meters and substations were processed locally at edge devices, reducing the need to transmit all data to a central server and ensuring low-latency responses to demand fluctuations.

Real-time stream processing: The provider used Apache Kafka to process real-time data streams from millions of smart meters and energy distribution points. This allowed the grid to respond dynamically to changes in energy demand, shifting energy loads in real time to prevent blackouts and optimize distribution.

Blockchain for data integrity: To enhance the security and integrity of the energy grid's operational data, the provider implemented a blockchain-based system to record all transactions and changes to the energy grid. The blockchain ensured that data could not be tampered with, providing a secure and auditable trail of all operations within the grid.

Automated data governance: The energy provider used Informatica's data governance platform to automate data quality checks, access controls and compliance with industry regulations. This allowed the provider to enforce governance policies consistently across the grid and ensure that only authorized personnel could access operational data.

Outcome: The modernization of the energy grid resulted in a highly efficient, secure, and scalable system that could respond to real-time changes in energy demand. By using decentralized data control, real-time processing, blockchain technology, and automated governance, the energy provider was able to reduce energy waste, prevent outages, and secure its operational data. The system now serves as a model for other national energy providers looking to implement smart grid technologies [65].

2.7.5 Big Data Control in E-Commerce

Industry context: E-commerce companies collect vast amounts of data from user interactions, purchase histories, and product reviews. These data are essential for providing personalized recommendations, improving user experience, and optimizing marketing strategies. However, managing and controlling such large-scale data across multiple regions while maintaining data quality, security, and privacy are a significant challenge.

Problem: A global e-commerce platform needed to integrate and control data from multiple regional websites, ensuring data quality and consistency across all platforms. Additionally, the company had to comply with data privacy regulations such as GDPR, while maintaining a high degree of personalization for customers.

Data control methods used

Data sharding for scalability: The platform implemented data sharding to partition its global dataset across different geographic regions. This approach allowed the company to scale its data infrastructure while ensuring that each region's data were stored and processed locally in compliance with local regulations.

Real-time personalization with online learning: To offer personalized recommendations, the platform used online learning algorithms that updated user models in real time based on their interactions and browsing behavior. This allowed the platform to provide accurate, personalized recommendations without needing to retrain models from scratch every time new data were collected.

Privacy-preserving analytics: To comply with GDPR, the platform implemented anonymization and data masking techniques to protect customer data. Sensitive information, such as payment details and personal identifiers, was masked before being used in analytics, ensuring that user privacy was maintained while still allowing for effective data analysis.

Metadata management for data consistency: The platform used a data catalog to manage metadata across its global dataset. This catalog ensured that all datasets were properly documented, versioned, and governed, providing consistency across the platform's multiple regional websites.

Outcome: The e-commerce platform successfully integrated its global data infrastructure while maintaining compliance with data privacy regulations. By using data sharding, online learning, privacy-preserving techniques, and metadata management, the company was able to offer personalized recommendations and a seamless user experience across all regions. The system's scalability and data control capabilities also enabled the platform to handle increasing volumes of data as its customer base grew [66].

2.8 Future Directions in Data Control

There is a rapid development in the field of data, in the recent years, with the advancements in technology, the increase in data volumes, the growing complexity of data-driven systems, and the rise in demand for privacy and security. The field of data control is rapidly evolving, driven by advancements in technology, increasing data volumes, the growing complexity of data-driven systems, and the rising demand for privacy and security. As data become more distributed and real-time, traditional methods of data control must adapt to new paradigms. Emerging technologies such as edge computing, federated learning, blockchain, and quantum computing will play key roles in shaping the future of data control. This section explores these emerging trends and technologies, outlining how they will influence the next generation of data control methods.

2.8.1 Decentralized and Distributed Data Control

As systems become more distributed across cloud, edge, and IoT devices, centralized data control architectures are becoming less feasible. The future of data control lies in decentralized and distributed systems that can ensure security, consistency, and governance without relying on a single point of control.

2.8.1.1 Edge Computing and Data Control at the Edge

In edge computing, data are processed closer to where it is generated, such as on IoT devices or local servers, rather than being sent to a centralized data center. This reduces latency and bandwidth usage, but it also introduces new challenges in data control, particularly around consistency, governance, and security across distributed nodes.

Data control challenges at the edge
Real-time processing: Edge devices need to process data in real time while maintaining high levels of accuracy and control. Traditional batch-processing models are insufficient for these use cases.
Data integrity and synchronization: Ensuring data integrity across distributed edge nodes, where data are processed in parallel, can be difficult. As data are aggregated at the edge, ensuring consistency and synchronization across different devices will be critical.

Scalability: Edge computing environments are highly scalable, but this scalability introduces complexity in terms of ensuring data governance and control across a rapidly expanding network of devices.

Future directions

Federated edge computing: Combining federated learning with edge computing will enable distributed model training without sharing sensitive data between edge devices. This approach could ensure data privacy while allowing edge devices to contribute to global models.

AI-driven data control: AI models deployed at the edge could provide dynamic data control based on real-time conditions, adjusting data collection, processing, and transmission based on context. For example, sensors in a smart city could adjust their data transmission frequency based on network congestion or priority levels [67].

2.8.1.2 Blockchain for Decentralized Data Control

Blockchain technology offers a promising approach to decentralized data control. It enables the creation of tamper-proof, transparent ledgers where data transactions can be securely recorded and shared across a distributed network without relying on a central authority. In the future, blockchain could provide a backbone for managing data integrity, provenance, and access control across distributed systems.

Potential applications

Data integrity and auditing: Blockchain can be used to record all transactions involving data, ensuring that any modifications to the data are transparent and tamper-proof. This could be particularly useful for critical industries such as finance, healthcare, and supply chain management, where data integrity is paramount.

Smart contracts for data governance: Smart contracts on blockchain platforms could enforce automated governance policies, such as access controls or data usage rules, without the need for human intervention. This could streamline compliance and security in complex, multiparty environments.

Challenges

Scalability of blockchain: While blockchain is secure and transparent, its scalability is still a challenge, particularly in environments where massive amounts of data are being processed. Future developments in blockchain technology, such as layer-2 solutions or sharding, will be necessary to make it viable for large-scale data control applications.

Interoperability: As multiple blockchains emerge, ensuring interoperability between different blockchain networks will be critical for decentralized data control. This may involve developing new standards or protocols to enable seamless data flow between different blockchain systems [68].

2.8.2 Privacy-Preserving Data Control

With growing concerns around data privacy and increasing regulatory requirements, the future of data control must prioritize privacy-preserving techniques. Advanced privacy-preserving technologies such as differential privacy, homomorphic encryption, and SMPC will become essential for enabling data sharing and collaboration without compromising privacy.

2.8.2.1 Differential Privacy

Differential privacy is already being used in many large-scale systems (e.g., Apple and Google) to protect user data while allowing aggregate analysis. However, future developments in differential privacy will focus on making the technique more scalable and widely applicable to various data control scenarios.

Challenges and innovations

Utility versus privacy trade-off: One of the key challenges in differential privacy is balancing data utility with privacy. Adding too much noise to the data to protect privacy can reduce its usefulness for analysis. Future innovations may focus on improving algorithms that optimize this trade-off for specific applications.

Scalability: As differential privacy becomes more widely adopted, particularly in big data systems, improving its scalability and efficiency will be critical. This could involve developing more efficient noise-adding mechanisms or designing differentially private systems that can handle streaming and real-time data.

Future applications

Privacy-preserving machine learning: Future machine learning models will incorporate differential privacy at scale, allowing organizations to build powerful models on sensitive data (e.g., healthcare, finance) without exposing individuals' information. Privacy-preserving machine learning will become a key component of AI systems that must comply with regulations such as GDPR [69].

2.8.2.2 Homomorphic Encryption and Secure Computation

Homomorphic encryption allows data to be processed while still encrypted, ensuring that sensitive information is never exposed even during computation. While homomorphic encryption is currently computationally expensive and difficult to scale, ongoing research aims to make it more practical for large-scale applications.

Applications in data control

Cloud computing: In the future, organizations could use homomorphic encryption to securely process sensitive data in the cloud without ever decrypting it. This would allow cloud providers to offer data processing services without compromising client data security.

Secure data sharing: Homomorphic encryption and SMPC could enable secure multiparty collaboration without sharing raw data. For example, multiple organizations could jointly analyze data for research purposes without revealing their proprietary or sensitive information to one another.

Challenges and future directions

Performance optimization: Current homomorphic encryption techniques are slow and resource-intensive. Future research will focus on optimizing these techniques to make them viable for real-time or large-scale data processing.

Hybrid models: Future data control systems may combine homomorphic encryption with other privacy-preserving techniques, such as differential privacy or federated learning, to balance efficiency, privacy, and security [70].

2.8.3 Real-Time Adaptive Data Control

As more systems move toward real-time data processing, the ability to control data adaptively in response to changing conditions will become increasingly important. Real-time adaptive data control will enable systems to dynamically adjust data collection, processing, and governance policies based on context, such as network conditions, user demand, or environmental factors.

2.8.3.1 AI-Driven Data Control

The future of data control systems is based by enabling adaptive and self-regulating data management frameworks, in which AI and machine learning play a critical role. The AI helps in detecting anomalies, monitors data streams, and makes real-time adjustments to ensure optimal data flow and security of the data.

Key capabilities
Anomaly detection: The AI models help in monitoring the real-time data, thus enabling it to detect the unusual patterns or inconsistencies that indicate data compromise, corruption, or system failure. This immediate response-based approach helps in preventing issues before they affect downstream systems.
Dynamic policy adjustment: Based on current conditions, AI dynamically adjusts the data governance policies dynamically. For example, if there is an anomaly detected in the system, the AI-driven system might restrict the data access due to the anomaly detected, or it might temporarily reduce data collection if network bandwidth is limited.

Future applications
Autonomous systems: AI-driven data control enables to manage sensor data stream in real time while maintaining the privacy and processes critical information immediately. This helps in AVs or drones, as it allows in prioritizing data and less important data are filtered for later analysis.
Smart cities: In smart cities, in order to process the data of millions of sensors in dynamic control for traffic management, public safety, and environmental monitoring, AI-driven data control would be a boon [71].

2.8.3.2 Context-Aware Data Control

When the systems, on the basis of current environment or situation, adjust their data collection and processing strategies, it is known as context-aware data control. In order to effectively manage and process the data at any given moment metadata, sensor inputs and external conditions are kept into consideration.

Examples of context-aware systems
Smart energy grids: Data control systems adjust the energy distribution in a smart grid, on the basis of current demand, weather conditions, or energy prices. In order to improve its efficacy, real-time data can be accessed from smart meters and sensors, which would allow the grid to balance supply and demand dynamically.
Healthcare systems: Patient data can be monitored dynamically on the basis of the criticality of the patient in a hospital. This can help in times of

accidents such as earthquakes or any event of heavy casualties. Another example in the healthcare system can be that real-time data of critical patients are monitored, and immediate analysis on the patient's condition requiring a fast response rather than waiting for check-ups could be prioritized [72].

2.8.4 Federated Learning and Collaborative Data Control

In order to enable secure, collaborative data control, federated learning will continue to play a critical role in the rise of collaboration of data-driven projects without the need of sharing the raw data. In this training model, with the help of federated learning techniques, preserving the privacy of the raw data allows decentralized devices or organizations to collaboratively train models without sharing their local data, thus preserving privacy while still benefiting from the collective knowledge of the group.

2.8.4.1 Federated Learning at Scale

Federated learning is already being used in applications such as mobile phones, where models are trained on device to improve user experiences without uploading sensitive data to central servers. However, as federated learning scales, new challenges and opportunities will arise, particularly in fields such as healthcare, finance, and government.

Applications

Healthcare research: Hospitals and research institutions could use federated learning to train models on patient data across multiple institutions without ever sharing sensitive health data. This would enable more accurate and diverse models while maintaining compliance with privacy regulations.

Financial services: Federated learning can be used to develop fraud detection models that allow the banks and financial institutions to share insights without compromising proprietary customer data [28].

2.8.4.2 Federated Governance and Data Control

With the increase in popularity of federated learning, federated governance also is becoming important. When multiple parties collaborate to manage data policies, access controls, and model updates across distributed system without a single authority, it is known as federated governance.

Future developments
Federated data markets: A new form of collaborative data economy where institutions can buy or sell model or updates without sharing raw data while safeguarding its privacy and proprietary information.
Cross-domain collaboration: Industries that generally do not share data such as healthcare and insurance could collaborate due to federated learning. This is to check whether management of access, compliance, and security in multiparty collaborations is ensured by federated governance [73].

2.8.5 Quantum Computing and Its Impact on Data Control

Quantum computing promises to revolutionize data control by offering exponentially faster processing power and enabling new cryptographic techniques that could redefine data security and privacy.

2.8.5.1 Quantum Cryptography for Data Security

Quantum cryptography, particularly quantum key distribution, could provide unbreakable encryption by using the principles of quantum mechanics. In the future, quantum cryptography will enable secure data control that is resistant to attacks from even the most powerful classic and quantum computers.

Quantum-safe data control
Postquantum encryption: As quantum computing advances, existing cryptographic techniques will become vulnerable. Future data control systems will need to incorporate postquantum encryption algorithms to protect against quantum attacks, ensuring long-term data security [74].

2.8.5.2 Quantum Machine Learning for Data Control

Quantum machine learning (QML) could provide powerful new tools for optimizing data control in large, complex systems. Quantum algorithms could be used to process massive datasets faster and more efficiently, enabling real-time control over even the most complex data environments.

Future applications
Real-time data processing: Quantum algorithms could optimize real-time data processing in fields such as autonomous systems, healthcare, and finance, enabling faster decision-making and more effective data control.

Optimizing data governance: QML models could optimize data governance strategies by processing vast amounts of metadata and access logs in real time, helping organizations identify inefficiencies and vulnerabilities in their data control systems [75].

2.9 Concluding Remarks

The success of data-driven modeling is fundamentally dependent on the data control of the system. The enhanced reliability and performance of the modern applications are the outcomes of effective data control methods, which include data integrity, privacy, governance, and the ability to handle the complexities of real-time processing and distributed systems. This chapter explores the core principles of data control, which includes versioning, auditing, collaborative data sharing, and advanced privacy-preserving techniques such as differential privacy and federated learning. Emerging technologies such as edge computing, blockchain, and AI-driven data control that are shaping the future of the field have also been addressed.

As the data volumes and complexity grow, the future advancements in decentralized systems, real-time adaptive control, and quantum computing will play a pivotal role in meeting the challenges of modern data environments. The adoption of these cutting-edge practices and technologies in the industry to remain competitive, secure, and compliant is the solution in the increasingly data-driven world. One can harness the full potential of their data while safeguarding privacy and ensuring regulatory compliance only by mastering advanced data control strategies.

References

1. Solomatine, D., See, L.M., Abrahart, R.J., Data-driven modelling: concepts, approaches and experiences, in: *Practical hydroinformatics: Computational intelligence and technological developments in water applications*, pp. 17–30, 2008.
2. Hassani, H. and MacFeely, S., Driving excellence in official statistics: unleashing the potential of comprehensive digital data Governance. *Big Data Cognit. Comput.*, *7*, 3, 134, 2023.
3. Montáns, F.J., Chinesta, F., Gómez-Bombarelli, R., Kutz, J.N., Data-driven modeling and learning in science and engineering. *C. R. Méc.*, *347*, 11, 845–855, 2019.

4. Yin, S., Li, X., Gao, H., Kaynak, O., Data-based techniques focused on modern industry: An overview. *IEEE Trans. Ind. Electron.*, *62*, 1, 657–667, 2014.
5. Xu, L., Jiang, C., Wang, J., Yuan, J., Ren, Y., Information security in big data: privacy and data mining. *IEEE Access*, *2*, 1149–1176, 2014.
6. Brunner, D., Legat, C., Seebacher, U., Towards Next Generation Data-Driven Management: Leveraging Predictive Swarm Intelligence to Reason and Predict Market Dynamics, in: *Collective Intelligence*, pp. 152–203, CRC Press, Boca Raton, FL, 2024.
7. Ncube, M.M. and Ngulube, P., Enhancing environmental decision-making: a systematic review of data analytics applications in monitoring and management. *Discover Sustain.*, *5*, 1, 290, 2024.
8. Yap, K.Y., Chin, H.H., Klemeš, J.J., Blockchain technology for distributed generation: A review of current development, challenges and future prospect. *Renew. Sustain. Energy Rev.*, *175*, 113170, 2023.
9. Patel, J., An effective and scalable data modeling for enterprise big data platform, in: *2019 IEEE International Conference on Big Data (Big Data)*, pp. 2691–2697, 2019.
10. Jiang, Y., Yin, S., Kaynak, O., Data-driven monitoring and safety control of industrial cyber-physical systems: Basics and beyond. *IEEE Access*, *6*, 47374–47384, 2018.
11. Solomatine, D.P. and Ostfeld, A., Data-driven modelling: some past experiences and new approaches. *J. Hydroinf.*, *10*, 1, 3–22, 2008.
12. Robinson, S., Narayanan, B., Toh, N., Pereira, F., Methods for pre-processing smartcard data to improve data quality. *Transp. Res. Part C: Emerg. Technol.*, *49*, 43–58, 2014.
13. Janssen, M., Brous, P., Estevez, E., Barbosa, L.S., Janowski, T., Data governance: Organizing data for trustworthy Artificial Intelligence. *Gov. Inf. Q.*, *37*, 3, 101493, 2020.
14. Bertino, E., Data security and privacy: Concepts, approaches, and research directions, in: *2016 IEEE 40th annual computer software and applications conference (COMPSAC)*, 2016, June, vol. 1, pp. 400–407.
15. Berberich, J., Köhler, J., Müller, M.A., Allgöwer, F., Data-driven model predictive control with stability and robustness guarantees. *IEEE Trans. Autom. Control*, *66*, 4, 1702–1717, 2020.
16. Madireddy, S., Balaprakash, P., Carns, P., Latham, R., Lockwood, G.K., Ross, R., Wild, S.M., Adaptive learning for concept drift in application performance modeling, in: *Proceedings of the 48th International Conference on Parallel Processing*, 2019, August, pp. 1–11.
17. Halbach, S., Sharer, P., Pagerit, S., Rousseau, A.P., Folkerts, C., Model architecture, methods, and interfaces for efficient math-based design and simulation of automotive control systems (No. 2010-01-0241). SAE Technical paper, 2010.

18. Salman, O., Elhajj, I., Kayssi, A., Chehab, A., An architecture for the Internet of Things with decentralized data and centralized control, in: *2015 IEEE/ACS 12th International Conference of Computer Systems and Applications (AICCSA)*, 2015, November, pp. 1–8.
19. Bader, S.R. and Maleshkova, M., SOLIOT—Decentralized data control and interactions for IoT. *Future Internet, 12*, 6, 105, 2020.
20. Nadal, S., Jovanovic, P., Bilalli, B., Romero, O., Operationalizing and automating data governance. *J. Big Data, 9*, 1, 117, 2022.
21. Sen, A., Metadata management: past, present and future. *Decis. Support Syst., 37*, 1, 151–173, 2004.
22. Patel, S., Rahevar, M., Parmar, M., Data provenance and data lineage in the cloud: A survey. *Int. J. Adv. Sci. Technol., 29*, 5, 4883–4900, 2020.
23. Singh, J., Bacon, J., Eyers, D., Policy enforcement within emerging distributed, event-based systems, in: *Proceedings of the 8th ACM International Conference on Distributed Event-Based Systems*, 2014, May, pp. 246–255.
24. Cao, J., Zhang, W., Tan, W., Dynamic control of data streaming and processing in a virtualized environment. *IEEE Trans. Autom. Sci. Eng., 9*, 2, 365–376, 2012.
25. Gedik, B., Generic windowing support for extensible stream processing systems. *Softw.: Pract. Exper., 44*, 9, 1105–1128, 2014.
26. Fan, L., Xiong, L., Sunderam, V., FAST: differentially private real-time aggregate monitor with filtering and adaptive sampling, in: *Proceedings of the 2013 ACM SIGMOD International Conference on Management of Data*, 2013, June, pp. 1065–1068.
27. Chen, X.Z., Chang, C.M., Yu, C.W., Chen, Y.L., A real-time vehicle detection system under various bad weather conditions based on a deep learning model without retraining. *Sensors, 20*, 20, 5731, 2020.
28. Zeng, T., Semiari, O., Chen, M., Saad, W., Bennis, M., Federated learning on the road autonomous controller design for connected and autonomous vehicles. *IEEE Trans. Wirel. Commun., 21*, 12, 10407–10423, 2022.
29. Wang, H. and Zhang, J., Blockchain based data integrity verification for large-scale IoT data. *IEEE Access, 7*, 164996–165006, 2019.
30. Monaco, S. and Normand-Cyrot, D., Advanced tools for nonlinear sampled-data systems' analysis and control. *Eur. J. Control, 13*, 2-3, 221–241, 2007.
31. Piga, D., Forgione, M., Formentin, S., Bemporad, A., Performance-oriented model learning for data-driven MPC design. *IEEE Control Syst. Lett., 3*, 3, 577–582, 2019.
32. Li, T., Yang, J., Ioannou, A., Data-driven control of wind turbine under online power strategy *via* deep learning and reinforcement learning. *Renew. Energy, 234*, 121265, 2024.
33. Cupelli, L., Cupelli, M., Ponci, F., Monti, A., Data-driven adaptive control for distributed energy resources. *IEEE Trans. Sustain. Energy, 10*, 3, 1575–1584, 2019.

34. Van Dongen, G. and Van den Poel, D., Evaluation of stream processing frameworks. *IEEE Trans. Parallel Distrib. Syst.*, *31*, 8, 1845–1858, 2020.
35. Li, K. and Li, G., Approximate query processing: What is new and where to go? a survey on approximate query processing. *Data Sci. Eng.*, *3*, 4, 379–397, 2018.
36. Gomes, H.M., Read, J., Bifet, A., Barddal, J.P., Gama, J., Machine learning for streaming data: state of the art, challenges, and opportunities. *ACM SIGKDD Explor. Newsl.*, *21*, 2, 6–22, 2019.
37. Costa, J., Silva, C., Antunes, M., Ribeiro, B., Adaptive learning for dynamic environments: A comparative approach. *Eng. Appl. Artif. Intell.*, *65*, 336–345, 2017.
38. Iwashita, A.S. and Papa, J.P., An overview on concept drift learning. *IEEE Access*, *7*, 1532–1547, 2018.
39. Val, O.O., Selesi-Aina, O., Kolade, T.M., Gbadebo, M.O., Olateju, O.O., Olaniyi, O.O., Real-Time Data Governance and Compliance in Cloud-Native Robotics Systems. *J. Eng. Res. Rep.*, *26*, 11, 222–241, 2024.
40. Nayak, A.K., Reimers, A., Feamster, N., Clark, R., Resonance: Dynamic access control for enterprise networks, in: *Proceedings of the 1st ACM Workshop on Research on Enterprise Networking*, 2009, August, pp. 11–18.
41. Fisher, O.J., Watson, N.J., Escrig, J.E., Witt, R., Porcu, L., Bacon, D., Gomes, R.L., Considerations, challenges and opportunities when developing data-driven models for process manufacturing systems. *Comput. Chem. Eng.*, *140*, 106881, 2020.
42. Yang, R. and Xu, J., Computing at massive scale: Scalability and dependability challenges, in: *2016 IEEE symposium on service-oriented system engineering (SOSE)*, pp. 386–397, 2016.
43. Dautov, R. and Distefano, S., Quantifying volume, velocity, and variety to support (Big) data-intensive application development, in: *2017 IEEE International Conference on Big Data (Big Data)*, pp. 2843–2852, 2017.
44. Ali, A.H., A survey on vertical and horizontal scaling platforms for big data analytics. *Int. J. Integr. Eng.*, *11*, 6, 138–150, 2019.
45. Sahiner, B., Chen, W., Samala, R.K., Petrick, N., Data drift in medical machine learning: implications and potential remedies. *Br. J. Radiol.*, *96*, 1150, 20220878, 2023.
46. Wares, S., Isaacs, J., Elyan, E., Data stream mining: methods and challenges for handling concept drift. *SN Appl. Sci.*, *1*, 1–19, 2019.
47. Li, J., Yu, H., Zhang, Z., Luo, X., Xie, S., Concept drift adaptation by exploiting drift type. *ACM Trans. Knowl. Discov. Data*, *18*, 4, 1–22, 2024.
48. Shukla, S., Hassan, M.F., Tran, D.C., Akbar, R., Paputungan, I.V., Khan, M.K., Improving latency in Internet-of-Things and cloud computing for real-time data transmission: a systematic literature review (SLR). *Cluster Comput.*, 26, 3, 2657–2680, 2023.

49. Han, G., Zeng, H., Di Natale, M., Liu, X., Dou, W., Experimental evaluation and selection of data consistency mechanisms for hard real-time applications on multicore platforms. *IEEE Trans. Ind. Inf.*, *10*, 2, 903–918, 2013.
50. Li, N., Qardaji, W., Su, D., On sampling, anonymization, and differential privacy or, k-anonymization meets differential privacy, in: *Proceedings of the 7th ACM Symposium on Information, Computer and Communications Security*, 2012, May, pp. 32–33.
51. Arockiam, L. and Monikandan, S., Data security and privacy in cloud storage using hybrid symmetric encryption algorithm. *Int. J. Adv. Res. Comput. Commun. Eng.*, *2*, 8, 3064–3070, 2013.
52. Schapke, S.E., Beetz, J., König, M., Koch, C., Borrmann, A., Collaborative data management, in: *Building Information Modeling: Technology Foundations and Industry Practice*, pp. 251–277, 2018.
53. Tian, H., Nan, F., Jiang, H., Chang, C.C., Ning, J., Huang, Y., Public auditing for shared cloud data with efficient and secure group management. *Inf. Sci.*, *472*, 107–125, 2019.
54. Pulicharla, M.R., Data Versioning and Its Impact on Machine Learning Models. *J. Sci. Technol.*, 5, 1, 22–37, 2024.
55. Brunner, M., Sillaber, C., Demetz, L., Manhart, M., Breu, R., Towards data-driven decision support for organizational IT security audits. *it-Inf. Technol.*, *60*, 4, 207–217, 2018.
56. Cruz, J.P., Kaji, Y., Yanai, N., RBAC-SC: Role-based access control using smart contract. *IEEE Access*, *6*, 12240–12251, 2018.
57. Samanthula, B.K., Elmehdwi, Y., Howser, G., Madria, S., A secure data sharing and query processing framework *via* federation of cloud computing. *Inf. Syst.*, *48*, 196–212, 2015.
58. Yu, H., Cai, H., Liu, Z., Xu, B., Jiang, L., An automated metadata generation method for data lake of industrial WoT applications. *IEEE Trans. Syst. Man Cybern.: Syst.*, *52*, 8, 5235–5248, 2021.
59. Heinis, T. and Alonso, G., Efficient lineage tracking for scientific workflows, in: *Proceedings of the 2008 ACM SIGMOD international conference on Management of data*, 2008, June, pp. 1007–1018.
60. Salamkar, M.A. and Immaneni, J., Data Governance: AI applications in ensuring compliance and data quality standards. *J. AI-Assisted Sci. Discovery*, *4*, 1, 158–183, 2024.
61. Thirunagalingam, A., Enhancing Data Governance Through Explainable AI: Bridging Transparency and Automation. *Int. J. Sustain. Dev. Through AI ML IoT*, *1*, 2, 1–12, 2022.
62. Philip, B.V., Alpcan, T., Jin, J., Palaniswami, M., Distributed real-time IoT for autonomous vehicles. *IEEE Trans. Ind. Inf.*, *15*, 2, 1131–1140, 2018.
63. Faridoon, A. and Kechadi, M.T., Healthcare Data Governance, Privacy, and Security-A Conceptual Framework. arXiv preprint arXiv:2403.17648, 2024.

64. Geib, M., Kolbe, L.M., Brenner, W., CRM collaboration in financial services networks: a multi-case analysis. *J. Enterp. Inf. Manage.*, *19*, 6, 591–607, 2006.
65. Diamantoulakis, P.D., Kapinas, V.M., Karagiannidis, G.K., Big data analytics for dynamic energy management in smart grids. *Big Data Res.*, *2*, 3, 94–101, 2015.
66. Pan, C.L., Liu, Y., Pan, Y.C., Research on the status of e-commerce development based on big data and Internet technology. *Int. J. Electron. Commer. Stud.*, *13*, 2, 027–048, 2022.
67. Cao, K., Liu, Y., Meng, G., Sun, Q., An overview on edge computing research. *IEEE Access*, *8*, 85714–85728, 2020.
68. Chen, Y., Chen, S., Liang, J., Feagan, L.W., Han, W., Huang, S., Wang, X.S., Decentralized data access control over consortium blockchains. *Inf. Syst.*, *94*, 101590, 2020.
69. Cortés, J., Dullerud, G.E., Han, S., Le Ny, J., Mitra, S., Pappas, G.J., Differential privacy in control and network systems, in: *2016 IEEE 55th Conference on Decision and Control (CDC)*, 2016, December, pp. 4252–4272.
70. Hallman, R.A., Diallo, M.H., August, M.A., Graves, C.T., Homomorphic Encryption for Secure Computation on Big Data, in: *IoTBDS*, 2018, March, pp. 340–347.
71. Davuluri, M., Navigating AI-Driven Data Management in the Cloud: Exploring Limitations and Opportunities. *Trans. Latest Trends IoT*, *1*, 1, 106–112, 2018.
72. Diaz, R.A.C., Ghita, M., Copot, D., Birs, I.R., Muresan, C., Ionescu, C., Context aware control systems: An engineering applications perspective. *IEEE Access*, *8*, 215550–215569, 2020.
73. Dolhopolov, A., Castelltort, A., Laurent, A., Implementing Federated Governance in Data Mesh Architecture. *Future Internet*, *16*, 4, 115, 2024.
74. Thayananthan, V. and Albeshri, A., Big data security issues based on quantum cryptography and privacy with authentication for mobile data center. *Procedia Comput. Sci.*, *50*, 149–156, 2015.
75. Zeng, Y.X., Shen, J., Hou, S.C., Gebremariam, T., Li, C., Quantum control based on machine learning in an open quantum system. *Phys. Lett. A*, *384*, 35, 126886, 2020.

3

Machine Learning Algorithms for Data-Driven Modeling

Souryadip Ghosh[1]*, Indrani Mukherjee[2] and Suparna Biswas[3]

[1]*Department of Computer Science & Engineering, OmDayal Group of Institutions, Uluberia, West Bengal, India*
[2]*Department of Computer Science & Engineering, Narula Institute of Technology, Kolkata, West Bengal, India*
[3]*Department of Computer Science & Engineering, Maulana Abul Kalam Azad University of Technology, Haringhata, West Bengal, India*

Abstract
Data-based modeling in different fields has seen significant application of machine learning. In this chapter, an overview of advanced machine learning algorithms meant for data-driven modeling is provided starting from basic concepts of machine learning. Techniques such as decision trees and support vector machines are examples of supervised learning that bears its algorithms, optimization methods, and realistic situations. As such, unsupervised learning algorithms such as k-means, hierarchical clustering, principal component analysis, and t-distributed stochastic neighbor embedding are also discussed together with their influential ramifications. Other areas touched upon include ensemble learning and association rule mining, as well as anomaly detection, among others. Examples presented showcase how machine learning algorithms help solve complicated issues across various fields with great significance and impact. With this regard, this chapter will continue to analyze future prospects and challenges in data-driven modeling through machine learning, vividly revealing its changing nature while providing suggestions for potential avenues leading toward more research and innovation.

***Keywords*:** Machine learning, supervised learning, unsupervised learning, decision trees, support vector machines, clustering, dimensionality reduction, t-SNE (t-distributed stochastic neighbor embedding)

**Corresponding author*: Souryadipghosh62@gmail.com

Arindam Mondal and Souvik Ganguli (eds.) Data-Driven Modeling, (81–98) © 2026 Scrivener Publishing LLC

3.1 Introduction

Machine learning has emerged as a crucial component of data-driven modeling. It is important to note that this chapter includes a comprehensive package that facilitates more efficient data-driven modeling. It consists of project-specific supervised and unsupervised learning approaches [1]. The chapter opens with machine learning, a topic that covers its main ideas and theories. The chapter emphasizes the idea of data-driven modeling in many domains, as well as the components of machine learning models and supervised, unsupervised, and reinforcement learning [2]. The thing is that the models covered in the chapter assume a foundational level of the modeling process. The models lay the ground for further elaboration. Changeover to unsupervised learning, the chapter closely examines the clustering techniques, especially k-means and hierarchical clustering. The algorithmic methods for clustering, including cluster fusion and iterative data point assignment, are covered in this chapter along with methods for figuring out the ideal number of clusters. It also covers dimensionality reduction techniques that make managing complicated datasets simple, such as principal component analysis (PCA) and t-distributed stochastic neighbor embedding (t-SNE).

They prove prosperously that by dimensionality reduction they could do more efficient data exploration and analysis having been able to extract from the enormous datasets important information and hence meaningful insights.

This chapter presents the methodology and foundational knowledge of machine learning for data-driven computational models across several disciplines. It covers supervised learning algorithms such as decision trees and support vector machines (SVMs), gives examples of clustering techniques such as k-means and hierarchical clustering, and refers to dimensionality reduction strategies such as PCA and t-SNE. Its usefulness to effective data preparation and analysis is demonstrated by empirical examples.

3.2 What is Machine Learning?

This portion is all about what is the machine learning methodology and how it replaced conventional engineering approaches as a cutting-edge tool in algorithmic design [2, 3]. Domain expertise is used in typical engineering workflows to create physics-based models, which are essential for improving algorithms such as those used to decode wireless fading

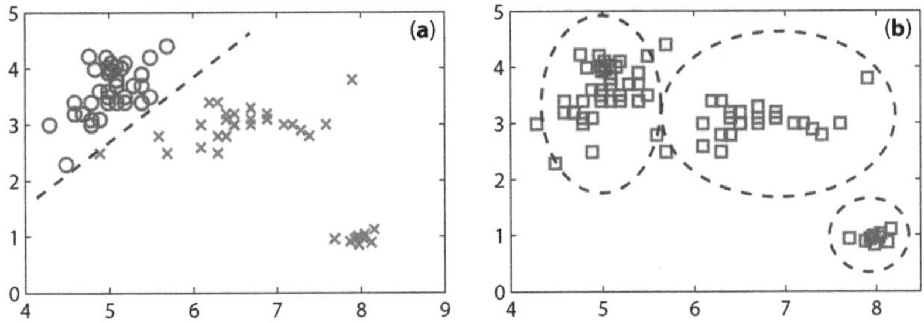

Figure 3.1 (a) Supervised learning and (b) unsupervised learning [2].

channels [2]. Machine learning, on the other hand, is more concerned with gathering instances of desired behavior than with domain knowledge [4]. As covered by Simeone [2], these instances serve as a training set for a learning algorithm, which uses them to build a trained "machine" that can carry out the intended task.

3.3 Classification of Machine Learning Methods

Machine learning techniques can be broadly categorized into three main classes, each serving distinct purposes:

3.3.1 Supervised Learning

In supervised learning, we have data for training. These data consist of two parts or pairs that include an input and outputs expected to be gotten (Figure 3.1(a)); the main goal is to find how connections can be made between input spaces and those of output. For example, a hyperplane concept as depicted in Figure 3.2 where in Figure 3.3(a), it shows the inputs as some points, whereas outputs may be circle or cross signs given at respective inputs; hence, what is required is a binary classifier.

3.3.2 Unsupervised Learning

This type of learning is completely different from its predecessor having no labeled datasets implying there are no expected outputs indicated [2]. In this instance, the aim in a two-dimensional setting such as that illustrated in Figure 3.3(b) would be clustering similar input points so as to give each individual point an index that will represent the cluster it belongs to.

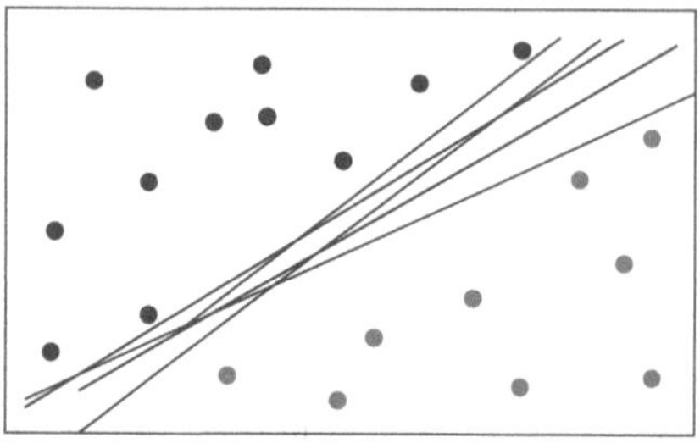

Figure 3.2 Hyperplane [3].

3.3.3 Reinforcement Learning

Reinforcement learning operates between supervised and unsupervised learning, receiving feedback after selecting outputs for inputs, rather than predefined outputs for every input [1, 2].

Supervised learning dominates due to its well-understood foundations, whereas unsupervised learning tackles direct observation without feedback, and reinforcement learning is used with clear feedback signals [2]. This chapter focuses on machine learning algorithms for data-driven modeling.

3.4 Supervised Machine Learning

Supervised machine learning is one of the key aspects of artificial intelligence and data science that seeks to redefine the way we look at data by developing various algorithms and techniques [1]. In this chapter, the adaptability of decision trees in classification and their parameter optimization will be examined for better machine learning applications.

3.4.1 Decision Tree for Classification

The classification of heterogeneous and uncertain data becomes a challenge when the data involved are incomplete, noisy, or even dirty. Various decision tree models such as C4.5, CART, CHAID, and ID3 are looked into in this part because of their abilities to manage different types of inputs and effectively handle missing information or inconsistencies for customized decision-making trees.

3.4.2 C4.5

C4.5 improves from ID3 algorithm using information gain ratio during attribute selection, minimizing bias toward attributes having many distinct values [17]. Thus, C4.5 becomes suitable for classifying heterogeneous data [3, 17, 24].

3.4.3 CART

CART extends decision trees for classification, regression with binary tree structures, using the index for attribute selection [3, 20]. Cost-complexity pruning is used to improve performance and interpretability [24].

3.4.4 CHAID

CHAID uses χ^2 tests on nominal attributes [3] to find important features enhancing the interpretability of resulting decision trees [19].

3.4.5 Iterative Dichotomizer 3

ID3, proposed by Quinlan, is a foundational decision tree algorithm that uses information entropy to select attributes, recursively partitioning data to maximize information gain, effective for small- to medium-sized datasets with nominal and numerical attributes [3, 18].

$$\mathbf{Entropy}(S) = -\Sigma\, \boldsymbol{p}(\boldsymbol{x})\mathbf{log2}\,\boldsymbol{p}(\boldsymbol{x}) \tag{3.1}$$

In the data collection, x symbolizes the collection of categories, whereas $p(x)$ denotes the ratio or possibility of the components in class x to the sum of all components in set S [3]. If $I(S) = 0$, entropy signifies that every object belongs to one class, and therefore, it is perfectly classified. As stated in Eq. (3.2), information gain (IG(S)) is a metric that captures how much uncertainty is removed from S by splitting it based on attribute A:

$$\mathbf{IG}(S) = \boldsymbol{I}(S) - \Sigma\, \boldsymbol{p}(\boldsymbol{t}).\boldsymbol{I}(\boldsymbol{t}) \tag{3.2}$$

Here, the proportion of the number of elements in class to the total number of elements in the set indicates that $I(t)$ indicates entropy of subset

t and $p(t)$ [3, 24]. Overall, ID3 offers a systematic approach to constructing decision trees tailored to dataset characteristics, making it a foundational algorithm in machine learning [18].

3.5 Support Vector Machine

SVM gained prominence in 1992 for classification and regression in predictive analysis, introduced by Vapnik, Guyon, and Boser at COLT-92. Using linear or nonlinear decision boundaries, SVM prevents overfitting by finding hyperplanes to separate data into classes, using kernel functions for effective classification in high-dimensional, nonlinear spaces.

Neural networks are widely used in classification and regression, pivotal in artificial intelligence, grouping data into networks for both supervised and unsupervised learning [3]. SVM handles large datasets and complex networks effectively, whereas multi-layer perceptron (MLP) utilizes recurrent and feedforward architectures for neural networks [8, 21].

3.5.1 SVM for Linear Classification

SVM is used for classification and regression, utilizing hyperplanes to separate samples in linear classification [1, 3]. Selecting the optimal hyperplane involves finding the boundary that effectively separates dataset categories, posing a balancing challenge. The process involves the following:

i. Define a function to generate the required hyperplane.
ii. Choose a hyperplane and compute its distance from both sides of the datasets.
   a. Whenever there is an increase in distance on either side of the previous hyperplane, it will serve as the selected decision boundary.
   b. The points that lie nearby to the hyperplane are termed as supporting vectors to help in decision boundary selection.
iii. Repeat the process until the best hyperplane [3] is found.

3.5.2 SVM for Nonlinear Classification

The effectiveness of SVM in linear classification is well-established. However, nonlinear classification is done through the kernel function so as to have a larger feature space that will classify the data [8].

i) **Soft margin classifier**: Not all datasets can be separated perfectly by a single hyperplane—hence case for which data points do not lie on same line—slack variables allow for curved decision boundaries, thus accommodating noise [15] and nonlinear separations [3].

$$y_i(w'x + b) \geq 1 - S_k \tag{3.3}$$

The equation represents the soft margin constraint in SVM for linear classification, where y_i denotes the target class label (−1 or 1) for the ith data point, and w' is the weight indicating the decision boundary direction in feature space. x_i represents the feature vector of the ith data point. The bias term b or intercept of the hyperplane determines its position in the feature space. S_k serves as a slack variable allowing flexibility in classification, accommodating nonlinear separability and outliers, aiming to maximize the margin. The inequality in Eq. (3.3) shows the condition for each data point I, where, to handle potentially large slack, a Lagrangian variable is introduced in Eq. (3.4) [9]:

$$min\ L = w'w - \Sigma\lambda k(yk(w'xk + b) + S_k - 1) + \alpha\Sigma s_k \tag{3.4}$$

where α is reduced, allowing more data points to be on the wrong side of the hyperplane, effectively treating them as outliers and resulting in a smoother decision boundary.

3.5.3 Kernel

In cases where linear data are present, a straightforward approach involves utilizing a separating hyperplane for classification [7]. For linear data, using a separating hyperplane suffices; nonlinear data require a kernel function to transform it into a higher-dimensional space for effective classification [3], as shown in Figure 3.3.

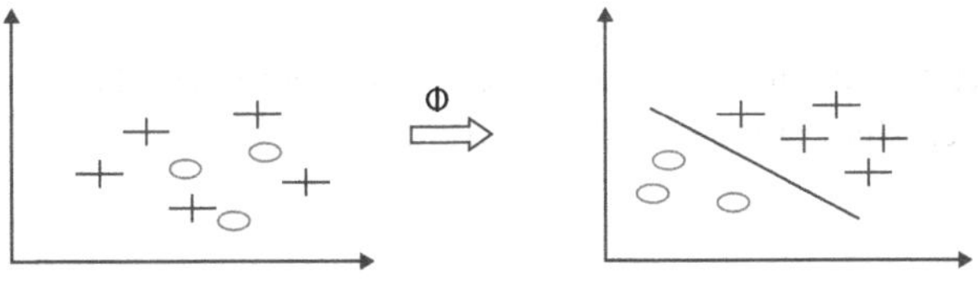

Figure 3.3 Use of kernels [3].

The mapping function defined by the kernel is represented in Eq. (3.5)

$$k(x, y) = \phi(x)\, x\, \phi(y) \tag{3.5}$$

where ϕ signifies the transformation in Eq. (3.5).

3.5.4 Unsupervised Machine Learning

Unsupervised learning techniques play a crucial role in extracting meaningful patterns and structures from datasets without the need for explicit guidance or labeled data. Unsupervised learning extracts patterns without labels. Clustering methods such as hierarchical clustering create tree structures for cluster analysis *via* dendrograms, whereas k-means iteratively refines centroids to categorize data into predefined clusters, aiming to minimize squared errors.

3.5.5 Clustering

Clustering is very important for data mining. It is used in grouping data into clusters through such techniques as hierarchy, partitioning, grid-based approach, and model-based and graph methods. This helps in interpreting data and compressing it without a teacher [13, 25].

3.5.6 K-Means

K-means stands as one of the simplest algorithms devised for addressing the clustering problem [25]. The method uses k-means clustering to categorize datasets into k clusters by adjusting centroids iteratively to minimize the squared error function J, quantifying discrepancies between data points and cluster centers for optimal results [13, 16].

$$J = \sum_{j=1}^{k} \sum_{i=1}^{n} \left\| x_i^{(j)} - c_j \right\|^2 \tag{3.6}$$

where it represents for measuring distance between data points, $x_i^{(j)}$, **around the** cluster center c_j in Eq. (3.6) [28].

Algorithm k-means

The procedure followed the algorithm:

1. Set K centroids in the data space. Locate K points represented by the topics that are being clustered.
2. Each object is assigned to the cluster centered at the nearest centroid.
3. After every object has been assigned, update the positions of the K centroids.
4. Repeat steps 2 and 3 until stationary centroids are obtained. This results into separation of objects into clusters so as to minimize metrics [28].

3.6 Hierarchical Clustering

Hierarchical clustering entails forming clusters in a tree or hierarchical structure. Each node within the tree denotes a distinct cluster, with the hierarchy represented by dendrograms. Hierarchical clustering uses divisive or agglomerative methods to form clusters hierarchically based on similarity, visualizing relationships with dendrograms [25]. It uses distance measures such as centroid, single, complete, or average linkage for merging or splitting clusters.

3.6.1 Methodologies for Determining the Optimal Number of Clusters

The optimal number of clusters aims to identify the most suitable partitioning of the data, whereas cluster quality metrics such as elapsed time, cohesion, and silhouette index evaluate the resulting clusters.

- **i.** **Elapsed time**: Time spent is important in cluster analysis as it shows quality and efficiency through minimum cluster creation time [25].
- **ii.** **Cohesion measurement**: Intracluster similarity is revealed by cohesion, which evaluates how well the objects are grouped, whereas the sum of squared error effectively measures the dispersal of clusters [25].

iii. **Silhouette index**: Intracluster similarity is graphically shown by the silhouette index, where silhouette widths ranging from −1 to +1 indicate how appropriate the clusters are assigned for each object [25]. Depending on the value of the silhouette width, three cases arise:

1. When a silhouette width approaches +1, correct assignment of objects to their clusters.
2. When a silhouette width approaches 0, it suggests possible indecisiveness regarding its cluster assignment.
3. Conversely, a silhouette width nearly equal to −1 signifies that the object is in the wrong cluster.

Clusters obtained using the silhouette index are typically more accurate compared to those obtained using other indices.

3.6.2 Dimensionality Reduction

Addressing the challenges posed by vast datasets has become a central focus of information technology in the modern era. To effectively manage, some techniques are used for simplification of the evaluation process, like-multidimensional scaling (MDS), PCA, and self-organizing map (SOM) are traditional methods for dimensionality reduction, vital for handling large datasets [10, 20]. t-SNE maps data into 2D or 3D, ideal for complex data such as genetics, whereas MDS analyzes proximity in lower dimensions, used in tasks such as magnetic resonance imaging segmentation. Recent advancements expand the use of classic MDS algorithms in diverse applications. This study evaluates K-nearest neighbors (KNN), edited nearest neighbor (ENN), and SVM with t-SNE and MDS on UCI datasets, assessing their effectiveness using metrics such as F-measure and G-mean for classification tasks.

3.6.3 t-Distributed Stochastic Neighbor Embedding

t-SNE stands out as one of the few algorithms adept at simultaneously preserving both local and global structures of data [10, 27]. Given a set of high-dimensional objects $(x_i), i = 1 \text{ to } N,$ and a function $(\boldsymbol{i}, \boldsymbol{j}),$ where $\boldsymbol{d}_{ij} = \left\|\boldsymbol{x}_i - \boldsymbol{x}_j\right\|^2$ represents the Euclidean distance [12], t-SNE initially computes the contingent probabilities $p_{j|i}$ among close data points objects x_i and x_j. The contingent probability is mathematically expressed as in Eq. (3.7) [27].

$$p_{j|i} = \frac{\exp\left(-\|x_i - x_j\|^2 / 2\sigma_i^2\right)}{\sum_{k\neq i}\exp(-\|x_i - x_k\|^2 / 2\sigma_i^2)} \tag{3.7}$$

Similarly, an analogous contingent probability $q_{j|i}$ is calculated for finding the low-dimensional data points y_i, where y_j represents the high dimensional set x_i and x_j, shown in Eq. (3.8) [27].

$$q_{j|i} = \frac{\exp\left(-\|y_i - y_j\|^2 / 2\sigma_i^2\right)}{\sum_{k\neq i}\exp(-\|y_i - y_k\|^2 / 2\sigma_i^2)} \tag{3.8}$$

t-SNE is one of the methods that have been widely used to visualize high-dimensional data in lower dimensions while preserving the local structures and revealing the hidden patterns within it in various fields such as bioinformatics, image processing, and text analysis classifications, among others [12, 27].

3.6.4 Multidimensional Scaling

According to multidimensional scaling techniques [27], multidimensional scaling is an approach for reducing dimensions that leads to new representations of smaller dimensions of data, which maintain distance information between pairs [21]. Given a dissimilarity matrix, $D_{ij} = d_{ij}$, where d_{ij} represents distance between i and j, the resulting matrix X as output, having the reduced dimension as d (typically $d = 1, 2,$ or 3) reduces loss called as strain, expressed as in Eq. (3.9).

$$\textbf{Strain} = \left(\frac{\sum_{i\neq j}(d_{ij} - \|x_i - x_j\|)^2}{\sum_{i\neq j} d_{ij}^2}\right)^{1/2} \tag{3.9}$$

MDS operates basis on principle that the matrix X is found through method eigen decomposition from $B = XX'$. Matrix is derived on the basis of D, dissimilarity matrix by performing double centering. Using a dissimilarity matrix, products are mapped to a lower-dimensional space where each point represents a product, reflecting similarities or dissimilarities based on customer perceptions. Visualizing products in a 2D or 3D plot using MDS helps marketers identify product similarities and customer perceptions based on proximity, facilitating segmentation by shared attributes. Conversely, products placed farther apart suggest distinct characteristics, guiding strategic product positioning, portfolio optimization, and targeted marketing campaigns to align with customer preferences [22].

3.7 Principal Component Analysis

This is a fundamental reduction technique and reduces dataset dimensionality by transforming data into orthogonal principal components ordered by variance, crucial for signal processing, pattern recognition, and data compression.

1. **Standardization**: Standardize the dataset centers each feature around 0 with a standard deviation of *1*, mitigating scale dominance in analysis.
2. **Covariance matrix computation**: Compute the covariance matrix to analyze relationships between standardized features.

   The covariance can be positive, 0, or negative; 0 indicates no direct relation.
3. **Eigen decomposition**: Using eigenvectors and eigenvalues, the covariance matrix is obtained.
4. **Selection of principal components**: Sort eigenvectors are ranked according to their eigenvalues in decreasing order, and the top ones are selected as principal components since they capture the highest variance in the data.
5. **Projection**: Project the dataset onto selected principal components, reducing dimensionality while preserving maximum variance.

PCA offers several benefits and aids in dimensionality reduction and noise reduction while visualizing high-dimensional data [11], crucial for extracting insights in bioinformatics and other domains using ML techniques such as t-SNE and MDS. Initially, a population size was chosen as the dataset, and cluster analysis was conducted on varying dataset sizes, which comprised 100 rows and 3 attributes, with subsequent scaling to 200, 300, and beyond. The methodology in Figure 3.4 used MATLAB R2009b, starting with a dataset of 100 rows and 3 attributes, scaling up to larger sizes such as 200 and 300 rows for cluster analysis [25].

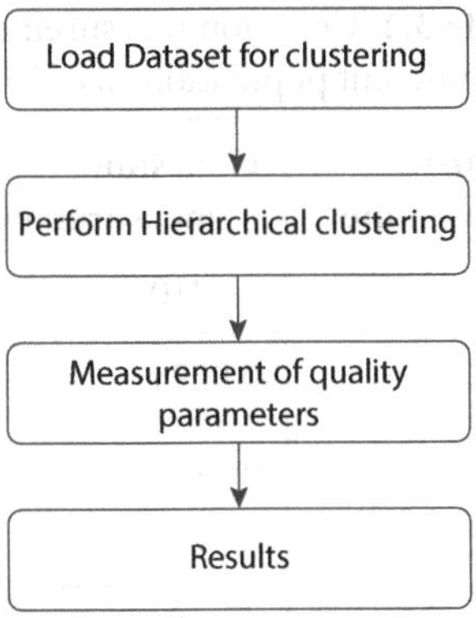

Figure 3.4 Steps of methodology used.

Table 3.1 For different population size–elapsed time [25].

Cluster volume	Elapsed time
100 × 3	0.092
200 × 3	0.010
300 × 3	0.012
400 × 3	0.020
500 × 3	0.031

The proposed methodology in Tables 3.1 and 3.2 integrates silhouette index, cohesion measurement, and elapsed time as key quality variable for cluster analysis. Metrics of the cohesiveness such as lack of cohesion of methods (LCOM) and loose class cohesion (LCC) assess how well objects are brought together in order to make dataset organization better, whereas silhouette index graphically represents cluster quality with variance in data points. The silhouette index graphically represents cluster quality through scattered data point visualization, whereas shorter processing times indicate higher-quality clusters [25].

Evaluation in terms of population size shows that, with an increase in dataset, elapsed time also increases; thus, 200-record volumes are recommended for best clustering applications. In addition, cohesion measurements were found to fluctuate as a result of changes in population size showing a relationship with cluster formation instead of dataset size. Lower cohesion at 100-record volumes, followed by increases at 200-record

Table 3.2 Cohesion measurement for different population size [25].

Cluster volume	Cohesion measurement
100 × 3	0.8210
200 × 3	0.8294
300 × 3	0.8219
400 × 3	0.8253
500 × 3	0.8215

volumes and subsequent decreases at higher volumes, underscored this observation. Cohesion measure based on object association suggests that better cluster quality translates to higher values. Consequently, cluster analysis should involve 200-record volumes only. The findings suggested relationships between parameters that could improve clustering while making more general conclusions regarding data processing techniques including optimizing systems.

3.8 Conclusion

This chapter extensively discusses machine learning methods that are important in recent modeling based on data. For instance, it explores supervised learning techniques such as classification tress and SVMs, which demonstrate their utility everywhere. Again, there is a focus on unsupervised learners including clustering algorithms such as clustering and reduction methods such as PCA and t-SNE and others. By presenting algorithms and providing case studies of their use, this chapter shows why it is essential for ML to be used in handling complex datasets so as to obtain vital information that leads to new developments in all areas.

Bibliography

1. Sarker, I.H., Machine Learning: Algorithms, Real-World Applications and Research Directions. *SN Comput. Sci.*, *2*, 160, 2021, https://doi.org/10.1007/s42979-021-00592-x.

2. Simeone, O., A Very Brief Introduction to Machine Learning With Applications to Communication Systems. *IEEE Trans. Cognit. Commun. Netw.*, *4*, 4, 2332–7731, 2018, https://doi.org/10.1109/TCCN.2018.2888019.
3. Somvanshi, M., Chavan, P., Tambade, S., Shinde, S.V., A Review of Machine Learning Techniques using Decision Tree and Support Vector Machine, in: *2016 International Conference on Computing Communication Control and automation (ICCUBEA)*, IEEE, Pune, India, 2016, Electronic ISBN: 978-1-5090-3291-4.
4. Angra, S. and Ahuja, S., Machine learning and its Applications: A Review, in: *2017 International Conference on Big Data Analytics and Computational Intelligence (ICBDAC)*, IEEE, 2017.
5. Abdualgalil, B. and Abraham, S., Applications of Machine Learning Algorithms and Performance Comparison: A Review, IEEE, 2020.
6. Kumar, M., Bhatia, A., Jain, P., Khan, S.A., Sharma, V., A Conceptual Introduction of Machine Learning Algorithms, in: *2023 1st International Conference on Intelligent Computing and Research Trends (ICRT)*, IEEE, 2023, Electronic ISBN: 979-8-3503-3677-1.
7. Burges, B. and Scholkopf, (Eds.), *Advances in Kernel Methods–Support Vector Learning*, MIT Press, 1998.
8. Thomas, R.N. and Gupta, R., A Survey on Machine Learning Approaches and Its Techniques, in: *2020 IEEE International Students' Conference on Electrical, Electronics and Computer Science (SCEECS)*, 2020, February 22-23, IEEE, pp. 1–6, https://doi.org/10.1109/SCEECS48394.2020.190.
9. Xiao, Q., Li, C., Tang, Y., Chen, X., Energy Efficiency Modeling for Configuration-Dependent Machining *via* Machine Learning: A Comparative Study. *IEEE Trans. Autom. Sci. Eng.*, *18*, 2, 717–730, 2021, https://doi.org/10.1109/TASE.2019.2961714.
10. Rosas–Arias, L., Sanchez–Perez, G., Toscano–Medina, L.K., Perez–Meana, H.M., Portillo–Portillo, J., A Graphical User Interface for Fast Evaluation and Testing of Machine Learning Models Performance, in: *2019 7th International Workshop on Biometrics and Forensics (IWBF)*, Cancun, Mexico, 2019, https://doi.org/10.1109/IWBF.2019.8739238.
11. Oreški, D. and Hajdin, G., A Comparative Study of Machine Learning Approaches on Learning Management System Data, in: *2019 International Conference on Control, Artificial Intelligence, Robotics & Optimization (ICCAIRO)*, Athens, Greece, 2019, https://doi.org/10.1109/ICCAIRO47923.2019.00029.
12. C M, S. and Prakash, J., Performance Analysis of Machine Learning and Deep Learning Models for Text Classification, in: *2020 IEEE 17th India Council International Conference (INDICON)*, New Delhi, India, 2020, https://doi.org/10.1109/INDICON49873.2020.9342208.
13. Durga Prasad, B.K., Choudhary, B., Ankayarkanni, B., Performance Evaluation Model using Unsupervised K-Means Clustering, in: *2020*

International Conference on Communication and Signal Processing (ICCSP), Chennai, India, 2020, https://doi.org/10.1109/ICCSP48568.2020.9182368.
14. Panda, P. and Behera, S., Data-driven model of Photovoltaic Module by Machine Learning Regression for Power Maximization, in: *2020 IEEE International Symposium on Sustainable Energy, Signal Processing and Cyber Security (iSSSC)*, Gunupur, Odisha, India, 2020, https://doi.org/10.1109/iSSSC50941.2020.9358893.
15. Pashentsev, A.V. and Vedishchev, V.V., Applying Big Data and Machine Learning Approach to Identify Noised Data, in: *2020 2nd International Conference on Control Systems, Mathematical Modeling, Automation and Energy Efficiency (SUMMA)*, Lipetsk, Russia, p. 384, 2020, https://doi.org/10.1109/SUMMA50634.2020.9280585.
16. Yang, F.-J., An Extended Idea about Decision Trees, in: *2019 International Conference on Computational Science and Computational Intelligence (CSCI)*, Las Vegas, NV, USA, p. 349, 2019, https://doi.org/10.1109/CSCI49370.2019.00068.
17. He, P., Chen, L., Xu, X.-H., FAST C4.5, in: *2007 International Conference on Machine Learning and Cybernetics*, IEEE, Hong Kong, China, p. 2841, 2007, https://doi.org/10.1109/ICMLC.2007.4370632.
18. Wang, Y.-Y., Li, Y.-B., Rong, X.-W., Improvement of ID3 algorithm based on simplified information entropy and coordination degree, in: *2017 Chinese Automation Congress (CAC)*, IEEE, Jinan, China, p. 1526, 2017, https://doi.org/10.1109/CAC.2017.8243009.
19. Mohapatra, S., Segmentation using Support Vector Machines, in: *2019 Second International Conference on Advanced Computational and Communication Paradigms (ICACCP)*, IEEE, Gangtok, India, 2019, https://doi.org/10.1109/ICACCP.2019.8882941.
20. Miao, L., Application of CART Decision Tree Combined with PCA Algorithm in Intrusion Detection, in: *2017 8th IEEE International Conference on Software Engineering and Service Science (ICSESS)*, IEEE, Beijing, China, p. 38, 2017, https://doi.org/10.1109/ICSESS.2017.8342859.
21. Calheno, R., Carvalho, P., Lima, S.R., Henriques, P.R., Merino, M.R., Improving conformance checking in process modelling: a multiperspective algorithm. *J. Supercomput.*, *79*, 18256–18292, 2023, https://doi.org/10.1007/s11227-023-05315-y.
22. Estañol, M., Munoz-Gama, J., Carmona, J., Teniente, E., Conformance checking in UML artifact-centric business process models. *Softw. Syst. Model.*, *18*, 4, 2531–2555, 2019, https://doi.org/10.1007/s10270-018-0681-6.
23. Song, M., Yang, H., Siadat, S.H., Pechenizkiy, M.J.E., S. w. A., A comparative study of dimensionality reduction techniques to enhance trace clustering performances. *Expert Syst. Appl.*, *40*, 9, 3722–3737, 2013.
24. Lu, Y., Ye, T., Zheng, J., Decision Tree Algorithm in Machine Learning, in: *2022 IEEE International Conference on Advances in Electrical Engineering*

and Computer Applications (AEECA), IEEE, 2022, https://doi.org/10.1109/AEECA55500.2022.9918857.
25. Nisha, and Kaur, P.J., Cluster Quality Based Performance Evaluation of Hierarchical Clustering Method, in: *2015 1st International Conference on Next Generation Computing Technologies (NGCT-2015)*, Dehradun, India, 4-5 September 2015.
26. Hinton, G.E. and Salakhutdinov, R., Reducing the dimensionality of data with neural networks. *Science, 313*, 5756, 504–507, 2006.
27. Sakib, S., Abu, M., Rahman, M.A., Performance Evaluation of t-SNE and MDS Dimensionality Reduction Techniques with KNN, ENN and SVM Classifiers, in: *2020 IEEE Region 10 Symposium (TENSYMP)*, Dhaka, Bangladesh, 5-7 June 2020.
28. Shah, S. and Singh, M., Comparison of a time efficient modified K-mean algorithm with K-Mean and K-Medoid algorithm, in: *2012 International Conference on Communication Systems and Network Technologies*, p. 435, 2012, https://doi.org/10.1109/CSNT.2012.100.

4

Neural Networks and Deep Learning in Data-Driven Modeling

Tanishka Chakraborty[1], Indrani Mukherjee[2*] and Suparna Biswas[3]

[1]*Department of Computer Science & Engineering, OmDayal Group of Institution Uluberia, West Bengal, India*
[2]*Department of Computer Science & Engineering, Narula Institute of Technology, Kolkata, West Bengal, India*
[3]*Department of Computer Science & Engineering, Maulana Abul Kalam Azad University, Kolkata, West Bengal, India*

Abstract

In deep learning methods to estimate system parameters and evaluate the global Lipschitz condition with respect to input/output data, it is possible for an unknown-dynamic iterative learning control system. Neuron models: M-P including habituation network neurons can enhance convolutional network performance *via* nonassociative training. A novel solution to this problem is a deep layer-by-layer supervised pretraining framework utilizing stacked supervised encoder–decoder, which jointly prelearns the feature extraction and also soft sensor modeling in industrial processes. The BLEU helps the architect to unroll higher computationally layers and connection between them in feed forward as well as recurrent neural network architectures. Leveraging offline data mining with hardware design results in intelligent memory systems, which balances energy efficiency and cost against classification accuracy during execution. The mixture of synaptic- and SRAM-type computation greatly improves power efficiency at only minor accuracy degradation for state-of-the-art deep learning models. Combining theoretical research and practical applications, this interdisciplinary effort ultimately leads to technological advances, driving technological advancements across various domains. Transfer learning, leveraging pretrained models, enhances learning efficiency and performance across tasks. Academics or educational field and industry together highlight the dynamic nature of technological progress and its societal impact.

**Corresponding author*: indranim849@gmail.com

Arindam Mondal and Souvik Ganguli (eds.) Data-Driven Modeling, (99–120) © 2026 Scrivener Publishing LLC

***Keywords*:** Neural network, deep learning architectures, data-driven modeling, recurrent neural network, transfer learning, pretrained models, convolutional neural network

4.1 Introduction

Today, machine learning (ML) and its close kin deep learning are practically ubiquitous in every walk of life—it affects more or less everything we do on a daily basis: from getting better results for web searches to improving what we see on social media; from recommendation systems when shopping online to consumer devices such as cameras and smartphones. Traditionally, ML methods were heavily dependent on the hand-engineered features made by domain experts, which was a slow and expert-driven process [1]. Representation learning changed that by allowing machines to learn the relevant features from actual data and as such solved years of infuriating feature engineering. Representation learning is a part of deep learning that, through layering nonlinear transformations inside the network (each subsequent layer form feature from binary information), it can transform representation into one data group to another more abstract level [1]. Each layer learns increasingly complex representations, with higher layers amplifying essential aspects for discrimination while suppressing irrelevant variations, exemplified in image analysis where lower layers are usually used for detection of simple features such as edges, and higher layers are used for combining these into recognizable objects. Deep learning's applications span diverse fields, achieving superhuman performance in recognizing image and speech and exceling in the field of natural language processing (NLP). In the field of healthcare, deep learning aids in analyzing medical images for disease detection and assists in genomics and drug discovery [2]. Deep learning faces hurdles such as the need for big labeled datasets, trouble explaining models, and heavy computer power needs. But better hardware and smarter methods keep tackling these problems. The field's future looks bright, with work on smarter learning tricks, artificial intelligence (AI) you can understand, and team-ups with Internet of Things and edge computing. These advances are set to spark new ideas and change what tech can do. Self-driving cars also benefit from deep learning. It helps process sensor info and makes snap choices boosting safety and how well these cars work. Banks use deep learning too. It spots fraud, trades stocks, and manages risk. This lets them dig through huge amounts of data and find hidden patterns. In show business, deep learning picks movies, songs, and other stuff you might like, giving each person their own mix.

When deep learning joins forces with virtual reality and augmented reality, it makes games and mockups feel more real and fun to use. Deep learning methods are getting better and better. We expect them to play a big role in science research. They will help break down tricky data in star science, weather science, and life science. As computers get stronger, and we have more data, plus new ways to learn and build networks, deep learning will grow faster. This will make it key in moving AI forward and bringing it into our daily lives. Schools and companies are working together to push deep learning research ahead. This shows how lively it is and how it could change society. It also means we need to keep putting money and effort into exploring what it can do. Deep learning is also making progress in nature sciences. It helps model complex living systems, guess how tiny particles will act, and find new materials quicker. In earth science, it helps track and model climate change. This leads to better guesses and smarter choices about rules. In schools, deep learning tech makes learning fit each student better. It adapts to what each student needs and offers smart tutoring systems that can boost how well students learn [5]. Deep learning plays a bigger part in cybersecurity now. It helps spot threats, find odd things, and build tough security systems to keep important information safe. As this tech gets better, it will become a key part of how we live. It will push new ideas and make things work better in many areas, from health care to making stuff moving people and things around and dealing with money [3]. Deep learning can change things in a big way. It is not just about what it can do tech-wise. It can also help create new ways to do business, shake up old industries, and come up with fresh answers to hard problems. We are at the start of a new tech age. Deep learning could make things better in so many ways. It might lead to a future where smart systems are a normal part of how we live. This could help us move forward and make life better for people all over the world. As we find ourselves on the threshold of a new technological age, the potential for deep learning to revolutionize and revolutionize various domains appears limitless, promising a great future where intelligent systems seamlessly integrate into each and every aspect of human life, driving progress, and improving the quality of life worldwide.

4.2 Basic Concept of Neural Network and Deep Learning

Neural networks find their motivation in the structure of the animal brain, particularly in that of human. This involves layers of interconnected units known as neurons. Each neuron takes in input signals, performs operations on them through an activation function, and after that forwards the output to the neurons in the following layer. The weights improve the ability of the network to perform a given task.

Deep learning is a very important part of ML, which combines the concept of neural networks with many layers. These deep neural networks (DNNs) are able to figure out the detailed patterns in data by utilizing a layered learning process. The most important thing is that the excellence of deep learning has automatically discovering. It automatically extracts features from raw data without any human intervention for feature engineering. Deep learning models discover intricate patterns and relationships hidden in high dimensional data by stacking multiple layers of nonlinear transformations.

4.2.1 Characteristics of Neural Network

Learning from data: In general, a neural network is subjected to be trained using examples as input–output pairs. While training has performed to the network, the network weights are adjusted to cut down the difference between the actual outputs and the expected values that it should produce, called the target values.

Nonlinearity: Neural networks allow the use of nonlinear activation functions and can thus establish nonlinear relationships between the inputs and outputs [1]. This nonlinearity allows the neural networks to approximate any arbitrary function that is required and to capture more data features.

Parallel distributed processing: While working together as a group, neural networks operate independently in that a neuron handles all its input independently as dictated by the network. This coordination of parallel processing allows neural networks to deal with enormous amounts of information and at the same time [2].

Adaptability: Neural networks are progressive; they are capable of producing changes as new data are fed to it or whenever there is a change to the environment without having to be reprogrammed [3]. Due to this flexibility, these two types of heuristics are appropriate to be applied on procedures, where circumstances are inconstant or stochastic.

Generalization: Neural networks strive to find a relationship between the training data it has been trained on and the test data so that they can classify or predict on incoming data. The second is generalization, which directly helps maintain the network's ability to accomplish practical tasks apart from the training set.

Hierarchy of features: In DNNs, features are learned by nesting one layer onto the other; they provide several layers of representation. The lower layers are often used to cool basic attributes, whereas the higher layers deal with more complex and abstract forms. This hierarchical feature learning allows for neural networks to extract bottom-up hierarchical features from data.
Robustness to noise: Neural networks are somewhat stable against noise and variability of input data to a certain extent. They can handle "noisy" or "imperfect" inputs and still yield sensible outputs; this is because they can learn robust representation [4].
Scalability: Neural networks do not have a limitation with size and dimensionality of data that they can operate on. New processor technologies such as graphics processing unit (GPUs) and tensor processing unit (TPUs) have added to the scalability of neural network training and predictions.

4.2.2 Characteristics of Deep Learning

Automatic feature learning: Most of the deep learning models are so capable to learn the features directly from raw input data, which is given to the model, and thus, they can decrease the role of human when it comes to feature extraction [5].
Hierarchical representation: DNNs learn a hierarchy, where the features computed in earlier layers are simple, and those computed by later layers are more abstract [1].
Scalability: Deep learning models used to scale the large datasets and complex tasks, leveraging parallel processing on powerful hardware such as GPUs and TPUs.
State-of-the-art performance: The area of speech and image recognition, reinforcement learning, and NLP have been greatly influenced by deep learning and its applications.

4.3 Applications of Neural Networks and Deep Learning in Data-Driven Modeling

There is a wider range of applications are available of involvement of neural network and deep learning in data-driven modeling. Those are as follows:

4.3.1 Image Recognition

Image recognition is a prominent application of deep learning that involves training the neural networks to identify objects, scenes, or patterns within images. Deep convolutional neural networks (CNNs) have many more contributions on the area in broader aspect such as in image recognition, and it is used to learn hierarchical features from raw pixel data automatically [1]. Also, Figure 4.1 defines image recognition, where the networks basically contain multiple layers of convolutional and the pooling operations, which are followed by the layers that are fully connected, used for classification [1]. It is possible to support great results in all fields of concern, including detecting objects, classifying images, or segmenting image semantically by exploiting large-scale annotated datasets and powerful computational resources.

4.3.2 Natural Language Processing

NLP provides the potential to the machines to understand, analyze, and generate human language. Among the many important developments in deep learning algorithms, for example, recurrent neural networks (RNNs) and transformers, much progress has been achieved by comparing the state of the art, which exists today in NLP. This has been due to their capacity to learn the patterns and semantic representations from the textual data.

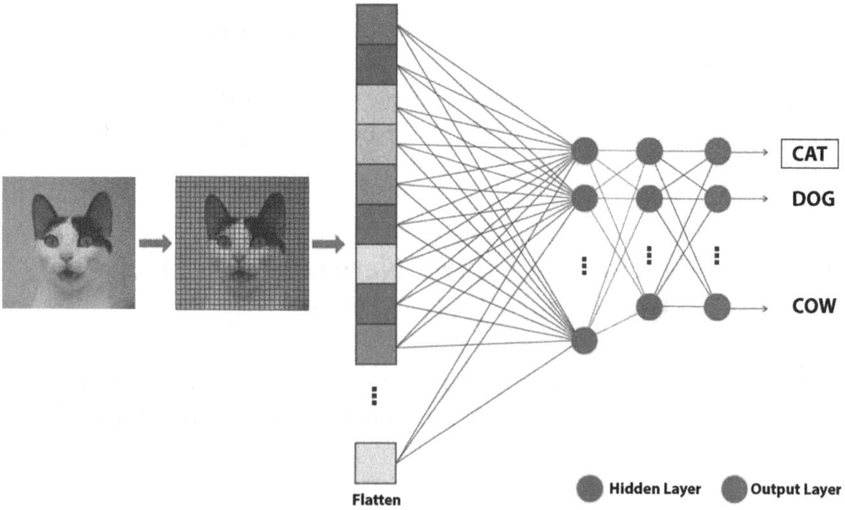

Figure 4.1 Image recognition [28].

RNNs, which incorporate feedback loops, are so good at dealing with sequential data that they can perform language modeling, sentiment analysis, and machine translation. RNNs rightly evolved hidden states breaking into sentences and have a number of sequential sentences in a row so that they can successfully treat the dependencies and relationships of the language data. And also, these enhanced RNN architectures mitigate gradient issues and improve performance in tasks requiring the long-range context retention.

4.3.3 Time-Series Prediction

The prediction of time series is forecasting future values using past data points collected over sequential time. Neal's deep learning models have some incredible features that allow them to learn temporal dependencies and patterns from data sequences. Deep learning models, especially RNNs and long short-term memory (LSTM) networks, have amazing abilities to record temporal dependencies and patterns from sequential data [7]. As Figure 4.2 has demonstrated, these models have a variety of applications in financial, healthcare, and climate science such as predicting the stock price, giving the prognosis of the diseases, and forecasting the weather.

4.3.4 Recommender Systems

Recommender systems functioning in a personalization mode focus on users and are based on users' preferences or similarities such as their past interactions with other items. Deep learning methods are used more and more frequently to make better performance of the recommender systems [8]. The

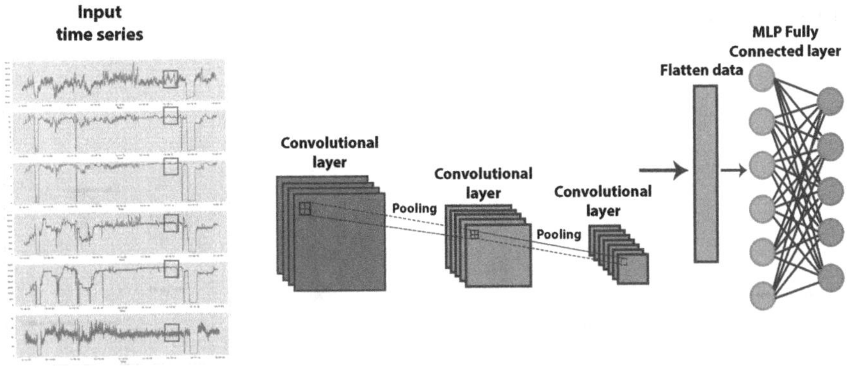

Figure 4.2 Time-series prediction system pipeline [29].

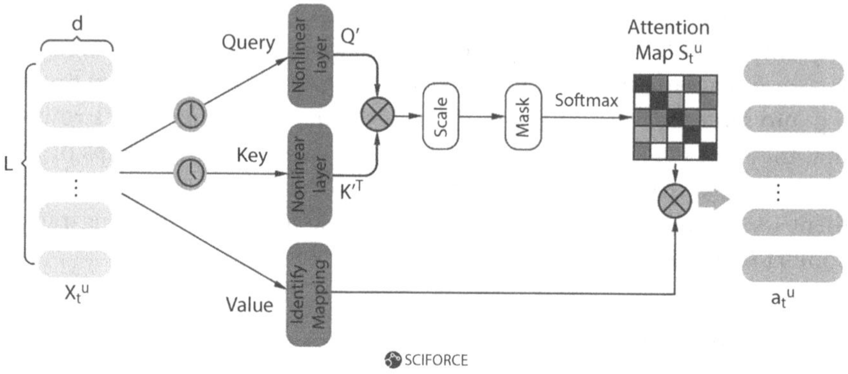

Figure 4.3 Way of recommender system pipeline [30].

ability of those models to use a complex interaction of user–item groups together with latent representations from sparse and high-dimensional data is evident in [8]. Figure 4.3 depicts that the recommender system actually works using neural networking and deep learning methods.

4.3.5 Anomaly Detection

Anomaly detection is one of the identifications of those rare events or patterns that are different from the normal behavior in a dataset. Deep learning models, for example, auto encoders and generative adversarial networks (GANs), are some of the best methods for anomaly detection because they learn representations of normal data distributions to be normal [9] (Figure 4.4). These models demonstrate the possibility of detecting anomalies in different domains such as cybersecurity, industrial systems, and healthcare, by capturing the subtle deviations and abnormalities from normal patterns.

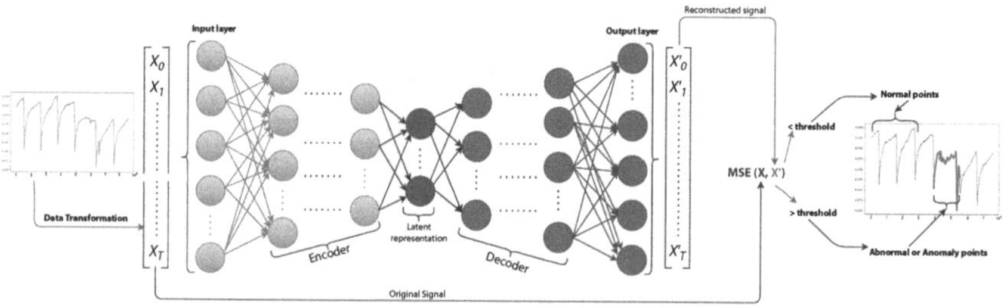

Figure 4.4 Anomaly detection pipeline [31].

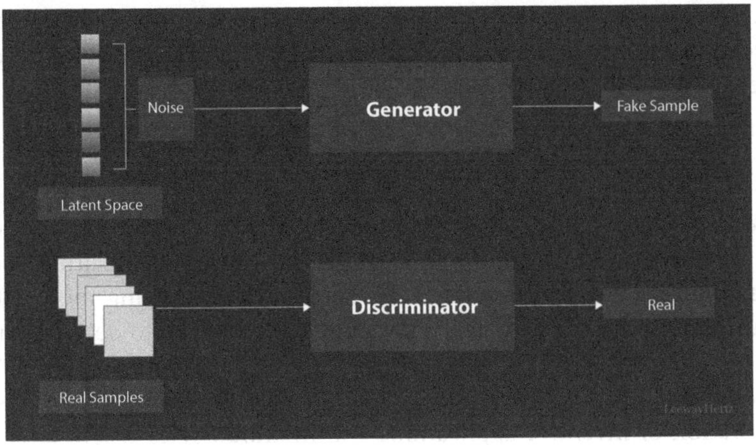

Figure 4.5 Structure of GAN devices [32].

4.3.6 Generative Adversarial Networks

GANs are basically defined as a group of deep learning models that basically consists of two neural networks, named as generator and discriminator, which are competitors with each other in a game. In Figure 4.5, there is a generator that aims to produce synthetic data samples that are very similar with the real data, whereas the discriminator concentrates to find the difference between the real samples and the fake samples [10]. GANs have shown exceptional potential in producing virtual photos, composing music, and generating text [10]. The main pros of GANs are that they can be highly efficient and also allow for color control of the emitted light. Liabilities comprise hurdles in managing growth and supplying 3D structure treatment.

4.3.7 Autonomous Driving

Autonomous driving systems leverage deep learning techniques to perceive the surrounding environment, decision-making, and navigations of vehicles without human interruption. CNNs are used for detection of an object, lane, and semantic segmentation from sensor data such as cameras, LiDAR, radar, etc., and many more [11]. End-to-end learning provides such approaches, where neural networks used to map sensor inputs to vehicle control commands have gained traction in autonomous driving research. Basically, these are the algorithms that are used for executing the processes such as long learning and short prediction and different types of regression algorithms for implementing various autonomous applications, for example, self-driving cars.

4.3.8 Health Monitoring Using Wearable Devices

Wearable devices equipped with sensors, such as accelerometers and heart rate monitors, collect continuous streams for monitoring health through physiological data. RNNs and CNNs are the deep learning models that are utilized in this context, analyze wearable sensor data to detect anomalies, predict health outcomes, and assist in disease management [12]. The increasing scholarly interest, as depicted in Figure 4.6, highlights a rising exploration of inventive applications and methodologies where wearable technologies intersect with ML algorithms. Concurrently, a noticeable thematic shift toward personalized wearable devices has surfaced, indicating researchers' growing emphasis on tailoring wearable solutions. The continuous academic research and personalization in wearable technology play a significant role in patient care. Figure 4.7 shows the three key sorts for some wearable devices, which include bioelectrical devices, bioimpedance devices, and electrochemical and electromechanical devices.

4.3.9 Attention Mechanisms in NLP

Attention mechanisms in NLP are what allow models to aim on specific relevant pieces of the input sequences when generating predictions. As shown

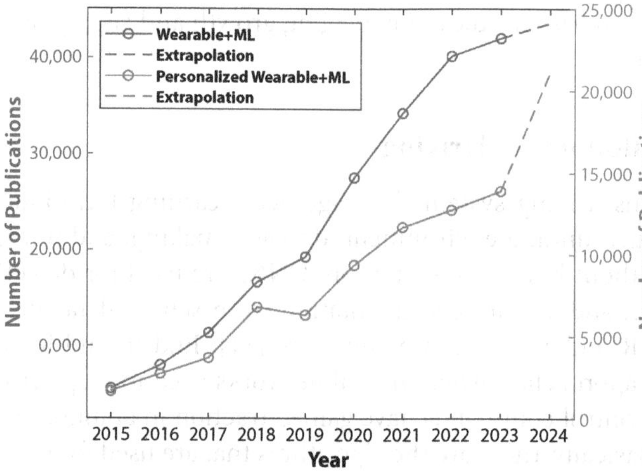

Figure 4.6 Utilizing or personalized wearable devices using machine learning [33].

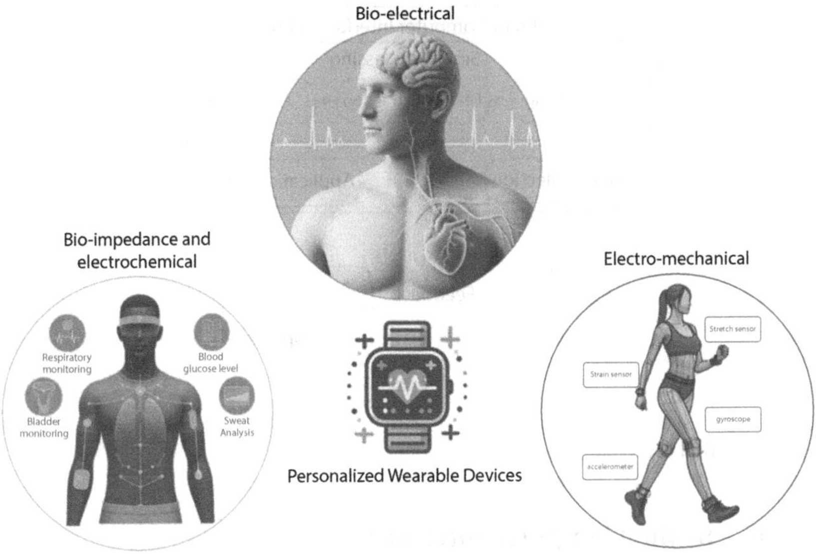

Figure 4.7 Illustration of three main categories of personalized wearable devices [33].

in Figure 4.8, such attention mechanisms have propelled great effectiveness in various tasks involving sequence-to-sequence models and include machine translation, text summarization, and question answering, among others. The transformer architecture, equipped with self-attention mechanisms, has become the de facto standard for many NLP tasks [13]. Some of the attention mechanisms are as follows: (a) self-attention, (b) multihead attention, (c) cross-attention, and (d) causal attention.

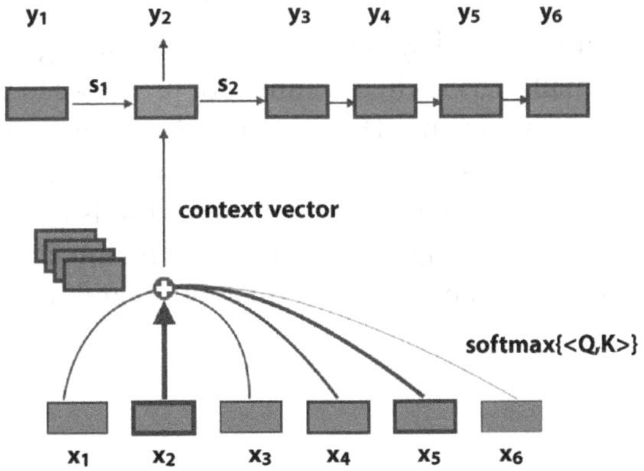

Figure 4.8 Attention mechanism [34].

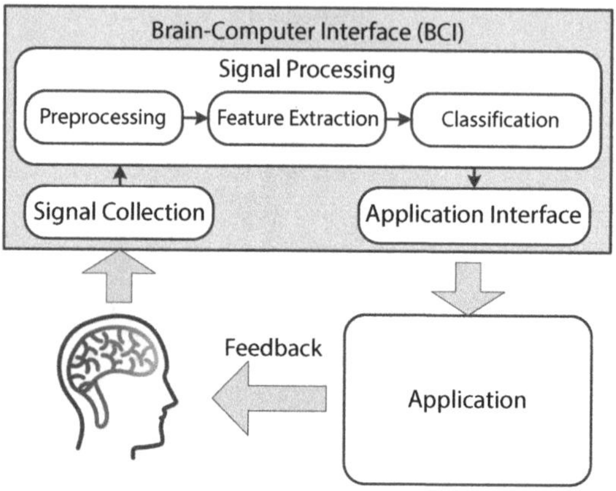

Figure 4.9 BCI principle [35].

4.3.10 Brain–Computer Interface

Brain and external devices have communicated with each other using brain–computer interfaces (BCIs), and it allows individuals to control computers, prosthetics, and other technology using neural signals. As shown in Figure 4.9, CNNs and RNNs have been utilized to interpret neural signals captured through electroencephalography data for motor imagery tasks, speech synthesis, and rehabilitation applications. BCI can help in technologies involved to help in mind-control prosthetic limbs/wheelchairs and many more; for example, it can help in aiding in the rehabilitation of stroke victims or those with spinal cord injuries.

4.3.11 Fault Diagnosis in Industrial Systems

Fault diagnosis in industrial systems involves identifying and diagnosing abnormalities or malfunctions in machinery or processes to prevent downtime and optimize maintenance (Figure 4.10). Anomalies are detected and equipment failures forecasted by analyzing sensor data and process metrics through the application of deep learning methods utilizing CNN and RNN. Fault detection and diagnosis methods are mainly divided into three types of categories: (a) quantitative, (b) qualitative, and (c) data- driven.

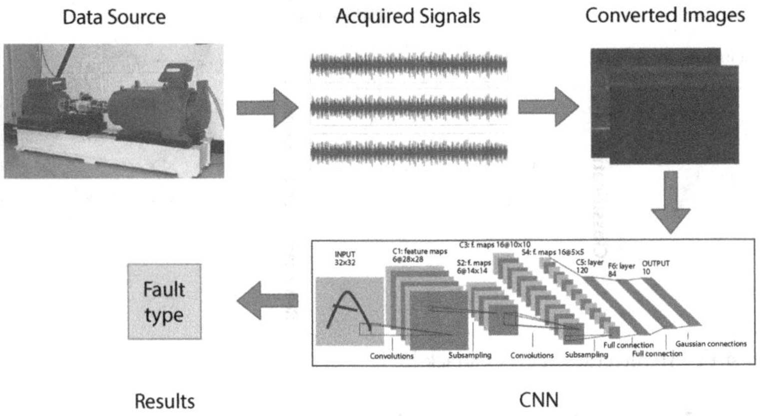

Figure 4.10 Fault diagnosis in industrial system [36].

4.3.12 Speech Recognition

Speech recognition is a process that involves converting human verbal language into text, enabling applications such as virtual assistants, voice-controlled devices, and dictation systems rely on advanced learning techniques to analyze the acoustic and phonetic characteristics of raw audio data. Deep learning models, such as CNNs and RNNs, enhance the accuracy and reliability of speech recognition systems [15].

4.3.13 Cybersecurity Applications

Cybersecurity applications can be explained as all the tasks are aimed at computer systems, networks, and data security from the cyber threats such as malware, phishing, and unauthorized access [16]. DNNs and CNNs are used to analyze network traffic, log data, and system behavior to find and stop security breaches in real time. It helps in threat detection and intrusion detection as well for the computer systems and networks. Such networks have the capability to detect insecure actions by assessing patterns and some features that are common with threats or intrusions. With discussing about the application of neural network in cyber security, Figure 4.11 shows the architecture of detecting cyber-attack using neural network.

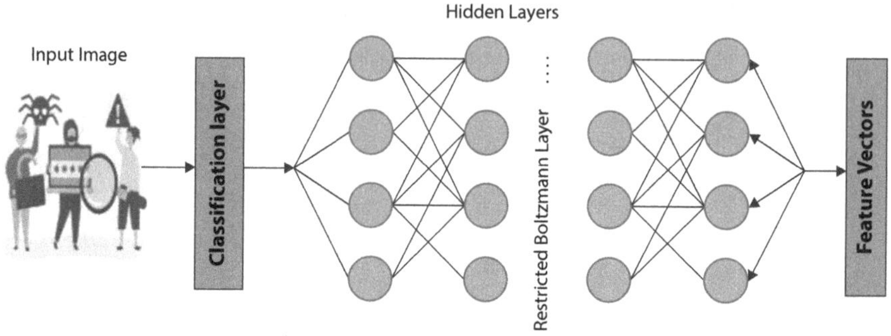

Figure 4.11 Architecture of cyber attack [37].

4.3.14 Energy Consumption Forecasting

A forecast of energy consumption entails the creation of predictions of the energy consumption patterns in the future in order to optimize the resource allocation, increase the energy efficiency, and help in the energy management decision-making process; some deep learning techniques play a significant role and observe the past energy consumption patterns and the external causes such as weather conditions and economic indicators to give a precise forecast of the energy demand in the future [17]. Figure 4.12 shows that MES is the multienergy system, which is responsible for the district of the buildings under consideration, supplied with both heating and power *via* a district heating network that links the main energy supply to the individual buildings in the district. The aggregate demand for heating and power throughout the district was measured at the points described below.

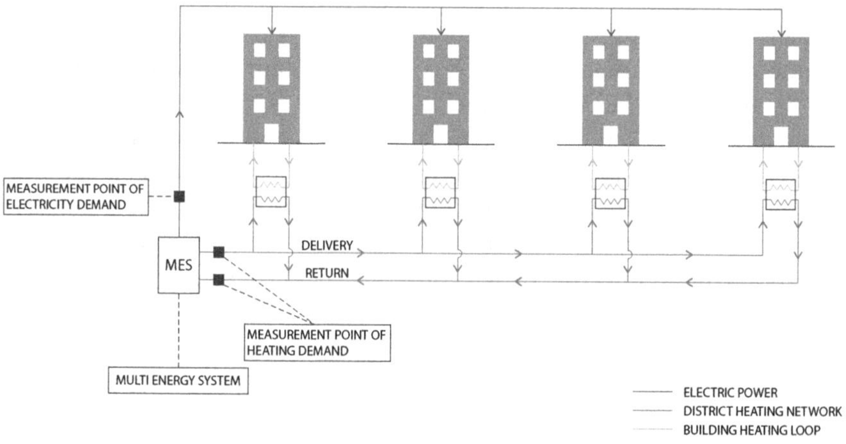

Figure 4.12 MES representation [38].

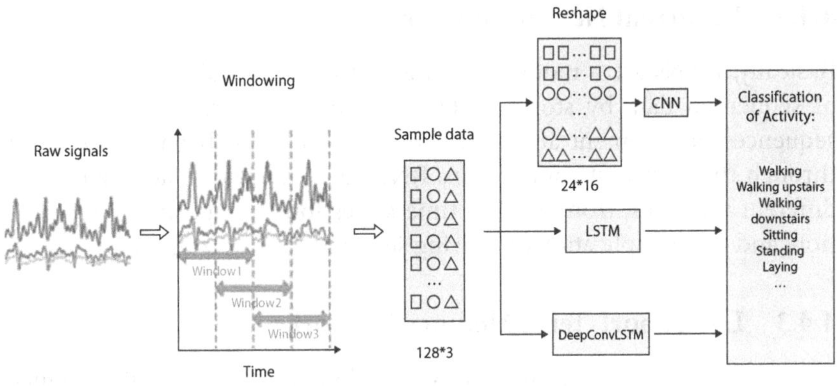

Figure 4.13 Human activity recognition system based on deep learning [39].

4.3.15 Human Activity Recognition

It refers to the procedure by which identification and classification of various activities performed by individual sensors detect and classify various human activities based on information gathered from wearable devices, smartphones, or Internet of Things sensors. Sensor readings by accelerometers and gyroscopes can be processed, for example, by deep learning models for the classification of activities such as walking, running, or cycling [18]. The most useful algorithm is decision tree algorithm, which is the most efficient algorithm for HAR (human activity recognition). Basically, decision tree algorithms are effective models for handling nonlinear relationships between features and labels. They can be utilized for classification tasks in HAR, particularly when analyzing sensor data from devices such as accelerometers or gyroscopes. Figure 4.13 shows the architecture of human activity recognition using deep neural network.

4.4 Techniques of Neural Networks and Deep Learning in Data-Driven Modeling

There are many important techniques present that are mostly used for this neural networks and deep learning in data-driven modeling.

4.4.1 Convolutional Neural Networks

CNNs excel at recognizing spatial hierarchies of features in images, which enhances their effectiveness for various tasks, including classifying images, recognizing objects, and dividing images into segments [19].

4.4.2 Recurrent Neural Networks

Basically, RNNs are a model of neural networks that allow the handling of sequential data by storing internal memory states. They take input sequences one element at a time, knowing what has been fed in so far through the recurrent connections. RNNs are now widely adopted across different branches, from NLP to time-series forecasting, speech recognition, and other applications requiring sequential data processing.

4.4.3 Long Short-Term Memory Networks

LSTM networks are a specialized kind of RNN, which are basically designed to specify the vanishing gradient problem. This enables them to learn long-term very effectively dependencies in sequential data. LSTM networks achieve this through the use of memory cells and various gating mechanisms, which enhance their ability to hold on to and manage information for longer periods, enabling a selective remembering or forgetting of information from time to time [21]. They show greater promise for actions in which temporal dynamics modeling is primarily involved, for example, machine translation, speech recognition, and time-series prediction.

4.4.4 Autoencoders

In supervised settings and dimensionality reduction, autoencoders are used. It has an encoder network that is used to take input data and transform them into a compressed design in a much lower-dimensional, and also, it helps to compress the input data into a latent space representation by containing an encoder network and a decoder network that helps to reconstruct the original data from the desired representation. They are commonly used for various applications, including data denoising, anomaly detection, and feature extraction.

4.4.5 Generative Adversarial Networks

GANs can be seen as a type of generative model that entails twin different types of neural networks known as the discriminator and the generator, which are in a competition with each other in a zero-sum game. The generator is trying to mimic the original data by providing fake data samples that are good enough to convince the discriminator, whereas the discriminator is trying to tell apart real samples from fake ones [10]. GANs find applications in image synthesis, data augmentation, and generative modeling, to name a few.

4.4.6 Deep Reinforcement Learning

This type of learning combines deep learning techniques with reinforcement learning principles. It basically enables the agents to develop optimal decision-making strategies by making interactions with their environment. Two prominent algorithms in the realm of deep reinforcement learning (RL) are deep Q-networks and proximal policy optimization that have performed quite well in many applications—from games to robotics and even navigating autonomous mechanisms.

4.4.7 Transfer Learning

Transfer learning is the type of ML technique that makes use of the knowledge learned from training a model on one task and applies it to another task that is similar. Transfer learning is a process of bringing pretrained models to new datasets or domains with few labeled data. Through the transfer of knowledge from large-scale datasets, transfer learning allows for faster convergence and better generalization to new tasks.

4.4.8 Data Augmentation

The process of expansion in the size of a training dataset using various transformations among the original data samples is called data augmentation techniques.

4.5 Methods of Neural Networks and Deep Learning in Data-Driven Modeling

In this data-driven modeling, several types of methods are used. But some methods are most important for this neural networks and deep learning in data-driven modeling. Those are discussed as follows:

4.5.1 Backpropagation

Backpropagation is an important training algorithm for neural networks. It iteratively updates parameters of the model so that it could minimize a selected loss function. The underlying operation is basically computing the gradient of loss, which is calculated for each parameter in the network. Once all the gradients are obtained, the parameters are adjusted in the direction opposite to the gradient.

4.5.2 Data Augmentation

The process of expansion in the size of a training dataset using various transformations among the original data samples is called data augmentation techniques [24].

4.5.3 Hyperparameter Optimization

Hyperparameter optimization is a manner of looking for the right set of hyperparameters to optimize a neural network's performance to its fullest on a validation dataset.

4.5.4 Ensemble Learning

Instead of using any single model, ensemble learning provides an ensemble of a group of individual models to achieve higher performance.

4.5.5 Attention Mechanisms

Attention mechanisms allow neural networks to emphasize the most crucial parts of input data when making a decision. Summarization of texts, translations for a machine, etc., can be a great example of such mechanisms [25]. Attention mechanisms are suitable for getting long-distance connections and for managing different lengths of input sequences, respectively [25]. In recent years, attention mechanisms have gained significant importance due to their effectiveness in an application area of NLP.

4.5.6 Capsule Networks

Capsule Networks (CapsNets) represent a novel neural network architecture introduced as an alternative to traditional CNNs. The goal of CapsNets is to rectify some shortcomings of CNNs, such as problems dealing with pose variations and hierarchical relationships between parts of objects [26]. Capsules are collections of neurons that represent different properties of an entity [26]. The capsules contain both the information of an entity and the instantiation parameters such as pose or deformation [26]. To demonstrate, by modeling hierarchical relationships explicitly between parts of the objects, it is believed that CapsNets will gain more robustness and interpretability than CNNs.

4.5.7 Neuroevolution

Neuroevolution is a method that uses the hybridization of neural networks and genetic algorithms to train and perfect the architectures of neural networks. In contrast to gradient-based optimization methods, neuroevolutionary uses biological evolution-inspired principles to explore the neural network architectures and configuration space [27]. Neuroevolution algorithms typically involve the generation of a population of candidate neural networks, their performance evaluation on a task, the selection of the best-performing networks, and, finally, the application of genetic operators, such as mutation and crossover, which are used to produce the next generation of offspring [27].

4.6 Conclusion

Neural networks and deep learning gave us data-driven modeling that is beyond our imagination. With all these techniques and methods, neural networks that have given power to researchers and practitioners to solve challenges once considered insurmountable have been addressed using neural networks, particularly in some areas such as time-series forecasting, NLP, image classification, and even in autonomous decision-making, and they have gone beyond the traditional limits and pushed the boundaries of what is possible in data-driven modeling.

CNNs have obtained a status of an irreplaceable foundation in computer vision, which has never been the case with CNNs before, because their performance in image recognition, object detection, and semantic segmentation is nearly flawless. Their competence in the learning of visual features respectively allows them to automatically acquire various levels of hierarchical representations, which in turn allows them applications from medical image analysis to self-driving car systems. Along the line, the two types of data, namely, RNNs and LSTM networks and their different types, possess great potential for the analysis of sequential and temporal data. These networks have found applications in machine translation, speech recognition, time-series forecasting, and reshaping industries.

In addition, the advent of attention mechanisms has brought a new dimension to NLP tasks, enabling models to select the appropriate portions of the input sequences and to attain the best performance in summarization of various texts, translation of machines and question answering tasks. CapsNets are the new miracle workers. They promise to distribute the data hierarchically, and thus, potentially, they can defeat the convolutional networks.

Brilliant minds from the field of AI have been continuously inventing different combinations of DNNs and reinforcement learning to create intelligent agents with incredible capabilities. Deep reinforcement learning technology has proven to be the best in AI demonstrating incredible results such as the ability to play board games and the control of robots.

Bibliography

1. LeCun, Y., Bengio, Y., Hinton, G., Deep learning, in: *Proceedings of the IEEE International Symposium on Information Theory*, F.R. Kschischang, B. Frey, H. Loeliger (Eds.), pp. 436–444), 2015.
2. Zhang, S., Chai, X., Liu, S., Lin, Q., Parallel computing in deep learning, in: *2015 IEEE International Conference on Cyber Technology in Automation, Control, and Intelligent Systems (CYBER)*, pp. 1280–1284, 2015.
3. Allen-Zhu, Z. and Li, Y., Backward Feature Correction: How Deep Learning Performs Deep (Hierarchical) Learning, in: *Proceedings of the 36th Conference on Learning Theory (COLT 2023). Proceedings of Machine Learning Research*, vol. 195, pp. 4598–4598, 2023.
4. Ma, C., Karam, L., Sejnowski, T., Robustness of deep neural networks to noise, in: *2018 IEEE International Conference on Acoustics, Speech and Signal Processing (ICASSP)*, pp. 1–5, 2018.
5. Bengio, Y., Courville, A., Vincent, P., Representation learning: A review and new perspectives. *IEEE Trans. Pattern Anal. Mach. Intell.*, 35, 8, 1798–1828, 2013.
6. Young, T., Hazarika, D., Poria, S., Cambria, E., Recent trends in deep learning based natural language processing. *IEEE Comput. Intell. Mag.*, 13, 3, 55–75, 2018.
7. Zhang, G., Patuwo, B.E., Hu, M.Y., Forecasting with artificial neural networks: The state of the art. *Int. J. Forecasting*, 14, 1, 35–62, 1998.
8. Zhang, Y. and Koren, Y., Efficient Bayesian hierarchical Poisson factorization for recommendation system, in: *Proceedings of the 25th ACM SIGKDD International Conference on Knowledge Discovery & Data Mining*, pp. 259–267, 2019.
9. Chandola, V., Banerjee, A., Kumar, V., Anomaly detection: A survey. *ACM Comput. Surv. (CSUR)*, 41, 3, 1–58, 2009.
10. Goodfellow, I., Pouget-Abadie, J., Mirza, M., Xu, B., Warde-Farley, D., Ozair, S., Bengio, Y., Generative adversarial nets, in: *Advances in Neural Information Processing Systems*, pp. 2672–2680, 2014.

11. Bojarski, M., Del Testa, D., Dworakowski, D., Firner, B., Flepp, B., Goyal, P., Zhang, X., End to end learning for self-driving cars. arXiv preprint arXiv:1604.07316, 2016.
12. Shoaib, M., Bosch, S., Incel, O.D., Scholten, H., Havinga, P.J., Fusion of smartphone motion sensors for physical activity recognition. *Sensors*, 16, 2, 257, 2016.
13. Vaswani, A., Shazeer, N., Parmar, N., Uszkoreit, J., Jones, L., Gomez, A.N., Polosukhin, I., Attention is all you need, in: *Advances in Neural Information Processing Systems*, pp. 5998–6008, 2017.
14. Lebedev, M.A. and Nicolelis, M.A., Brain–machine interfaces: past, present and future. *Trends Neurosci.*, 29, 9, 536–546, 2006.
15. Hinton, G., Deng, L., Yu, D., Dahl, G.E., Mohamed, A.R., Jaitly, N., Kingsbury, B., Deep neural networks for acoustic modeling in speech recognition: The shared views of four research groups. *IEEE Signal Process Mag.*, 29, 6, 82–97, 2012.
16. Xu, B., Wang, N., Chen, T., Li, M., Empirical evaluation of rectified activations in convolutional network. arXiv preprint arXiv:1505.00853, 2018.
17. Yu, W. and Lai, L.L., Forecasting of seasonal energy consumption using a hybrid ARIMA and support vector machine methodology. *Energy Convers. Manage.*, 76, 617–627, 2013.
18. Anguita, D., Ghio, A., Oneto, L., Parra, X., Reyes-Ortiz, J.L., A public domain dataset for human activity recognition using smartphones, in: *ESANN*, pp. 437–442, 2013.
19. Krizhevsky, A., Sutskever, I., Hinton, G.E., ImageNet classification with deep convolutional neural networks, in: *Advances in Neural Information Processing Systems*, pp. 1097–1105, 2012.
20. Hochreiter, S. and Schmidhuber, J., Long short-term memory. *Neural Comput.*, 9, 8, 1735–1780, 1997.
21. Graves, A., Mohamed, A.R., Hinton, G., Speech recognition with deep recurrent neural networks, in: *Acoustics, Speech and Signal Processing (ICASSP), 2013 IEEE International Conference on*, pp. 6645–6649, 2013.
22. Mnih, V., Kavukcuoglu, K., Silver, D., Rusu, A.A., Veness, J., Bellemare, M.G., Petersen, S., Human-level control through deep reinforcement learning. *Nature*, 518, 7540, 529–533, 2015.
23. Rumelhart, D.E., Hinton, G.E., Williams, R.J., Learning representations by back-propagating errors. *Nature*, 323, 6088, 533–536, 1988.
24. Shorten, C. and Khoshgoftaar, T.M., A survey on image data augmentation for deep learning. *J. Big Data*, 6, 1, 60, 2019.
25. Haykin S., *Neural Networks and Learning Machines.* 3rd ed. Pearson Education, Upper Saddle River, NJ, 2009.
26. Sabour, S., Frosst, N., Hinton, G.E., Dynamic routing between capsules, in: *Advances in Neural Information Processing Systems*, pp. 3856–3866, 2017.
27. Stanley, K.O. and Miikkulainen, R., Evolving neural networks through augmenting topologies. *Evol. Comput.*, 10, 2, 99–127, 2002.

28. Orbofi, A.I., Deep learning is revolutionizing image recognition.
29. Casolaro, A., Capone, V., Iannuzzo, G., Camastra, F., Deep learning for time series forecasting: Advances and open problems. *Information,* 14, 11, 598, 2023, doi: 10.3390/info14110598.
30. Sciforce. *Deep learning-based recommender systems.* Sciforce Blog, Published 2020. Accessed September 10, 2025. https://medium.com/sciforce/deep-learning-based-recommender-systems-b61a5ddd5456.
31. Nicholaus, I.T., Park, J.R., Jung, K., Lee, J.S., Kang, D.K., Anomaly detection of water level using deep autoencoder. *Sensors,* 21, 19, 6679, 2021. doi:10.3390/s21196679.
32. LeewayHertz, Generative adversarial networks (GANs): A deep dive into the architecture and training process. *LeewayHertz Blog.* Published 2021. Accessed September 10, 2025. https://www.leewayhertz.com/generative-adversarial-networks.
33. Olyanasab, A. and Annabestani, M., Leveraging machine learning for personalized wearable biomedical devices: A review. *J. Pers. Med.,* 14, 2, 203, 2024, doi:10.3390/jpm14020203.
34. Odaibo, S., Attention mechanisms in deep learning, The Blog of RETINA-AI Health, Inc.
35. Peksa, J. and Mamchur, D., State-of-the-art on brain-computer interface technology. *Sensors,* 23, 13, 6001, 2023. doi:10.3390/s23136001.
36. Qiu, S., Cui, X., Ping, Z., Shan, N., Li, Z., Bao, X., Xu, X., Deep learning techniques in intelligent fault diagnosis and prognosis for industrial systems: A review. *Sensors,* 23, 3, 1305, 2023. doi:10.3390/s23031305.
37. Dixit, P. and Silakari, S., Deep learning algorithms for cybersecurity applications: A technological and status review. *Comput. Sci. Rev.,* 38, 100317, 2020. doi:10.1016/j.cosrev.2020.100317.
38. Manno, A., Martelli, E., Amaldi, E., A shallow neural network approach for the short-term forecast of hourly energy consumption. *Energies,* 15, 3, 958, 2022. doi:10.3390/en15030958.
39. He, J., Zhang, Q., Wang, L., Pei, L., Weakly supervised human activity recognition from wearable sensors by recurrent attention learning. *IEEE Sens. J.* 19, 6, 2287–2297, 2019. doi:10.1109/JSEN.2018.2885796.

5

Advances in Time-Series Analysis: Techniques and Applications for Predictive Forecasting

A. UmaDevi[1], Jagendra Singh[2*], Shrinwantu Raha[3], Nazeer Shaik[4], Anil V. Turukmane[5] and Ishaan Singh[6]

[1]*Department of Management Studies, SRM Valliammai Engineering College, Tamil Nadu, India*
[2]*School of Computer Science Engineering and Technology, Bennett University, Greater Noida, India*
[3]*Department of Geography, Bhairab Ganguly College, Belgharia, India*
[4]*Department of CSE, Srinivasa Ramanujan Institute of Technology – Autonomous, Anantapur, India*
[5]*School of Computer Science and Engineering, VIT - AP University, Amaravati, India*
[6]*School of Computer Science, Ryan International School, Ghaziabad, India*

Abstract

Advances in time-series analysis (TSA) have revolutionized the field of predictive forecasting for powerful techniques and applications across diverse domains. This chapter presents some of the most recent methodologies that enhance the precision and reliability of time-series predictions. Key strategies include exponential smoothing state space models, autoregressive integrated moving average, and advancements in machine learning (ML) algorithms, such as long short-term memory networks and Prophet. These are developed to capture seasonality, identify trends, and detect anomalies in time-series data. Furthermore, it points to the integration of hybrid models that combine age-old statistical methods with the latest machine learning methods and demonstrate extraordinary improvements in forecast precision. Real-world applications of these advanced techniques cut across many sectors, including finance, where they help in predicting stock prices and economic indicators; healthcare for patient monitoring and forecasting

**Corresponding author*: jagendrasngh@gmail.com

Arindam Mondal and Souvik Ganguli (eds.) Data-Driven Modeling, (121–142) © 2026 Scrivener Publishing LLC

disease outbreaks; and environmental science for climate, weather, and so on. This chapter also discusses the importance of real-time data processing and the role of big data technologies in handling large-scale time-series datasets. Emphasis is usually on the practical implications, with the application of these techniques shown through case studies that demonstrate the implementation of the strategies, practical effects, and, most importantly, success in the real world. New advances in the TSA landscape have opened not only horizons for better predictive capability but also new avenues for further research and development for critical data-driven decision-making processes.

***Keywords*:** Predictive forecasting, time-series analysis (TSA), long short-term memory (LSTM) networks, autoregressive integrated moving average (ARIMA), hybrid models, real-time data processing

5.1 Introduction

Time-series analysis (TSA) is one of the most powerful statistical procedures dealing with the analysis of succession of data observed or recorded over successive periods, usually at regular time intervals. It has been designed to bring out underlying patterns and characteristics in the data that can then be used in making forecasts. Time-series data result from the process of measuring snacks in finance, economics, environmental studies, health sciences, and social sciences. It is any data in which the temporal ordering of observations involves the basis of the investigation, and it becomes pretty essential in carrying out tasks such as forecasting, monitoring, and anomaly detection [1, 2]. The essential elements in the TSA are trend, seasonality, and noise. This explains the trend of the long-term series and indicates whether the data point increases, decreases, or remains at a constant level over time.

Seasonality: Regular fluctuations observed daily, monthly, or yearly, probably under the influence of seasonal factors.

Irregular variations: Fluctuations strongly carry the component of randomness and hence may not follow any typical systematic pattern [3].

TSA uses different documented approaches in modeling and forecasting data, which is shown in Figure 5.1. The traditional methods include those using statistics *via* autoregressive integrated moving average (ARIMA), exponential smoothing state space model (ETS), and seasonal decomposition of time series (STL [seasonal trend decomposition using LOESS]), the most commonly used over the past years. ETS is specific and especially based on exponential smoothing to implement trend and seasonality

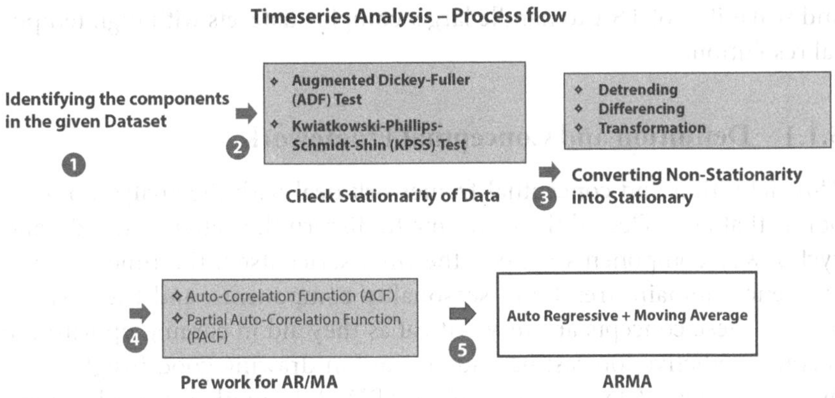

Figure 5.1 Time-series analysis and forecasting.

components. Recently, the developments in machine learning (ML) have greatly improved TSA. New techniques, such as long short-term memory (LSTM) networks, which belong to the family of recurrent neural networks (RNNs), are particularly useful with sequential data and for capturing long-term dependencies. Another critical model in forecasting is Prophet, developed by Facebook, which has a very intuitive and flexible approach toward time-series forecasting that finds ideal use in business cases with strong seasonal effects and missing data [4, 5].

Hybrid models amalgamate traditional statistical analytics with advanced ML algorithms to develop a model that gives better predictive performance than either of the methods working alone. These models are pretty helpful specifically when the characteristics of the data are complex and multifaceted. In addition to time-series forecasting and modeling, TSA is generally used for anomaly detection, that is, in the location of rare observations that differ markedly from normal behavior. For instance, TSA has great practical importance in network security, fraud detection, and equipment monitoring to prevent significant losses and enable companies to be more effective. The list is long, varied, and practical. Finance uses it to predict stock prices, manage risks, and forecast changes in economic conditions. Healthcare is an application area where time-series models help to monitor the vital signs of the patient, predict outbreaks, and forecast the number of resources that would be demanded in hospitals. Environmental scientists exploit the techniques for weather forecasts and climate modeling and tracking natural phenomena [6, 7]. The recent advent of big data and real-time data processing technologies has further expanded the scope and scalability of TSA to handle large, complex datasets with high temporal resolution.

5.1.1 Definition and Conceptual Framework

TSA definition and conceptual framework deal with the analysis of data points that are collected through time to discern the patterns, trends, and cycles. Key components include the time series itself, the time domain, frequency domain, trend and seasonality components, and the ARIMA model. These concepts are very critical as they aid in coming up with the correct predictive forecasting and also aid in drawing good insight from time-dependent data. Understanding ARIMA is another critical dimension of TSA. ARIMA is an all-inclusive model composed of three parts: autoregression (AR), differencing (I), and moving average (MA). The AR component represents the influence of a past observation on the present value [8, 9].

The MA component represents the influence of the lags of error terms on the present value. The act of differencing ensures a time series is stationary; this is important for proper modeling and forecasting. Additive to this, there is the trend and seasonality. Seasonality, on the other hand, refers to the periodic fluctuations that often occur at regular time intervals—for example, the monthly or yearly patterns. Followed by this, there is the time domain and the frequency domain. The time domain is the sequence by which the observations are represented against time, to graphically represent the behavior of the data. The frequency domain comprises ways of transforming data into frequency components using techniques such as Fourier analysis.

That is facilitated using a framework that comprises several essential components. On one side is the time series itself. Such observations may be on any variable, for instance, an economic indicator, climate data, or stock prices. At the lowest level, TSA forms the analysis of the data gathered over time. Most data points are reported at regular frequencies. Thus, it is possible to observe patterns of change in the values over time. The primary aim is to try and identify the underlying patterns, trends, and repeating cycles in the data. TSA is the most critical predictive forecasting that gives an insight into the pattern and tendencies lying hitherto within a dataset. In this section, we define and describe TSA's conceptual framework, its key features, and standard processes [10, 11].

5.1.2 Importance and Applications

TSA is fundamental to data analysis, and it plays a critical role in understanding and forecasting temporal patterns within a wide range of areas. This is because it can model and predict future values from observed past data, which is handy in making decisions relating to finance, economics, healthcare, and environmental science, among others. TSA aids in detecting trends, seasonal variations, and cyclical behaviors that do not show under a different statistical method but by examining the behavior pattern of data points over time. The capacity of TSAs to decode the underpinning structure of timed data can proffer lots of help in forecasting in both short and long terms. It can give organizations power in rational decision-making, operation optimization, and risk control. TSA in finance is used for the extensive forecasting of stock prices, interest rates, and economic indicators [12–14].

Tools that might assist in solving market volatility, such as ARIMA and GARCH, could go a long way in forecasting future movement, thus helping investment strategies and risks. In the healthcare sector, it is used to monitor some critical functions of a patient, predict outbreaks of diseases, and manage resources in a hospital with patients. It can help detect the early onset of a medical condition in men by analyzing patient time-series data, thus enabling timely interventions. Besides, models for infectious diseases can be developed by forecasting disease spread to ensure necessary measures are taken promptly. The environmental scientists also use TSA while modeling climate conditions, weather prediction, and monitoring ecological changes. For instance, using historical climate data, the scientists can forecast future climate trends and the relationship between human activities and the environment [15].

TSA uses not only in these traditional areas but is also applicable in marketing, manufacturing, and urban planning. In marketing, TSA is used to forecast the behavior of consumers, determine the ideal inventory level, and plan promotion activities. Businesses can optimize their marketing strategies by analyzing sales patterns and trends in what the customers have preferred over time, thus increasing the satisfaction level of different customers. In manufacturing, TSA is used in demand forecasting, quality control, and maintenance planning. Predictive maintenance models interpret machinery data and cross-reference such data to predict possible failures to avoid significant downtimes, which can be costly. Urbanists use TSA to research traffic and population growth patterns and the usage of resources in effective urban planning and the development of infrastructure [16, 17].

As the volume and variety of data continue to grow, the importance of TSA will only increase, driving innovation and efficiency across multiple sectors. By harnessing the power of TSA, organizations can unlock valuable insights, improve predictive accuracy, and stay ahead in an increasingly data-driven world [18].

5.2 Foundational Techniques in TSA

The goal is to analyze data points collected or recorded at specific time intervals to uncover patterns, trends, and other critical information that can be used for forecasting future values. Foundational techniques in TSA have evolved over the years, offering robust tools to manage the inherent complexities of time-dependent data.

5.2.1 AR Models

The AR model of order p assumes that a value at time t depends linearly on p values at previous times, with an additive stochastic term. The simplicity involved in this makes AR models particularly useful in the context of understanding and forecasting time-series data where the dependence on the past is linear. An AR model can be fitted into several methods, among which are the Yule–Walker equations, method of moments, and maximum likelihood. The choice of the order is critical because it will always impact the complexity and performance of the model. Model selection criteria such as AIC (Akaike information criterion) and BIC (Bayesian information criterion) are considered for optimal order [19, 20]. Applications of AR models have widespread applications across numerous fields:

a) **Finance**
AR models are capable of producing asset price forecasts and interest rates, as well as other economic indicators. It also allows modeling and forecasting financial time series where dependencies in time happen very frequently. The AR model assumes that the value at any point in time depends linearly on its previous values, added to a stochastic error term. Beyond that, its simplicity results from the AR models being quite helpful when applied to the understanding and forecasting of time-series data that exhibit linear dependence on past observations. The parameter estimation can be done by the Yule–Walker equations, method of moments, or maximum likelihood. Order selection is an essential decision that impacts the

complexity of a model. Typically, model selection criteria such as AIC or BIC are used to decide on the optimal order.

b) **Economics**

The AR model is significant for macroeconomic forecasting. They are applied to predict some critical macroeconomic indicators such as the GDP, inflation, and unemployment rates. These predictions also occupy an essential place in the process of making policy decisions and inform the judgment of the analyst. On the other hand, AR models help to display data from the past to understand past tendencies in the economy to facilitate the ability to predict the appearance of new trends. This has been said to equip the government and financial institutions in proper planning, exemplary policy implementation, and setting of measures to reduce the possibility of economic shocks. Thus, AR models bear a high degree of onus to maintain economies at a stable level toward sustainable growth.

c) **Engineering**

AR models are general models used on signals to analyze and predict their behavior over time. AR models are applied in many fields: the study of transmission in telecommunications, control systems in predictive nature, and the response of systems in speech recognition technologies, which increase accuracy by modeling speech patterns. Such kinds of models use some past data to predict future data points and become very crucial in those tasks wherein the historical data analysis is used to forecast future trends.

d) **Environmental science**

AR models have been found to rank as one of the best tools in making predictions of environmental and climatic factors such as temperature, precipitation, and concentration of pollutants. Such predictions form a basis for improved resource management and preparedness for disasters. In aid of making better response decisions to the challenge of the environment is the insight into future conditions based on attributable past data that the AR models provide. This is highly significant for fields such as agricultural planning, urban planning, and public health—where the reduction of risks could be made, and the optimal use of resources could be done by the prediction of changes in climate and environmental conditions.

Advantages and limitations

There is simplicity, ease of implementation, and interpretability in AR models. AR models present a straightforward methodology to model time-series data when the linear relationship is quite clear. Some of them are enclosed in the assumptions made within AR models, for instance, about linearity and stationarity. They might perform poorly for nonlinear trends or structural changes in the time series. To handle these restrictions, AR models are typically integrated with other techniques, such as MA ensemble models, yielding more complicated models such as ARMA and ARIMA.

5.2.2 MA Models

Essential tools under the umbrella of time series analysis (TSA) are moving average (MA) models, which smooth short-run fluctuations in data while highlighting longer-term trends or cycles. Conceived in the process of analyzing and forecasting temporal data, MA models belong to the broad class of linear time-series models and are, in particular, very useful for capturing and intrinsically modeling randomness in time-series data. Also, because they have fewer parameters than the more complex models, they are very friendly concerning computation and interpretation. Simplicity has its downside, however; until now, it has been mentioned that MA models are suitable for stationary time-series data; i.e., statistical properties such as mean and variance of time-series data do not vary with time. For nonstationary series, usually, the series is differenced or transformed to make it stationary before fitting an MA model. MA models are part of a more general ARIMA structure. They assist the AR components in the modeling of both the dependency on past values and the dependency on old errors [21, 22].

Integrating AR and MA models in ARMA and ARIMA frameworks provides a versatile approach for a wide range of time-series forecasting tasks, a graphical representation of which is shown in Figure 5.2. The practical applications of MA models can take on endless and diverse scopes. In a financial context, using these techniques supports stock price and economic indicator analysis for smoothing random fluctuations to see the underlying trends. In manufacturing and quality control, they can monitor process stability and detect the presence of any type of anomaly [23].

5.2.3 ARIMA Models

One of the great strengths of ARIMA is its ability to adapt to most of the patterns within time series, such as trends, seasonality, and irregular fluctuations. For example, sales data that show seasonal patterns can be well represented with ARIMA models to enable business people to have a forewarning of peak times and procure inventory accordingly. ARIMA is also a precious tool in economic forecasting, where both trends and cycles in the data have very complex behaviors over time. However, ARIMA has a few

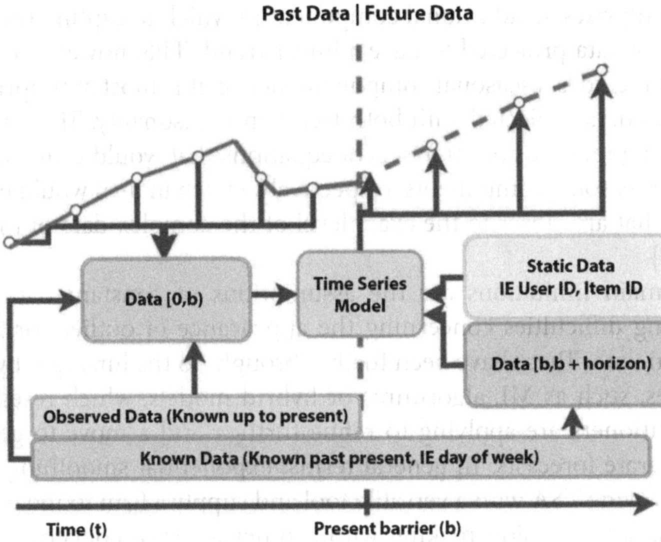

Figure 5.2 Time-series forecasting with time-series prediction platform.

associated limitations, including its assumption of linearity and stationary data under most circumstances, which are often incorrect. In many cases, alternative models, such as the ML algorithms or some other hybrid methods, offer, for highly nonlinear or dynamic data patterns, better predictive performance. However, ARIMA remains an essential tool in the hands of time-series analysts, serving up-to-data, rich insights, and forecasts in diverse domains [24, 25].

5.2.4 Exponential Smoothing Methods

These forecasting methods apply exponentially decreasing weights to older observations, allowing for more accurate and responsive predictions. One of the simplest methods of exponential smoothing is SES (simple exponential smoothing), in that it upholds the forecast with a weighted average of the past observations, whereby the weight decreases exponentially with the age of the past observation. SES is very suitable for data representing a negligible trend and season time-series dataset in that it is computationally simple and therefore fast and easy to estimate, then commonly used for forecasts. As we advance beyond simple exponential smoothing, we get time-series smoothing methods that are more sophisticated, such as double exponential smoothing (DES) and triple exponential smoothing (TES), which are known as the Holt–Winters methods [26].

DES comprises an additional component in which to capture the trend. It works for data projected to have a linear trend. TES, however, expands DES, as it includes a seasonal component; hence, it is most appropriate for time-series data projected with both trend and seasonality. These include the updating methods of three sets of equations that would estimate level, trend, and seasonal components, respectively, which in turn would provide forecasts that are closer to the exact level of the complex data of the time series [27].

Their main limitations are the assumptions of constant parameters and solving difficulties concerning the appearance of outliers or radical changes in data. These have been further brought to the limelight by other techniques, such as ML algorithms or hybrid models, which researchers and practitioners are applying to refine further, and a move to generate more accurate forecasts. In general terms, exponential smoothing methods still provide TSA with a versatile tool and supply a firm foundation for forecasting and decision-making within other areas of concern, such as finance, supply chain, and healthcare.

5.2.5 Seasonal Decomposition of Time Series

STL decomposition is an abbreviation for seasonal trend decomposition using LOESS. It is one of the most potent techniques in TSA and is generally used in understanding and extracting seasonal components within a given time-series dataset. This method decomposes a time series into these three: seasonal, trend, and residual. In general, it captures the nature of the seasonal component as recurring patterns or cycles through time. These cycles may happen within some period, for example, daily, monthly, or yearly. These patterns are highly crucial in that they underlie the behavior of the series and can give information of valuable meaning about seasonal spikes related to sales during holidays or because of weather patterns in the year. This extraction of the seasonal component allows for analysis and forecasting of future seasonal variation to a greater degree and hence allows analysis on better predictions and determination [28].

The second component extracted from the STL is the trend, which can be described as the long-term direction or general pattern of the data. Trends may indicate the underlying tendency for growth or decline in the time series, which helps analysts determine patterns of slow-moving changes over time. Detection of the trend component is essential to trace the long-term patterns and strategic decisions that would be taken in correspondence with the general modus direction of the data. Finally, the residual component, also referred to as the remainder of the irregular component, exhibits erratic variations or noise in data that persist after the removal of the seasonal or trend components. Analysis of the residual component studies how the model fits the data and what further patterns or anomalies remain, which are possibly of interest. Overall, STL provides a holistic framework for breaking down time-series data into its essential elements for further interpretation by analysts to draw out more meaning, improve forecast accuracy, and be confident of the best data-driven decision.

5.2.6 State Space Models and Kalman Filtering

TSA offers a flexible framework, making it ideal for modeling complex dynamic systems and extracting meaningful insights from noisy data. The basic idea behind state space models is that the states are unobservable and are structures that evolve, driven by some transition or state equations, while the observations are generated by an underlying state function composed with an amount of noise. This separation between the latent states and the observed data means that a detailed representation of the dynamics underlying the data can be given while it provides the possibility of estimating and predicting it well. One of the most essential advantages of state space models is their full ability to deal with nonstationary and poorly linear data, thus allowing the implications of such to reach into such diverse realms as finance, economics, engineering, and environmental science. Kalman filter is a recursive algorithm for estimating the state of a dynamic system given a stream of noisy measurements. The state space model can be more easily placed in the center of the Kalman filter. This means that the updating of the state estimate by new observations, with this built-in prior knowledge and uncertainty, will further enhance the accuracy of estimation with time [29, 30].

One of the properties that make the Kalman filter quite popular is adaptive. On the other hand, the dynamics that are responsible for the changes in dynamics or handling the missing data are data that are regularly sampled, which indeed is most important for real-time applications. Besides the obvious utility for estimation and prediction, the filtering carried out by state space models, and so on, these methods allow the integration of exogenous factors into the model and incorporation of the complex structure of the system, hence increasing the model's predictability and model durability. In all these aspects, state space models and Kalman filtering have a high level of smartness for TSA because they are versatile in modeling dynamic systems, extracting valuable information from noisy data, and providing a base for making sound decisions in numerous fields.

5.2.7 Spectral Analysis and Fourier Transform

Spectral analysis, up to the Fourier transform, provides the essential tools for TSA. Here, it is possible to decompose signals into their essential frequency components and represent the signal in a way that is simpler and more informative about underlined patterns and features. The aim is therefore to give a view of the frequency content of a time-series signal. It goes a long way in giving one knowledge of cyclical patterns or periodicity and identification of trends. The Fourier transformation, being one of the significant mathematical operations in spectral analysis, is a process of converting time-domain signals into their corresponding representations in the frequency domain, at the same time retaining the amplitude and phase of the various frequency components in their respective signals. It is majorly used to uncover dominant frequencies, periodic variation, and noise or irregularities within data. By breaking signals into their component frequencies, analysts can focus on the most critical periodic features, be it daily, weekly, or yearly cycles. What is even more, it provides spectral analysis, which enables anomaly detection when an unusual frequency component is recognized. That is to say, it can help detect anomalous events by finding the outlying observations. The Fourier transform also supports the filtering operation used either to isolate or remove determined bands of frequency in data preprocessing and noise reduction [31].

Spectral analysis is also used for signal processing and system identification in nearly all of the applications described above. The approach is widely used in engineering and physics to study vibrations, oscillations, and signals from various sensors to identify resonant frequencies and structural weaknesses. Applied in telecommunication, spectral analysis is used for signal modulation and the allocation of bandwidths that ensure efficiency in the performance of communication systems. Besides, it carries implications for the neuroscience and biomedical research application with diagnostic and medical monitoring instrumentation in rapport with brainwave patterns, heart rate variability, and physiological signals. Similarly, the uses of spectral analysis and Fourier transform relate to environmental science through the study of climate data, seismic signals, and natural phenomena of importance for the prediction of climate and detection of earthquakes, as well as environmental monitoring.

5.2.8 ML Techniques

TSA has extensively been driven by the usage of ML techniques in extracting patterns that guide more focused and precise forecasts. The most significant research issue based on deep learning models is time-series forecasting models such as RNN and LSTM networks. The inaccuracy of the conventional models is mostly due to their inability to model sequential data, thereby exposing the innate abilities of RNNs in capturing temporal dependencies. LSTMs are a specific type of RNN. It solves the vanishing gradient problem and can store information over a long duration, hence making it applicable to data that are time-dependent series presentations and have long-time dependencies.

The capability to catch complex patterns and nonlinear relationships within time-series data makes the LSTM model adequate, with accuracy and robustness in prediction, compared to traditional statistical techniques. Another critical technique using ML for TSA is ensemble methods, such as gradient boosting machine (GBM) and random forests. This implies combining a set of individual essential learners to enhance the predictive qualities and generalization of the model to avoid overfitting. As an example, GBM implements an iterative process in the reduction of weak learner prediction errors, leading to predictive solid performance in the forecast of time-series data. The random forest model works by aggregating the prediction of members from many decision trees, thus taking the crowd's wisdom for a very reliable prediction. Ensemble methods are more valuable for time series having noise and heterogeneity, the involvement of essential but complex structures, and the possibility of time-series outliers. More generally, ML techniques provide TSA with a large toolbox, each with its strengths in capturing different temporal data characteristics and increasing the forecasting accuracy; these are all very interesting.

ML techniques have been applied across various domains with remarkable success. In finance, for example, LSTM networks have been utilized for stock price prediction, leveraging historical market data to forecast future trends and identify profitable trading opportunities. Financial forecasting applications of GBMs have included predicting economic indicators and optimizing investment portfolios. Among the most critical applications of ML in the healthcare domain is its use in monitoring patients and predicting disease onset by collecting time-series data using medical sensors and electronic health records. LSTM networks effectively use temporal data for early diagnosis of health issues. The field of environmental science uses ML techniques in climate modeling and weather forecasting to support disaster preparedness and resource allocation efforts.

5.3 Applications of TSA

TSA finds application in many fields shown in Figure 5.3 because meaningful inferences could be extracted from the temporal data. TSA in finance plays a significant role in forecasting stock prices, exchange rates, and economic indicators. The commonly used techniques to model and forecast financial time-series data are models such as ARIMA and ETS. Such models consider historical patterns and trends in data to make the analyst an informed decision concerning investments, risk management, and portfolio optimization. Moreover, advanced ML algorithms, such as LSTM networks and Prophet, have also gained popularity in capturing complicated patterns and nonlinear interrelations in financial data to enhance the predictions made. Instead, TSA is more valuable in the banking and insurance industries for (a) credit risk estimation, (b) fraud detection, and (c) customer behavior analysis to help the cause of operations efficiency and the risk mitigation strategy.

In the healthcare sector, TSA plays a role in patient monitoring, forecasting outbreaks of diseases, and making appropriate healthcare resource allocations. The time-series inpatient data patterns can lead to the prediction of disease progression, early warning, and tailoring of treatment plans. In clinical aspects, time-series models such as ARIMA, STL, and ML with random forests and support vector machine applications are used in forecasting patient admissions and estimating healthcare demand and optimal resource allocation in hospitals. Moreover, TSA is instrumental in epidemiology for tracking infectious diseases, modeling transmission dynamics, and assessing the impact of interventions. With the advent of wearable devices and electronic health records, TSA has become more accessible, allowing for continuous monitoring of patients' health status and proactive intervention strategies, ultimately improving healthcare outcomes and patient care.

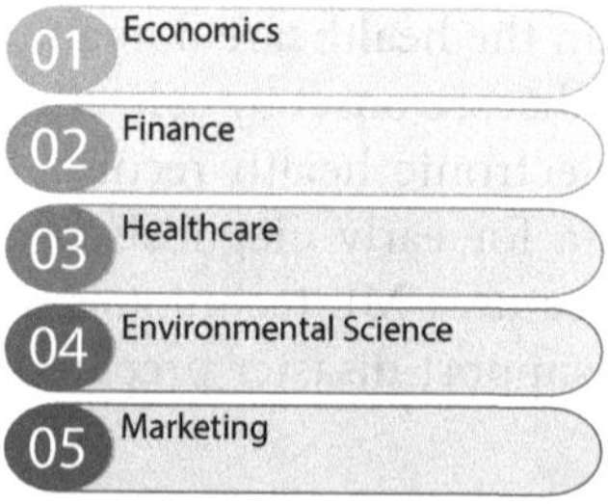

Figure 5.3 Applications of time-series forecasting.

5.3.1 Economic and Financial Forecasting

TSA plays a crucial role in economic and financial forecasting, offering valuable insights into trends, patterns, and future predictions. TSA helps economists and policymakers make informed decisions about monetary policy, fiscal policy, and business strategies. For example, in GDP forecasting, TSA techniques such as ARIMA models are commonly used. ARIMA models capture the underlying patterns and dynamics in GDP data, including seasonality, trends, and cyclical fluctuations. By analyzing historical GDP data using ARIMA models, economists can forecast future GDP growth rates and anticipate economic expansions or contractions. This information is crucial for governments, central banks, and businesses to formulate appropriate policies and strategies to manage economic conditions effectively.

Stock price forecasting, for instance, is a prominent application of time series analysis (TSA) in finance. Mainly, this involves the use of techniques such as moving average convergence divergence (MACD), relative strength index (RSI), and exponential moving average (EMA) in the analysis of historical stock price data to identify potential trends and therefore trading opportunities. Consequently, traders and investors rely heavily on these TSA tools to make buy or sell decisions, manage risks, and optimize portfolio performances.

Furthermore, TSA is very instrumental in risk management and financial modeling. For example, in the credit risk modeling of banks and financial institutions, TSA is applied to assessing probability of default (PD) and loss given default (LGD) for a book of loans. Using the analysis of historical data on loan performance through time-series models or Markov chains, risk analysts can approximate the possibility of loan borrowers' default and the potential losses that would arise thereof. This gives an indication to the banks of adequate capital reserves, fixes the risk-based pricing for the loans, and structures the risk mitigation strategies. This means economic and financial forecasting using TSA is wide and diversely applied, including GDP forecasting, prediction of stock prices, risk management, and financial modeling. Insights drawn from TSA provide policymakers in governments, central banks, financial institutions, or businesses the power to decide how to operate in complex economic environments, how to maximize investments, and how to minimize risks.

5.3.2 Healthcare and Epidemiology

ML algorithms, such as neural networks and SVM, are established in epidemiology for predicting diseases and early detection. Thus, the capacity of these algorithms is very high—considering all nonlinearities in the data structure—leading to better prediction accuracy. For example, LSTMs have worked very well in making predictions about outbreaks of infectious diseases based not only on social media data but also on environmental and healthcare records. Such a multidimensional approach can help to understand and predict the dynamics of the disease, thus coming up with robust public health measures. TSA also supports the surveillance and monitoring of chronic diseases. For instance, patients' health data such as vital signs, laboratory results, and medication adherence are collected over time and analyzed for time-series techniques in monitoring the progress of the disease, evaluation of the effectiveness of treatment, and identification of possible complications. For example, for the management of diabetes, TSA helps in predicting blood glucose levels, optimizing insulin dosages, and avoiding hypoglycemic or hyperglycemic episodes, all of which end up resulting in improved patient outcomes and quality of life.

Overall, TSA is a cornerstone of modern healthcare and epidemiology, enabling proactive disease management, resource optimization, policy formulation, and personalized patient care. By harnessing the power of data-driven insights, healthcare professionals and policymakers can address public health challenges effectively, improve health outcomes, and enhance the resilience of healthcare systems in an ever-evolving landscape.

5.4 Future Directions and Emerging Trends

Future directions and emerging trends in TSA encompass a broad spectrum of developments that are shaping the landscape of predictive modeling, forecasting, and data-driven decision-making. These advancements are driven by technological innovations, the integration of ML with traditional statistical methods, and the increasing availability of complex and high-dimensional time-series data. In this discussion, we explore several key areas that represent the forefront of TSA.

5.4.1 Deep Learning and Neural Networks

Deep learning techniques, particularly neural networks, have gained significant attention and adoption in TSA. Models such as long short-term memory (LSTM) networks and gated recurrent units (GRUs) have shown remarkable performance in capturing temporal dependencies and patterns in sequential data. Future directions in this area involve the development of more complex architectures, such as transformer-based models, which can handle long-range dependencies and nonlinear dynamics more effectively.

5.4.2 Probabilistic Forecasting

Probabilistic prediction methods are now coming to the fore on account of point predictions, as well as estimation of uncertainty. Although progress has been made with Bayesian and Gaussian processes and ensemble-type techniques that can make probabilistic point forecasts in the form of associated confidence intervals, prediction intervals, and quantile forecasts, more developed probabilistic forecasting will be centralized in handling complex data structures in the form of consistent probabilistic forecasting, integrating external information and domain knowledge, and improving calibration, reflecting well the actual uncertainties in the predictions.

5.4.3 Anomaly Detection and Outlier Analysis

Anomaly detection in time-series data is crucial and has a wide range of applications, such as fraud detection, network monitoring, and fault diagnosis. Designing anomaly detection robust algorithms, which can adapt to pattern changes in data and real-time streaming data, will differentiate between the natural anomalies and noise. Although the aim of such improvements is toward the better accuracies and reliabilities of the anomaly detections needed for both effective monitoring and intervention strategies across a variety of domains, techniques are currently under exploration for anomaly detection in domains such as isolation forests, one-class SVMs, and deep learning–based approaches.

5.4.4 Interpretable and Explainable Models

As the complexity of time-series models increases, there is a growing need for interpretability and explainability. Explainable artificial intelligence (XAI) principles are being integrated into TSA to enhance trust, facilitate domain experts' understanding of model decisions, and enable stakeholders to act upon model recommendations confidently.

5.4.5 Multivariate and High-Dimensional TSA

With the proliferation of multisource data and high-dimensional time series, there is a shift toward developing techniques that can effectively model dependencies and interactions across multiple variables. Multivariate TSA methods, including dynamic Bayesian networks, vector AR models, and copulas, are being extended to handle high-dimensional data with spatio-temporal correlations, missing values, and irregular sampling intervals.

Real-time and streaming data analysis
The increasing prevalence of real-time data streams from Internet of Things devices, sensors, and online platforms necessitates efficient and scalable TSA methods. Future directions in this domain involve the development of streaming algorithms that can process data in real time, adapt to concept drift, and update models dynamically. Techniques such as online learning, mini–batch processing, and distributed computing frameworks are being utilized to handle large-scale streaming time-series data effectively.

5.4.6 Integration with Domain-Specific Knowledge

TSA is becoming more intertwined with domain-specific knowledge and expertise across various industries. Researchers are focusing on developing domain-adaptive models that can leverage domain-specific features, constraints, and contextual information to improve forecasting accuracy and decision-making. Hybrid models that combine statistical techniques with domain knowledge, such as causal inference methods and domain-specific feature engineering, are emerging as powerful tools for addressing complex real-world challenges. These models leverage the strengths of both data-driven approaches and expert insights, enabling more accurate and interpretable predictions.

5.4.7 Ethical and Fair TSA

A trend is developing toward considerations of ethical aspects and justness in model development as the TSA model gains importance and new applications in essential areas, including healthcare, finance, and social systems. The discovery of ethical AI frameworks, bias detection techniques, and fairness-aware algorithms is being worked out in the mentioned efforts that allow the time-series models not to keep discriminating, respect privacy standards, and keep the well-being of the society at the forefront. Efforts are geared at designing transparent, accountable, and justifiable models, whereby the power of TSA would be exercised with responsibility, protecting individual rights and promoting social good.

5.4.8 Automated ML for Time Series

This has, in turn, fast-tracked automation by automated ML (AutoML) platforms and tools designed specifically for time-series data. AutoML solutions are now purposely designed to automate the features of feature engineering, model selection, hyperparameter tuning, and model evaluation, saving time and expertise in coming up with an accurate time-series model. The integration of AutoML with interpretability and customization features is a promising direction for democratizing TSA across diverse user groups.

5.4.9 Continuous Learning and Model Adaptation

Traditional time-series models often assume stationary data distributions, which may not hold true in dynamic and evolving environments. Future directions in TSA include continuous learning paradigms that enable models to adapt and learn from new data while retaining knowledge from past observations. Incremental learning techniques, transfer learning frameworks, and adaptive forecasting algorithms are being developed to address concept drift, data shifts, and evolving trends in time-series data streams.

5.5 Conclusion

In short, the proliferation of TSA has changed predictive forecasting across scores of applications. On this note, the move of TSA has revolutionized traditional predictive modeling from ARIMA models to more advanced techniques, such as deep learning and ensemble learning. Big data technologies have increased the scalability and efficiency of TSA, already enabled through cloud computing, and businesses and thus have a chance to handle large datasets and easily make real-time forecasting. In the future, TSA will be pushed toward new dimensions of innovation and development. Other emerging trends are in interpretability AI models, causal inference techniques, and explainable forecasting methods, gaining strength from more comprehensive data revolution, fostering transparency, accountability, and actionable insights. Moreover, the confluence of TSA with reinforcement learning and the paradigm of learning online are changing how organizations adapt to their environments and optimize their resource allocations in real-time. In other words, the journey of TSA from foundational principles to its latest applications implies a continued quest for accuracy, ability, and relevance in predictive forecasting. As the data systems grow, evolve with new technologies, and become more integrated, the role of TSA as a key foundational answer to predictive analytics remains of importance in driving strategic decisions and opening up new opportunities for businesses.

References

1. Masini, R.P., Medeiros, M.C., Mendes, E.F., Machine Learning Advances for Time Series Forecasting. *J. Econ. Surv.*, 37, 1, 76–111, 2023.
2. Kaur, J., Parmar, K.S., Singh, S., Autoregressive Models in Environmental Forecasting Time Series: a Theoretical and Application Review. *Environ. Sci. Pollut. Res.*, 30, 8, 19617–19641, 2023.
3. Raparthy, M. and Dodda, B., Predictive Maintenance in Iot Devices Using Time Series Analysis and Deep Learning. *Dandao Xuebao/Journal Ballistics*, 35, 01–10, 2023.
4. Bilal, K. and Sajid, M., Blockchain Technology: Opportunities & Challenges. *2022 International Conference on Data Analytics for Business and Industry, ICDABI 2022*, pp. 519–524, 2022, Https://Doi.Org/10.1109/ICDABI56818.2022.10041562.
5. Bharadiya, J.P., Exploring the Use of Recurrent Neural Networks for Time Series Forecasting. *Int. J. Innov. Sci. Res. Technol.*, 8, 5, 2023–2027, 2023.
6. Alghamdi, W., Mayakannan, S., Sivasankar, G.A., Ravi Naik, B., Venkata Krishna Reddy, C., Turbulence Modeling Through Deep Learning: an In-Depth Study of Wasserstein Gans. *Proceedings of the 4th International Conference on Smart Electronics and Communication, ICOSEC 2023*, pp. 793–797, 2023, Https://Doi.Org/10.1109/ICOSEC58147.2023.10275878.
7. Yadav, C.S., Pradhan, M.K., Gangadharan, S.M.P., Chaudhary, J.K., Khan, A.A., Haq, M.A., Alhussen, A., Wechtaisong, C., Imran, H., Alzamil, Z.S., Pattanayak, H.S., Multi-Class Pixel Certainty Active Learning Model for Classification of Land Cover Classes Using Hyperspectral Imagery. *Electron. (Switzerland)*, 11, 17, 2799, 2022, Https://Doi.Org/10.3390/Electronics11172799.
8. Kumar, R., Lexical Co-Occurrence and Contextual Window-Based Approach With Semantic Similarity for Query Expansion. *Int. J. Intell. Inf. Technol.*, 13, 3, 57–78, 2017, Https://Doi.Org/10.4018/IJIIT.2017070104.
9. Osama, O.M., Alakkari, K., Abotaleb, M., El-Kenawy, E.S.M., Forecasting Global Monkeypox Infections Using LSTM: a Non-Stationary Time Series Analysis, in: *2023 3rd International Conference on Electronic Engineering (ICEEM)*, IEEE, pp. 1–7, 2023, October.
10. Sharan, A., Co-Occurrence and Semantic Similarity Based Hybrid Approach for Improving Automatic Query Expansion in Information Retrieval, in: *Lecture Notes in Computer Science (Including Subseries Lecture Notes in Artificial Intelligence and Lecture Notes in Bioinformatics)*, vol. 8956, 2015, Https://Doi.Org/10.1007/978-3-319-14977-6_45.
11. Singh, R., Collaborative Filtering Based Hybrid Music Recommendation System. *Proceedings of the 3rd International Conference on Intelligent Sustainable Systems, ICISS 2020*, pp. 186–190, 2020, Https://Doi.Org/10.1109/ICISS49785.2020.9315913.

12. Hajirahimi, Z. and Khashei, M., Hybridization of Hybrid Structures for Time Series Forecasting: a Review. *Artif. Intell. Rev.*, 56, 2, 1201–1261, 2023.
13. Singh, M., Learning Based Driver Drowsiness Detection Model. *Proceedings of the 3rd International Conference on Intelligent Sustainable Systems, ICISS 2020*, pp. 698–701, 2020, Https://Doi.Org/10.1109/ICISS49785.2020.9316131.
14. Stefenon, S.F., Seman, L.O., Aquino, L.S., Dos Santos Coelho, L., Wavelet-Seq2Seq-LSTM With Attention for Time Series Forecasting of Level of Dams in Hydroelectric Power Plants. *Energy*, 274, 127350, 2023.
15. Yadav, A. and Kumar, S., A Review of Physical Unclonable Functions (Pufs) and Its Applications in Iot Environment, in: *Lecture Notes in Networks and Systems*, vol. 356, 2022, Https://Doi.Org/10.1007/978-981-16-7952-0_1.
16. Farayola, O.A., Adaga, E.M., Egieya, Z.E., Ewuga, S.K., Abdul, A.A., Abrahams, T.O., Advancements in Predictive Analytics: a Philosophical and Practical Overview. *World J. Adv. Res. Rev.*, 21, 3, 240–252, 2024.
17. Bohat, V.K., Neural Network Model for Recommending Music Based on Music Genres. *2021 International Conference on Computer Communication and Informatics, ICCCI 2021*, 2021, Https://Doi.Org/10.1109/ICCCI50826.2021.9402621.
18. Chen, Z., Ma, M., Li, T., Wang, H., Li, C., Long Sequence Time-Series Forecasting With Deep Learning: a Survey. *Inf. Fusion*, 97, 101819, 2023.
19. Aggarwal, R., Tiwari, S., Joshi, V., Exam Proctoring Classification Using Eye Gaze Detection. *3rd International Conference on Smart Electronics and Communication, ICOSEC 2022 - Proceedings*, pp. 371–376, 2022, Https://Doi.Org/10.1109/ICOSEC54921.2022.9951987.
20. Raza, S.M. and Sajid, M., Vehicle Routing Problem Using Reinforcement Learning: Recent Advancements, in: *Lecture Notes in Electrical Engineering*, p. 858, 2022, Https://Doi.Org/10.1007/978-981-19-0840-8_20.
21. Zhuang, D., Gan, V.J., Tekler, Z.D., Chong, A., Tian, S., Shi, X., Data-Driven Predictive Control for Smart HVAC System in Iot-Integrated Buildings With Time-Series Forecasting and Reinforcement Learning. *Appl. Energy*, 338, 120936, 2023.
22. Kumar, S. and Pathak, S.K., A Comprehensive Study of XSS Attack and the Digital Forensic Models to Gather the Evidence. *ECS Trans.*, 107, 1, 7153–7163, 2022, Https://Doi.Org/10.1149/10701.7153ecst.
23. Karim, F.K., Khafaga, D.S., Eid, M.M., Towfek, S.K., Alkahtani, H.K., a Novel Bio-Inspired Optimization Algorithm Design for Wind Power Engineering Applications Time-Series Forecasting. *Biomimetics*, 8, 3, 321, 2023.
24. Benti, N.E., Chaka, M.D., Semie, A.G., Forecasting Renewable Energy Generation With Machine Learning and Deep Learning: Current Advances and Future Prospects. *Sustainability*, 15, 9, 7087, 2023.
25. Sajid, M., Gupta, S.K., Haidri, R.A., Artificial Intelligence and Blockchain Technologies for Smart City, in: *Intelligent Green Technologies for Sustainable Smart Cities*, 2022, Https://Doi.Org/10.1002/9781119816096.Ch15.

26. Sharan, A., Relevance Feedback-Based Query Expansion Model Using Ranks Combining and Word2Vec Approach. *IETE J. Res.*, 62, 5, 591–604, 2016, Https://Doi.Org/10.1080/03772063.2015.1136575.
27. Gruver, N., Finzi, M., Qiu, S., Wilson, A.G., Large Language Models Are Zero-Shot Time Series Forecasters, in: *Advances in Neural Information Processing Systems*, vol. 36, 2024.
28. Habbak, H., Mahmoud, M., Metwally, K., Fouda, M.M., Ibrahem, M., II, Load Forecasting Techniques and Their Applications in Smart Grids. *Energies*, 16, 3, 1480, 2023.
29. Kumar, V., Kedam, N., Sharma, K.V., Mehta, D.J., Caloiero, T., Advanced Machine Learning Techniques to Improve Hydrological Prediction: a Comparative Analysis of Streamflow Prediction Models. *Water*, 15, 14, 2572, 2023.
30. Liu, X., Hu, J., Li, Y., Diao, S., Liang, Y., Hooi, B., Zimmermann, R., Unitime: a Language-Empowered Unified Model for Cross-Domain Time Series Forecasting, in: *Proceedings of the ACM on Web Conference 2024*, pp. 4095–4106, 2024, May.
31. Borré, A., Seman, L.O., Camponogara, E., Stefenon, S.F., Mariani, V.C., Coelho, L.D.S., Machine Fault Detection Using a Hybrid CNN-LSTM Attention-Based Model. *Sensors*, 23, 9, 4512, 2023.

6

Ensemble Methods for Data-Driven Modeling in Agriculture and Applications

Khalil Ahmed[1], Mithilesh Kumar Dubey[1]*, Kajal[1] and Devendra Kumar Pandey[2]

[1]School of Computer Application, Lovely Professional University, Phagwara, Punjab, India
[2]School of Bioengineering and Biosciences, Lovely Professional University, Phagwara, Punjab, India

Abstract

One of the ancient civilizations, farming endured remarkable change recently due to being driven by information methods and technological breakthroughs. A variety of farm themes, including handling crops, the condition of the soil, watering, controlling pests, and the distribution of resources, are represented through methods based on data in statistical modeling, which is an attempt to replicate actual farming processes and structures. Growing food has developed from old methods into advanced technologies that integrate artificial intelligence (AI), machine learning (ML), and statistical analysis. Data-driven methods and collective ML have become highly effective instruments for the Agri-domain amid the several strategies used in this transition. The current study provides a thorough investigation of learning strategies in the field of agricultural data-driven modeling. An in-depth discussion of the theoretical underpinnings of ensemble learning is provided in this work, along with an explanation of the concepts underlying widely used tactics such as bagging, boosting, and stacking; their practicality and effectiveness in resolving important issues in crop data analysis, from precise farming to identifying diseases and harvest rate foresight, clarify the constraints and potential applications of collaboration in farming for increasing productivity in the future.

**Corresponding author*: mithilesh.21436@lpu.co.in

Arindam Mondal and Souvik Ganguli (eds.) Data-Driven Modeling, (143–164) © 2026 Scrivener Publishing LLC

Keywords: Ensemble methods, agriculture, data-driven techniques, machine learning, artificial intelligence, Internet of Things, data modeling, sustainable development goals (SDGs)

6.1 Introduction

Technological developments have brought significant transformations in the farm industry; driven-by-data modeling has emerged as a critical element of innovation in the past few years. Agriculture's conventional methods, which formerly relied solely on experience and intuition, are now going through a dramatic transition. In agricultural operations, data analysis and modeling become increasingly important.

This move toward methods based on data aims to address pressing issues such as limited resources, environmental sustainability, and food security by transforming agricultural activities' production, administration, and optimization [1]. Agriculture plays a key role in the 2030 Plan for Sustainability by helping to link the 17 sustainable development goals (SDGs) [2]. Despite producing more, the farming industry faces unforeseen difficulties that endanger the entire human race. Due to rising populations and shifts in the environment, farmland is moving away from traditional methods toward data-driven, resource-efficient practices [3]. To fulfill the objectives of the SDGs, growers must immediately implement these agricultural practices [4]. Water, fertilizer, and pesticides are examples of resource- and data-optimized inputs that can be used to promote climatic and ecological results [5, 6]. Agriculturists can better manage assets, produce better crops, handle chemicals and energy commodities more efficiently, and reduce hazards by utilizing such ensemble techniques using statistical modeling.

At present, the emergence of intelligence-driven agriculture has provided growers access to vast amounts of data derived from aerial photographs, aerial vehicles, and estimates [7]. These kinds of data provide valuable information about crop wellness, soil biology, seasonal variations, and agriculture operations as a whole. However, the sheer volume and range of it make it difficult to get significant insight without the use of sophisticated analytical techniques. These days, data-driven farming techniques are seen as an essential technological development that enables more efficient use of land [8]. In food production, the primary goals of data-driven approaches are to increase outputs while reducing the negative effects of excessive herbicide and pesticide usage as well as ineffective practices. Data-driven modeling, which offers a comprehensive toolkit for converting raw data to perceptive insights and statistical analysis, is essential to overcoming this difficulty [9], maximizing the use of resources, reducing pitfalls, and increasing crop productivity by applying advanced farming methods while taking informed decisions [10]. Agricultural structures are increasingly relying progressively more on driven by data methods, technologically advanced devices, and automated farm gear.

Precise farming is facilitated, whereby agricultural techniques are tailored to the specific needs of specific plants or areas of land [11]. Growers can apply specific actions such as proper watering, fertilization, and insect management by analyzing geographical and time-dependent variations in the composition of soil, moisture levels, and nutrient content [12]. Furthermore, informed by data modeling holds great potential for enhancing efficiency further along the crop value line. Through the optimization of resource utilization, reduction of junk, and reduction of harmful practices, these techniques provide more flexible and resilient agriculture [13]. By leveraging data-driven models for maximizing alternate tillage methods, sales patterns, and customer demands, producers can make tactical choices that strike a balance between protecting the environment and profitability. A new approach to resource management and food production that is sustainable is provided by data-driven modeling, which represents an abrupt shift in farming [14]. By utilizing analytical tools and information, growers can take advantage of novel opportunities for improved output, effectiveness, and adaptability in the midst of growing global challenges [15]. To fully realize the promise of agriculture and embark on this data-driven future, collaboration, ingenuity, and flexibility will be crucial.

Although there exist some barriers preventing data-driven modeling from being widely used in the farming industry, such as connectivity, security concerns, the need for specific tools and knowledge, and other issues, data-driven modeling is a potential technique [16]. To overcome these problems in the agricultural ecology, cooperation across scholars, policymakers, manufacturers of technology, and growers directly is needed.

6.1.1 Data Analysis Solutions for Data Modeling in Agriculture

The agricultural industry has come a long way from the days when it depended only on referrals from other farmers to what it is today, which is driven by data [12]. These days, farmers may utilize their insights along with an abundance of past data to form a rational decision regarding the crops and how to cultivate them. With the advancement in technology in agriculture, data analytics is being integrated into traditional agricultural processes to improve productivity, reduce anomalies, and minimize risks associated with handling perishable goods [17]. To make agriculture more productive and cost-effective at every stage of the process, data analysis is being used in this field of work. Every step of the value chain is affected, including supply chain management, crop selection, cultivation techniques, and also harvesting [18].

Farm managers and owners now have access to vast amounts of crop data in real time to direct farmers' actions because sensors and connected equipment interact with one another on the farm using innovative techniques leveraged by artificial intelligence (AI) and machine learning (ML) algorithms [19]. Massive data collection in agriculture is revolutionizing the way that livestock are cared for, creating effective risk assessment modules, opening up the possibility of urban farming to more people, and accelerating labor, and land [20]. The application of data-driven modeling and ML techniques in agriculture offers numerous significant benefits. To produce a profitable harvest, farmers can select a strain of crop that is most suited for the weather, seasons of precipitation, and soil type by using smart crop data. Based on data analysis, hybrid varieties or breeds that are most resistant to disease and spoiling can be suggested. These cultivars or breeds are best suited to the soil and climate [21]. The data modeling aims to create a standardized, organized information environment for agriculture, assisting agribusinesses, government agencies, and farms in implementing a geographic information system (GIS); facilitating information sharing; ensuring legal compliance; and serving as a resource that helps farmers in seeking information for the agriculture related to the crop growth, fertilizers used, pest and insect disease damage, etc. [22]. The data analysis solution for data modeling in agriculture is represented in Figure 6.1, in which a systematic approach is applied to data for the implementation of a graphical user interface (GUI) to farmers for monitoring crops and fields.

The above strategy is data-driven and stems from the process of knowledge discovery in general. The accuracy of the entire analysis depends on the initial stage, that of gathering the data. The kind of data that should be gathered, how it should be gathered, and how to keep it up to date during its entire life cycle need to be carefully considered. Data include a lot of ambiguous aspects, and this becomes much more complicated in data analysis [23]. Because there are no accepted guidelines for how the data should be combined, unified, and proper for analysis, as well as for selecting analytical methods, the second phase—data representation and analysis, is extremely complex. Ultimately, making decisions is an exhausting procedure where the knowledge that has been extracted is combined with the knowledge of agronomists and farmers, as well as cultivating

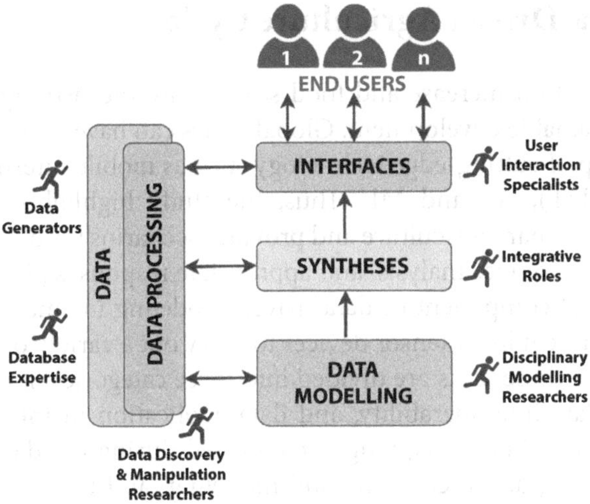

Figure 6.1 Data analysis solution for data modeling in agriculture.

constraints and regulations, to create new management processes that seek to boost production quality and productivity while minimizing environmental impact. The graphical representation of data analytics methods for crop yield monitoring is shown in Figure 6.2.

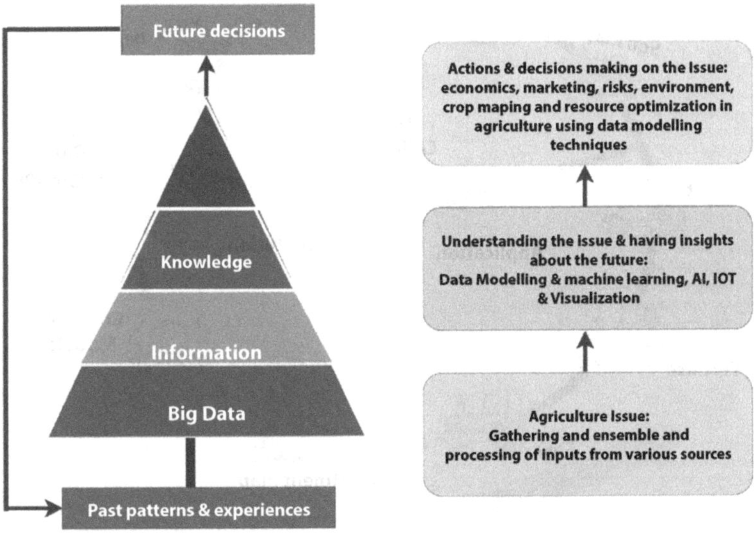

Figure 6.2 Data analysis paradigms for crop monitoring in agricultural fields.

6.2 Data-Driven Agriculture Cycle

Global population increase and food scarcity are the two biggest limitations to sustainable development. Global issues can have practical answers with the help of cutting-edge technology such as mobile internet, Internet of Things (IoT), AI, and ML. Thus, the study highlights data-driven approaches to smart agriculture and provides scenarios for data collection, transmission, storage, analysis, and appropriate responses [24]. The IoT is a fundamental component of data-driven modeling in smart agriculture systems because it links sensor devices to carry out a variety of fundamental functions. These tasks are divided into three categories, including data collecting, data interoperability, and data application in the agricultural industry. Soil and crop mapping is completed during the data collection stage; data integration, crop and soil modeling, and treatment mapping are done during the interpretation step [25]. The final phase of the aforementioned activity is application, which involves using machines and robots for automation throughout the seed sowing to harvesting processes.

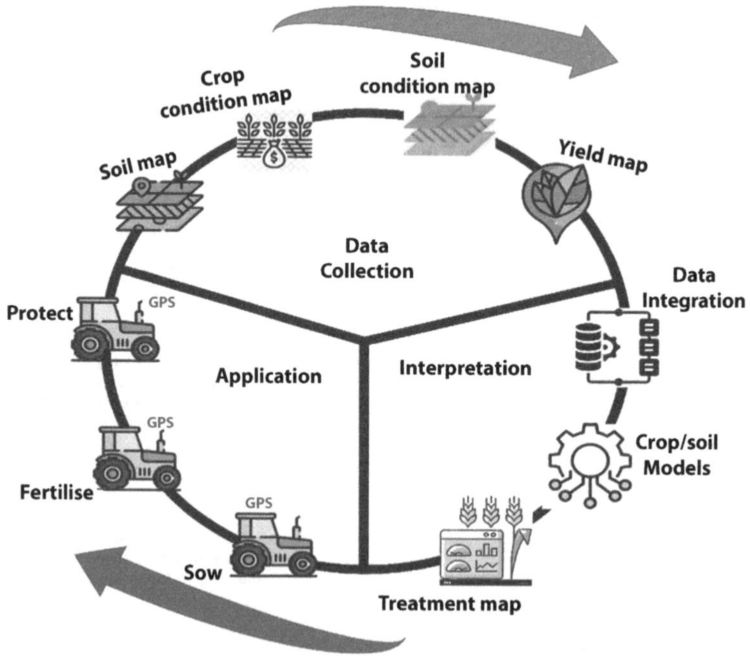

Figure 6.3 Data-driven agriculture cycle.

Above is a detailed discussion of each of the aforementioned stages in the data-driven agriculture cycle (Figure 6.3).

6.3 Cloud-Based Event and Data Management in Data-Driven Modeling

The field of data management and analytics in agriculture has seen a radical transformation in recent years with the introduction of data-driven modeling using ensemble approaches. Scalability, adaptability, and accessibility are features that make cloud-based solutions suited for processing massive amounts of agricultural data and carrying out intricate computational operations. A strong infrastructure for managing events and data streams in real time is provided by cloud computing, IoT, ML, and AI [26]. Cloud platforms can handle transactional systems, because of their distributed architecture and elastic scalability. Event-driven architectures set off automated reactions to particular events or modifications in data streams as analytics for agricultural decision-making is represented in Figure 6.5. These serverless computing models provide scalable and affordable ways to process events in real time and address challenging issues in agriculture, such as gathering, interpreting, and using data [27]. High-throughput, low-latency data access is provided by Azure Cosmos DB, facilitating effective querying and analysis. With the help of these managed database services, infrastructure management is no longer necessary, freeing up data scientists and analysts to concentrate on concluding the data to prevent crop damage and accomplish sustainable objectives by using crop data to track issues facing the agriculture sector, which lead to yield loss [28]. Cloud-based environments enable the development and deployment of data-driven models at scale, supported by ML frameworks such as TensorFlow and PyTorch. Managed services such as Amazon Sage Maker streamline the workflow, providing scalability, reliability, and automation. Pipelines for end-to-end data processing and modeling require the assembling and orchestration of cloud-based services [29]. Workflow automation and orchestration across many services and environments are made possible by cloud-native orchestration solutions, among others. These technologies ensure the scalability and dependability of data processing pipelines by offering functionality for scheduling, monitoring, and error management. Communication and cooperation within the cloud ecosystem are made easy through integration with other cloud services including message queues, notification systems, and monitoring tools for agriculture

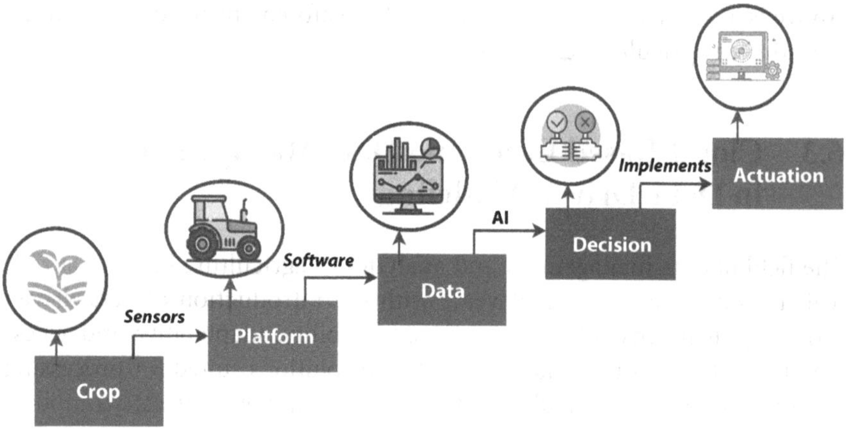

Figure 6.4 Analytics for agricultural decision-making.

automation and decision-making process as depicted in Figure 6.4. Cloud-based event and data management are crucial for scalable data-driven modeling. It allows organizations to handle events, process real-time data, and develop sophisticated models [30]. As data volume and velocity increase, cloud-based solutions remain indispensable.

6.4 Ensemble Methods for Data-Driven Modeling in Agriculture

Ensemble methods are approaches that generate a final forecast by combining the predictions of several different separate models. Ensemble approaches are based on the general rule of heaps, which claims that the total cognition of multiple models often surpasses the intellect of a single model. When several factors come together to influence outcomes in farming, such as crop DNA, soil characteristics, and climate variables, the ensemble approach is especially pertinent.

One of the array techniques' key benefits is its capacity to lessen excessive fitting, a common complex modeling issue with large datasets and limited size of samples. By leveraging a range of models that represent different aspects of the actual data dispersion, ensembles can exhibit improved robustness for distortion and instability as well as an increased ability to extrapolate to hitherto unknown data [31]. Furthermore, specialists can tailor the ensemble layout to the particular characteristics of the farming sector they are researching due to the freedom that ensemble methods offer in model building. Figure 6.5 summarizes ensemble tactics for data-driven modeling in agro. The theory underlying ensemble learning is first presented, along with a summary of the various ensemble concepts. Next, this study explores the use of ensemble approaches in several agricultural areas such as disease detection, pest management, precision agriculture, and crop yield prediction [32]. We present a survey of state-of-the-art ensemble techniques for each application domain, highlighting their advantages and disadvantages as well as empirical research proving their practical effectiveness.

6.4.1 Random Forest

The intriguing combination of mathematics and technology termed AI has grown tremendously, and one particularly noteworthy technique is the random forest. A cooperative group of trees of choices known as random forests cooperates to produce just one result. The above method is for controlled learning. Since Leo Breiman introduced random forest in 2001, it has grown to be a mainstay for those interested in ML. Forest-based tools are adaptable and can be used to solve regression and classification problems in agriculture as shown in Figure 6.6. It is trained using the bagging method, which combines many learning models to improve the final result. When it comes to assisting the agriculture sector in achieving sustainability, this approach has a significant benefit. The introduction of heterogeneity among trees in random forests, which are commonly used for regression and classification purposes, lowers the danger of overfitting and enhances prediction accuracy [33]. They manage intricate data, lessen overfitting, and produce accurate forecasts in a range of conditions.

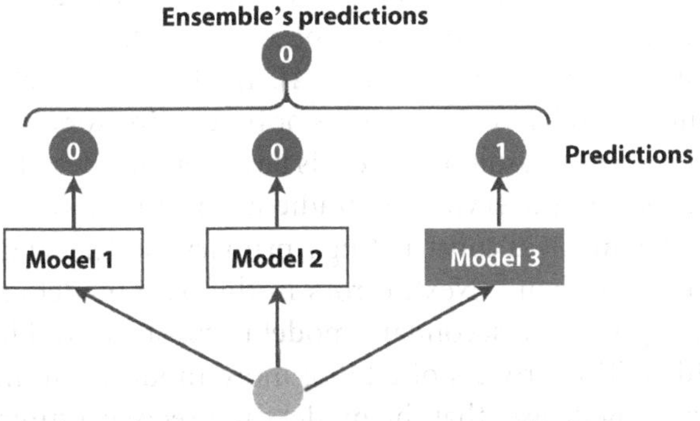

Figure 6.5 Overview of ensemble learning.

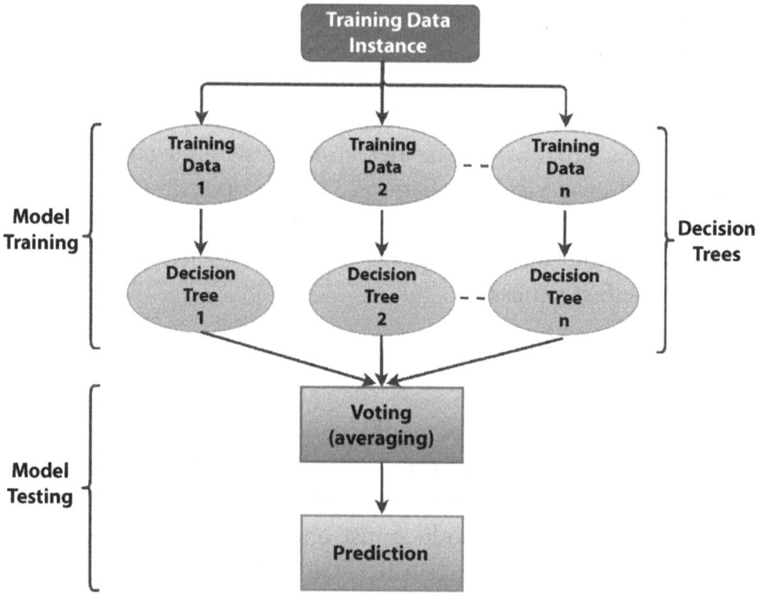

Figure 6.6 Working of random forest in disease prediction in the agriculture sector.

6.4.2 Gradient-Boosting Machines

Gradient-boosting machine (GBM) is a category of algorithms for ML that have gained significant traction and adaptability. They have shown exceptional effectiveness in agricultural applications, including ranking and recommendation systems, regression, and classification. Among the technologies most frequently utilized in the agriculture field for creating predictive models for a variety of challenges from pre-harvesting to the harvesting stage are machine learning, deep learning, remote sensing, IoT-based monitoring systems, and computer vision techniques, which enable accurate forecasting, early detection of pests and diseases, yield estimation, and optimized resource management [34]. The boosting strategy uses several rudimentary model's weak learners or base estimators in combination to produce the desired result because it is based on the idea of collaborative learning; the working overview of gradient boosting is shown in Figure 6.7. The first step involves constructing a primary model using the training datasets that are on hand. Next, errors in the base model are identified. Following this process, a secondary model is constructed. Finally, a third model is added. This process of adding more models continues until we have a full training dataset that the model can precisely estimate [34].

6.4.2.1 *Loss Function*

However, a wide range of ML error functions can be used, contingent on the type of activities being performed in agriculture. How the loss function is used depends on the desired characteristics of the conditional distribution, such as robustness. Usually, the loss function in GBM is distinguished between actual values and the values predicted by the model. It lessens this difference, which guides the model's learning process.

6.4.2.2 *Weak Learners*

An ML model known as a weak learner does marginally superior to randomized picking. A weak learner makes a lot of mistakes when interpreting data and performs miserably.

6.4.2.3 *Additive Model*

Statistical models known as additive models combine several simpler models to produce a more versatile and complicated model. They are frequently used in the analysis of data with intricate correlations between variables, such as the identification of fruit, leaf, and root diseases in the agricultural sector.

6.4.3 AdaBoost

Researchers have applied ensemble learning to image-based crop disease recognition to enhance the generalization performance of the recognition approach for sustainability in agriculture. Enhancing the recognition

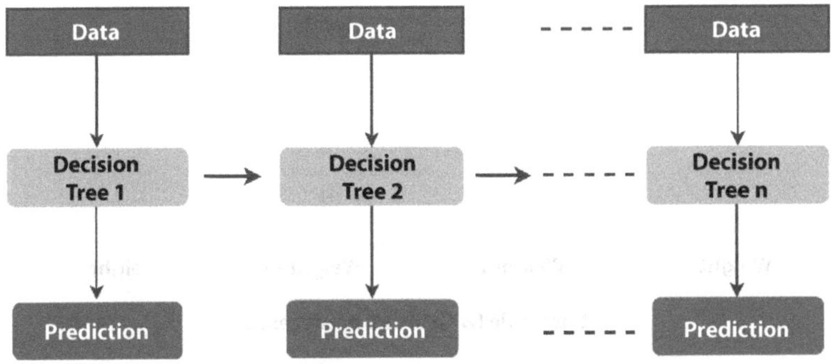

Figure 6.7 Working overview of gradient-boosting machine.

method's generalization performance using ensemble learning is a successful strategy for enhancing crop yield to meet the increasing demand of food around the globe. Recent years have seen impressive results from computational algorithms, especially deep learning (DL) models, in a variety of computer vision work, including the agricultural industry. In this sector, various convolutional neural networks have become a mainstream option for object detection and classification within images. Achieving high classification accuracy is still difficult, though, because plant diseases are complex and diverse. In the ML field, ensemble learning method that mixes different models to produce collective predictions has received a lot of attention as a solution to this challenge. Accuracy and robustness are increased through ensemble learning, which takes advantage of the diversity and complementary qualities of different models [35]. One of them, AdaBoost, operates a little differently from other boosting algorithms as depicted in the figure below. AdaBoost is a formidable method of team learning that builds an effective classifier from several poor learners as represented in Figure 6.8. It focuses on examples that prior learners incorrectly identified and trains weak learners iteratively on various subsets of their instructional data. AdaBoost begins by giving each training example the same weight. It trains a weak learner in each iteration and modifies the instance's weights according to the accuracy of the prediction. Examples that were incorrectly categorized are given greater weights, which compels later learners to pay attention to them. It produces a strong classifier that outperforms any one weak learner through the integration of several weak learners [36]. The above is accomplished by making use of the weakest learners' variety and their capacity to fix one another's errors.

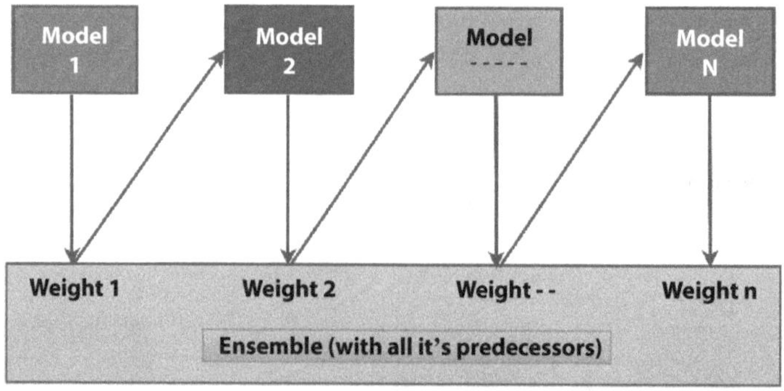

Figure 6.8 Working of AdaBoost algorithm.

6.4.3.1 XGBoost

XGBoost is an approach to ML that has gained popularity and widespread usage in agriculture because it is capable of handling enormous datasets as well as attaining contemporary outcomes for numerous tasks related to technique that delivers a more powerful prediction by combining the estimates of several weak models. It is a useful tool to manage real-world data containing value gaps in agriculture, especially visual datasets for pathogen recognition, due to its capacity to deal with incorrect values effectively. This feature removes the requirement for a lot of preprocessing. Moreover, models may be trained rapidly on large datasets due to its inherent computational capacity [37]. In the agricultural sector, scalability, efficiency, handling of data that are incomplete, and clarity are the key benefits associated with these boosting algorithms. Despite this, there are many drawbacks, including duration and computing expenses, tuning of hyperparameters, excessive fitting, and cost of computation [38].

6.4.4 Bagging

The model average is calculated using the models of uniform weak learners. Boot pooling enhances ML reliability and efficiency in statistical regression and classification. Tree-based techniques are widely used. Through the continual addition of weak models, boosters create models until every training dataset is accurately forecasted; a working overview of the bagging technique is represented in Figure 6.9.

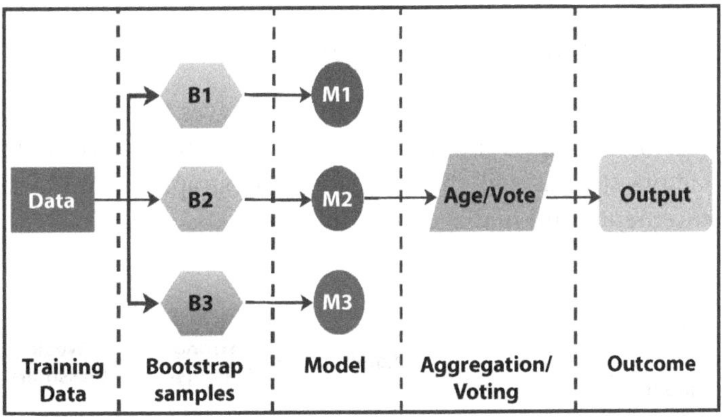

Figure 6.9 Working model of begging ensemble classifiers in agriculture.

6.4.5 Boosting

Boosting techniques are comparable to bagging techniques, but they prioritize the successive fitting of several weak learners, placing greater weight on data that earlier models performed poorly, as represented in Figure 6.10. This responsive method can be successfully applied to classification as well as regression problems, producing a strong learner with reduced error. Because they can fit several complicated models successively and have a reduced computing expense, little variance but highly biased models are frequently utilized for promoting [39]. Because concurrent processes can become prohibitively expensive when utilizing shallow decision trees as foundation models, this is especially crucial. In summary, how these meta-algorithms generate and combine the weak learners throughout the orderly procedure is different. Although gradient boosting modifies the value of these observations, adaptive boosting modifies the weights assigned to each training dataset observation [40]. The primary distinction between the two approaches is from how they approach the optimization task of identifying the optimal model that can be expressed as a weighted sum of weak learners.

6.5 Applications of Data Modeling in Agriculture

Ensemble ML, which entails building numerous models and integrating their projections to make more precise and reliable outcomes, can be applied to a variety of challenges in cultivation from sowing of seed to harvesting and marketing and enhancing crop procedures. Several tasks of collective ML models are covered below.

6.5.1 Field and Resource Management

Field and zone management in agriculture involves the strategic division and management of agricultural land into smaller units or zones based on various factors such as soil characteristics, topography, water availability, crop requirements, and management practices.

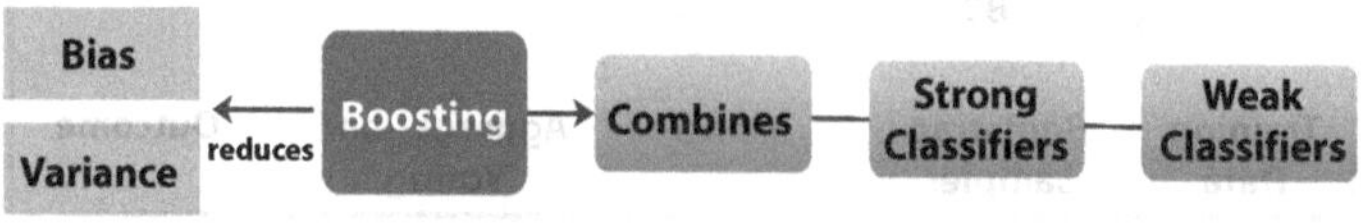

Figure 6.10 Illustration of machine learning boosting techniques.

Optimizing productivity, resource use efficiency, and environmental sustainability. Soil mapping and analysis are crucial for field and zone management, identifying soil properties such as texture, fertility, pH, organic matter content, and drainage, thereby identifying variability [41]. Precision agriculture technologies such as GPS, GIS, remote sensing, and on-farm sensors are crucial for field and zone management, enabling farmers to collect spatially explicit data on soil properties, crop health, and moisture levels.

Pesticides and irrigation water at different rates, optimizing resource use efficiency, and reducing environmental impacts. Variable rate application (VRA) technology also aids in crop selection and rotation based on management zone characteristics, allowing for better performance in specific soil types and topographic conditions and reducing nutrient depletion risk [42]. Field and zone management techniques optimize water use efficiency by implementing site-specific irrigation strategies using soil moisture sensors, weather data, and evapotranspiration models. They also aid in pest and disease management by identifying areas susceptible to infestations or diseases, implementing integrated pest management practices, and implementing conservation practices such as contour farming, terracing, cover cropping, and buffer strips. These strategies are tailored to each management zone's conditions and needs. Data-driven decision-making processes, integrating information from soil tests, crop monitoring, remote sensing, and historical yield data help farmers identify patterns, trends, and opportunities for improvement and resource management [43].

6.5.2 Environmental Sustainability and Food Safety

Ensemble learning techniques, resource optimization strategies, and increased accuracy of predictive models contribute to environmental sustainability in agriculture. Solutions for managing noxious species and conducting intelligent protection are made possible by ensemble learning approaches, which forecast the location and frequency of bugs, threatened species, and introduced species. Their contributions to protecting biodiversity and rehabilitating ecosystems involve integrating predictions from multiple models trained on external variables, assessing the suitability of habitats for various taxa, and identifying key conservation areas or potential sites for ecosystem restoration. Through the integration of estimates from several models trained on different hydrology and atmospheric variables, ensemble learning approaches can enhance air safety monitoring, resource management, and mitigation efforts by enhancing water safety forecasts [44].

Moreover, carbon retention modeling can be supported by ensemble approaches, which enhance forecasts for greenhouse gas stocks and fluxes in terrestrial ecosystems by combining data from satellite imagery, ground-based sensors, and weather data. Ensemble learning techniques can improve methods for managing waste by incorporating information on garbage generation, layout, and disposal techniques. Ensemble approaches can lessen their adverse environmental impacts, advance the adoption of circular economy ideas, and ensure food safety by improving the accuracy of waste creation forecasts and supporting the creation of more efficient agricultural product reuse, composting, and waste into energy systems [45].

6.5.3 Crop Yield Prediction

Ensemble approaches are capable of capturing intricate linkages and increasing prediction accuracy by merging several models that were trained on various subsets of data or with various algorithms [46]. Ensemble learning combines predictions from many classifiers trained on distinct attributes or subsets of data to detect illnesses and pests in crops. For instance, models trained on crop photos may recognize disease symptoms visually, whereas models trained on environmental information such as temperature and humidity can pinpoint insect infestation–friendly circumstances [47].

The use of ML ensemble approaches, which combine data from several sources such as satellite imaging, remote sensors, and on-farm sensors, can improve precision agriculture methods. Farmers can use ensemble models to create more precise maps of crop health, soil characteristics, and yield potential by combining data from many sources.

6.5.4 Agriculture Market and Associated Risk Management

Because of its inherent volatility, the agriculture industry is highly influenced by global market trends, crop diseases, weather patterns, policy decisions, and technological breakthroughs, all of which create uncertainty and require robust predictive models for effective planning and decision-making. Estimating agricultural market changes with accuracy and controlling associated risks efficiently are critical for farmers, dealers, and investors to ensure profitability and sustainability. In earlier times, marketers made decisions based on experience, instinct, and professional judgment. Nonetheless, advanced tactics are required due to the agricultural markets' growing complexity and dynamism [48]. Machine learning

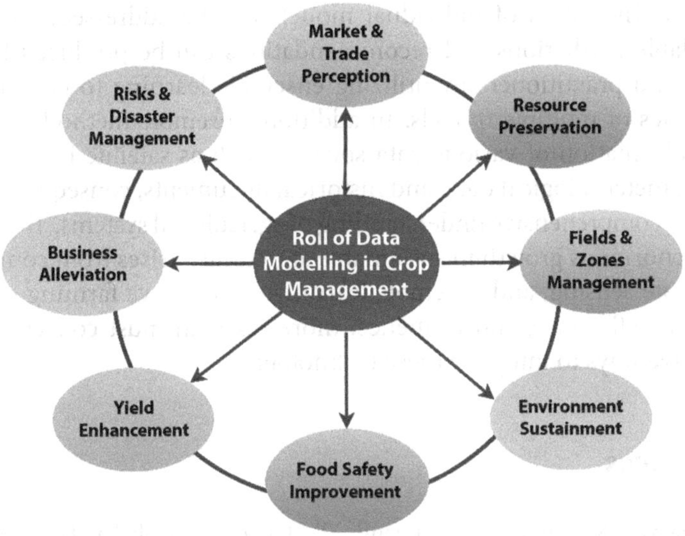

Figure 6.11 Data modeling and ensemble learning application in the agriculture sector.

ensemble approaches have become extremely useful instruments for managing risks and farm price forecasting in recent years. Machine learning ensemble methods use the combined knowledge of several models to improve risk management and prediction accuracy in agriculture tasks. Using a combination of ensemble approaches can extract a wide range of connections and patterns from agricultural market data [49].

Through this research, we seek to clarify how AI ensemble approaches may help those involved in farming make better judgments, lower risks, and manage the complexities associated with agricultural markets, clearly indicated in Figure 6.11. Market players may maximize resource allocation, adjust to changing conditions, and ultimately support the resilience and sustainability of the agriculture sector by utilizing the power of data-driven models [50].

6.6 Conclusion and Future Directions

Ensemble learning outperforms single-model learning in many categories by combining numerous categorization algorithms and decreasing bias and modeling variability to increase prediction ability. This chapter presents ensemble learning techniques, which, when paired with advanced data modeling techniques, show promise for creating sustainable farming practices. The limits of individual models can be addressed, and more dependable predictions and recommendations can be produced by academics and practitioners by utilizing ensemble learning to combine the capabilities of multiple models. In addition, ensemble methods facilitate the amalgamation of various data sources, such as satellite imaging, IoT sensors, meteorological data, and historical documents, consequently promoting a comprehensive understanding of agricultural systems. The potential for enormous growth in sustainable agriculture arises from combining AI, remote sensing, and ensemble learning. To improve farming systems' scalability, efficiency, and resilience, more research must concentrate on innovative ways to integrate these technologies.

References

1. Charvat, K., Junior, K.C., Reznik, T., Lukas, V., Jedlicka, K., Palma, R., Berzins, R., Advanced visualisation of big data for agriculture as part of databio development, in: *IGARSS 2018-2018 IEEE International Geoscience and Remote Sensing Symposium*, IEEE, pp. 415–418, 2018, July.
2. Ladha, J.K., Jat, M.L., Stirling, C.M., Chakraborty, D., Pradhan, P., Krupnik, T.J., Gerard, B., Achieving the sustainable development goals in agriculture: The crucial role of nitrogen in cereal-based systems. *Adv. Agron., 163*, 39–116, 2020.
3. Linaza, M.T., Posada, J., Bund, J., Eisert, P., Quartulli, M., Döllner, J., Lucat, L., Data-driven artificial intelligence applications for sustainable precision agriculture. *Agronomy, 11*, 6, 1227, 2021.
4. Roop, R., Weaver, M., Fonseca, A.P., Matouq, M., Innovative Approaches in Smallholder Farming Systems to Implement the Sustainable Development Goals, in: *SDGs in the Americas and Caribbean Region*, pp. 971–998, Springer International Publishing, Cham, 2023.
5. de Paul Obade, V., Gaya, C., Obade, P.T., Challenges and opportunities of digital technology in soil quality and land management research. *Environ. Climate-Smart Food Prod.*, 285–317, 2022.
6. Shaikh, T.A., Rasool, T., Lone, F.R., Towards leveraging the role of machine learning and artificial intelligence in precision agriculture and smart farming. *Comput. Electron. Agric., 198*, 107119, 2022.
7. Velamuri, A., Data-Driven Management in Agriculture, in: *Encyclopedia of Digital Agricultural Technologies*, pp. 267–276, Springer International Publishing, Cham, 2023.
8. Ahmed, K., Dubey, M.K., Pandey, D.K., Singh, S., Fuzzy and Data Mining Methods for Enhancing Plant Productivity and Sustainability, in: *Microbial Data Intelligence and Computational Techniques for Sustainable Computing*, pp. 205–216, Springer Nature Singapore, Singapore, 2024.

9. Jha, K., Doshi, A., Patel, P., Shah, M., A comprehensive review on automation in agriculture using artificial intelligence. *Artif. Intell. Agric.*, *2*, 1–12, 2019.
10. Gómez-Chabla, R., Real-Avilés, K., Morán, C., Grijalva, P., Recalde, T., IoT applications in agriculture: A systematic literature review, in: *2nd International conference on ICTs in agronomy and environment*, Springer International Publishing, Cham, pp. 68–76, 2018, December.
11. Chang, C.L., Chung, S.C., Fu, W.L., Huang, C.C., Artificial intelligence approaches to predict growth, harvest day, and quality of lettuce (Lactuca sativa L.) in a IoT-enabled greenhouse system. *Biosyst. Eng.*, *212*, 77–105, 2021.
12. Rozenstein, O., Cohen, Y., Alchanatis, V., Behrendt, K., Bonfil, D.J., Eshel, G., Lowenberg-DeBoer, J., Data-driven agriculture and sustainable farming: friends or foes? *Precis. Agric.*, *25*, 1, 520–531, 2024.
13. Bachmann, N., Tripathi, S., Brunner, M., Jodlbauer, H., The contribution of data-driven technologies in achieving the sustainable development goals. *Sustainability*, *14*, 5, 2497, 2022.
14. Kamble, S.S., Gunasekaran, A., Gawankar, S.A., Achieving sustainable performance in a data-driven agriculture supply chain: A review for research and applications. *Int. J. Prod. Econ.*, *219*, 179–194, 2020.
15. Chergui, N., Kechadi, M.T., McDonnell, M., The impact of data analytics in digital agriculture: a review, in: *2020 International Multi-Conference on: Organization of Knowledge and Advanced Technologies (OCTA)*, IEEE, pp. 1–13, 2020, February.
16. Paul, K., Chatterjee, S.S., Pai, P., Varshney, A., Juikar, S., Prasad, V., Dasgupta, S., Viable smart sensors and their application in data driven agriculture. *Comput. Electron. Agric.*, *198*, 107096, 2022.
17. Dineva, K. and Atanasova, T., Cloud data-driven intelligent monitoring system for interactive smart farming. *Sensors*, *22*, 17, 6566, 2022.
18. Janssen, S., Porter, C.H., Moore, A.D., Athanasiadis, I.N., Foster, I., Jones, J.W., Antle, J.M., Towards a new generation of agricultural system models, data, and knowledge products: building an open web-based approach to agricultural data, system modelling and decision support. AgMIP. *Towards a New Generation of Agricultural System Models, Data, and Knowledge Products.*, *91*, 2015.
19. Ahmed, K., Dubey, M.K., Dubey, S., Guarding Maize: Vigilance Against Pathogens Early Identification, Detection, and Prevention, in: *Microbial Data Intelligence and Computational Techniques for Sustainable Computing*, pp. 301–318, Springer Nature Singapore, Singapore, 2024.
20. Naseem, M., Alam, M., Ahmad, K., Singh, V., Mahroof, M., Ahamad, G., Machine learning approaches for automatic irrigation system in hilly areas using wireless sensor networks, 2022.
21. Koshariya, A.K., Rameshkumar, P.M., Balaji, P., Cavaliere, L.P.L., Dornadula, V.H.R., Singh, B., Data-Driven Insights for Agricultural Management: Leveraging Industry 4.0 Technologies for Improved Crop Yields and

Resource Optimization, in: *Robotics and Automation in Industry 4.0*, pp. 260–274, CRC Press, 2024.

22. Chattopadhyay, S., Carroll, M.E., Ganapathysubramanian, B., Singh, A.K., Sarkar, S., Data driven ensemble learning for soybean yield prediction, in: *2nd AAAI Workshop on AI for Agriculture and Food Systems*, 2023.
23. Ok, A.O., Akar, O., Gungor, O., Evaluation of random forest method for agricultural crop classification. *Eur. J. Remote Sens.*, *45*, 1, 421–432, 2012.
24. Naseem, M., Singh, V., Ahmed, K., Mahroof, M., Ahamad, G., Abbasi, E., Architecture of automatic irrigation system in hilly area using wireless sensor network: a review, in: *2022 2nd International Conference on Emerging Frontiers in Electrical and Electronic Technologies (ICEFEET)*, IEEE, pp. 1–6, 2022, June.
25. Kumar, J.S., Santhosh, P.S., Kowshik, T., Maheswari, G., Deep Learning Based Crop Yield Prediction and Disease Identification, in: *2024 International Conference on Advances in Data Engineering and Intelligent Computing Systems (ADICS)*, IEEE, pp. 1–5, 2024, April.
26. Branstad-Spates, E.H., Castano-Duque, L., Mosher, G.A., Hurburgh Jr., C.R., Owens, P., Winzeler, E., Bowers, E.L., Gradient boosting machine learning model to predict aflatoxins in Iowa corn. *Front. Microbiol.*, *14*, 1248772, 2023.
27. Li, C., A gentle introduction to gradient boosting. *URL: http://www.ccs.neu.edu/home/vip/teach/MLcourse/4_boosting/slides/gradient_boosting.pdf*, *59*, 2016.
28. Ying, C., Qi-Guang, M., Jia-Chen, L., Lin, G., Advance and prospects of AdaBoost algorithm. *Acta Autom. Sin.*, *39*, 6, 745–758, 2013.
29. Mathanker, S.K., Weckler, P.R., Bowser, T.J., Wang, N., Maness, N.O., AdaBoost classifiers for pecan defect classification. *Comput. Electron. Agric.*, *77*, 1, 60–68, 2011.
30. Mallikarjuna Rao, G.S., Dangeti, S., Amiripalli, S.S., An efficient modelling based on XGBoost and SVM algorithms to predict crop yield, in: *Advances in Data Science and Management: Proceedings of ICDSM 2021*, Springer Nature Singapore, Singapore, pp. 565–574, 2022.
31. Premasudha, B.G., Thara, D.K., Tara, K.N., ML based methods XGBoost and random forest for crop and fertilizer prediction, in: *2022 14th International Conference on Computational Intelligence and Communication Networks (CICN)*, IEEE, pp. 492–497, 2022, December.
32. Ribeiro, M.H.D.M. and dos Santos Coelho, L., Ensemble approach based on bagging, boosting and stacking for short-term prediction in agribusiness time series. *Appl. Soft Comput.*, *86*, 105837, 2020.
33. Hakim, L., Sartono, B., Saefuddin, A., Bagging based ensemble classification method on imbalance datasets. *Repositories-Dept. Statistics IPB Univ.*, 670–676, 2017.
34. Chauhan, S., Mahawar, S., Jain, D., Udpadhay, S.K., Mohanty, S.R., Singh, A., Maharjan, E., Boosting sustainable agriculture by arbuscular mycorrhiza

under stress condition: mechanism and future prospective. *Biomed Res. Int.*, *2022*, 1, 5275449, 2022.
35. Nagesh, O.S., Budaraju, R.R., Kulkarni, S.S., Vinay, M., Ajibade, S.S.M., Chopra, M., Kaliyaperumal, K., Boosting enabled efficient machine learning technique for accurate prediction of crop yield towards precision agriculture. *Discover Sustain.*, 5, 1, 78, 2024.
36. Silva, V.C., Rocha, M.S., Faria, G.A., Xavier Junior, S.F.A., de Oliveira, T.A., Peixoto, A.P.B., Boosting algorithms for prediction in agriculture: an application of feature importance and feature selection boosting algorithms for prediction crop damage. *agriRxiv*, 2021, 20210437677, 2021.
37. Mahlein, A.K., Plant disease detection by imaging sensors–parallels and specific demands for precision agriculture and plant phenotyping. *Plant Dis.*, *100*, 2, 241–251, 2016.
38. Haq, Z.U., Ullah, H., Khan, M.N.A., Naqvi, S.R., Ahad, A., Amin, N.A.S., Comparative study of machine learning methods integrated with genetic algorithm and particle swarm optimization for bio-char yield prediction. *Bioresour. Technol.*, *363*, 128008, 2022.
39. Ngige, G.A., Ovuoraye, P.E., Igwegbe, C.A., Fetahi, E., Okeke, J.A., Yakubu, A.D., Onyechi, P.C., RSM optimization and yield prediction for biodiesel produced from alkali-catalytic transesterification of pawpaw seed extract: Thermodynamics, kinetics, and Multiple Linear Regression analysis. *Digit. Chem. Eng.*, 6, 100066, 2023.
40. Drinkwater, L.E., Schipanski, M., Snapp, S., Jackson, L.E., Ecologically based nutrient management, in: *Agricultural Systems*, pp. 203–257, Academic Press, 2017.
41. Kumar, S., Meena, R.S., Sheoran, S., Jangir, C.K., Jhariya, M.K., Banerjee, A., Raj, A., Remote sensing for agriculture and resource management, in: *Natural Resources Conservation and Advances for Sustainability*, pp. 91–135, Elsevier, 2022.
42. Kuethe, H., Briggeman, B., Paulson, D., L. Katchova, A., A comparison of data collected through farm management associations and the agricultural resource management survey. *Agric. Financ. Rev.*, 74, 4, 492–500, 2014.
43. Dubman, R., Variance Estimation with USDA's Farm Costs and Returns Surveys and Agricultural Resource Management Study Surveys, 2000.
44. Carvalho, F.P., Pesticides, environment, and food safety. *Food Energy Secur.*, 6, 2, 48–60, 2017.
45. Sunardi, S., Ghulam, I., Istiqomah, N., Fadilah, K., Safitri, K., II, Abdoellah, O.S., Environmental Sustainability and Food Safety of the Practice of Urban Agriculture in Great Bandung. *Int. J. Sustain. Dev. Plann.*, 18, 3, 2023.
46. Van Klompenburg, T., Kassahun, A., Catal, C., Crop yield prediction using machine learning: A systematic literature review. *Comput. Electron. Agric.*, 177, 105709, 2020.

47. Dahikar, S.S. and Rode, S.V., Agricultural crop yield prediction using artificial neural network approach. *Int. J. Innov. Res. Electrical Electronics Instrum. Control Eng.*, 2, 1, 683–686, 2014.
48. Heiman, A. and Hildebrandt, L., Marketing as a risk management mechanism with applications in agriculture, resources, and food management. *Annu. Rev. Resour. Econ.*, 10, 253–277, 2018.
49. Novickytė, L., Income risk management in agriculture using financial support. *Eur. J. Sustain. Dev.*, 7, 4, 191–191, 2018.
50. Saroj, and Paltasingh, K.R., What promotes production contract in Indian agriculture? Managing Market Risk Versus Profit Orientation. *Agric. Econ.*, 55, 1, 140–153, 2024.

7

Artificial Intelligence–Enabled Ensemble Machine Learning Approaches for Solanaceae Crops

Kajal[1], Mithilesh Kumar Dubey[1*], Khalil Ahmed[1] and Devendra Kumar Pandey[2]

[1]*School of Computer Application, Lovely Professional University, Phagwara, Punjab, India*
[2]*School of Bioengineering and Biosciences, Lovely Professional University, Phagwara, Punjab, India*

Abstract

Farming is a crucial part of the economic growth of every nation providing food, fiber, and raw materials for various industries. Increasing global population and rising demands for food are putting pressure to increase yields in agriculture as agriculture faces several challenges due to biotic and abiotic stress including plant diseases. Sustainable agriculture has emerged as a novel approach to address current challenges for global food security. Machine learning makes it possible to learn without explicit programming. Ensemble methods are popular approaches for enhancing the prediction ability of a machine learning model. Tomatoes, potatoes, eggplants, and bell and chili peppers are some of the widely planted solanaceous crops and are significant important crops from a commercial and nutritional perspective, but these crops are affected by multiple diseases that result in significant losses in yield and fruit quality, thus adversely affecting human well-being through economic and agricultural loss. This chapter discusses the challenges, opportunities, and future directions of artificial intelligence–enabled ensemble machine learning approaches with knowledge-driven agriculture for sustainably improving the productivity of crops.

**Corresponding author*: mithilesh.21436@lpu.co.in

Arindam Mondal and Souvik Ganguli (eds.) Data-Driven Modeling, (165–186) © 2026 Scrivener Publishing LLC

***Keywords*:** Artificial intelligence, machine learning, ensemble learning, Solanaceae crops, data modeling, precision agriculture, Internet of Things (IoT)

7.1 Introduction

The development of new farming techniques is how the agriculture sector, a crucial worldwide industry, is responding to the expanding population's desire for food and jobs [1]. This study shed light on how machine learning ensemble approaches can help agriculture sector stakeholders reduce risks, make better decisions, and successfully negotiate the intricate agricultural markets through this investigation. Market players may adjust to shift circumstances, allocate resources optimally, and eventually enhance their versatility by utilizing the influence of data-driven modeling. These days, precise agriculture is seen as a crucial technological advancement that makes it possible to use agricultural resources more effectively [2]. Increasing harvest or quality yields while lowering input costs is one of the aide's main objectives. Another is to reduce the detrimental impact of farming on the ecosystem, which includes overuse of fertilizers and pesticides and ineffective watering. This is made possible by intelligent sensors, instrumentation, and machinery or ensemble of all that are starting to become increasingly important in agricultural systems. These systems are impacted by a variety of factors, including environmental factors, soil properties, supply of water, harvesting techniques, plant diseases, and invasive plants, as well as other pests. Sophisticated tools for PA will soon be available through the combination of artificial intelligence (AI) algorithms, decision support tools, and ensemble-based machine learning techniques with automated data gathering and analysis. Furthermore, aerial and terrestrial robotic systems will also enhance precision monitoring, support automated data collection, and assist in targeted intervention for improved agricultural management [3]. The 2030 Plan of Action for sustainability, which unites the 17 Sustainable Goals including halting global warming, eliminating poverty, and protecting natural resources, is heavily dependent on agriculture [4]. Even with increased output, the agricultural industry is confronted with fresh difficulties that pose a threat to global human civilization. With the complexity of climate change and population increase, the industry is shifting to data-driven management and automation to grow larger harvests while using fewer resources [5]. Farmers must adopt nature-based, technological, digital, and space-based solutions to optimize water, pesticides, fertilizers, climate, and environmental consequences, requiring the acceptance of core technologies such as machine learning and data-driving techniques [6]. These methods assist farmers in risk reduction, resource management, and improved crop production while maximizing the use of energy and pesticides. Across a wide range of applications, AI and robotics are significantly assisting or replacing human participation in the agriculture sector [7]. Automation's capacity to perform a variety of activities independently, such as weeding, watering, and plant monitoring, is one way that robotics has affected agricultural output and management. In agriculture, drones are used to track crop development, detect weeds, and evaluate the health of crops and systems for irrigation. Collective learning and data-driven approaches are integrated with all of these techniques to achieve accurate prediction.

To satisfy current needs without endangering the capacity of future generations to satisfy their own, sustainable agriculture places a high priority on socially, economically, and environmentally sound techniques. Sustainable agriculture can be approached interestingly by combining data-driven approaches and ensemble learning [8]. By using data on crop health, climate patterns, and soil conditions, farmers may make informed decisions about irrigation, pest management, and resource allocation [9]. This data-driven approach makes it feasible to reduce environmental impact, optimize crop productivity, and practice long-term environmental responsibility. A viable approach to sustainable agriculture is the combination of data-driven techniques with ensemble learning [10].

7.2 Overview of Solanaceae Crops

In the Solanaceae crop, also referred to as the nightshade family, there are more than 4000 members spread throughout 106 taxa. There are many different kinds throughout the world, with the genus *Solanum*, which has more than 2000 species, being the most prominent. The Solanaceae family of plants is one of the largest and most lucrative [11]. One of the main plant families that generate food species is Solanaceae. South America has the highest concentration of this diversity. In addition to its many uses in pharmacology, traditional medicine, decorative gardening, and other fields, Solanaceae species are essential food plants in many parts of the world. For instance, solanaceous food crops were planted on 28 million hectares globally in 2010 alone, yielding about 540 million tons of food [12]. Nevertheless, this is restricted to the basic crop species of potatoes, tomatoes, aubergines, and capsicums. The past few years have seen an increase in population, which has increased demand for both the supply and bearing. The Food and Agriculture Organization (FAO) projects that in 2050 food output needs an increase by 80% to counteract the food shortage. Solanaceae crops are essential to national economies and human nourishment. They go by the name "Nightshade family" alternatively. The Solanaceae family offers a wider range of habitat, morphology, and ecology with 98 genera and 2700 species [13]. There are several different types of regularly grown plants in the family of Solanaceae [14]. The Solanaceae family, which is home to many different plant species that are significant both commercially and nutritionally, is substantially responsible for the world's agricultural output. Because they provide vital vitamins, minerals, and antioxidants, solanaceous crops are critical for human sustenance [15]. Because these plant species are widely cultivated and have a long cultural history, they have become indispensable components of many regional, national, and international culinary traditions. In addition to their nutritional value, crops of the Solanaceae family support millions of farmers globally and are essential to the world's economy [16]. Problems such as the susceptibility to illnesses such as bacterial wilt in tomatoes and late blight in potatoes must be resolved if Solanaceae agriculture is to continue for a long time. According to the FAO 2019 data, harvested areas and production of well-known Solanaceae family crops are represented in Figure 7.1.

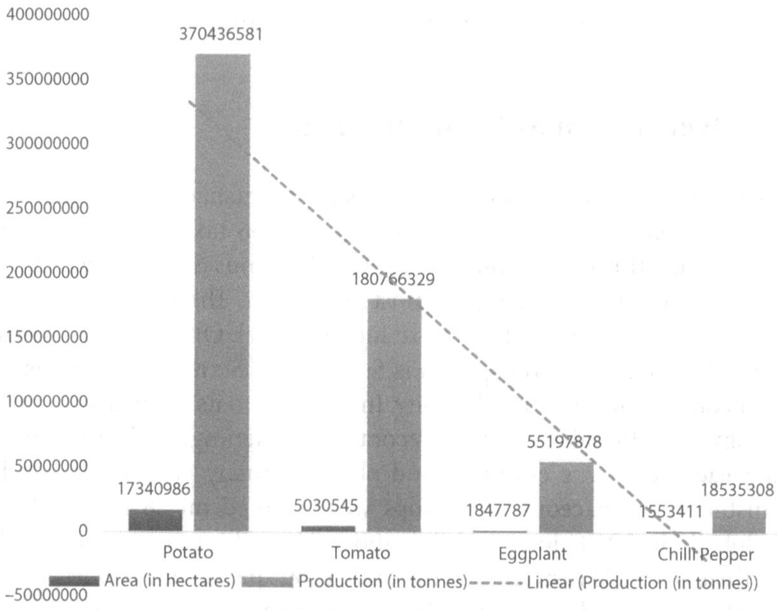

Figure 7.1 Harvested areas and production of popular Solanaceae family crops.

7.3 Data Modeling in Agriculture

To be more precise, data modeling is necessary to make use of vast volumes of agricultural data for optimization and knowledgeable decision-making. In the era of digital transformation, agriculture is positioned at the intersection of data-driven innovation and sustainable development. Data modeling, a key element of modern analytics, has the potential to completely transform some agricultural management processes [17], through examination of data modeling applications in agriculture, focusing on potential benefits for productivity increases, environmental sustainability, and resource allocation optimization. This paper synthesizes recent research, case studies, and technological advancements to investigate different methods, challenges, and possible uses of data modeling in agriculture [18]. Technological developments and crop mapping are revolutionizing traditional farming practices, improving precise water and soil management, and advancing the environmental sustainability of agriculture.

The endeavor investigates different collective learning-based data and modeling techniques for agricultural management, such as supply chain optimization, insect control, crop yield prediction, and resource allocation. The integration of Internet of Things (IoT), AI, and remote sensing technologies to improve sustainability and productivity is also covered [19]. Three main obstacles are interpretability, scalability, and heterogeneity of data. The study suggests the following five thematic groupings for a GIS design for agricultural data models: farm production, agribusiness, facilities, cadastre, and basemap. This strategy makes it easier to comply with rules and create a geographic database for agriculture. Data model is classified into two broad ways as discussed below and shown in Figure 7.2.

More specifically, data modeling is required to leverage the massive volumes of agricultural data for intelligent decision-making and optimization. Agriculture is positioned at the nexus of data-driven innovation and sustainable development in the age of digital transformation. A fundamental component of contemporary analytics, data modeling can alter a

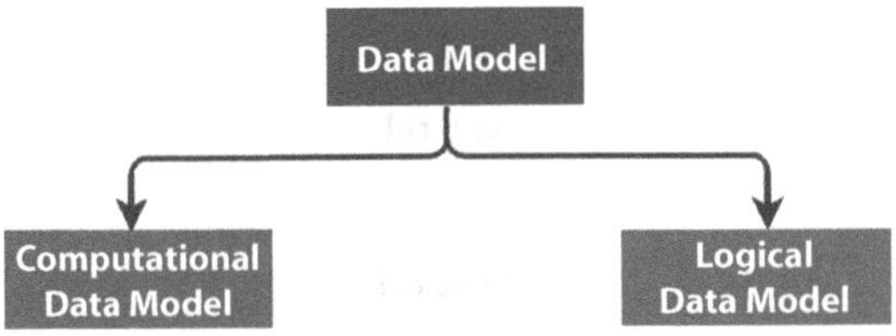

Figure 7.2 Types of data modeling.

variety of agriculture management procedures. The Solanaceae family has a wide variety of crops that are important to agriculture, trade, and nutrition worldwide. The Solanaceae family of crops, which includes potatoes, tomatoes, eggplants, peppers, and eggplants, is crucial for sustaining agricultural economies and providing essential foods. Data modeling offers an agriculturalist an orderly framework for grouping, integrating, and assessing different types of data pertinent to crop management and production [20]. A data model, which shows the relationships between various data units and attributes, provides an effective means of collecting, storing, and utilizing agricultural data. Given the unique development patterns, environmental sensitivity, and management requirements of Solanaceae crops, a specialized data model can offer vital insights and help to producers, academics, and other groups associated with the cultivation of these crops.

7.3.1 Life Cycle of Data Modeling

An organized process called the Data Modeling Lifecycle directs the creation, application, and upkeep of data models inside an entity. To make sure the data model satisfies the farmer's needs and is in line with agricultural goals, it consists of several phases, each with distinct tasks and expectations. Below is a thorough breakdown of the most important stages of the Data Modeling Lifecycle as shown in Figure 7.3.

7.3.1.1 Conceptual Data Model

Conceptual data modeling is most useful, as the name implies, during the conceptual stage when an agriculture platform creates a general plan to iron out the finer points later to improve crop productivity and realize sustainable agriculture [21]. Constructed by data architects and agricultural experts, the conceptual data model documents the interactions between

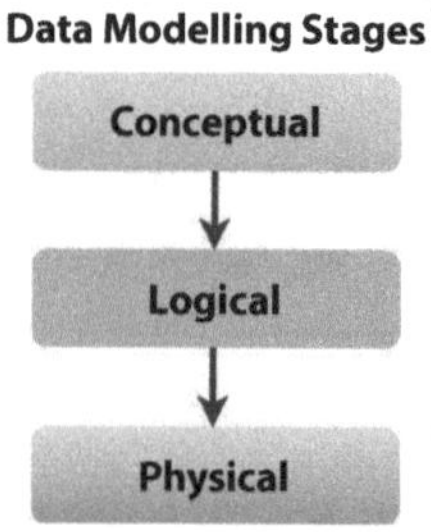

Figure 7.3 Data modeling lifecycle stages.

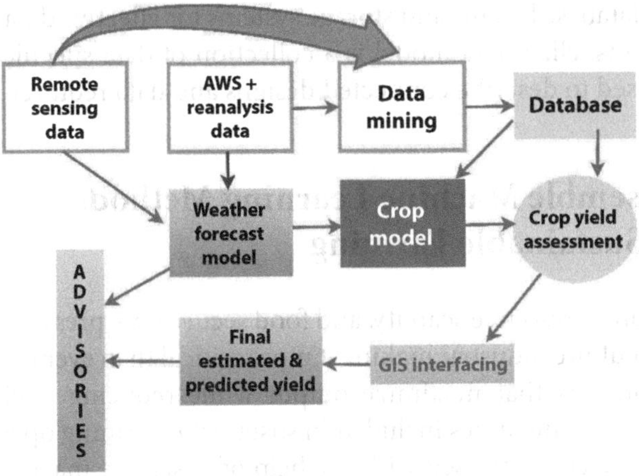

Figure 7.4 Conceptual data model in agriculture.

crop entities, offering a data-centric view of the agriculture industry. It is independent of both technology and application, showcasing the model's current and future states. The color scheme is the most effective way to differentiate between the as-is and to-be states [22]. It is used to clarify and convey high-level conceptual linkages. Conceptual data models are used in data modeling to organize concepts and rules based on use-case requirements. Although less detailed, they are useful for farmers outside the tech bubble [23]. They provide a starting point for developing context-rich diagrams, with complexity peaking with physical data models.

The main benefit of this stage is that, from the perspective of time and resource management, the conceptual-based model can assist the pertinent stakeholders in better understanding what is needed to achieve their intended business result [24]. The basis for complicated data modeling enables analysts to include needs and constraints that are crop database data requirements for a logical data model. Quest's Data Modeler also has a plethora of strong automation features that expedite the procedure, lower the chance of human error, and boost productivity [25]. The diagram of conceptual data modeling in agriculture is shown Figure 7.4.

7.3.1.2 Logical Data Model

In agriculture, logical data modeling increases crop productivity by precisely illustrating the connections between various agricultural processes [26]. Physical data modeling transforms logical models into physical schemas depending on selected database management system (DBMS), designing database layouts and storage systems for effective data extraction [27]. In a nutshell, a data model is a collection of data specifications and diagrams used to describe connected designs and data requirements.

7.4 Ensemble Machine Learning Methods in Sustainable Farming

Climate change, resource scarcity, and food security are pressing issues facing the agriculture industry, making it more critical than ever to implement creative solutions that maximize output while reducing environmental effects [28]. The difficulties included in sustainable farming operations can now be effectively addressed with the help of ensemble machine learning techniques. Ensemble approaches provide reliable and accurate solutions for a variety of agricultural activities, such as predicting crop production, managing pests, evaluating soil health, and optimizing water resources [29]. They do this by combining the predictive strengths of numerous models. By examining current studies and case studies, the study investigates how ensemble methods such as random forests, gradient boosting, etc., solve agricultural issues to improve the accuracy of predictions and decision-making.

Ensemble learning techniques based on the task performed in the agriculture sector including Solanaceae crop are divided into two broad terms such as basic ensemble learning and advanced ensemble learning techniques as shown in Figure 7.5.

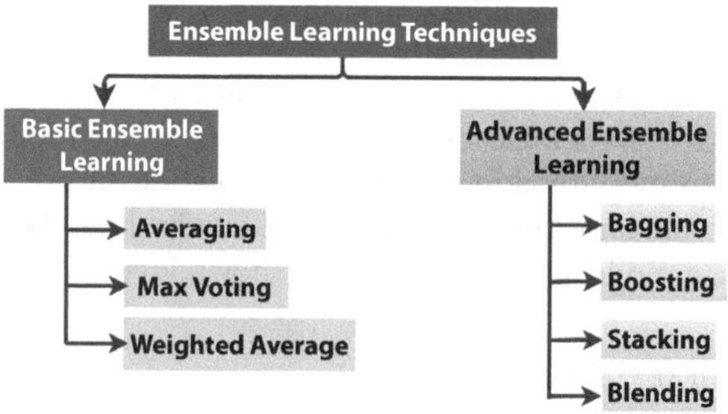

Figure 7.5 Classification of ensemble learning techniques.

7.4.1 Basic Ensemble Learning Techniques

When using ensemble learning methods, different machine learning algorithms are combined to produce weak predictions based on features extracted from a variety of data projections based on Solanaceae crops from disease detection to fruit quality checking. These results are then fused with different voting mechanisms to achieve better performances for the Solanaceae crop than would be possible with any one constituent algorithm working on its own [30]. It can define the basic methods of combining several learners to generate a more powerful and accurate predictive model as the core technique of ensemble learning. These techniques are typically useful as a first step in group learning before moving on to more sophisticated techniques [31]. However, these basic techniques are the best fits for many agricultural tasks; for example, the majority voting technique is an optimum solution for many classification problems because it provides robustness, minimizes overfitting, is compatible with various models, and has many other advantages; thus, before diving into the more sophisticated techniques, one must obtain some practical experience with the elementary ensemble learning methods. In the following sections, look at the technical aspects of elementary ensemble learning methods. The framework of basic ensemble learning techniques is shown in Figure 7.6.

7.4.1.1 Max Voting

Max voting, often used for issues related to classification, represents one of the most basic techniques to combine estimations obtained from various machine learning algorithms [32]. Each base model anticipates and votes

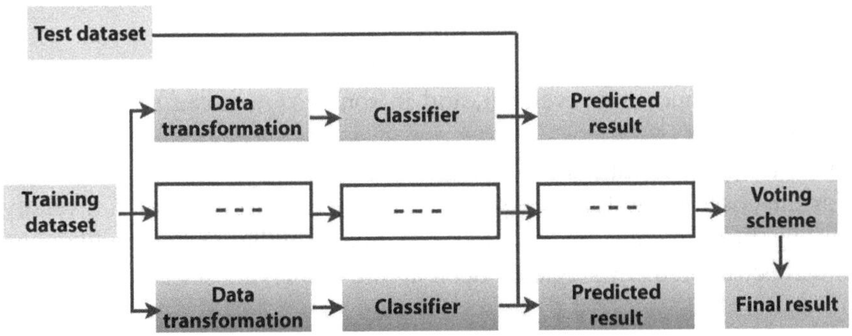

Figure 7.6 Framework of basic ensemble learning techniques.

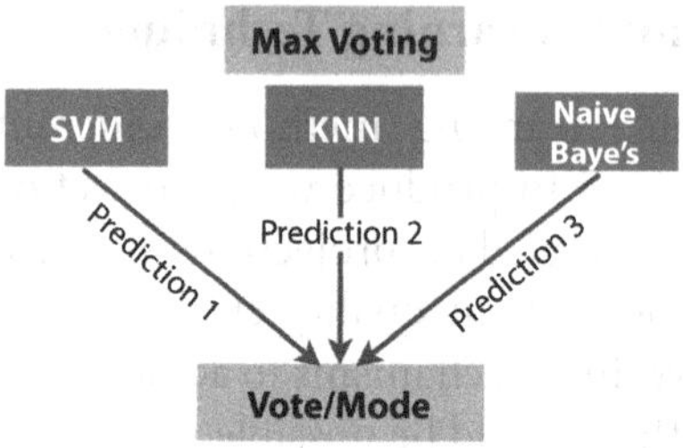

Figure 7.7 Max voting ensemble learning technique.

for each specimen; the sampling class with the highest number of votes becomes the final predictive class as shown in Figure 7.7. To optimize its advantages, the max voting categorization strategy that combines several models to make accurate predictions needs diversity among base models.

7.4.1.1.1 Advantages of Max Voting Techniques

Robustness

Mixing forecasts from several models can reduce the risk of depending too much on a single model that may be inaccurate or overfitted.

Increased accuracy

Because ensembles average out mistakes, they usually attain greater accuracy than individual models.

Simplicity

It is easy to apply and comprehend the maximum voting approach.

7.4.1.1.2 Disadvantages of Max Voting Techniques

Operational cost

It can be costly to train several models and use each one to make predictions.

Diminished results

Adding more models to the ensemble does not always result in a significant performance improvement, and in some cases, it can even have the opposite effect.

Wide range of demands

For the ensemble to function successfully, there must be enough diversity among the individual models. The performance of the ensemble will not be much better than any single model if all the models are similar.

7.4.1.2 *Averaging*

Instead of building a single model, averaging in machine learning refers to the procedure that entails building several models and combining them into one to get the desired output. Individual model errors are averaged out, and an ensemble of models often performs better than any single model [33]. Ensemble averaging is a basic form of parliamentary machine. It belongs to one of the two primary groups of static committee machines, together with boosting. Compared to traditional network layout, which creates many networks but keeps only one, ensemble averaging keeps lesser-satisfactory models but gives them less weight. The theory of ensemble averaging depends on two features of artificial neural networks.

By merging low-bias and high-variance networks into one, ensemble averaging creates a new network that frequently performs better than a single model [34]. Several models can contribute to a forecast in proportion to their perceived performance or level of trust, thanks to weighted average ensembles. Nevertheless, in contrast to chance, this method necessitates expertise from every member of the ensemble. Weighted ensembles enable the model's performance to be used to weigh each member's contribution to the final forecast. Using a holdout validation dataset is a more reliable method, as this one may lead to an overfit model.

7.4.1.3 *Weighted Average*

Not every model makes an equal contribution to the group. Weighted average assembling gives each model a weight according to how well it performs on its own. This guarantees that the final prediction is more influenced by models with higher accuracy. The working of the weighted average ensemble model is represented in Figure 7.8. The fundamental averaging method is expanded upon by weighted averaging [35]. There are other ways to find the weights, including grid search and cross-validation. As in the averaging strategy, train several machine learning models. Based on each model's performance, give it a weight; models that perform better are given greater weights [36]. Using each model, make predictions. Multiply the prediction of each model by the corresponding weight. Compute the weighted forecasts to obtain the ultimate. You can minimize the contributions of poorer models and highlight the predictions of more accurate models by using weighted averaging [37]. This method has some benefits, such as increased precision in comparison to individual models, decreased fluctuation, and overfitting, which enhanced resilience to noise and anomalies.

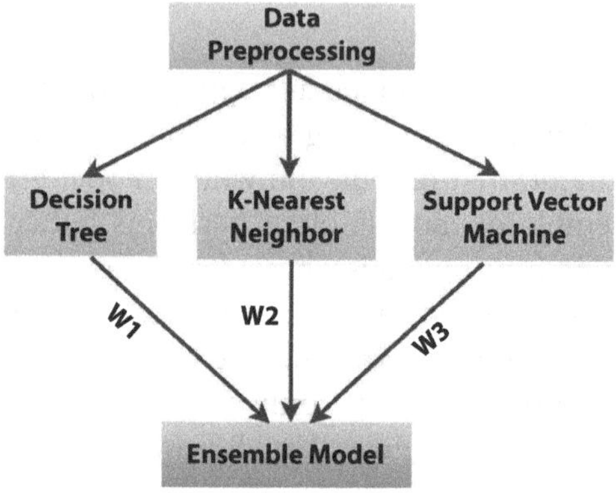

Figure 7.8 Weighted average ensemble model.

7.4.2 Advanced Ensemble Learning Techniques

Advanced ensemble learning approaches apply several models to increase prediction accuracy. The predictions of multiple base models are combined by ensemble methods to create a stronger learner that frequently outperforms any one model alone. The following are some popular sophisticated ensemble learning strategies in machine learning.

7.4.2.1 Stacking

Stacking is an ensemble learning method that enhances performance by combining several models. It essentially teaches a meta-model how to optimally mix the findings of individual initial models by training it on its projections. One technique for grouping multiple categories or predictive models is stacking. Models about the same issue often yield different predictions, highlighting the importance of comparing their assumptions, methodologies, and outcomes to ensure robust and reliable conclusions [38]. The concept behind this approach is that various models that can learn only a portion of the issue space can be used to tackle a learning problem. As a result, you may create a variety of learners and utilize them to create an intermediate prediction for every taught model. Next, a new model is added that trains from the interim judgments and predicts the same objective [39] as represented in Figure 7.9. The name comes from the idea that this last model is stacked on top of all of the others. As a result, you may perform better overall, and frequently you will produce a superior model than all of the intermediary models combined. But take note that, as is frequently the situation when using any machine learning technique,

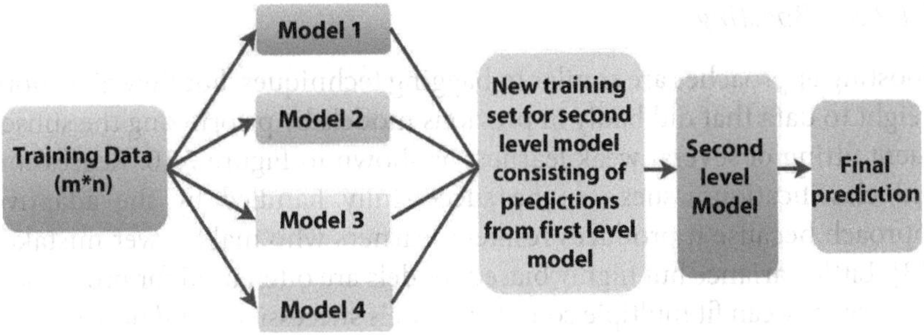

Figure 7.9 Stacking in artificial intelligence–enabled data modeling.

Table 7.1 Merits and demerits of stacking in ensemble learning techniques.

Stacking techniques	
Advantages	**Disadvantages**
Simplicity	Limited access
Efficiency	Potential for overflow
Last in, first out	Not suitable for random access
Limited memory usage	Limited capacity

it does not offer you any assurance. Stacking involves dividing training data into K-folds, fitting a base model to K-1 parts, and fitting the entire train dataset to the basic model [40]. The second-level model uses predictions from the train set to predict the test set. The merits and demerits of stacking in ensemble learning techniques are shown in Table 7.1.

7.4.2.2 Blending

Blending is a tactic that is comparable to stacking with a specific configuration. It is thought of as a stacking method that uses cross-validation for obtaining sample forecasts of the meta-model. Using this strategy, learning models are developed on the sets used for training after the data used for training have been divided into various sets for both training and validation [41]. Estimates are then produced for the dataset and validation set. After that, a new model is built using the validated predictions as features and applied to the test set to produce final predictions using the values for prediction as characteristics [42].

7.4.2.3 Boosting

Boosting approaches are similar to bagging techniques, but they give more weight to data that did badly in previous models by prioritizing the subsequent fitting of several weak learners as shown in Figure 7.10. Regression and classification issues can be successfully handled by the adaptive approach because it produces resilient learners who make fewer mistakes [43]. Little variance but highly biased models are often used for promotion because they can fit multiple complex models successively and have a lower computing cost. This is particularly important when using shallow decision trees as foundation models for concurrent processes, as they might become prohibitively expensive [44]. In conclusion, these meta-algorithms differ in how they produce and aggregate the weak learners throughout the systematic process. Table 7.2 explains the merits and demerits of boosting in ensemble learning techniques. A summary of bagging, boosting, and stacking ensemble learning techniques is described in Table 7.3.

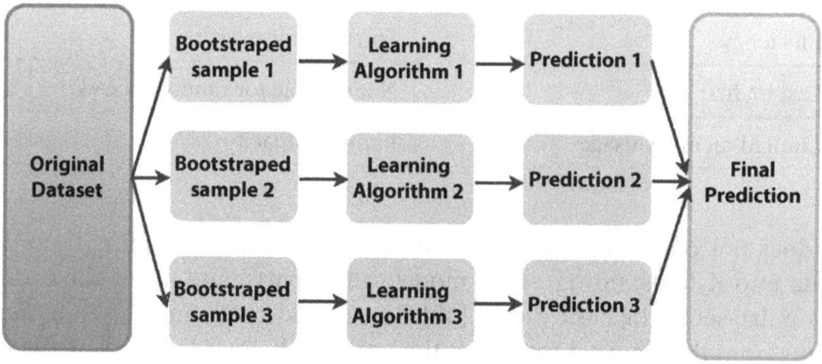

Figure 7.10 Demonstration of bagging and boosting techniques.

Table 7.2 Merits and demerits of boosting in ensemble learning techniques.

Boosting techniques	
Advantages	**Disadvantages**
Reduces bias and variance	An excessive number of inferior models could make them harder to understand
Improves accuracy	High computational cost required
Versatility	Sensitive to outliers leads to overfitting
Handles imbalanced datasets	Less interpretable as compared to linear models

Table 7.3 Summary of bagging, boosting, and stacking ensemble learning techniques.

	Bagging	**Boosting**	**Stacking**
Process	In bagging, multiple base learners are created and trained using substitution on random portions of the training data	Boosting creates several base learners in a progressive fashion. Each learner after that concentrates more on the examples that the earlier learners mislabeled	The dataset is used by base learners to generate predictions, which are then inputted into the meta-learner together with the original features
Base learners	Base learners in bagging are trained independently of each other	The base learners in boosting are typically weak learners	Base learners in stacking can be diverse
Prediction, aggregation	Prognosis	Weighted summing, where each learner's weight depends on their performance	Meta-learner techniques
Purpose	Aims to reduce variance by averaging the predictions	Aims to reduce bias by combining multiple weak learners into a strong learner that can capture complex patterns in the data	Aims to improve predictive performance by leveraging the diverse perspectives of multiple base learners and learning how to best combine their predictions

(Continued)

Table 7.3 Summary of bagging, boosting, and stacking ensemble learning techniques. (*Continued*)

	Bagging	Boosting	Stacking
Example	Random forest	AdaBoost, gradient boosting machines, etc.	Stacking is a flexible technique and can involve various base learners and meta-learners, depending on the problem

7.5 Application of Data Modeling and Ensemble Learning in Solanaceae Crops

The dataset is utilized by base learners to generate predictions, which are then combined with the original features as input by the meta-learner. In agriculture, data modeling and ensemble learning techniques are important because they facilitate decision-making, increase crop yields, and optimize resource allocation. Some of the common applications are discussed in Figure 7.11.

Figure 7.11 Application of data modeling and ensemble learning in agriculture.

7.5.1 Disease Detection and Diagnosis

Diseases in Solanaceae crops are a major economic loss in agriculture. Crop disease detection is a significant agricultural task allowing for rapid response to reduce losses in crops by early disease identification and diagnosis. Novel sensors, biosensors, and remote sensing techniques are being developed to detect early infections, detect infections at asymptomatic stages, and provide instantaneous results [45]. These innovative techniques aim to decrease the usage of costly pesticides for crop protection, hence increasing agricultural sustainability and safety with combined machine learning techniques.

7.5.2 Yield Prediction and Optimization

Predicting crop yields is a significant but challenging issue that is essential for sustainability. Forecasts of crop yields are useful to a wide range of hierarchies. Numerous climatic and biological factors affect crop production; therefore, developing a trustworthy and interpretable prediction model is challenging [46].

Crop production prediction involves various techniques, such as statistical models and field surveys, empowered by data modeling and machine learning techniques [47]. Field surveys aim to understand plant, environment, and management interactions [48]. For the utilization of resources and increase to be sustainable, crop yield prediction is vital. It is difficult to create a trustworthy prediction model because of several crop-specific and environmental parameters.

7.5.3 Supply Chain Optimization

By examining past sales information, buyer demand projections, and freight, data modeling approaches may optimize a supply network for crops. Participants can minimize debris, raise revenue, and boost the quality of goods by streamlining the handling of inventory, transportation routes, and warehouses [49]. In general, the use of data modeling and machine learning in the cultivation of crops can result in more lucrative, effective, and environmentally friendly farming practices that are advantageous to both growers and clients.

7.6 Conclusion and Future Directions

Among the main factors determining the effectiveness of collective learning is the model's ability to reduce prejudice and unpredictability. Many categorization techniques can be combined to lower error without increasing model heterogeneity. Research has indicated that group learning does better than single-model learning in numerous domains. There are numerous ensemble techniques available to enhance classification algorithms. The main difference between any two ensemble procedures is how the initial models are combined and taught. This chapter gives a thorough introduction to ensemble learning methods, which hold great promise for developing sustainable farming practices when paired with sophisticated data modeling methods. By combining the advantages of many models through collaborative learning, academics and industry professionals may conquer the limits of each model and offer more reliable predictions and suggestions. Ensemble techniques also make it easier to integrate data from a variety of sources, including satellite imagery, meteorological data, historical documents, and IoT sensors. This helps to advance our comprehension of agricultural systems as a whole. Hybrid and mapping with ensemble learning have the potential to significantly increase sustainable agriculture; creative approaches for combining these tools with enhanced effectiveness, adaptability, and resilience need to be the focus of future studies.

References

1. Javaid, M., Haleem, A., Khan, I.H., Suman, R., Understanding the potential applications of Artificial Intelligence in the Agriculture Sector. *Adv. Agrochem.*, *2*, 1, 15–30, 2023.
2. Ahmed, K., Dubey, M.K., Dubey, S., Guarding Maize: Vigilance Against Pathogens Early Identification, Detection, and Prevention, in: *Microbial Data Intelligence and Computational Techniques for Sustainable Computing*, pp. 301–318, Springer Nature Singapore, Singapore, 2024.
3. Schuster, E.W., Kumar, S., Sarma, S.E., Willers, J.L., Milliken, G.A., Infrastructure for data-driven agriculture: identifying management zones for cotton using statistical modelling and machine learning techniques, in: *2011 8th International Conference & Expo on Emerging Technologies for a Smarter World*, IEEE, pp. 1–6, 2011, November.
4. Kumar, D., Singh, R.B., Kaur, R., Kumar, D., Singh, R.B., Kaur, R., SDG 2: Case Study–Crop Modelling for Sustaining Agricultural Productivity. *Spatial Inf. Technol. Sustain. Dev. Goals*, 169–197, 2019.

5. Malhi, G.S., Kaur, M., Kaushik, P., Impact of climate change on agriculture and its mitigation strategies: A review. *Sustainability*, *13*, 3, 1318, 2021.
6. Shrestha, S., Effects of climate change in agricultural insect pest. *Acta Sci. Agric.*, *3*, 12, 74–80, 2019.
7. Dash, P.B., Naik, B., Nayak, J., Vimal, S., Socio-economic factor analysis for sustainable and smart precision agriculture: An ensemble learning approach. *Comput. Commun.*, *182*, 72–87, 2022.
8. Abdallah, E.B., Grati, R., Boukadi, K., A machine learning-based approach for smart agriculture *via* stacking-based ensemble learning and feature selection methods, in: *2022 18th International Conference on Intelligent Environments (IE)*, IEEE, pp. 1–8, 2022, June.
9. Kamble, S.S., Gunasekaran, A., Gawankar, S.A., Achieving sustainable performance in a data-driven agriculture supply chain: A review for research and applications. *Int. J. Prod. Econ.*, *219*, 179–194, 2020.
10. Svobodová, B. and Kuban, V., Solanaceae: A family well-known and still surprising. *Phytochemicals Vegetables*, 296–372, 2018.
11. Añibarro-Ortega, M., Pinela, J., Alexopoulos, A., Petropoulos, S.A., Ferreira, I.C., Barros, L., The powerful Solanaceae: Food and nutraceutical applications in a sustainable world, in: *Advances in Food and Nutrition Research*, vol. 100, pp. 131–172, Academic Press, 2022.
12. Hubert, B., Rosegrant, M., Van Boekel, M.A., Ortiz, R., The future of food: scenarios for 2050. *Crop Sci.*, *50*, S–33, 2010.
13. Khafagi, A., El-Ghamery, A., Ghaly, O., Ragab, O., Fruit and seed morphology of some species of Solanaceae. *Taeckholmia*, *38*, 1, 123–140, 2018.
14. Knapp, S., Chiarini, F., Cantero, J.J., Barboza, G.E., The Morelloid clade of Solanum L. (Solanaceae) in Argentina: nomenclatural changes, three new species and an updated key to all taxa. *PhytoKeys*, *164*, 33, 2020.
15. Knapp, S., A revision of the Solanum havanense species group and new taxonomic additions to the Geminata clade (Solanum, Solanaceae). *Ann. Mo. Bot. Gard.*, 405–458, 2008.
16. Altaf, M.A., Behera, B., Mangal, V., Singhal, R.K., Kumar, R., More, S., Lal, M.K., Tolerance and adaptation mechanism of Solanaceous crops under salinity stress. *Funct. Plant Biol.*, *51*, 1, 2022. NULL-NULL.
17. Ahmed, K., Dubey, M.K., Pandey, D.K., Singh, S., Fuzzy and Data Mining Methods for Enhancing Plant Productivity and Sustainability, in: *Microbial Data Intelligence and Computational Techniques for Sustainable Computing*, pp. 205–216, Springer Nature Singapore, Singapore, 2024.
18. Antle, J.M., Basso, B., Conant, R.T., Godfray, H.C.J., Jones, J.W., Herrero, M., Wheeler, T.R., Towards a new generation of agricultural system data, models and knowledge products: Design and improvement. *Agric. Syst.*, *155*, 255–268, 2017.
19. Coble, K.H., Mishra, A.K., Ferrell, S., Griffin, T., Big data in agriculture: A challenge for the future. *Appl. Econ. Perspect. Policy*, *40*, 1, 79–96, 2018.

20. Tyrychtr, J. and Vasilenko, A., Transformation econometric model to multidimensional databases to support the analytical systems in agriculture. *Agris On-line Pap. Econ. Inf.*, 7, 3, 71–7, 2015.
21. Gómez-Sal, A., Belmontes, J.A., Nicolau, J.M., Assessing landscape values: a proposal for a multidimensional conceptual model. *Ecol. Modell.*, *168*, 3, 319–341, 2003.
22. Naseem, M., Alam, M., Ahmad, K., Singh, V., Mahroof, M., Ahamad, G., Machine learning approaches for automatic irrigation system in hilly areas using wireless sensor networks, 2022.
23. Henriyadi, H., Esichaikul, V., Anutariya, C., A Conceptual Model for Development of Small Farm Management Information System: A Case of Indonesian Smallholder Chili Farmers. *Agriculture*, *12*, 6, 866, 2022.
24. Kukar, M., Vračar, P., Košir, D., Pevec, D., Bosnić, Z., AgroDSS: A decision support system for agriculture and farming. *Comput. Electron. Agric.*, *161*, 260–271, 2019.
25. Shahhosseini, M., Hu, G., Archontoulis, S.V., Forecasting corn yield with machine learning ensembles. *Front. Plant Sci.*, 11, 1120, 2020.
26. Rincy, T.N. and Gupta, R., Ensemble learning techniques and its efficiency in machine learning: A survey, in: *2nd international conference on data, engineering and applications (IDEA)*, IEEE, pp. 1–6, 2020, February.
27. Mohammed, A. and Kora, R., A comprehensive review on ensemble deep learning: Opportunities and challenges. *J. King Saud Univ. Comput. Inf. Sci.*, *35*, 2, 757–774, 2023.
28. Escorcia-Gutierrez, J., Gamarra, M., Soto-Diaz, R., Pérez, M., Madera, N., Mansour, R.F., Intelligent agricultural Modelling of soil nutrients and pH classification using ensemble deep learning techniques. *Agriculture*, *12*, 7, 977, 2022.
29. Izmailov, P., Podoprikhin, D., Garipov, T., Vetrov, D., Wilson, A.G., Averaging weights leads to wider optima and better generalization. *arXiv preprint arXiv:1803.05407.*, 2018.
30. Sloczynski, T., *A general weighted average representation of the ordinary and two-stage least squares estimands* (No. 11866). IZA Discussion Papers, 2018.
31. S., AM, Joe, IR, P. R. A. V. E. E. N, Venkatraman, S., & Kumar S, P., Improved tomato leaf disease classification through adaptive ensemble models with exponential moving average fusion and enhanced weighted gradient optimization. *Front. Plant Sci.*, 15, 1382416, 2024.
32. Sharif, M., Khan, M.A., Iqbal, Z., Azam, M.F., Lali, M., II, Javed, M.Y., Detection and classification of citrus diseases in agriculture based on optimized weighted segmentation and feature selection. *Comput. Electron. Agric.*, *150*, 220–234, 2018.
33. Chen, J., Zeb, A., Nanehkaran, Y.A., Zhang, D., Stacking ensemble model of deep learning for plant disease recognition. *J. Ambient Intell. Hum. Comput.*, *14*, 9, 12359–12372, 2023.

34. Elizabeth, C.P. and Baulkani, S., Color Space Blending With Deep Learning Networks In The Identification Of Plant Leaves. *Plant Arch.*, *22*, 2, 09725210, 2022.
35. Mockshell, J. and Kamanda, J., Beyond the agroecological and sustainable agricultural intensification debate: Is blended sustainability the way forward? *Int. J. Agric. Sustain.*, *16*, 2, 127–149, 2018.
36. Naseem, M., Singh, V., Ahmed, K., Mahroof, M., Ahamad, G., Abbasi, E., Architecture of automatic irrigation system in hilly area using wireless sensor network: a review, in: *2022 2nd International Conference on Emerging Frontiers in Electrical and Electronic Technologies (ICEFEET)*, IEEE, pp. 1–6, 2022, June.
37. GT, P.K. and Sabeena, J., Agriculture soil classification and fertilizer recommendation using adaboost and bagging approaches, in: *2018 IADS International Conference on Computing, Communications & Data Engineering (CCODE)*, pp. 7–8, 2018, February.
38. Ribeiro, M.H.D.M. and dos Santos Coelho, L., Ensemble approach based on bagging, boosting and stacking for short-term prediction in agribusiness time series. *Appl. Soft Comput.*, *86*, 105837, 2020.
39. Ruß, G. and Brenning, A., Data mining in precision agriculture: management of spatial information, in: *Computational Intelligence for Knowledge-Based Systems Design: 13th International Conference on Information Processing and Management of Uncertainty, IPMU 2010, Dortmund, Germany, June 28-July 2, 2010*, vol. *Proceedings 13*, Springer Berlin Heidelberg, pp. 350–359, 2010.
40. Nagesh, O.S., Budaraju, R.R., Kulkarni, S.S., Vinay, M., Ajibade, S.S.M., Chopra, M., Kaliyaperumal, K., Boosting enabled efficient machine learning technique for accurate prediction of crop yield towards precision agriculture. *Disc. Sustain.*, *5*, 1, 78, 2024.
41. Silva, V.C., Rocha, M.S., Faria, G.A., Xavier Junior, S.F.A., de Oliveira, T.A., Peixoto, A.P.B., Boosting algorithms for prediction in agriculture: an application of feature importance and feature selection boosting algorithms for prediction crop damage. *agriRxiv*, 2021, 20210437677, 2021.
42. Mahlein, A.K., Plant disease detection by imaging sensors–parallels and specific demands for precision agriculture and plant phenotyping. *Plant Dis.*, *100*, 2, 241–251, 2016.
43. Haq, Z.U., Ullah, H., Khan, M.N.A., Naqvi, S.R., Ahad, A., Amin, N.A.S., Comparative study of machine learning methods integrated with genetic algorithm and particle swarm optimization for bio-char yield prediction. *Bioresour. Technol.*, *363*, 128008, 2022.
44. Ngige, G.A., Ovuoraye, P.E., Igwegbe, C.A., Fetahi, E., Okeke, J.A., Yakubu, A.D., Onyechi, P.C., RSM optimization and yield prediction for biodiesel produced from alkali-catalytic transesterification of pawpaw seed extract: Thermodynamics, kinetics, and Multiple Linear Regression analysis. *Digit. Chem. Eng.*, *6*, 100066, 2023.

45. Drinkwater, L.E., Schipanski, M., Snapp, S., Jackson, L.E., Ecologically based nutrient management. *Agric. Syst.*, 203–257, 2017.
46. Thudi, M., Palakurthi, R., Schnable, J.C., Chitikineni, A., Dreisigacker, S., Mace, E., Varshney, R.K., Genomic resources in plant breeding for sustainable agriculture. *J. Plant Physiol.*, *257*, 153351, 2021.
47. Ge, H., Gray, R., Nolan, J., Agricultural supply chain optimization and complexity: A comparison of analytic vs simulated solutions and policies. *Int. J. Prod. Econ.*, *159*, 208–220, 2015.
48. Van Klompenburg, T., Kassahun, A., Catal, C., Crop yield prediction using machine learning: A systematic literature review. *Comput. Electron. Agric.*, 177, 105709, 2020.
49. Dahikar, S.S. and Rode, S.V., Agricultural crop yield prediction using artificial neural network approach. *Int. J. Innov. Res. Electrical Electronics Instrum. Control Eng.*, 2, 1, 683–686, 2014.

8

Dynamic Multitask Transfer Learning with Adaptive Feature Sharing for Heterogeneous Data and Continual Learning

Toufique Ahammad Gazi

Department of Computer Science & Engineering, School of Engineering & Technology, Adamas University, Kolkata, West Bengal, India

Abstract

Investigations have revealed that attention processes can be modulated and adapted for different goals or operations. The model's flexibility enables it to learn multiple representations for each task and may possibly resume data with them. Further, the relative weights of corresponding factors may also be made changeable. The suggested model has the characteristic of meta-learning methodologies where it will have the potential to learn across new and emerging policy problems within the same domain effectively. KD stands for knowledge distillation, which acts as a transfer of information from a large model to a small one, which is really good for continual learning, whereas on the other hand, ensemble learning takes many models and joins them to work better performing while reducing on catastrophic forgetting. The model's usage of data from different activities to generate predictions is analyzed using two techniques: relevance analysis techniques, such as layer-wise relevance propagation, and attention visualization. It is necessary to learn model compression techniques such as quantization and pruning in order to lessen the amount of processing needed but not the rate. Thus, this approach facilitates the model's ability to learn from different types of inputs and build on previously gained knowledge while incorporating new tasks. All such fields including sentiment analysis, medical diagnostics for auto and half auto mode, robotics, and many other fields with different types of data and need for continuous learning can be applied with the proposed methodology. The capability of multitask

Email: tag.bismillah@gmail.com

Arindam Mondal and Souvik Ganguli (eds.) Data-Driven Modeling, (187–202) © 2026 Scrivener Publishing LLC

transfer learning has demonstrated using information across related activities. Nonetheless, current methods often struggle with schema, or the employment of different types of data, or data kinds, and continual learning or the capability to learn new tasks while maintaining existing ones. Hence, to counter these problems, a new multitask transfer learning method with dynamic feature sharing is proposed in this study.

Keywords: Attention visualization, transfer learning, dynamic feature sharing, meta-learning, knowledge distillation, continual learning

Introduction

Machine learning has massive limitations, especially where deep learning models are crucial, which require huge amounts of data to be labeled and trained. We can note that manual data classification is very time consuming, for example, in the medical picture analysis. On this regard, multitask transfer learning (MTTL) makes use of information from other related tasks so that it overcomes this obstacle. Based on the supposed similarity in the fundamental aspects of the tasks that comprise MTTL, the framework trains a single model based on several of them. This strategy is said to have latter shown to boost the performance on each of the tasks as opposed to training individual models. As earlier seen, depending on the type of task that is being addressed, MTTL incorporates various contexts such as supervised learning (label prediction), unsupervised learning (pattern recognition), and reinforcement learning (changing behavior to get the most rewards). It can be likened to how humans learn, where information obtained at one task can be used in another—just such as how one learns squash and tennis. Accompanying the acronym MTL are related notions that are different from MTL and include multilabel learning—training on many labels for the same instance, and transfer learning—when one task is used to solve another. In MTL, several tasks contribute to the improvement

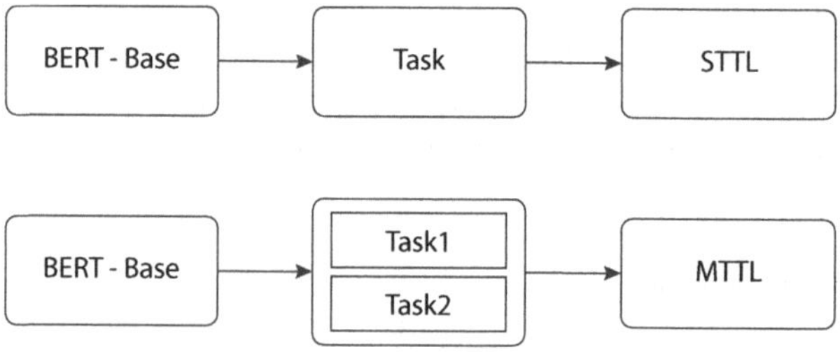

Figure 8.1 Single and multitask model.

of the others' performance. The following paper offers an extensive analysis of MTL by describing and discussing the theory, domains of utilization, types of models, and different scenarios.

Continual learning (CL), one of the uncommon paradigms in machine learning, aims at handling data streams where there is no natural access to prior data, which is a challenge of most classification paradigms. Compared to traditional machine learning, CL trains the models incrementally over the mini-batches of data potentially up to one data sample at a time. Because each batch is used only once, it looks such as a stream of data, and it is unclear what data will be used next. This step removes the conventional training (Figure 8.1), validation, and test set split used in most of the machine learning pipelines. Such pipelines' objective is to achieve the best performance on the entire dataset through the validity and testing sets. But CL is not content with optimizing for the current data; it also tries to optimize for not forgetting past data.

In general, the weaknesses of classic machine learning methods are as follows: the prior knowledge about the data is needed; it is hard to select suitable model functions; there are problems related to the management of complex machinery; and the noisy data can also pose problems. Traditionally, conventional MTTL performs all operations through the implementation of the shared layers of the network. However, negative transfer may be observed to occur from this tactic if the tasks are not well matched properly. One way would be to transmit only lower levels of features of general attributes and having branches for a higher level of particulars of the tasks. Therefore, manual specification of such designs is not feasible because the number of possible designs that is conceivable is immense. The solution to this chapter lies in the automatically determination of the branching architecture as well as the selective sharing.

Dynamic feature sharing: It has methods such as the attention mechanisms that dynamically alter the proportions of features presented to different jobs. This means that a specific form of learning associated with a particular task can still go on alongside a second form of learning that consists of the transfer of information from one activity to another.

Meta-learning for faster adaptation: It is possible that the model would acquire knowledge at a highly competent rate on new, unseen tasks within the same domain through the use of meta-learning techniques.

Deep learning's attention mechanism: Thus, by focusing on elements of the input sequence and affecting the model's output through computational attention, deep learning contributes positively to the field of machine translation. This increases the score for particular segments of inputs that are far more significant than others, thus improving a model's recall ability in responding to queries just such as our brains have selective hearing. The picture recognition, the machine translation, and the question answering that are the sub-branches of natural language processing (NLP) tasks make use of attention mechanisms. Due to their capacity to direct consideration only on relevant information, they are an effective means for boosting the result of deep learning models.

The chapter comprises literature evaluation and review, research method, assessment and analysis of the model, and the last and conclusion part. Also explained is how learning continuity contributes to the concept.

Literature overview

MTTL is one of the most recognized machine learning strategies that has the focus of enhancing learning effectiveness and the resultant generalization capability. It makes it easier for models to utilize the same data for numerous operations in C#. In general, the previous MTTL designs used both the soft and the hard approach of parameter sharing to accomplish this. In hard parameter sharing, the hidden layers of the models are shared across tasks, whereas in soft parameter sharing, the models are constructed for individual tasks but are given a prior that is shared with other related tasks. These techniques demonstrated good performance in various fields including natural language processing, computer vision, and speech recognition [1, 2, 10, 16, 17].

Nevertheless, it is essential to note that conventional MTTL methods noted here have some disadvantages as well. The source also has a weak point that each task is assumed to have a constant input. This is usually far from the truth in the real world where data are often characterized by high variability, for example, in one of many-task learning where the subtasks are text summarization, and picture classification, and then the input modalities are contrasting, that is, text and photographs. Circumstances for which standard MTTL techniques are not very applicable are that MTTL cannot sufficiently manage such a large number of different inputs in complex, realistic situations [3, 5, 6, 18].

The other drawback of classic MTTL approaches is that they are not suitable for the conditions of continuous learning. In continuous learning, models are trained in a process of tasks, where at the same time there is learning of new tasks, there is need to retain knowledge of past tasks that were conducted. However, in most cases, those general MTTL methods operate under catastrophic forgetting, or in other words, learning of new tasks leads to a dramatic decrease in performance of previously learned ones. This is especially the case for those applications that call for model refresh at some time due to changes in conditions or preferences of users [7–9, 19].

Difference in the style of the input and the output speech and poor accommodation of multiple input modalities and continuous learning are some of the limitations of MTTL models that have been developed in the past years. Multimodal learning is arguably one of the viable approaches that seek to combine data from various input modalities with a view of enhancing the performance of a task. For example, in visual question and answering, instead of feeding the model with only the question's text, the multimodal MTTL model can use the question's text and the picture that is linked to the question to give more correct answers. These models are capable of handling the cross-modal relationship and the input heterogeneity because they fuse the data from multiple modalities. In Figure 8.2, there is a comparison between the traditional approach and transfer learning.

Moreover, the following progression in MTTL is essential: the use of attention processes. Attention helps models to decide where to look or attend to, during the information processing, which is important especially when it comes to information selection for a particular task. This is especially handy in MTTL scenarios because one activity may need a different type of data from the others stored in the common representations. Thus, by following the concept of attention, MTTL models can optimally adjust their capacity to focus on the relevant features on which their tasks depend, and hence, they perform better and more comprehensively [11–13].

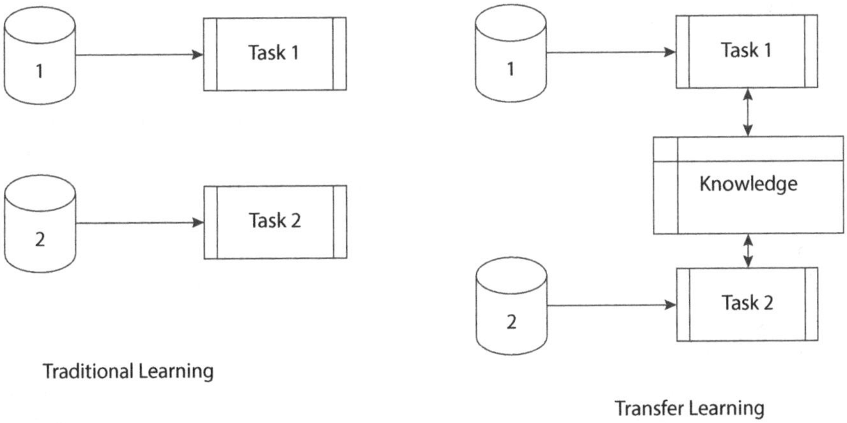

Figure 8.2 Different learning process.

Self-supervised learning approach: In order to enable continuous learning, which is considered as the key to the success of MTTL research, there are several typical solutions such as knowledge distillation and ensemble learning. For improving the robustness and, consequently, preventing catastrophic forgetting, ensemble learning implies the prediction of several models trained in parallel. The system as a whole is capable to learn new tasks and, at the same time, remain sensitive to the material from previous lessons due to the presence of a variety of models with different focuses. On the other hand, knowledge distillation looks more into the aspect of transferring knowledge from complex models to simple ones. Therefore, the knowledge stored in a substantial MTTL model is distilled to a compressed model, which can benefit from the representations that the larger model has acquired [4, 12–14, 20].

This is because as MTTL models are used in critical areas and becoming complex, there is a need for explain ability and interpretability. The objective of explainable artificial intelligence (XAI) techniques is to enable consumers to understand how the model makes its prediction of MTTL to warrant trust and credibility. Out of these techniques, layer-wise relevance propagation (LRP) has been used with MTTL models. Compared to the other models, LRP provides a deeper understanding of how the model uses data from multiple tasks and domains by identifying what contribution each characteristic of the input data makes to the model's prediction. Another useful technique for deciphering MTTL models is attention visualization, which shows the areas of the input that the model concentrates on for each job [15, 16].

Methodology

MTTL framework

As discussed above, the proposed dynamic MTTL with adaptive feature sharing has many detailed key components. First, multimodal learning module is utilized to ensure that all the data sources, including the texts and the visuals, are in one form, so that the input of the MTTL model is in order. Second, the model may transmit relevant characteristics in a task-specific manner by using adaptive feature sharing; this proceeds with the aid of attention processes. This makes it possible for the model to selectively attend to features pertinent to the task at hand and other features that are inseparable. To deal with the CL problem of catastrophic forgetting and promote CL, the given framework adopts CL strategies including ensemble learning. There are multiple models trained in parallel in ensemble learning, and their success rates are combined to enhance robustness.

This also includes using knowledge distillation, which transfers common knowledge to make complicated models of MTTL and enable effective continuous learning. The methods used under explain ability and interpretability are the LRP and the attention visualization. Some of them help to explain how the MTTL model fuses information from many tasks and modalities with the supporting results, increasing openness and confidence in the model's decision-making. That is why the following elements ensure the basic structure of the proposed framework for dynamic MTTL with adaptive feature sharing. Adaptive feature sharing selectively attends to the task-related information and utilizes mappings to enhance performance and generalize across tasks. Cross-modal interactions are enabled by a multimodal learning module; many input modalities are dealt with by aligning and merging data such as text and pictures.

Task connection: This comes in light with how successful the implementation of MTTL is depending on the degree of relationship that is believed to exist in the tasks. Understanding the relatedness of instances is going to be used later when constructing the so-called MTTL models.

Dictionary of tasks: Classification, regression, clustering, semisupervised, active learning, reinforcement learning, online learning, and multiview dealing are some of the several types of tasks in machine learning. The MTTL setting depends on activities to be performed at a given time and will be explained comprehensively in the following sections. In the case of the supervised learning tasks, there is a dataset containing corresponding labels and input features as vectors. Homogenous feature—when all the tasks lie in the same feature space or have the same number of features, then the state is called MTL. That is all that is left: heterogeneous-feature MTL. "Heterogeneous MTL" is broader at the same time; it is applicable to tasks of various types (classification, regression, etc.), whereas "homogeneous MTL" means the tasks of the same type. Subsequently, MTL makes use of the homogeneity of tasks and features by default.

Neural networks in deep learning take in information through the channels that comprised interconnected nodes, which can hinder the search of meaningful data the deeper they go. Attention mechanisms ease this by making it possible for the model to concentrate on some aspects of the input. Think about machine translation. In a typical seq2seq setting, an encoder and a decoder would struggle. The encoder reduces the length of the original sentential input into a unique context vector that the decoder utilizes to posit the complete translation. Thus, attention helps enhance this decoder's ability to generate each word in the target language while focusing the attention on specific parts of the input phrase (through attention weights).

Knowledge about the sequence-to-sequence data and how the models of that type work is essential to the understanding of attention. The concept of attention was first used when a model that comprised an encoder–decoder architecture together with an additive attention was published. Now let us consider the case of machine translation where x is the source sentence of length n, and y as the target sequence of length m. In a bidirectional sequence paradigm, there would be two hidden states: forward and backward—to the beginning of Adriana's life. As a result, in order for preceding or subsequent words to influence attention, researchers express the encoder state as simply the concatenation of such states. The decoder hidden state is represented by "st," which depends on a context vector "ct," the previous target element and the previous state of the decoder. This context vector is equal to alignment scores to each of hidden states of the input sequence ("hi"). Thus, the alignment score is another feed-forward neural network, which was trained on the rest of the model data. The relevance score for each input–output pair is calculated in this network. Subsequently, another set of probabilities of which the values are relative weights of each of the source hidden state and each of the output state is computed through SoftMax. The implication of this is that the model may attend to some of the parts of the input sequence that are very relevant to the output that is being generated at that particular time courtesy of the attention mechanism. For a better understanding, the same model has been depicted in Figure 8.3, known as scaled dot-product attention.

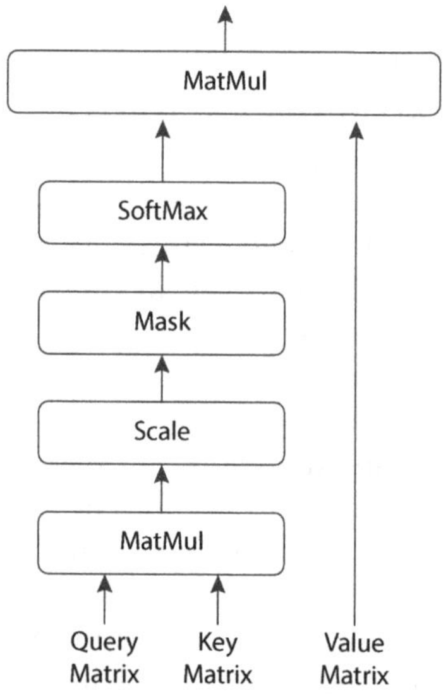

Figure 8.3 Basic attention model.

Experimental setup

To assess the system, a variety of datasets with different input types shall be ingested, and thus, the iterative learning will be performed. Others are VQA that is a combined modality job that involves questions and graphics that is a lifelong language learning task that involves the model learning from a sequence of language problems. We will make the comparison with single-task learning, other state-of-the-art CL approaches, and conventional MTTL methods. Output measures for performance will consist of objective measures tied to the activities for at least 30 consecutive days, including forgetting rate and mean accuracy for learner's continuous learning tasks, and task-specific measures containing accuracy for classification tasks, and BLEU (Bilingual Evaluation Understudy) score for learners' language production tasks.

Training and optimization

Due to this, the MTTL model is learned synchronously on multiple tasks with the mutual goal of perfecting performance on a given task as well as allowing for flexibly sharing relevant features. As for the lifelong learning where tasks are presented one at a time in a continuous manner, both the methods for ensemble learning and knowledge distillation will be applied to reduce forgetting and enhance successful learning. To avoid overfitting a model and to ensure that the features adapt well, the gradient-based optimization technologies will be adopted in improving the model together with the regularization techniques. Thus, the integration of the mentioned methodological elements in the proposed framework is for ensuring the dynamic and effective MTTL with explainable and interpretable predictions in the given heterogeneous and continuously learning scenarios.

A novel feature sharing framework is the driving force behind the presented recommendation at its core; there is a dynamic feature sharing system designed to support the transfer of knowledge with a focus on the specific task at hand. This technique uses gating networks and task-specific attention. The task-specific attention allows varying the contribution of the corresponding aspects for the particular task based on the analysis of the common feature representation. This can be thought of as rotating spotlights to shine or highlight important areas of a shared feature map for every activity. The type of continuous learning that exists is referred to as layer-wise relevance. Layer-wise relevance is a type of continuous learning that employs several key techniques, including CL-knowledge distillation, which transfers knowledge from more complex models to simpler models, ensemble learning, which strengthens methods and allows them to retain information from previous tasks, and decision justification through propagation and attention visualization. By incorporating all of these components, the framework should facilitate the MTTL that must be dynamic and efficient, learn from multiple data sources of disparate varieties, operate in the conditions of the continuing learning, and produce the results that are easily explainable and comprehensible by the end-users. Subsequently, gating networks act as filters and operate to allow access only to the common area and dealing with the issues of the flow of information to the modules that are exclusive to a particular activity. Thus, the negative transfer from irrelevant characteristics is avoided, and beneficial elements for one job or another can be exchanged selectively. The specific interaction of attention and gating is in this model as a part of a common feature space where transfer of information is learned and can happen with subsequent specialization for various tasks.

The attention mechanisms and gating networks change the contribution of the features in a way that is specific to the particular task and focuses on them. According to the papers cited, attention processes allow models to look at some of the specific components related to reconsidering problems by engaging in attention-based reasoning tasks. The given techniques result in neural networks' ability to concentrate on the necessary segments of a sequence, which, in turn, contributes to the improvement of neural network functioning due to the increase in the model's ability to manage and understand complicated input. Gating networks, in contrast, regulate the

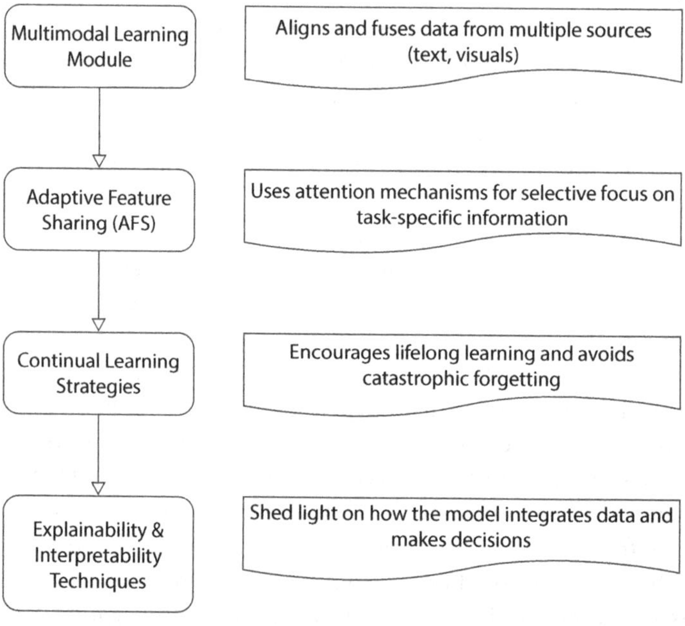

Figure 8.4 Phases of proposed model.

Table 8.1 Proposed model description.

Component	Description	Purpose
1. Multimodal learning module	Combines and aligns data from several sources (text, images)	Allows for the management of various input modalities
2. Adaptive feature sharing (AFS)	Selectively focuses on information relevant to a task using attention processes	Enhances generalization and performance via shared representations
2.1. Attention processes	Examine similar feature representation	Adapts characteristics dynamically to each activity, preventing negative transfer and fostering the transmission of just certain knowledge
2.2. Gating networks	Manage the flow of information between modules that are task-specific and shared.	Sustains performance over successive tasks
3. Continual learning strategies	Prevents catastrophic forgetting and promotes lifelong learning	Increases resilience and retention of information
3.1. Ensemble learning	Trains many models at once and compiles predictions	Effectively supports ongoing education
3.2. Knowledge distillation	Converts information from sophisticated models to simpler ones	Builds transparency and confidence in model judgments
4. Explain ability and interpretability techniques	Provide insight on the model's decision-making and data integration processes	Explains the process of model reasoning
4.1. Layer-wise relevance propagation (LRP)	Finds characteristics that are relevant to task performance	Provide information on how the model handles particular data items
4.2. Attention visualization	Shows the attention processes' focal point	Provides insights into how the model attends to specific data points

circulation of information within a model with the help of decision-making about which parts of it should be saved in memory or, vice versa, chosen for a particular task. As discussed, they are responsible for managing gating of strategies of input and output, thus ensuring that feature contribution is controlled in a way that lends only the appropriate and relevant input information to the specifics of the particular task the model is executing. This dynamic alteration of feature contribution is achieved by gating networks and task-specific attention processes, which in turn enhance the model's viability and accuracy across various systems and tasks. The flowchart in Figure 8.4 shows the proposed model flow to realize the objective of the chapter. Table 8.1 provides an explanation of Figure 8.4 expansion as follows:

Model analysis and interpretation

However, many of the subcomponents of the MTTL framework are entirely innovative, such as its modern take on multitask learning. MTTL is flexible compared with normal MTTL that is designed with a single appearance for all activities. High levels of transformer models are allowed, and there is also the opportunity to involve certain sections such as CNNs (convolutional neural networks) and RNNs (recurrent neural networks). Due to the flexibility, MTTL can perform a set of tasks from low-skilled to the knowledge-intensive tasks adequately.

The main strength of MTTL's design is the ability to effectively share more significant features. The model gathers numerous general characteristics and then, during the decoding, applies attention mechanisms to change the importance of these features for each particular job. Each activity involves imagining that there is a spotlight on the areas relevant to the current activity on the map jointly developed by all the learners. This lets MTTL focus on a job-specific knowledge while using general knowledge at the same time. Moreover, visualization is used to update and selectively erase undesired memories in the MTTL so that catastrophic forgetting in lifelong learning is avoided; besides, meta-learning is incorporated into the MTTL for efficient task acquisition. MTTL presents an attractive solution in the approach to the integration of the aforementioned components with optimized training techniques for multitask learning, especially when there is complex and/or heterogeneous data and/or continuous learning. Table 8.2 shows a comparative analysis of the transfer learning models.

Future directions

Adaptive characteristic in dynamic multitask transfer learning sharing for CL and heterogeneous data: Transfer learning procedures are used

Table 8.2 A comparative analysis of several methods for MTTL and DMTTL.

Component	Proposed approach—potential baseline 3 (DMTTL)	Potential baseline 1 (standard MTTL)	Potential baseline 2 (single task learning)
Model architecture	Transformer-based (such as ViT, BERT) or submodules tailored to a particular job (CNN, RNN)	All tasks have a common architecture (e.g., CNN, RNN)	Distinct models (e.g., CNN for pictures, RNN for text) for every job
Dynamic feature sharing	Common encoder for extracting general features and particular focus on tasks for dynamic weighting	All tasks sharing of static features	Not sharing features with other tasks
Meta-learning	Pretraining on relevant tasks using Model-Agnostic Meta-Learning (MAML) to facilitate quicker adaption	No particular approach; every new task requires retraining the model across all tasks	No set plan; every task requires a different model that is trained from start
Continual learning strategies	Knowledge distillation from bigger models and ensemble approaches to enhance performance	Depends on starting every new activity with zero knowledge	Depends on picking up new skills from start for every activity
Training and optimization	Loss function for many tasks including regularization methods	Loss function specific to a single activity and regularization strategies	Every task's own loss function as well as regularization strategies

in situations where data are expensive, limited, or irregular. In this way, models might remain accurate and useful even if conditions that preceded the model's construction have changed. Of the important strategies, group learning refers to an approach that recognizes the value of learning in groups, whereas active learning is a concept that embraces learning practices that stimulates students' interest. Precisely, transfer learning enables information to be transitioned from one task or context to another with the use of previously learned information and does not allow overtraining or undertraining. It is therefore observed that models perform well in the framework of heterogeneous transfer learning with nonoverlapping domain feature spaces of the source and destination. This technique is essential for applications such as a photo identification, the use of the natural language processing, and the recommender systems. To improve them in dynamic and diverse data situations in the future, the adjustments of the features spaces, the selection of the source and the destination domains, and the variations of the parameters of the models could be proposed.

Conclusion

It is therefore recommended that this chapter presents a paradigm that embraces all the required models in the enhancement of learning results. The identified sources state that the objectives of dynamic MTTL in the future, taking into account adaptive feature sharing for heterogeneous data, and continuous learning are to improve the efficiency and dynamism of models in changing and diverse data conditions. Such candidates include the use of feature space projection, adjusting the model's parameters, and optimizing the setting of the SSP and the DDP to enhance its performance. Furthermore, combining ideas such as progressive meta-task schedulers, dynamic distribution adaptation, and meta-learning frameworks might even push the field further by approaching concerns with sudden changes in distribution or the target mission. As seen in multitask learning contexts with related and unrelated data, these approaches intended to enhance learning of many tasks and domains while at the same time achieving reliable and competent sharing of knowledge and features.

References

1. Pan, S.J. and Yang, Q., A survey on transfer learning. *IEEE Trans. Knowl. Data Eng.*, 22, 10, 1345–1359, 2010.

2. Hernández-Lobato, J.M. and Hernández-Lobato, D., Learning feature selection dependencies in multi-task learning, in: *Advances in Neural Information Processing Systems*, vol. 26, pp. 746–754, 2013.
3. Ahmed, A., Das, A., Smola, A.J., Scalable hierarchical multitask learning algorithms for conversion optimization in display advertising, in: *In Proceedings of the 7th ACM International Conference on Web Search and Data Mining*, Association for Computing Machinery, pp. 153–162, 2014, March.
4. Zhang, X., Convex discriminative multitask clustering. *IEEE Trans. Pattern Anal. Mach. Intell.*, 37, 7, 1513–1528, 2015.
5. Wan, J., Zhang, Z., Yan, J., *et al.*, Sparse Bayesian multi-task learning for predicting cognitive outcomes from neuroimaging measures in Alzheimer's disease, in: *Proceedings of the IEEE Conference on Computer Vision and Pattern Recognition*, Institute of Electrical and Electronics Engineers, pp. 940–947, 2012, June.
6. Zheng, V.W., Pan, S.J., Yang, Q., Pan, J.J., Transferring multidevice localization models using latent multi-task learning, in: *AAAI*, vol. 8, pp. 1450–1455, 2008, July.
7. Liu, A., Su, Y., Nie, W., Kankanhalli, M.S., Hierarchical clustering multitask learning for joint human action grouping and recognition. *IEEE Trans. Pattern Anal. Mach. Intell.*, 39, 1, 140–154, 2017.
8. Puniyani, K., Kim, S., Xing, E.P., Multi-population GWA mapping via multitask regularized regression. *Bioinformatics*, 26, 17, i386–i392, 2010.
9. An, Q., Wang, C., Shterev, I., Wang, E., Carin, L., Dunson, D.B., Hierarchical kernel stick-breaking process for multi-task image analysis, in: *Proceedings of the 21st International Conference on Machine Learning (ICML 2008)*, pp. 16–23, 2008, July.
10. Alamgir, M., Grosse-Wentrup, M., Altun, Y., Multitask learning for brain-computer interfaces, in: *Proceedings of the Thirteenth International Conference on Artificial Intelligence and Statistics (AISTATS)*, vol. 9, pp. 17–24), 2010.
11. Collobert, R. and Weston, J., A unified architecture for natural language processing: Deep neural networks with multitask learning, in: *Proceedings of the 25th international conference on machine learning (ICML '08)*, pp. 160–167, 2008, July.
12. Wang, Y., Wipf, D.P., Ling, Q., Chen, W., Wassell, I.J., Multi-task learning for subspace segmentation, in: *Proceedings of the 28th International Conference on Machine Learning (ICML 2015)*, pp. 1574–1582, 2015, July.
13. Ruder, S., An overview of multi-task learning in deep neural networks [arXiv preprint arXiv:1706.05098]. [cs.LG], 2017, June 15.
14. Seltzer, M.L. and Droppo, J., Multi-task learning in deep neural networks for improved phoneme recognition, in: *2013 IEEE International Conference on Acoustics, Speech and Signal Processing (ICASSP)*, IEEE, pp. 6965–6969, 2013.
15. Kendall, A., Gal, Y., Cipolla, R., Multi-task learning using uncertainty to weigh losses for scene geometry and semantics, in: *Proceedings of the IEEE*

Conference on Computer Vision and Pattern Recognition (CVPR), pp. 7482–7491, 2018.
16. Dong, X. and Williamson, D.S., An attention enhanced multi-task model for objective speech assessment in real-world environments, in: *2020 IEEE International Conference on Acoustics, Speech and Signal Processing (ICASSP)*, pp. 911–915, 2020.
17. Long, M., Zhang, H., Deng, J., Ye, P., Learning transferable features with deep auto encoders. *IEEE Trans. Pattern Anal. Mach. Intell.*, 39, 4, 1083–1093, 2017.
18. Zhang, Y., Li, D., Xu, Z., Zhan, Y., He, X., Curriculum multi-task learning for knowledge distillation. *Proceedings of the IEEE/CVF Conference on Computer Vision and Pattern Recognition (CVPR)*, pp. 8177–8186, 2020.
19. Li, W., Wang, Z., Liu, J., Zeng, Z., Li, H., Multi-task learning for stock trend prediction, in: *International Conference on Neural Information Processing*, Springer, Cham, pp. 301–313, 2020.
20. Lu, J., Cheng, H., Tang, Y., Zhou, J., Deep multi-task learning for protein-protein interaction prediction, in: *Proceedings of the 2019 ACM SIGKDD Conference on Knowledge Discovery and Data Mining*, pp. 3445–3454, 2019.

9

Forecasting Solar Power Generation in the Future by ARIMA Approach and Stationary Transformation

Sudeep Samanta

Department of Electrical Engineering, MCKV Institute of Engineering, Liluah, Howrah, West Bengal, India

Abstract

This chapter presents an innovative process of daily solar energy output prediction using autoregressive integrated moving average (ARIMA) model. The appeal of the ARIMA model is found in its simplicity, although it requires time-series data to be stationary. Therefore, our approach involves transforming our nonstationary and seasonal data into a stationary format to leverage ARIMA effectively. Developing the model entails using advanced statistical techniques. Time-series forecasting proves invaluable when there is limited knowledge about how explanatory variables impact output. Such models rely solely on past values of the dependent variable. Once established, the model serves as a predictive tool for future values. Time-series methodologies, especially the ARIMA model, are commonly researched and continually refined in the forecasting domain. The best performing ARIMA model is chosen and assessed using the metrics such as Akaike information criterion and the residual sum square error. Assessment of error demonstrates the effective performance of this method. The outlined approach is evaluated based on 5-kW solar panel, and the result is validated with historical time-series data.

***Keywords*:** Solar panel, time-series forecasting, ARIMA model, stationary transformation, power generation

Email: Sudeep0809@gmail.com

Arindam Mondal and Souvik Ganguli (eds.) Data-Driven Modeling, (203–220) © 2026 Scrivener Publishing LLC

Introduction

Global electricity demand is rising steadily, although traditional fossil fuel sources are limited and supply significantly to carbon emissions. These factors, alongside technological innovations, have stimulated the growing adoption of decentralized renewable energy sources [1, 2]. As the grid evolves toward greater intelligence, the integration of renewable energy resources is expected to further expand. Among these, photovoltaic (PV) solar energy project is particularly promising [3]. Nevertheless, similar to other renewable sources, inherently solar energy exhibits uncertainty due to its dependence on variables such as solar irradiance, humidity, temperature, and geographic location. This uncertainty emphasizes the critical role of forecasting in the operational and strategic planning of PV systems [4, 5]. Precise forecasts of solar energy generation can mitigate uncertainty and enhance demand-side management [6, 7]. Given its stochastic nature, solar power generation is commonly modeled using time-series methods.

Researchers use various approaches to predict the energy production of PV modules. These techniques generally fall into four categories: (a) statistical approaches utilizing historical data for time-series forecasting (e.g., autoregressive integrated moving average [ARIMA]) [8], (b) machine learning (ML) techniques based on feature extraction, such as artificial neural networks (ANNs) [9], (c) physical models leveraging satellite imagery and numerical weather predictions [10], and (d) hybrid approaches that combine elements of the aforementioned methods [11].

In recent decades, many researchers give their constant effort to enhance the efficiency and energy utilization of solar panels through a range of techniques and strategies. Accurate energy forecasting on existing solar system is crucial for uses such as demand management, predictive model control, fault identification, energy optimization, and management also. The field of energy forecasting models has garnered significant interest, particularly with progress in artificial intelligence (AI) and ML [12]. These systems have found extensive application in infrastructure of energy consumption and high voltage alternating current (HVAC) systems with air conditioning, ventilation, and heating, supporting a range of functions.

Traditional methods for forecasting solar power generation often focus solely on identifying data correlations without exploring deeper insights. With the proliferation of data in modern power systems, these conventional approaches often struggle to provide precise forecasts. In response, deep learning (DL) techniques have appeared as robust tools for tasks such as pattern identification, trend analysis, and forecasting applications.

DL methods are gaining popularity for its capability to capture dependencies within time-stamped data. Different DL models containing deep belief networks, Boltzmann machines, convolutional neural network, and recurrent neural network (RNN) have been suggested [13, 14]. Among these, RNNs are particularly effective for modeling time-dependent data and have demonstrated success across diverse domains. An alternative RNN variant, known as long short-term memory network, prevents information over extended periods by addressing the challenges inherent in solar energy forecasting.

Runge and Zmeureanu [9] reviewed energy estimation and projections for buildings, evaluating physical models with ML and statistical approaches. Their study focuses that ML-based models offer greater accuracy and versatility than statistical models. Support vector machines were identified as surpassing ANNs, suggesting optimization as a promising area for future research. Runge *et al.* [10] explored the application of AI and comprehensive models in predicting building energy consumption. They analyzed how AI techniques are applied to forecast entire building loads using hourly data, highlighting widespread adoption beyond building energy studies. Their findings underscored the enhanced performance of integrated methods in energy prediction. Van Deventer *et al.* [15] and Seyedmahmoudian *et al.* [16] conducted comparative studies of various PV energy forecasting models, evaluating their strengths and weaknesses.

Time-series forecasting methods prove invaluable when the influence of explanatory variables on output is unclear. These methods utilize historical values of dependent variable to forecast future outcomes, contributing to their extensive study and ongoing refinement in forecasting. Among the prominent models, ARIMA stands out for its simplicity and the well-known Box–Jenkins methodology [17, 18]. This simplicity arises from assuming a linear relationship between past and present time-series values. However, this linear assumption limits ARIMA's effectiveness with nonlinear real-world data, despite its capability to handle various types of time series.

In this chapter, the author explores seasonal and nonseasonal ARIMA models for forecasting daily solar energy output from a 10-kW rooftop solar panel at MCKV Institute of Engineering, West Bengal, India. The time-series data are adjusted for stationarity, model parameters are determined through analysis, and validation is performed using standard tools such as the Akaike information criterion (AIC) and residual sum of squared error (RSSE). Accuracy of the presented model is further assessed through comprehensive error analysis.

ARIMA model–based time-series forecasting

a) ARIMA modeling

The correlation between the current value and its historical values of a dependent variable of ARIMA model may be represented through linear expression. The time-series data, which will be used for ARIMA model, must exhibit stationarity in nature.

Achieving strong stationarity can be complex, so this paper assumes weak stationarity when the time series meets this criterion. Weak stationarity indicates that key statistical measures such as mean and variance remain stable over a period. To transform stationary time series from a nonstationary one, different methods including differencing, logging, and deflating are adopted. The primary goal of these transformations is to aim for adjustment of the necessary data for satisfying the requirements of weak stationarity and preparing it suitable for ARIMA modeling.

ARIMA model can be classified into seasonal and nonseasonal categories. If any dataset exhibits seasonality, then the seasonal ARIMA model is considered for capturing recurring fluctuations effectively. In the other case, if the dataset is nonseasonal, then nonseasonal ARIMA model is considered for overall forecasting purposes [19, 20]. Better understanding of the difference between nonseasonal and seasonal ARIMA model is very important for accurate modeling the underlying pattern of the dataset. To enhance the forecast precision of the time-series dataset with periodic variations, seasonal ARIMA model incorporates seasonal components.

Conversely, nonseasonal ARIMA models are suited for time series lacking seasonal trends. In summary, comprehending stationarity and selecting the appropriate ARIMA model variation are essential steps in time-series analysis and forecasting. These considerations ensure that the model captures the data's dynamics effectively, leading to reliable predictions and insights.

The nonseasonal ARIMA model is expressed according to Equation (9.1),

$$\hat{c}_t = \epsilon + \theta_1 c_{t-1} + \theta_2 c_{t-2} + \ldots + \theta_p c_{t-m} - \sigma_1 e_{t-1} - \sigma_2 e_{t-2} - \ldots - \sigma_q e_{t-r} \tag{9.1}$$

In an ARIMA model, the model parameters m, n, and r relate to the autoregressive lag variables, differencing, and moving average (MA) lag components, respectively. Here, MA coefficients represented by σ, the autoregressive coefficients are denoted by θ, and ϵ represents the constant term.

According to the values of m, n, and r, an ARIMA method can manifest as a purely auto regressive (AR) model, pure MA model or the ARMA (autoregressive moving average) framework [21]. Seasonality in a time series signifies the occurrence of a repetitive pattern, identified by its period denoted as K. For instance, monthly solar energy production frequently shows increased values during summer months, thus $K = 12$ in such scenarios.

ARIMA models are very much suitable for forecasting both nonseasonal and seasonal time-series data. During dealing with seasonal variations, a compound structure incorporates both seasonal and nonseasonal variations, generally known as a seasonal ARIMA model.

This model is typically formulated as follows:

$$\text{ARIMA}(m,n,r)*(M,N,R)K \tag{9.2}$$

here,

M = AR process order for seasonal data
N= differencing order for seasonal data
R = MA process order for seasonal data
K = seasonal period length

The specifics of this forecasting model are accentuated by introducing a backshift operator B for time-series analysis:

$$B_{c_t} = c_{t-1} \tag{9.3}$$

Here, c_t and c_{t-1} represents consecutive two time-series data points. Hence, B^j is known as

$$B^j{}_{ct} = c_{t-j} \tag{9.4}$$

Further, using θ(B) as AR operator, defined as polynomial expression in the backshift operator:

$$\theta(B) = 1 - \theta_1 B - \theta_2 B^2 - \ldots - \theta_p B^m \tag{9.5}$$

Similarly, σ(B) denotes the MA operator, expressed as a polynomial in backshift operator:

$$\sigma(B) = 1 - \sigma_1 B - \sigma_2 B^2 - \ldots - \sigma_p B^r \tag{9.6}$$

The accurate equation of the seasonal ARIMA model is provided below:

$$\theta(B)[1 - \Theta_1 B^k - \ldots - \Theta_P B^{MK}](1-B)^n (1-B^K)^N c_t = \sigma(B)$$
$$[1 + \Sigma_1 B^K + \ldots + \Sigma_Q B^{RK}]x_t \tag{9.7}$$

b) Selection of model parameter

The primary stages of ARIMA model are to check the stationarity for time-series data to be required for future data forecasting. To check the stationarity, autocorrelation factor (ACF) and partial autocorrelation factor (PACF) of time-series data are plotted.

Basically, ACF identifies the correlation between given time-series value and different time lag values. It helps to choose the order of the MA terms in ARIMA model. whereas in the other case, PACF finds the correlation among time-series value and the delayed version of itself, which is not explained by intermediate lags [22]. It helps to choose the order of MA components in the ARIMA model.

However, PACF considers correlation only at specific lag values, disregarding correlations with other values at different lags. To determine stationarity, one looks for either a lack of significant values in the ACF after several lags or a sharp decline in the PACF after the initial lag. However, real-world data often present more complexity and may not exhibit immediate stationarity. In such cases, a systematic method such as the augmented Dickey–Fuller (ADF) test is utilized for confirming stationary nature. This test is commonly referred to as unit root test and examines whether the characteristic equation has a unit root. The stationary time-series results for the absence of unit root; otherwise, the dataset is deemed nonstationary. Now, generalized expression for assessing stationarity *via* ADF test [23] is given below:

$$\partial C_t = \epsilon + \beta t + \rho C_{t-1} + \partial_1 C_{t-1} + \ldots + \partial_p C_{t-m} + e_t \tag{9.8}$$

In this case, β symbolizes the tendency, whereas e_t denotes a series of nondependent random variables with a mean of 0 and the variance of 1. The hypothesis is proposed as follows:

Zero hypotheses or H_0: $|\xi| = 0$ (for nonstationary)
Alternative hypotheses or H_1: $|\xi| \neq 0$ (for stationary)

The determination of acceptance or rejection of the null hypothesis hinges on p value. In the current study, 95% confidence level is adopted. For $p \geq 0.05$, it indicates that, falling within the confidence interval, time-series data are deemed as fluctuating, hence affirming the zero hypotheses. Again, if $p < 0.05$, time-series dataset is considered as stationary, leading to rejection of zero hypotheses.

c) Model determination and evaluation

After confirmation of the preliminary stationarity verification of time series, differencing process is applied if the series exhibits nonstationarity. If the original time series is already showing stationarity ($n = 0$), no differencing is needed. Differencing is iteratively applied until stationarity is achieved, with this study focusing exclusively on differencing without exploring alternative transformation techniques. Following each differencing step, stationarity is verified using plots of ACF, PACF, or ADF test methods.

The parameters m and r are determined based on essential terms identified by the respective plots of PACF and ACF. Still, these parameters may not yield optimal system configuration for every case. Seasonal attributes are also inferred from the plots of ACF and PACF. The critical ultimate stage before making forecast is selecting optimal ARIMA modeling. Various criteria are typically used to evaluate the model fit of the established system, including [24]:

***a)* AIC**

AIC can be formulated as follows:

$$\text{AIC} = 2k - 2\ln(L) \tag{9.9}$$

Here, L represents the maximum value obtained from the maximum likelihood estimation function; again, k denotes the number of estimated parameters. When the model achieves the lowest AIC value, it is regarded as the most efficient.

***b)* Corrected Akaike information criterion**

Corrected Akaike information criterion (CAIC) can be formulated as follows:

$$\mathrm{AIC_c} = \frac{i+k}{i-k-2} - 2\ln(L) \tag{9.10}$$

where i is the total number of data points.

***c)* Bayesian information criterion**

The Bayesian information criterion (BIC) can be formulated as follows,

$$\mathrm{BIC} = \frac{k\ln(i)}{i} - 2\ln(L) \tag{9.11}$$

where L, k, and i are the same as mentioned above.

***d)* RSSE**

The RSSE is computed as the addition of the squared terms of all residuals, which represent basically differences between actual values and their corresponding forecasted values. Mathematically, the RSSE for an ARIMA model is expressed as follows:

$$\mathrm{RSSE} = \Sigma_{t=1}^{i}(c_t - \hat{c}_t)^2 \tag{9.12}$$

where c_t represents actual observed value for time step t, and $\hat{c}_t$ represents forecasted value at time t generated by ARIMA model. This RSSE provides a quantitative indicator of how effective the ARIMA model fits with data; lower RSS values indicate a better fit.

Preparation of dataset

Total solar energy output in kWh per day is used for this work as target variable. Generated energy data were collected over an entire year, from August 1, 2022, to July 31, 2023, from a 5-kW solar plant with 20 PV panels located on the rooftop of MCKV Institute of Engineering, Liluah, West Bengal, India, shown in Figure 9.1.

Figure 9.1 5-kW roof top solar plants.

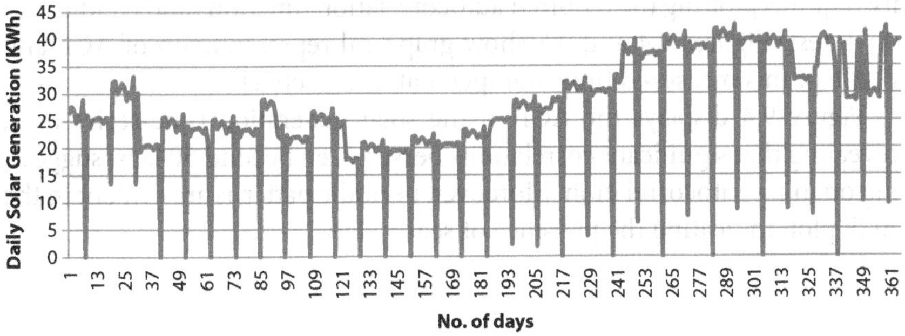

Figure 9.2 Daily solar energy generation data throughout the year.

Initially, the dataset saved in the form of .csv file and after that imported and graphed as a time series for further processing. As shown in Figure 9.2, there are some missing data points because the solar panel was not functional on those days.

To address this, we processed the data to fill in the gaps by linear interpolation technique, as depicted in Figure 9.3. This presented time-series data are subsequently used for analyzing the proposed work.

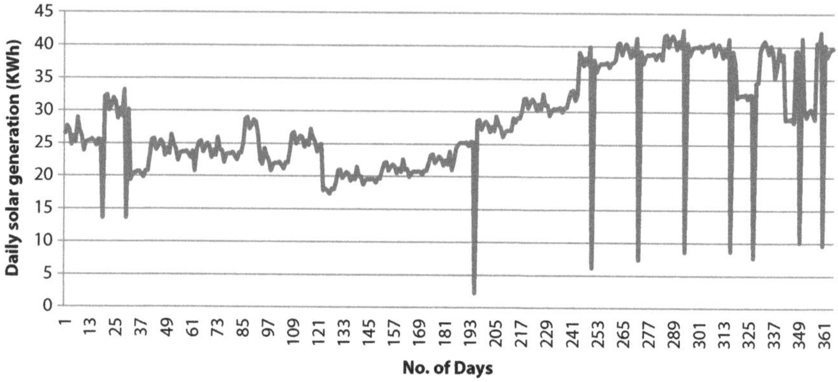

Figure 9.3 Daily solar energy generation data interpolating missing values.

Analysis

The initial assumption on the stationarity characteristics of our dataset can be done by observing Figure 9.3, which suggests two trends—one downward and one upward. However, a definitive decision regarding stationarity requires plotting the required autocorrelation functions and conducting ADF test. Figures 9.4 and 9.5 show graphical representation of ACF and PACF of this measured time-stamped data, respectively.

Figure 9.4 displays the ACF of the solar generation time-series data, revealing that significant correlations persist even beyond 50 lags, suggesting ongoing autocorrelation. Moreover, periodic patterns are evident in the ACF plot, indicating the presence of seasonality.

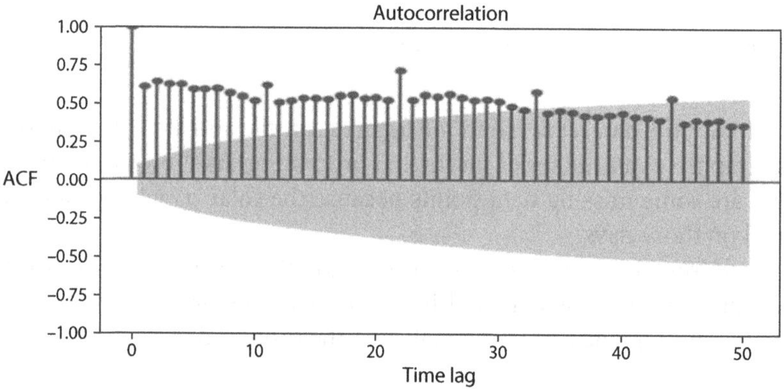

Figure 9.4 ACF plotting of solar generation data.

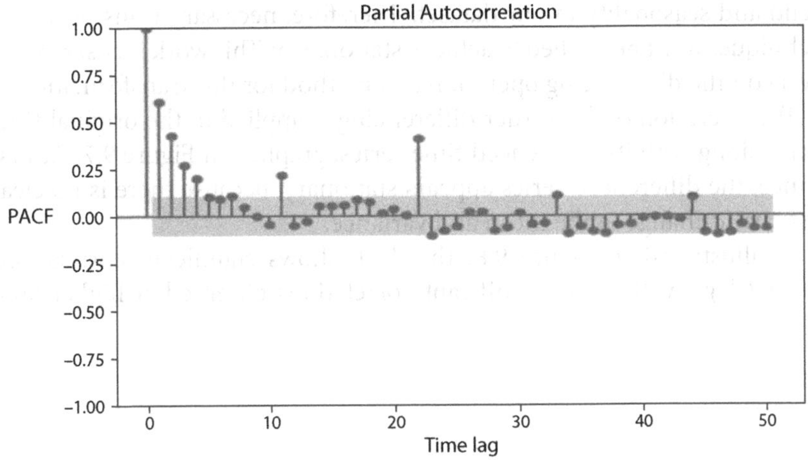

Figure 9.5 PACF plotting of solar generation data.

In Figure 9.5, the PACF plot shows no abrupt cutoff, which supports the graphical analysis indicating nonstationary characteristics of the time-stamped data. Nevertheless, for confirming nonstationarity conclusively, an ADF test is conducted. Obtained *p* value of 0.617 indicates that the zero hypotheses cannot be dismissed, affirming the nonstationary nature of the time-stamped data. The time series exhibiting both tendency and seasonal patterns inherently displays nonstationarity due to systematic fluctuations in its mean and variance.

Figure 9.6 displays the seasonal component, trending component of power generation of time-series data, clearly showing the presence of both

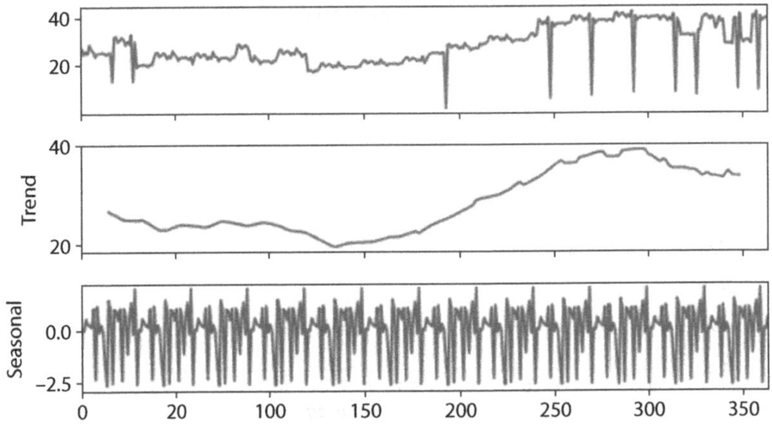

Figure 9.6 Trend and seasonality of solar generation data.

trend and seasonality in our dataset. Therefore, necessary transformation techniques must be applied to achieve stationarity. This work focuses exclusively on the differencing operation as a method for this transformation.

The operation of first-order differencing is applied to the original time series along with its differenced time series, graphed in Figure 9.7. At first glance, the differenced series appears stationary, because there is no clear systematic change in the mean and variance.

As illustrated in Figure 9.8, the ACF shows significant correlations up to 3 lags, with fewer significant correlations observed at higher lags.

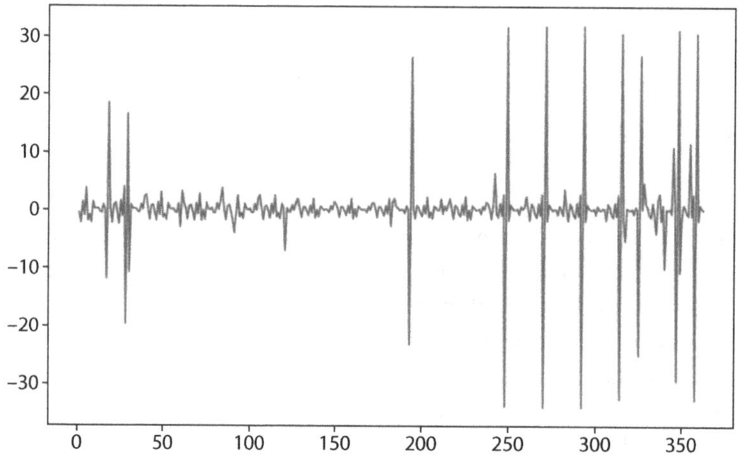

Figure 9.7 Solar generation time-series output after differentiation.

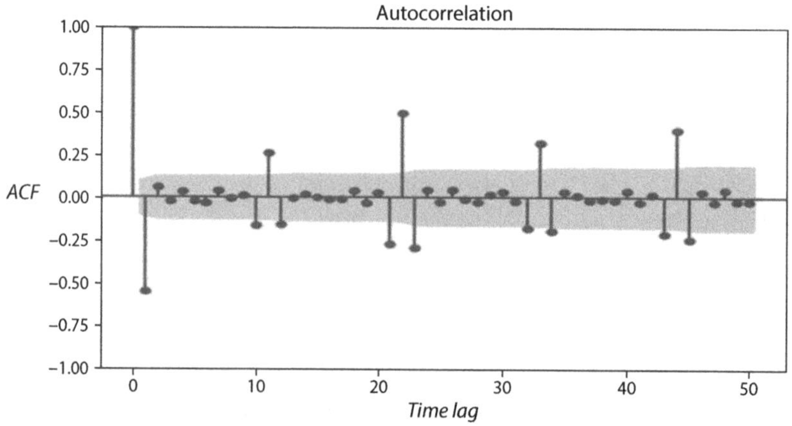

Figure 9.8 ACF of solar generation time-series data after differentiation.

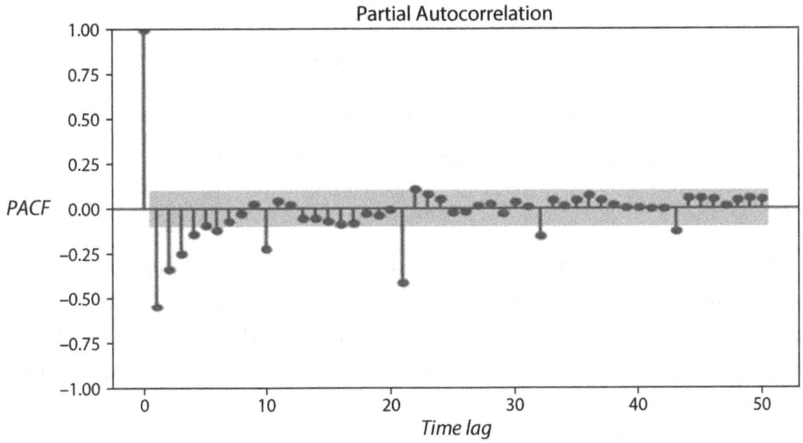

Figure 9.9 PACF of solar generation time-series data after differentiation.

Similarly, in Figure 9.9, the PACF of differenced series displays significant values up to 5 lags, whereas few significant values were observed at increased lags.

These plots demonstrate the potential stationary behavior of differenced series data, a hypothesis later verified by the ADF test. The significant lags observed in the plots of ACF and PACF serve as primary indicators for determining the orders of AR and MA model in the ARIMA framework. Following this, an ADF test is conducted upon differenced time series, yielding a p value of 0.00048, which dismisses the zero hypotheses and confirms the stationarity of reconstructed time-series dataset. Thus, initial differencing of the cleaned original time series has successfully achieved stationarity.

Validation of the proposed model

The duration of the seasonal pattern is not discernible from Figures 9.8 and 9.9. Therefore, the *auto.arima()* function is initially used on time-series data to determine the optimal seasonality. This routine identified the model *ARIMA(0,1,2)(0,0,2)30*. After testing alternative cycle lengths, a periodicity of 30 proved superior, minimizing the AIC.

Further, the *auto.arima()* function was run excluding consideration of seasonal behavior, but the seasonal framework consistently outperformed the nonseasonal model across all information metric, which aligns with inherent seasonality of our time series. As a result, all subsequent analyses in this study will focus exclusively upon the seasonal framework. Table 9.1 outlines the result.

Table 9.1 Outputs of auto.arima() function.

Dataset	AIC	CAIC	BIC
Nonseasonal	2416.48	2416.14	2428.58
Seasonal	2407.96	2407.23	2414.32

The relevant terms identified on the plots of PACF and ACF provide approximate estimation regarding nonseasonal orders of AR and MA models. Therefore, based on Figures 9.8 and 9.9, the estimated orders for this analysis are approximately 3 for AR and 5 for MA. Nonetheless, models with higher order increase both computational costs and complexity. To prioritize simplicity and efficiency, we constrain the orders at 3 for nonseasonal MA and AR model and orders of 2 for seasonal MA and AR model. Thus, the imposed boundaries are as follows:

$$0 \leq m,r \leq 3$$
$$0 \leq M, R \leq 2$$

ARIMA model is developed according to the above criteria, and the outcomes of the top 10 models are presented in Table 9.2. Due to space constraints, not all model outcomes are presented. Table 9.2 highlights that

Table 9.2 Performance of ARIMA model for different parameter values.

m	n	r	M	N	R	K	AIC	RSSE
0	1	1	0	0	1	30	2546.33	19,495.46
0	1	1	1	0	1	30	2533.68	19,488.21
0	1	2	1	0	1	30	2500.62	18,000.14
0	1	2	0	0	1	30	2564.97	22,645.31
0	1	2	1	0	1	30	2502.32	18,000.21
0	1	2	1	0	1	30	2482.16	16,483.32
1	1	2	2	0	1	30	2486.11	16,512.34
1	1	3	1	0	1	30	2484.52	16,492.76
1	1	3	2	0	2	30	2516.34	19,277.53
2	1	3	2	0	1	30	2684.88	20,143.41

the *ARIMA (0, 1, 2)(1, 0, 1)30* model surpasses others considering both RSSE and AIC.

Therefore, the proposed model equation is represented as:

$$(1-\Theta_1 B^{30})(1-B)^1 c_t = (1-\sigma_1 B-\sigma_2 B^2)(1+\Sigma_1 B^{30})x_t \qquad (9.13)$$

Ultimately, Equation (9.14) is used to predict the daily overall solar power production for any specific day.

$$\hat{c}_t = c_{t-1} + \Theta_1 c_{t-30} - \Theta_1 c_{t-31} + x_t + \sigma_1 x_{t-1} + \sigma_2 x_{t-2} + \Sigma_1 x_{t-30} + \sigma_1 \Sigma_1 x_{t-31} + \sigma_2 \Sigma_1 x_{t-32} \qquad (9.14)$$

The estimated values of Θ_1, σ_1, σ_2, and Σ_1 are 0.644, −0.518, −0.287, and −1. In this study, we compared previous 1 month (30 days) forecasted values in our dataset with the original values, as illustrated in Figure 9.10.

Following the forecasting process, we evaluated the model's root mean square error for our model, which was calculated to be 7.44%.

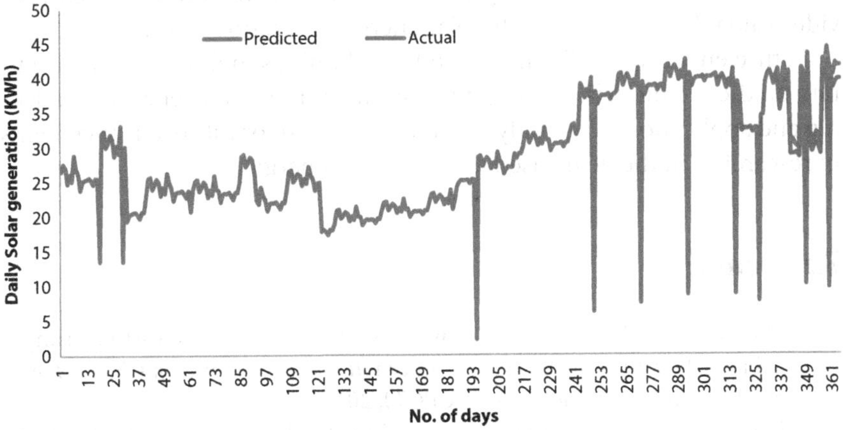

Figure 9.10 Actual versus predicted result for the last 30 days.

Conclusion

In this work, the author undertook the design and analysis of an ARIMA model to predict daily solar energy generation in the research institution. The ARIMA method, broadly acknowledged in time-series data analysis, was used. Despite encountering a slightly higher mean absolute percentage error than anticipated, this does not necessarily indicate flaws in the model but suggests potential influencing factors warranting further investigation.

During the analysis of the original time-series data, notable fluctuations were observed, particularly within the last 30 days of the dataset, likely influenced by external factors such as weather patterns or seasonal variations affecting solar energy generation. To mitigate such volatility, the author suggests exploring the effectiveness of using MAs of solar outputs instead of daily data, aiming for more stable and accurate predictions. Future research will focus on refining smoothing techniques to better manage these fluctuations. These approaches can adapt to evolving volatility patterns over time, promising more precise and dependable forecasts.

The present work underlays on advance solar energy forecasting after identification of limitations of current models used. After exploring different advanced modeling techniques such as ARCH and GARCH, addressing the challenge related to heteroscedasticity and data volatility, the model enhances the accuracy of daily solar energy prediction. In summary, the research focuses on enhancing the robustness of the model, which provides valuable insights on daily solar energy generation forecasting.

Future endeavors will build upon these findings to develop more accurate predictive models, driving innovations in renewable energy forecasting and application. This study also focuses a path for future advancements in researches in the field based on renewable energy.

References

1. Majumder, I., Behera, M.K., Nayak, N., Solar power forecasting using a hybrid EMD-ELM method. *2017 International Conference on Circuit, Power and Computing Technologies (ICCPCT)*, 2017.
2. Kabir, E., Kumar, P., Adelodun, A., Kim, H., Solar energy: Potential and future prospects. *Renew. Sustain. Energy Rev.*, 82, 894–900, 2018.
3. Sobri, S., Koohi-Kamali, S., Rahim, N.A., Solar photovoltaic generation forecasting methods: a review. *Energy Convers. Manage.*, 156, 459–497, 2018.

4. Antonanzas, J., Osorio, N., Escobar, R., Urraca, R., Martinez-de-Pison, F.J., Antonanzas-Torres, F., Review of photovoltaic power forecasting. *Sol. Energy*, 136, 78–111, 2016.
5. Fara, L., Diaconu, A., Dragan, F., Trends, challenges and opportunities in advanced solar cells technologies and PV market. *J. Green Eng.*, 4, 157–186, 5, 2016.
6. Diagne, H.M., David, M., Lauret, P., Bolan, J., Solar irradiation forecasting: state-of-the-art and proposition for future developments for small-scale insular grids. *Proceedings of the WREF 2012-World Renewable Energy Forum*, Denver, Colorado, pp. 65–76, 2012.
7. Paulescu, M., Mares, O., Paulescu, E., Stefu, N., Pacurar, A., Calinoiu, D., Gravila, P., Pop, N., Boata, R., Nowcasting solar irradiance using the sunshine number. *Energy Convers. Manage.*, 79, 690–697, 2014.
8. Atique, S., Noureen, S., Roy, V., Subburaj, V., Bayne, S., Macfie, J., Forecasting of total daily solar energy generation using ARIMA: a case study. *2019 IEEE 9th Annual Computing and Communication Workshop and Conference (CCWC)*, Las Vegas, NV, USA, pp. 0114–0119, 2019.
9. Runge, J. and Zmeureanu, R., Forecasting energy use in buildings using artificial neural networks: a review. *Energies*, 12, 17, 507–518, 2019.
10. Qing, X. and Niu, Y., Hourly day-ahead solar irradiance prediction using weather forecasts by LSTM. *Energy*, 148, 461–468, 2018.
11. Wu, Y.-K., Chen, C.-R., Abdul Rahman, H., A Novel Hybrid Model for Short-Term Forecasting in PV Power Generation. *Int. J. Photoenergy*, 14, 9, 238–249, 2014.
12. Poulos, M. and Papavlasopoulos, S., Automatic stationary detection of time series using auto-correlation coefficients and LVQ Neural Network. *2013 Fourth International Conference on Information, Intelligence, Systems and Applications (IISA)*, pp. 1–4, 2013.
13. Eseye, A.T., Zhang, J., Zheng, D., Short-term photovoltaic solar power forecasting using a hybrid Wavelet-PSO-SVM model based on SCADA and Meteorological information. *Renew. Energy*, 118, 357–367, 2018.
14. Wang, K., Qi, X., Liu, H., A comparison of day-ahead photovoltaic power forecasting models based on deep learning neural network. *Appl. Energy*, 251, 512–521, 2019.
15. Van Deventer, W., Jamei, E., Thirunavukkarasu, G.S., Seyedmahmoudian, M., Soon, T.K., Horan, B., Mekhilef, S., Stojcevski, A., Short-term PV power forecasting using hybrid GASVM technique. *Renew. Energy*, 140, 367–379, 2019.
16. Seyedmahmoudian, M., Jamei, E., Thirunavukkarasu, G.S., Soon, T., Mortimer, M., Horan, B., Stojcevski, A., Mekhilef, S., Short-term forecasting of the output power of a building-integrated photovoltaic system using a metaheuristic approach. *Energies*, 11, 5, 348–357, 2018.

17. Wu, J. and Chan, C.K., The prediction of monthly average solar radiation with TDNN and ARIMA. *2016 International Conference on Machine Learning and Applications*, Boca Raton, FL, USA, 2016.
18. Zhang, G., Time series forecasting using a hybrid ARIMA and Neural Network model. *J. Neuro Comput.*, 50, 159–175, 2003.
19. Ghofrani, M. and Suherli, A., Time series and renewable energy forecasting. *Time Ser. Anal. Appl.*, 48, 5, 77–92, 2017.
20. Flores, J., Engel, P., Pinto, R.C., Autocorrelation and partial autocorrelation functions to improve Neural Networks models on univariate time series forecasting. *International Joint Conference on Neural Networks (IJCNN)*, Brisbane, QLD, Australia, 2012.
21. Halim, S., Bisono, I., Thia, C., Automatic seasonal autoregressive moving average models and unit root test detection. *2007 IEEE International Conference on Industrial Engineering and Engineering Management*, 2007.
22. Sansa, I., Boussaada, Z., Bellaaj, N.M., Solar Radiation Prediction Using a Novel Hybrid Model of ARMA and NARX. *Energies*, 14, 6920, 2021.
23. Guermoui, M., Melgani, F., Gairaa, K., Mekhalfi, M., A comprehensive review of hybrid models for solar radiation forecasting. *J. Clean. Prod.*, 15, 2, 365–369, 2020.
24. Shadab, A., Said, S., Ahmad, S., Box–Jenkins multiplicative ARIMA modeling for predictionof solar radiation: a case study. *Int. J. Energy Water Resour.*, 3, 305–318, 2020.

10

Prognosticating Plays: ANN-Enabled Score Projection with the Help of FIS

Susmit Chakraborty* **and Sourish Harh**

Department of Computer Science and Engineering (CS&DS), Brainware University, Barasat, West Bengal, India

Abstract

Artificial neural networks (ANNs) are designed to look and behave like biological neural networks. They consist of neurons organized into layers, connected by weighted connections, and use activation functions for introducing nonlinearity. This work adopts the use of an ANN-based fuzzy logic system (FLS) method in which a prediction of the match score of a player is made having been trained in the supervised manner. A feedforward neural network with 300 cricketer's previous data is utilized to train the ANN model. Cricketer's database has listed six feature variables where the options are age, higher score, average score, strike rate of the player and the opponent team, and match place. These qualities in combination define the output variable, which is the cricketers' scores. Thus, the FLS that ANN trains determines the fuzzy sets necessary to make a prediction. FLS creates the projected rating of a cricketer. Finally, the prediction result is tested with the help of root mean square error criteria to judge the effectiveness of the proposed system. The entire project is drawn and modeled on MATLAB 2020A platform.

Keywords: Artificial neural networks (ANNs), fuzzy logic system (FLS), deep learning (DL), training and testing, score prediction, RMSE

10.1 Introduction

As a branch of computer science, artificial intelligence (AI) is the general undertaking of developing computer systems to carry out tasks that would

**Corresponding author*: susmit.eee@gmail.com

Arindam Mondal and Souvik Ganguli (eds.) Data-Driven Modeling, (221–238) © 2026 Scrivener Publishing LLC

otherwise be done by human beings [1]. Thus, machine learning is a branch of AI that is based on programs providing the computer with the ability to change its behavior based on data received, instead of being directly instructed what to do. It is used in analytical processing of data, control of business processes, individualization, and prognosis, among others. Machine learning is finding utility in industries as diverse as healthcare, finance, commerce, and autonomous vehicles, transforming businesses with access to insights and enabling efficiencies [1]. Artificial neural networks (ANNs) portray the shape and characteristic of the human mind, comprising interconnected nodes. Trained with statistics, they excel in responsibilities such as sample reputation, class, and regression across various fields [2]. Fuzzy-AI models combine AI with fuzzy information technology to provide efficient information processing. It harnesses the ability of AI to mimic human intelligence and deal with uncertainty and promises to be used extensively in information technology [3]. ANFIS, short for adaptive neuro-fuzzy inference system, combines neural networks with fuzzy logic to model complex systems. It learns from data through supervised learning and abstract reasoning, so that ANFIS, which is good at capturing nonlinear relationships and dealing with uncertainty, finds applications in various industries such as control systems, prediction, and classification tasks [4, 5]. A hybrid auto-regressive moving average (ARMA)/ANN model that uses data from a weather prediction model is proposed by Voyant *et al.* in [6]. The emphasis is on the multilayer perceptron inside the ANN. By optimizing its architecture and combining it with an ARMA model, the model outperformed classic predictors across Mediterranean locations. The hybrid model outperforms the naive persistence predictor at 26.2%. It has also been evaluated for forecast reliability using confidence intervals [6]. To forecast biomass higher heating value, authors in [7] proposes a novel model based on the ANFIS. This attempt seeks to analyze 444 data points of various kinds of biomass materials that consist of proximate analysis components. Thus, the subclustering-based ANFIS model was found to be most accurate as compared with available literature, with or during the testing phase [7]. Another research work conducted for the turning operation using stainless steel 202 involved an ANFIS-based prediction, and parametric analysis was done using Taguchi L16 DOE with the turning parameters as feed rate, spindle speed, and depth of cut [8]. The issue on the ability to predict hydraulic impact hammers performance, particularly by means of soft-computing technique, namely, ANN and ANFIS, was introduced by Melih Iphar [9]. The information collected from a metro tunnel work that is situated in Istanbul, Turkey, is applied in generating the prediction models using the ANN, ANFIS, and the multiple regression technique.

It is also probable that the efficiency of the ANFIS model is higher than both ANNs and regression-based models for analytical assessment and clarification of the relation between the impact hammer performance and the obtained field test indices such as Schmidt hammer rebound hardness (SHRH) and rock quality designation (RQD) [9]. Boyacioglu *et al.* [10] have discussed the prediction of stock market return through ANFIS prediction control. Boyacioglu *et al.* used six indicators as input variables and an additional three indices. Empirical data demonstrate that the ANFIS model achieves a highly satisfactory accuracy of 98.3% in predicting the returns experienced by the ISE National-100 Index. It implies that the ANFIS neural network technology possesses immense potential for economists as well as practitioners who are dealing with stock market forecasting [10]. Zhao *et al.* investigate an optimal ANFIS model for forecasting pile pullout resistance in [11]. Kalsi *et al.* demonstrated an ANN and ANFIS-based model to predict the drying behavior of leaf in a hot-air dryer [12]. Recently, Li *et al.* predicted the shear strength of concrete beams using ANFIS-assisted GA-PSO blended modeling [13]. ANFIS and ANN models are also used to predict heliostat tracking errors by Sarr *et al.* [14]. ANFIS estimates air pollution in Yonar's current research, as cited in [15]. Patel *et al.* projected flood flow in the Panam-basin using ANFIS and ANN in [16]. Kumar *et al.* established an ANFIS for forecasting COVID-19 epidemic peak and infected cases in India in recent research [17]. The author highlights the effectiveness of the ANFIS scheme to predict the output of different real-life problems. In this chapter, the authors try to develop a model that predicts the score of a player based on some feature variables such as age, highest score, strike rate, and average score of batsmen, as well as the match venue and the opponent team. The data are taken from open sources such as the Kaggle platform. Seventy percent of the data are used in the course of training, with the remaining 30% being used to validate the created model. The multiple linear regression model is used in this work to predict the run of a batsman. The predicted score is evaluated by comparing it with the actual score. Root mean square error (RMSE) is the evolutionary matrix, which is considered here for evaluation purposes.

10.2 System Model

Figure 10.1 illustrates the workflow of the recommended model for forecasting the score of a player. A set of labeled data is used to train an ANFIS model. The dataset contains six feature variables, such as age, highest score, average score, and strike rate of batsmen, as well as match venue

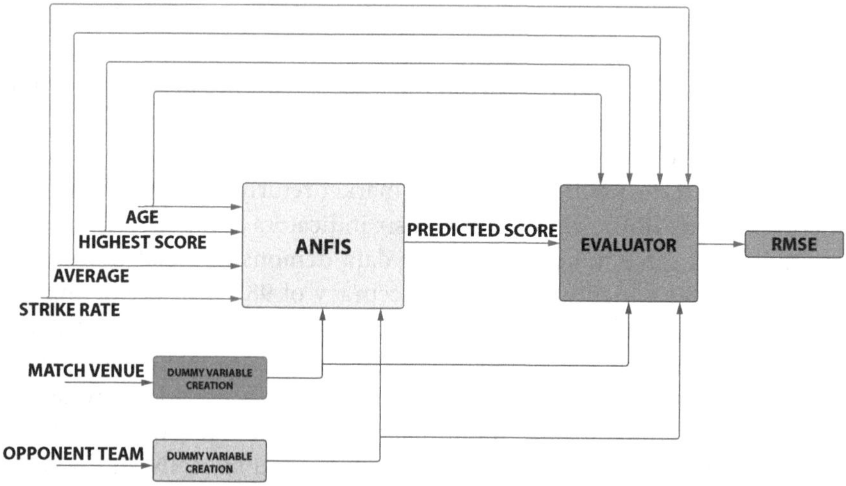

Figure 10.1 Schematic of the system model.

and opponent team name. Depending on these attributes, an ANFIS model is built and tested on a 20% dataset for evaluation. The predicted score is compared with their actual values, and an evolutionary matrix called RMSE [18] is considered to check the efficacy of the model. The mathematical view for RMSE is prescribed in Eq. (10.1).

$$\text{RMSE} = \sqrt{\frac{1}{n}\sum_{j=1}^{n}(R_A - R_P)^2} \tag{10.1}$$

where n identifies total number of the batsman whose score has been evaluated (20% of the total batsman), and R_A and R_P are the actual and predicted score, respectively.

10.3 ANFIS Controller

In order to solve complicated problems, AI techniques (such as NN, fuzzy technology, evolutionary algorithms, etc.) are increasingly being integrated into complementary hybrid frameworks [18]. This is known as intelligent systems or soft computing research. The basic concepts of the theory of fuzzy sets are fuzzy rules of if-then and imprecise reasoning, which handle ambiguity and information granularity. Although genetic algorithms rely on a systematic random search and are essential for optimization, neural networks may learn and adapt by modifying the connections between layers [19]. ANN and fuzzy inference systems (FISs) came together to produce neuro-fuzzy approaches, which are now widely used as a framework for problem solving in the real world. A neuro-fuzzy system is built on the foundation of a fuzzy system that was trained using a neural network–based learning method. From the perspective of FIS, the ability to learn is advantageous. But, from the perspective of ANN, the creation of a linguistic rule basis will be beneficial. There are various ways to combine ANN with FIS, and the choice is frequently based on the applications [20–23]. This study will focus on the ANFIS, a groundbreaking neuro-fuzzy system that is used to predict the score of a player based on previous data. There are six feature variables, such as age, highest score, average run, and strike rate of the player, as well as match venue and opponent team information; the last two attributes create 18 dummy variables using Python. A total of 22 features, including dummy variables and excluding the match venue and opponent team, are used to train this forecasting model of the score of the players. The proposed model contains a multilayer ANFIS, as depicted in Figure 10.2.

Figure 10.2 depicts the structure of ANFIS, which consists of five levels. This picture depicts an ANFIS framework with two input parameters and one output, consisting of four functions for membership and four rules. In this chapter, instead of two real-life inputs, a total 22 inputs are considered. For simplicity of the calculation, authors initially consider only two inputs. After stepwise analysis, the authors map the ANFIS system with all features considered in this work. The layer structure of the ANFIS is illustrated below using the ANFIS structure shown in Figure 10.2.

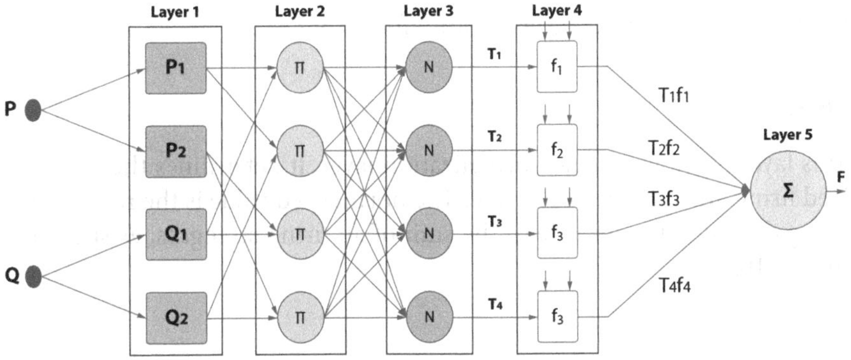

Figure 10.2 A simple ANFIS controller.

10.3.1 Layer 1

This component is known as the fuzzification layer. The fuzzification layer uses membership functions to generate fuzzy clusters from input data. Parameters that define the shape of a membership function are referred to as premise parameters. {X, Y, Z} is the premise attribute set. The membership degrees of each function of membership are determined using the settings specified in (10.2) and (10.3). The couple of membership degrees acquired from this layer are displayed as μ_x and μ_y.

$$\mu P_i(P) = gbellmf(P : X,Y,Z) = \frac{1}{1+\left|\frac{P-Z}{X}\right|^{2Y}} \tag{10.2}$$

$$O_i^1 = \mu\ P_i\ (P) \tag{10.3}$$

where O_i^1 expresses the layer 1 output for i = 1,2,3...

10.3.2 Layer 2

This layer is known as the rule layer. Firing attributes (T_i) for the regulations are calculated using membership metrics from the fuzzification tier. The T_i values are calculated through the multiplication of the membership quantities as follows:

$$O_i^2 = T_i = \mu\ P_i\ (P)\,.\mu Q_1(Q) \tag{10.4}$$

where O_i^2 expresses the layer 2 output for i = 1,2,3.....

10.3.3 Layer 3

This layer is known as the normalization layer. It determines the normalized firing attributes for each rule. The normalized value is the ratio of the firing degree of the ith rule to the sum of all firing strengths, as specified in Eq. (10.5).

$$O_i^3 = T_1 = \frac{T_1}{T_1 + T_2 + T_3 + T_4} \tag{10.5}$$

O_i^3 is considered to be the third layer output with $i \in \{1,2,3,4\}$.

10.3.4 Layer 4

This layer is known as the defuzzification layer. The measured scores for rules are determined at each node within this layer, as shown in Eq. (10.6). This number is calculated using the first-order polynomial specified in Eq. (10.6), which defines the layer 4 output.

$$O_i^4 = T_i f_i = T_i = (a_i u + b_i v + s_i) \tag{10.6}$$

The measure set is represented by $\{a_i, b_i, c_i\}$, whereas T_i represents the normalization layer's output. These are known as the consequence variables. Every rule has one more repercussion variable than inputs to be processed. Here, for two inputs, the count of the consequence parameters is 3.

10.3.5 Layer 5

It is known as the accumulation layer. The real output of ANFIS is calculated by adding the outputs acquired for every rule in the defuzzification phase. The final output of the controller is expressed in Eq. (10.6).

$$O_i^5 = \Sigma_i T_i f_i = \frac{\Sigma_i T_i f_i}{\Sigma_i T_i} \tag{10.7}$$

Figure 10.2 consists of two inputs with two membership functions, resulting in a total of four normalization layers and four output functions. The score predictor model has a total of four inputs (age, highest score, average, and strike rate) with three membership functions and 18 dummy inputs for opponent and venue with two membership values (0 and 1). Therefore, the number of normalization layers is as follows:

$$3^4 \times 2^{18} = 165888$$

Output of the ANFIS in score predictor model can be mapped with Eq. (10.6) and can be expressed in Eq. (10.7).

$$O_i^5 = \Sigma_i T_i f_i = \frac{\Sigma_i T_i f_i}{\Sigma_i T_i} = \frac{T_1 f_1 + T_2 f_2 + \dots\dots\dots\dots\dots\dots\dots + T_{165888} f_{165888}}{T_1 + T_2 + \dots\dots\dots\dots\dots\dots\dots + T_{165888}} \tag{10.8}$$

10.4 Results and Analysis

The score prediction model of a player is trained using the ICC World Cup 2023 database, where a total 10 teams with 150 players and 10 match venues are available. The dataset contains a total of 22 feature variables, including 18 dummy variables. Raw data are collected from the ICC World Cup official site, and it is preprocessed using the Jupyter Notebook platform. The structured data train the prediction model using the ANFIS toolset available in MATLAB 2020A. In this chapter, the authors discuss the results and their analysis in three subsections. Section 10.4.1 emphasizes the data preprocessing using Python code in the Jupyter Notebook. Section 10.4.2 analyzes the ANFIS model on the MATLAB 2020A platform. Section 10.4.3 is devoted to the evaluation of the model using the testing dataset in MATLAB 2020A.

10.4.1 Data Preprocessing in Jupyter Notebook

Some important python libraries are imported before starting any process with the dataset. The following python codes are used in this regard.

```
import pandas as pd
import numpy as np
import matplotlib.pyplot as plt
import seaborn as sns
```

The first two lines are two essential libraries required for any activity in Python [24]. The following two codes are used to visualize the result in Python [25]. Data are imported using the pd.read() method using the csv file of the dataset. The following second line is used to check the head of the dataset considered here, and the data head is illustrated in Figure 10.3.

	Age	Highest Score	Average	Strike Rate	Match Venue	Opponent Team	Score
0	23	119	29.346881	78	Lucknow	PAK	142
1	28	84	30.361677	78	Pune	NZ	20
2	22	187	35.456528	78	Ahmedabad	AUS	46
3	31	191	35.567704	78	Bengaluru	SA	178
4	19	191	38.812149	78	Lucknow	NED	103

Figure 10.3 Dataset head view.

Dataset features can be obtained using the following code: The statistical description of the dataset is analyzed using the following Python code. Figure 10.4 shows the statistical observations in the dataset.

```
ds = pd.read_csv("Dataset_1.csv")
ds.head()
print(ds.columns)
ds.describe()
```

```
count=ds.isnull().sum()
print(count)
```

Above, two python codes are used to check for the missing value in the dataset. The code returns the result of zero missing value in the dataset as depicted in Figure 10.5.

The first column of the figure represents all features available in the dataset, including the output variable (score), and the second column is

	Age	Highest Score	Average	Strike Rate	Score
count	500.00000	500.000000	500.000000	500.000000	500.000000
mean	29.57000	146.452000	38.281045	113.674000	88.142000
std	7.44338	40.999825	7.594693	21.705437	49.618119
min	17.00000	77.000000	25.015020	78.000000	0.000000
25%	23.00000	111.000000	31.730001	94.000000	49.500000
50%	29.00000	144.500000	37.420964	113.000000	88.000000
75%	36.00000	182.000000	44.998069	134.000000	129.000000
max	42.00000	218.000000	54.003337	150.000000	178.000000

Figure 10.4 Statistical description of the dataset.

```
Age                 0
Highest Score       0
Average             0
Strike Rate         0
Match Venue         0
Opponent  Team      0
Score               0
dtype: int64
```

Figure 10.5 Null value observation.

the count of the missing value, which is zero for all variables. A scatterplot between all numerical features such as "age," "highest score," "average," and "strike rate" is obtained using the following two Python codes: The scatterplots obtained between all the aforementioned features are illustrated in Figure 10.6.

```
sns.pairplot(ds, vars=['Age', 'Highest Score', 'Average', 'Strike Rate'])
plt.show()
```

Figure 10.6 declares completely scattered correlations among numerical features in the dataset. There is no visible pattern obtained from the pairplots. No correlations among numerical features as well as the output variable can also be verified by observing the heat map shown in Figure 10.7.

In Figure 10.7, the lighter shade identifies the negligible correlations among the numerical features available in the dataset. After visual observation of the dataset, the author uses the following two codes for generating dummy variables for two categorical features, such as "opponent" and "venue" of the match.

```
Match_venue=pd.get_dummies(ds['Match Venue'],drop_first=True)
Opponents=pd.get_dummies(ds['Opponent Team'],drop_first=True)
```

Dummy variables are concatenate to the main dataset using the following python codes.

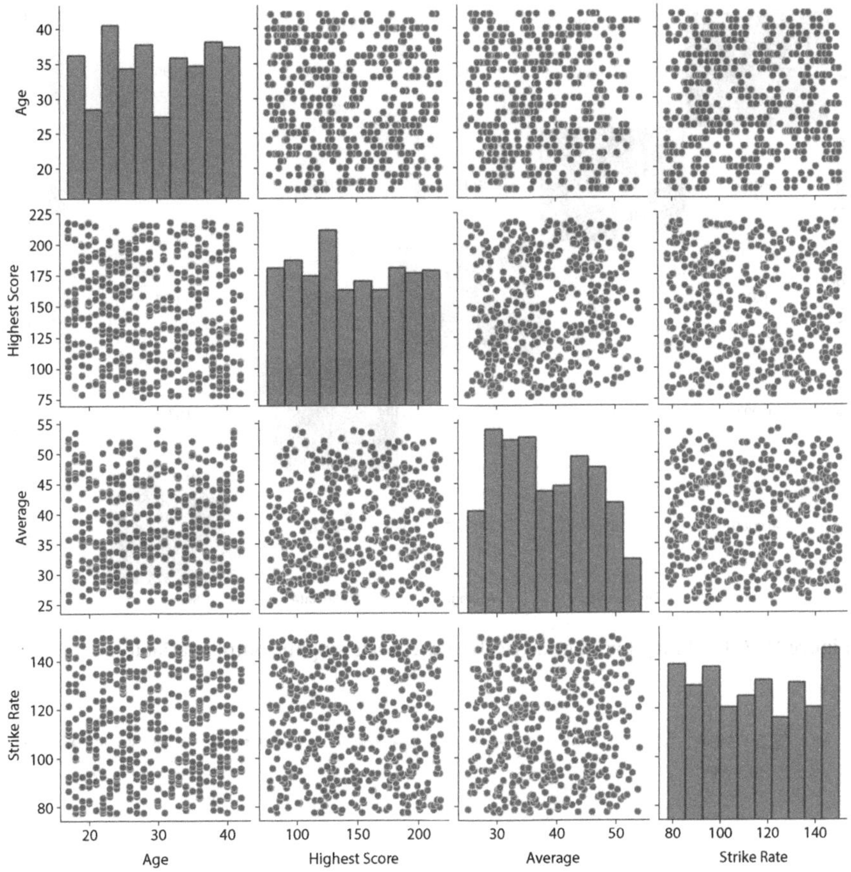

Figure 10.6 Pair-plot among numerical features.

```
ds=pd.concat([ds,Match_venue],axis=1)
ds=pd.concat([ds,Opponents],axis=1)
```

Dummy variables create 18 more features with 0 or 1 value. Then there is no use of the actual feature variables ("opponent" and "venue"); therefore, authors drop the features using the following codes.

```
ds.drop(['Match Venue'],axis=1,inplace=True)
ds.drop(['Opponent Team'],axis=1,inplace=True)
```

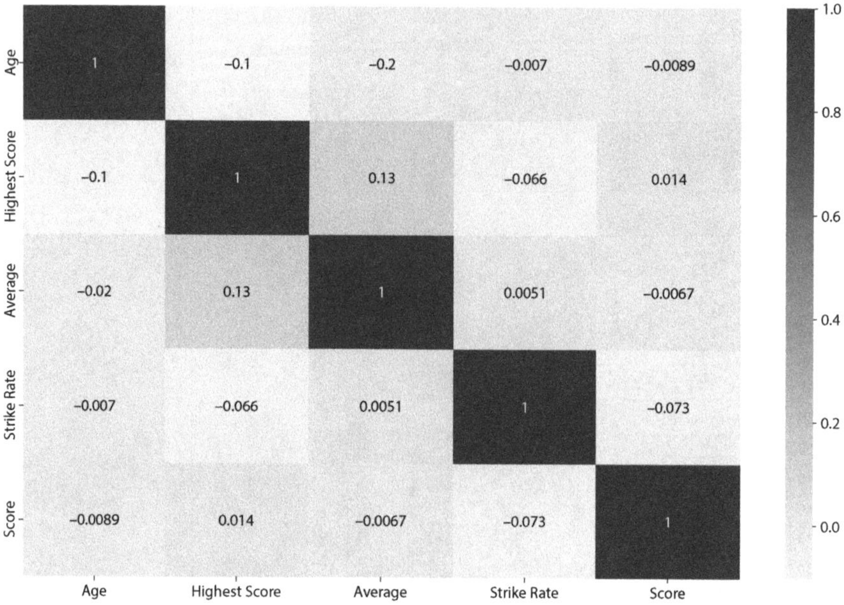

Figure 10.7 Heat map for all numerical features including the output variable.

	Age	Highest Score	Average	Strike Rate	Score	Bengaluru	Chennai	Delhi	Dharamsala	Hyderabad	...	Pune	AUS	BAN	ENG	IND	NED	NZ	PAK	SA	SL
0	23	119	29.346881	78	142	0	0	0	0	0	...	0	0	0	0	0	0	0	1	0	0
1	28	84	30.361677	78	20	0	0	0	0	0	...	1	0	0	0	0	0	1	0	0	0
2	22	187	35.456528	78	46	0	0	0	0	0	...	0	1	0	0	0	0	0	0	0	0
3	31	191	35.567704	78	178	1	0	0	0	0	...	0	0	0	0	0	0	0	0	1	0
4	19	191	38.812149	78	103	0	0	0	0	0	...	0	0	0	0	0	1	0	0	0	0

5 rows × 23 columns

Figure 10.8 Head of the preprocessed dataset.

Preprocessed dataset is now ready for training the ANFIS model and the dataset head looks as Figure 10.8.

10.4.2 ANFIS Model Building in MATLAB 2020A

A preprocessed dataset trains the ANFIS model in a MATLAB environment. In the training scheme, 1000 epochs are considered with a "sugeno"-type fuzzy model [26]. A total of 22 features produce a "fis" file, which is used to predict the score of a player. The simulation model that is used in MATLAB is illustrated in Figure 10.9.

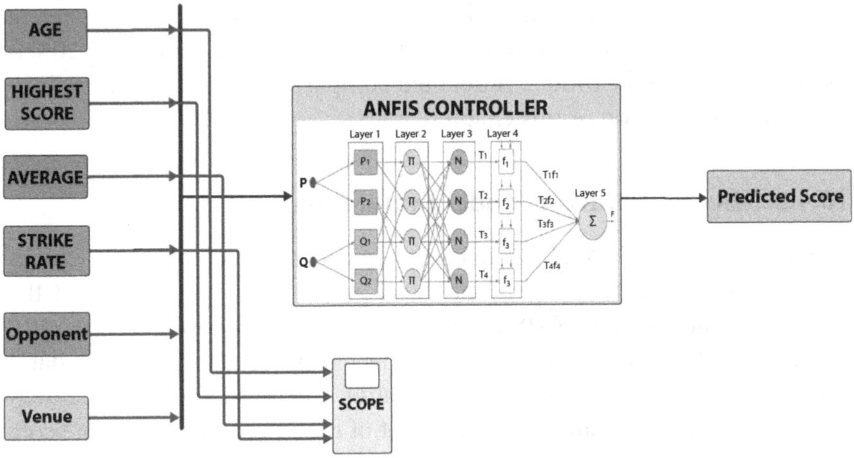

Figure 10.9 Simulation schematic of the proposed score predictor model.

Figure 10.9 identifies six input blocks, such as age, highest score, average, strike rate, opponent, and venue. The authors use a few datasets from test data randomly and observe the scores of the respective players. Inputs can be observed in the scope connected to the figure. The ANFIS predictor model operates using the tested dataset and produces a score. Table 10.1 shows 10 test results, which are evaluated in the next subsection.

Table 10.1 Test dataset with predicted score using proposed model.

Age	Highest score	Average	Strike rate	Predicted score
17	187	44.63499	94	151
35	129	50.1847	84	88
41	161	53.43257	179	172
24	92	30.40821	200	71
30	79	43.17138	141	81
32	78	43.84547	147	164
23	150	43.9474	110	131
24	182	46.05287	124	56
41	175	49.06465	91	60
20	118	25.79874	83	85

Table 10.1 shows the predicted score on the test dataset. Eighty percent of the entire data set is utilized for training, whereas the remaining 20% is used for verifying the model. A detailed comparison and analysis are done in the next subsection of this chapter.

10.4.3 Score Predictor Model Evaluation

In this subsection, 20% of the datasets are tested and compared with the actual score of the respective dataset. A graphical visualization and the model evaluation using RMSE are made in this subsection. Figure 10.10 depicts a scatterplot of the true and expected outcomes of the test dataset. The scatterplot identifies a linear relationship between real and anticipated scores, which evaluates the good fit of the proposed model for score prediction.

The authors also observe the graphical comparison between predicted and actual scores in Figure 10.11, which further evaluates the goodness of the model. The proposed model predicts the scores near their actual values.

Referring to Eq. (10.1) and the data from Table 10.1, the RMSE value of the recommended model is 3.4521, which signifies that, on average, the model's forecasting differs from the true values by approximately 3.1521 runs. For example, if a player scores 100 in a particular match, the proposed model predicts the score between 97 and 103, rounding to the nearest integer value.

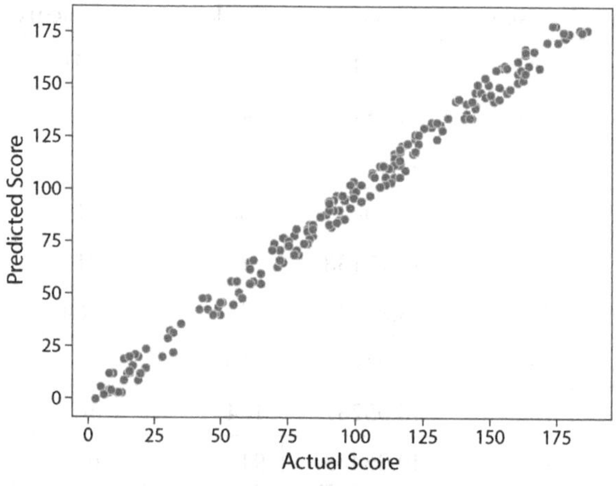

Figure 10.10 Scatterplot between predicted and actual score of test dataset.

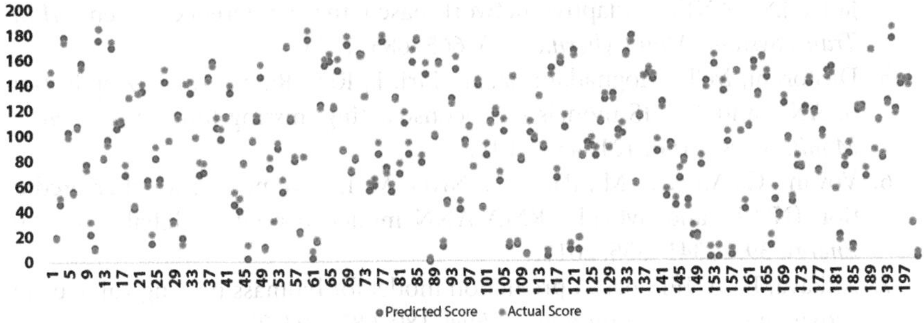

Figure 10.11 Observation of the actual and predicted scores of test dataset.

10.5 Conclusion

This chapter emphasizes the application of the ANFIS model to predict an interesting trendy task, which is the score of a player. ICC World Cup 2023 data are used to train the fuzzy system, and using an ANN, the model operates with the unseen data or test dataset. The Jupyter Notebook platform is utilized here to preprocess the dataset and visualize the optimized dataset. The processed dataset is further separated into training and testing sets. Eighty percent of the dataset is utilized for training, with the remaining 20% used to test or evaluate the proposed model. The model is simulated on the MATLAB platform, and the predicted scores are obtained as outputs. The ultimate stage of this chapter evaluates the proposed model using the RMSE value. Visualization of the predicted and actual scores also evaluates the model as a good fit. The authors finally conclude that the proposed model may be a viable solution for predicting the score of any player in the world of trendy games using a technology-based method instead of people's normal predictions.

References

1. Bell, J., What is machine learning? Machine Learning and the City: Applications in Architecture and Urban Design, 207-216, 2022.
2. Hopfield, J.J., Artificial neural networks. *IEEE Circuits Devices Mag.*, 4, 5, 3–10, 1988.
3. Lin, S., Fuzzy-AI model, in: *Fuzzy-AI Model and Big Data Exploration: A Methodological Philosophy in Solving Problems in Digital Era*, pp. 15–46, Springer Berlin Heidelberg, Berlin, Heidelberg, 2022.

4. Jang, J.S., ANFIS: adaptive-network-based fuzzy inference system. *IEEE Trans. Systems Man Cybern.*, 23, 3, 665–685, 1993.
5. Dastorani, M.T., Moghadamnia, A., Piri, J., Rico-Ramirez, M., Application of ANN and ANFIS models for reconstructing missing flow data. *Environ. Monit. Assess.*, 166, 421–434, 2010.
6. Voyant, C., Muselli, M., Paoli, C., Nivet, M. L., Numerical weather prediction (NWP) and hybrid ARMA/ANN model to predict global radiation. *Energy*, 39, 1, 341–355, 2012.
7. Akkaya, E., ANFIS based prediction model for biomass heating value using proximate analysis components. *Fuel*, 180, 687–693, 2016.
8. Shivakoti, I., Kibria, G., Pradhan, P.M., Pradhan, B.B., Sharma, A., ANFIS based prediction and parametric analysis during turning operation of stainless steel 202. *Mater. Manuf. Processes*, 34, 1, 112–121, 2018.
9. Iphar, M., ANN and ANFIS performance prediction models for hydraulic impact hammers. 27, 1, 23–29, 2012, doi: 10.1016/j.tust.2011.06.004.
10. Boyacioglu, M.A. and Avci, D., An adaptive network-based fuzzy inference system (ANFIS) for the prediction of stock market return: the case of the Istanbul stock exchange. *Expert Syst. Appl.*, 37, 12, 7908–7912, 2010.
11. Zhao, Y., Gor, M., Voronkova, D.K., Touchaei, H.G., Moayedi, H., Le, B.N., An optimized ANFIS model for predicting pile pullout resistance. *Steel Compos. Struct.*, 48, 2, 179, 2023.
12. Kalsi, B.S., Singh, S., Alam, M.S., Sidhu, G.K., Comparison of ANN and ANFIS modeling for predicting drying kinetics of Stevia rebaudiana leaves in a hot-air dryer and characterization of dried powder. *Int. J. Food Prop.*, 26, 2, 3356–3375, 2023.
13. Li, J., Yan, G., Abbud, L.H., Alkhalifah, T., Alturise, F., Khadimallah, M.A., Marzouki, R., Predicting the shear strength of concrete beam through ANFIS-GA–PSO hybrid modeling. *Adv. Eng. Software*, 181, 103475, 2023.
14. Sarr, M.P., Thiam, A., Dieng, B., ANFIS and ANN models to predict heliostat tracking errors. *Heliyon*, 9, 1, 2023.
15. Yonar, A. and Yonar, H., Modeling air pollution by integrating ANFIS and metaheuristic algorithms. *Model. Earth Syst. Environ.*, 9, 2, 1621–1631, 2023.
16. Patel, M. and Parekh, F., Forecasting of Flood Flow of Panam River Basin using Adaptive Neuro-Fuzzy Inference System (ANFIS) and ANN with Comparative Study. *J. Adv. Res. Appl. Sci. Eng. Technol.*, 32, 2, 346–359, 2023.
17. Kumar, R., Al-Turjman, F., Srinivas, L.N.B., Braveen, M., Ramakrishnan, J., ANFIS for prediction of epidemic peak and infected cases for COVID-19 in India. *Neural Comput. Appl.*, 35, 10, 1–14, 2023.
18. Abdolrasol, M.G., Hussain, S.S., Ustun, T.S., Sarker, M.R., Hannan, M.A., Mohamed, R., Milad, A., Artificial neural networks based optimization techniques: A review. *Electronics*, 10, 21, 2689, 2021.
19. Karim, I.U., Akkash, M.F., Raha, S., Approximate reasoning with fuzzy soft set. *Iran. J. Fuzzy Syst.*, 19, 4, 107–124, 2022.

20. Sharifi, H., Roozbahani, A., Hashemy Shahdany, S.M., Evaluating the performance of agricultural water distribution systems using FIS, ANN and ANFIS intelligent models. *Water Resour. Manage.*, 35, 1797–1816, 2021.
21. Precious, J.G., Selvan, S., Avudaiammal, R., Classification of abnormalities in breast ultrasound images using ANN, FIS and ANFIS classifier: a comparison, in: *Journal of Physics: Conference Series*, vol. 1916, IOP publishing, p. 012015, 2021, May.
22. Ayed, N. and Bougatef, K., Performance Assessment of Logistic Regression (LR), Artificial Neural Network (ANN), Fuzzy Inference System (FIS) and Adaptive Neuro-Fuzzy System (ANFIS) in Predicting Default Probability: The Case of a Tunisian Islamic Bank. *Comput. Econ.*, 64, 3, 1–33, 2023.
23. Sharifi, H., Roozbahani, A., Hashemy Shahdany, M., Development of ANN, FIS and ANFIS models to evaluate the adequacy index in agricultural water distribution systems (Case study: Rudasht irrigation network). *Iran. J. Ecohydrol.*, 7, 3, 635–646, 2020.
24. Miller, C., *Hands-On Data Analysis with NumPy and pandas: Implement Python packages from data manipulation to processing*, Packt Publishing Ltd, Birmingham, UK, 2018.
25. Khandare, A., Agarwal, N., Bodhankar, A., Kulkarni, A., Mane, I., Analysis of python libraries for artificial intelligence, in: *Intelligent Computing and Networking: Proceedings of IC-ICN 2022*, Springer Nature Singapore, Singapore, pp. 157–177, 2023.
26. Benić, J., Pender, A., Kasać, J., Stipančić, T., Sugeno-Type Fuzzy Ontology PI Controller for Proportional Electrohydraulic System. *IFAC-PapersOnLine*, 56, 2, 8732–8737, 2023.

11

Designing a PID Controller for the Two-Area LFC Problem Using Gradient Descent–Based Linear Regression

Susmit Chakraborty[1]* and Arindam Mondal[2]

[1]*Department of Computer Science and Engineering (CS&DS), Brainware University, Barasat, West Bengal, India*
[2]*Department of Electrical Engineering, Dr. B. C. Roy Engineering College, Durgapur, West Bengal, India*

Abstract
The technique for creating a linear model for the proportional integral derivative (PID) parameters of a PID controller (PIDC) is presented in this study. The method optimizes parameters through the use of the gradient descent technique and is based on linear regression. The designed PIDC is used to control a two-area hybrid power system (2-AHPS) network. The 2-AHPS consists of solar, ocean-thermal units as renewable sources along with the conventional power plants as thermal and hydro unit. A thorough review of the literature reveals that PID tuning techniques have been developed and performed better, with several advancements achieved. However, none of the literature points out a linear modeling of PID parameters for load frequency control problem. The key feature of this approach is that the tuning parameters are dependent on a limited set of chosen transient specifications. The whole system with the proposed controller is trained in Jupyter Notebook and the 2-AHPS along with the proposed scheme is sketched and tested in MATLAB platform. The simulation results are analyzed using the acquired time-domain parameters such as settling time, overshoot, undershoot, peak-overshoot, and peak-undershoot.

***Keywords*:** Linear regression (LR), linear modeling, gradient descent (GD) method, load frequency control (LFC), power system (PS)

**Corresponding author*: susmit.eee@gmail.com

Arindam Mondal and Souvik Ganguli (eds.) Data-Driven Modeling, (239–256) © 2026 Scrivener Publishing LLC

11.1 Introduction

The concept of proportional integral derivative controllers (PIDCs) represents a significant turning point in the evolution of control theory [1–3]. An American scientist, E. A. Sperry, created an apparatus that corrects the perturbations caused in sea during anomalous variations in sea level while conducting several tests with gyroscopic compasses [4]. This is among the first known instances of a PIDC in history. However, Nicolas Minorsky published a theoretical article on PIDC for the first time in 1922 [5]. Since then, proportional integral derivative (PID) has dominated the sector of control because of its easy-to-understand layout and simplicity of use. However, the prevailing consensus is that it falls short of performance requirements. Astrom and Hagglun discuss several methods established to ascertain PIDC settings for single-input single-output systems in the work "Automatic Tuning of PID Regulators." [6]. Ho provides an in-depth analysis of the several well-known PID tuning formulas, including the Cohen–Coon technique, the integral time-weighted absolute error (ITAE), integral absolute error (IAE), and the Ziegler–Nichols rule [7]. PIDCs are a very effective way to get the plant to produce the required amount in both steady state and dynamic response. This feature has made the use of PIDCs quite common. The primary tuning techniques used in both business and academic research are presented in the references [8, 9]. The Ziegler–Nichols and Cohen–Coon are two traditional techniques that are still in use; they both use analytical techniques for tuning and analysis. Additional analytical techniques are detailed in [10] Toscano and Lyonnet [10]. Typically, these techniques make use of heuristics [11] or sophisticated technique algorithms such as Firefly Swarm Optimization (FSO) [12], Levenberg–Marquardt Algorithm (LMA) [13], Big Bang–Big Crunch (BB-BC) [14], and Particle Swarm Optimization (PSO) [15]. A quicker self-tuning approach for PIDCs was presented by A. Besharati Rad *et al.* as an alternative to the ZN methodology for auto-tuning using Newton–Raphson search technique, which is effortless to use and does away with the need for laborious root-solving processes for the characteristic equation [16]. Mitsukura *et al.* use advanced genetic process to tune the PIDC [17]. Adaptive genetic algorithm-based self-tuning of PID parameters is also presented by Zhao and Xi [18]. These methods need the presence of a population that meets an evolutionary condition. So, it is clear that numerous studies on PID tuning enhancements have been published in the literature. However, in cases when they were not taught, their reliance on the model caused them to fail. Wang *et al.* have described a universal tuning approach for building PIDCs in managing a wide class of linear self-governing systems [19]. All of these traditional tunning methods take large calculation as well as time to tune the controller parameters. Some intelligent data-based tunning may be possible for PIDC. Machine learning (ML)–based tunning is a hot cake in recent research. Recently, reinforcement learning–based tunning is observed in [20]. Chowdhury *et al.* introduced TD3-based reinforcement learning for PIDC optimization [21]. Although some intelligent data–fed optimization techniques are available, the critical evaluation and prominent application are not made with the data modeled PIDC. Authors marked this gap and worked with ML-based PIDC tunning for load frequency control (LFC) problem. The authors of this work provide a method for linearly modeling PID parameters using the GD-based linear regression (LR), aiming to model PID parameters concerning transitory specifications of the two-area hybrid power system (2-AHPS) to obtain a dynamic control signal.

11.2 Plant Model

With two independent units in each area, the 2-AHPS is the one that has to be regulated in this chapter. Every region combines conventional energy sources (thermal or hydropower plants) with renewable energy sources (solar or ocean-thermal power plants). A thermal power plant and a solar photovoltaic unit are located in the first region [12], whereas an ocean-thermal unit and a hydro power unit are located in the second area [14]. The model's simulation scheme is shown in Figure 11.1.

11.3 PID Controller

Figure 11.1 shows the stimulation error signal in a simple feedback controller, which is a variation between the reference signal and real-time output. A PIDC provides an indicator of the real-time error, a measurement of previous accumulated errors, and an indication of future error or fluctuation in the error in the form of a proportional control signal. In terms of a mathematical equation, it can be expressed as Eq. (11.1).

$$g(t) = C_p e_a(t) + C_i \int_0^t e_a(\omega) d\omega + C_d \frac{d}{dt} e_a(t) \tag{11.1}$$

where $g(t)$ identifies the real-time control signal, and $e_a(t)$ is the dynamic error observed in 2-AHPS. Three controller parameters named as constant

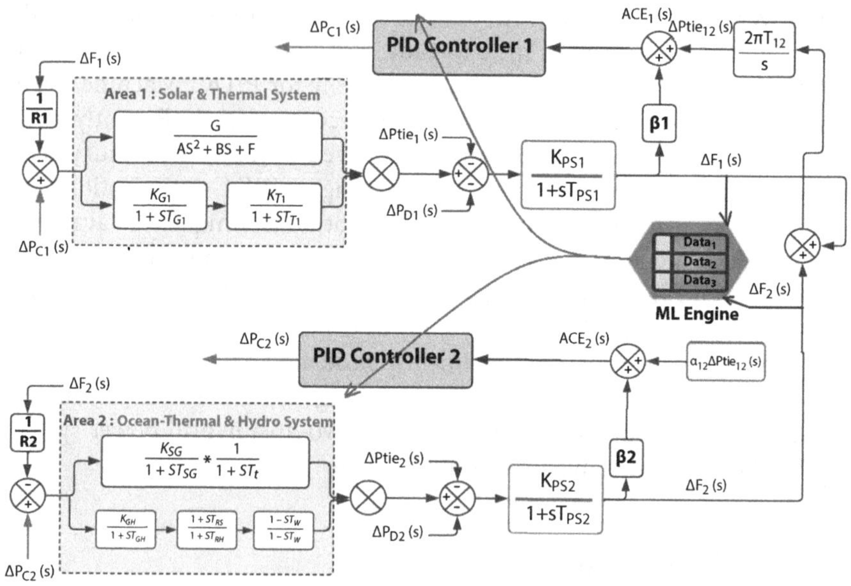

Figure 11.1 ML-based simulation schematic of the 2-AHPS.

of proportionality, integration, and derivative are denoted by C_p, C_i, C_d, respectively. The PIDC can be realized in Figure 11.2.

In the Laplace domain, Eq. (11.1) may be penned as Eq. (11.2), which is also termed as the transfer function of the system.

$$Q_{PID} = \frac{G(s)}{E(s)} = C_p + sC_d + \frac{C_i}{s} \tag{11.2}$$

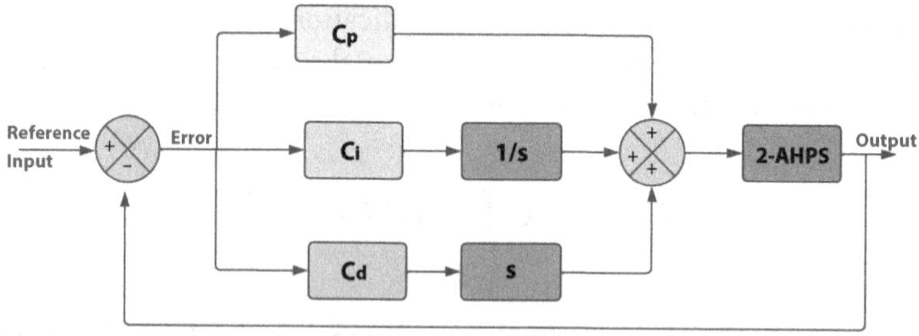

Figure 11.2 2-AHPS with PIDC schematic.

These three parameters are needed to be adjusted as per the dynamic error found in the system. Tunning of the parameters is done based on the ML approach, more prominently LR model [22] with GD method.

11.4 LR Model

A system may be modeled mathematically using LR [22], which establishes a relationship between feature variables and the dependent variable [22]. This is a popular strategy for fitting data to obtain a prediction model. In this regression model, three-time domain specifications such as rise time (t_R), peak time (t_P), and settling time (t_S) are considered as three feature variables. The PID parameters C_p, C_i, and C_d are the target parameters that need to be optimized. Eqs. (11.3), (11.4), and (11.5) are three LR equations that are considered as three hypotheses to get a succinct model.

$$C_p = at_R + bt_P + ct_S \tag{11.3}$$

$$C_i = dt_R + et_P + ft_S \tag{11.4}$$

$$C_d = gt_R + ht_P + it_S \tag{11.5}$$

where *a*, *b*, *c*, *d*, *e*, *f*, *g*, *h*, and *i* are nine coefficients of three time domain features for predicting three PID parameters, respectively.

Three ML engines (MLEs) are considered simultaneously to train the model obeying Eqs. (11.3), (11.4), and (11.5). MLEs work on the principle of GD approach [23]. In order to develop the linear model of the PID parameters, one training set has been considered with the system output data when the system is controlled by using FSO-, BB-BC–, and PSO-tunned PIDC. Accumulation of the response using different algorithms makes the training unbiased. Tables 11.1, 11.2, and 11.3 illustrate the training data for predicting the PID parameters such as C_p, C_i, and C_d, respectively. While tunning one parameter, the other two parameters remain constant.

LR model is established in the Jupyter Notebook platform. The following programs are used for building the model:

```
from sklearn.linear_model import LinearRegression
lm = LinearRegression()
lm.fit(X_train, y_train)
print(lm.summary())
```

Table 11.1 Training dataset for C_p with $C_i = 0.010$ and $C_d = 0.677$.

Serial number	t_R	t_P	t_S	C_p
1	0.751385	2.751385	4.751385	0.663
2	0.521849	2.521849	4.521849	0.670
3	0.906269	2.906269	4.906269	0.638
4	0.83855	2.83855	4.83855	0.647
.....	.....	.....	.....	.....
.....	.....	.....	.....	.....
998	1.089084	5.089084	9.089084	0.339
999	0.703705	4.703705	8.703705	0.418
1000	1.694562	5.694562	9.694562	0.305

Table 11.2 Training dataset for C_i with $C_p = 0.732$ and $C_d = 0.677$.

Serial number	t_R	t_P	t_S	C_i
1	0.902123	2.902123	4.902123	0.014
2	0.450398	2.450398	4.450398	0.013
3	0.775725	2.775725	4.775725	0.014
4	0.41169	2.41169	4.41169	0.012
.....	.....	.....	.....	.....
.....	.....	.....	.....	.....
998	1.570115	7.570115	13.57012	0.182
999	0.784893	6.784893	12.78489	0.177
1000	0.454635	6.454635	12.45464	0.163

First line is used to import the module named “LinearRegression” from the package “sklearn.linear_model.” Second line is for initializing the LR with a variable named “lm.” “lm.fit()” method is to train the model using the training dataset illustrated in Tables 11.1, 11.2, and 11.3. The last code is

Table 11.3 Training dataset for C_d with $C_p = 0.732$ and $C_i = 0.010$.

Serial number	t_R	t_P	t_S	C_d
1	0.837728	2.837728	4.837728	0.634
2	0.67409	2.67409	4.67409	0.609
3	0.277144	2.277144	4.277144	0.584
4	0.83082	2.83082	4.93082	0.641
.....	.....	.....	.....	.....
.....	.....	.....	.....	.....
998	0.195088	4.195088	8.195088	0.882
999	0.777743	4.777743	8.777743	0.896
1000	1.470151	5.470151	9.470151	0.911

to get the evaluation report of the linear model obtained. Table 11.4 depicts the coefficients of Eqs. (11.3), (11.4), and (11.5). Regression parameters are predicted with the action of the GD method as per the equation drawn in Eq. (11.6).

$$\Delta C(t) = \frac{1}{2t}\sum\nolimits_{j=1,\ \ k\subseteq\{p,i,d\}}^{t} \left(C_k(t)^j - y_k(t)^j\right) \tag{11.6}$$

where t is the number of training samples that are gathered using three traditional algorithms-tunned PID parameters for the same 2-AHPS. $\Delta C(t)$ is considered as the cost function considered for all three parameters tunning. $C_k(t)^j$ identifies the PID parameter for the iteration sequence j, and $y_k(t)^j$ is the actual parameter obtained from different optimization used here.

Table 11.4 Linear regression coefficients.

a	b	c	d	e	f	g	h	i
0.784	1.126	0.871	0.086	0.872	1.352	1.82	0.88	1.52

11.5 Result Analysis

A 2-AHPS with one renewable and one nonrenewable type unit in each area is simulated using MATLAB using the MLE, which is formed by the training in Jupyter Notebook platform. In this section, the results obtained in both the phases such as training in Jupyter Notebook and simulation in MATLAB are analyzed.

11.5.1 ML Phase in Jupyter Notebook

In this phase, three PID parameters are trained separately. The model starts with the initializing modules such as numpy [24] and pandas [25], as well as importing the respective csv datasets. Visualizing the data with the help of pair-plot for all three parameters is done in the next step. Figures 11.3, 11.4, and 11.5 illustrate the correlations among feature variables (t_R, t_P, and t_S) along with the output variables (C_p, C_i, and C_d). Nondiagonal plots of the pair-plots define independency among all feature variables to the output variable. There is no straightforward relation drawn from the plots as all datasets are scattered over the region. However, feature variables are highly correlated to each other, which is quite a natural fact.

Standardization of the feature variables is the next step where "MinMaxScaler" module from "sklearn.preprocessing" is used. In the next step, correlations are observed using a heat map method [26]. Heat map basically is a visual analysis that deals the correlation matrix between all variables of a dataset. Figures 11.3, 11.4, and 11.5 illustrate the heat map for the three parameters of PIDC. Lighter shade defines no correlations, whereas darker shade identifies a correlation between corresponding two features. It is quite natural to get a strong correlation between each two-time domain specifications and can easily be seen from the heat maps depicted in Figures 11.6, 11.7, and 11.8.

Standardized dataset is directly used to generate corresponding linear model for all of the PID parameters using the "statsmodels.api.OLS" method. Table 11.4 is the final output of the training phase. The evaluation reports of the models are depicted in Figures 11.9, 11.10, and 11.11, respectively, for the three parameters of the PIDC.

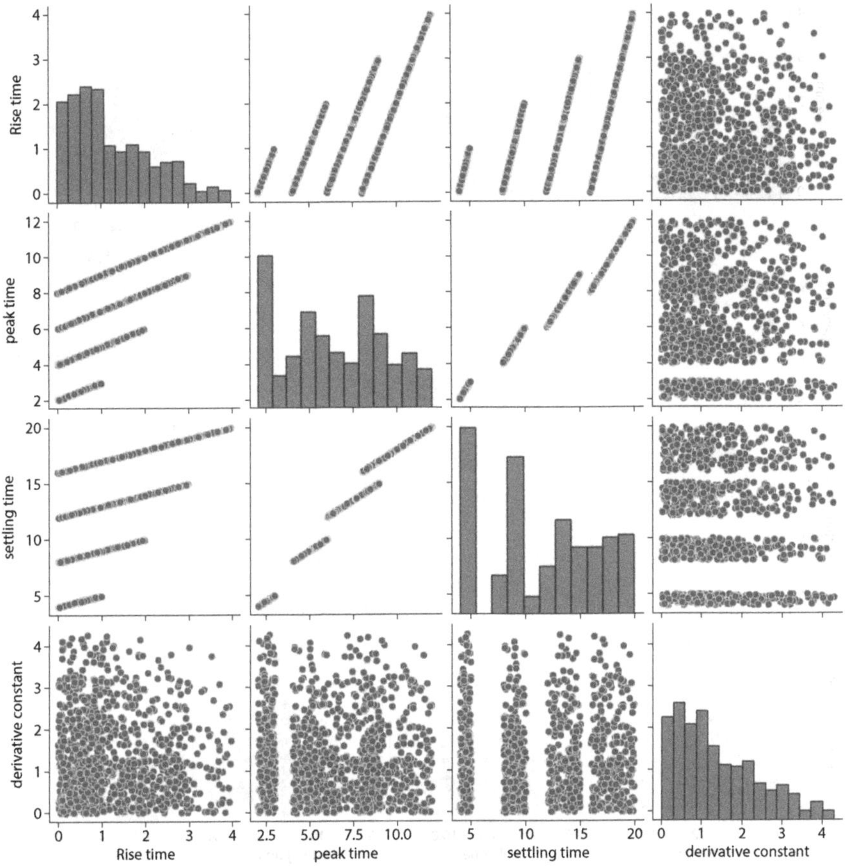

Figure 11.3 Pair-plot for derivative constant model.

Figures 11.9, 11.10, and 11.11 infer the summary report of the models, which are built using LR method. Reports show that acceptable R^2 values such as 0.864, 0.854, and 0.839 are obtained for the models of C_p, C_i, and C_d, respectively. Corresponding p values of the feature variables are also within acceptable range [27] as depicted in Figures 11.9, 11.10, and 11.11.

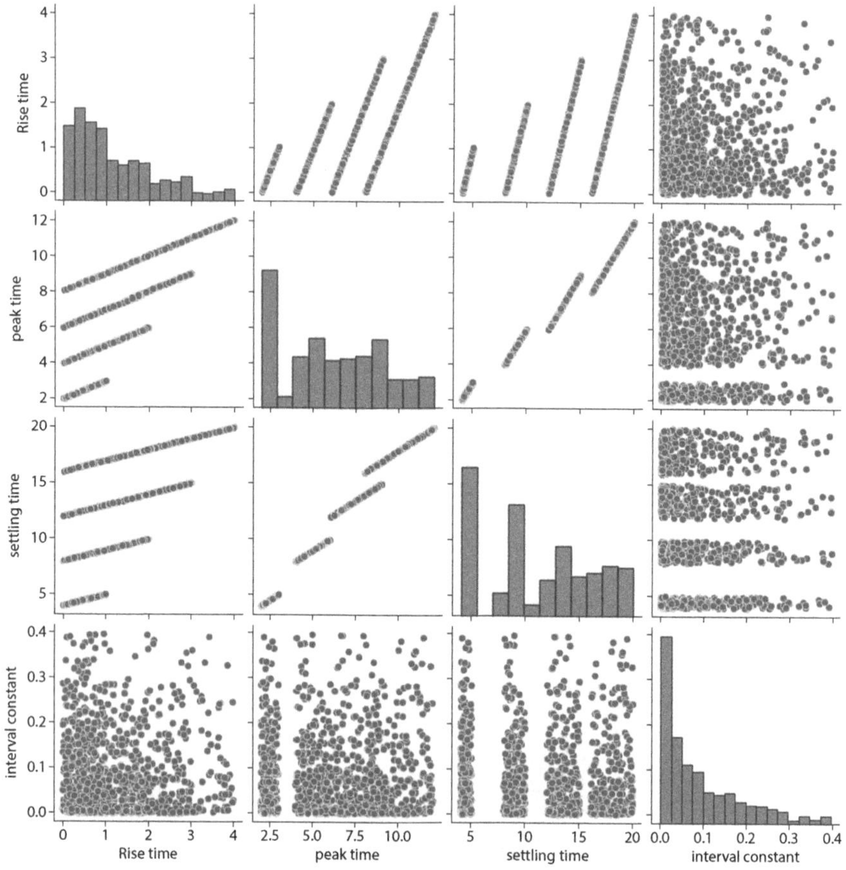

Figure 11.4 Pair-plot for integral constant model.

11.5.2 Simulation Phase in MATLAB

After training phase, the chapter enters into the simulation phase to test the model with the same 2-AHPS. Two MLEs are considered to tune the PID parameters in real-time simulation. MATLAB version 2020A with Intel Core i7 at 2.80 GHz processor with 16 GB RAM simulates the MLE-assisted 2-AHPS. Figure 11.12 depicts the frequency errors of two areas (ΔF_1 *and* ΔF_2) of the 2-AHPS controlled by FSO-tunned PID, BB-BC–tunned PID, and LR-tunned PIDC. It is clearly observed that the LR-tunned PID outperforms the other two methods of control. Table 11.5 illustrates the details of the time domain output features such as t_R, t_P, t_S as well as two additional parameters such as peak-overshoot (POS) and peak-undershoot (PUS).

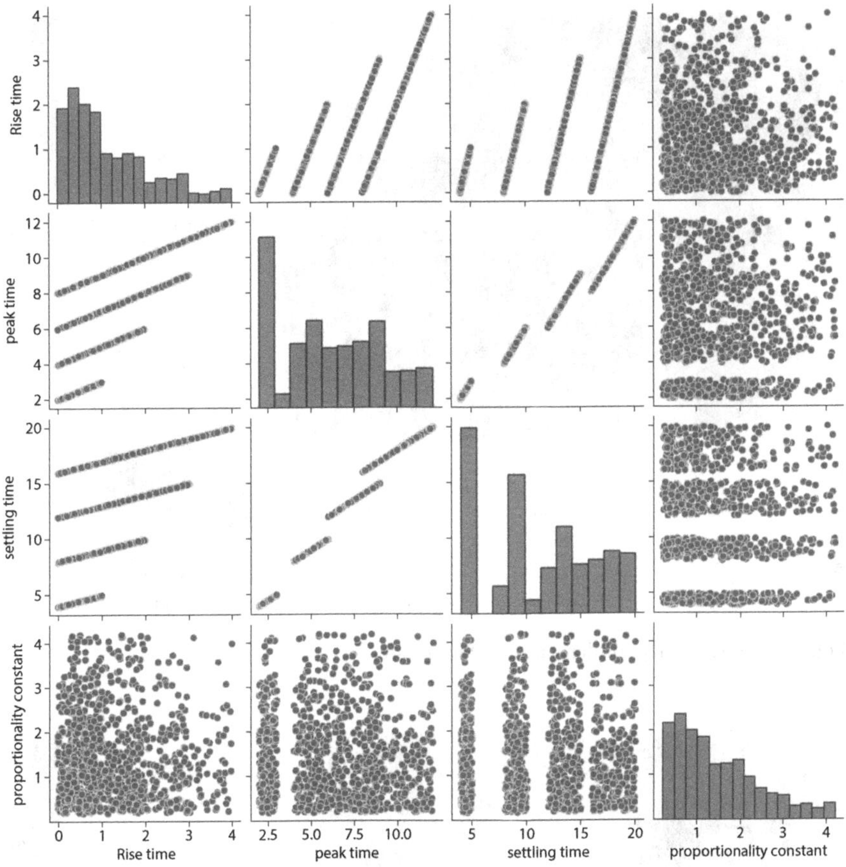

Figure 11.5 Pair-plot for proportionality constant model.

Table 11.5 reveals that the proposed method of control gives very accurate results with minimum frequency errors in both the areas. LR:PID outperforms FSO:PID and BB-BC:PID with approximately 68%, 69%, and 77% better t_R, t_P, t_S, respectively, in ΔF_1. Similar results are observed in ΔF_2 where LR:PID shows 98% and 80% better results than FSO:PID and BB-BC:PID for t_P, t_S, respectively, and t_R remains zero when the system is controlled using LR:PID method; 62% and 25% betterment in POS are found with LR:PID method than the other two control strategies, respectively. In case of PUS, it is found that the proposed method outperforms the other two control schemes with approximately 99% improved result.

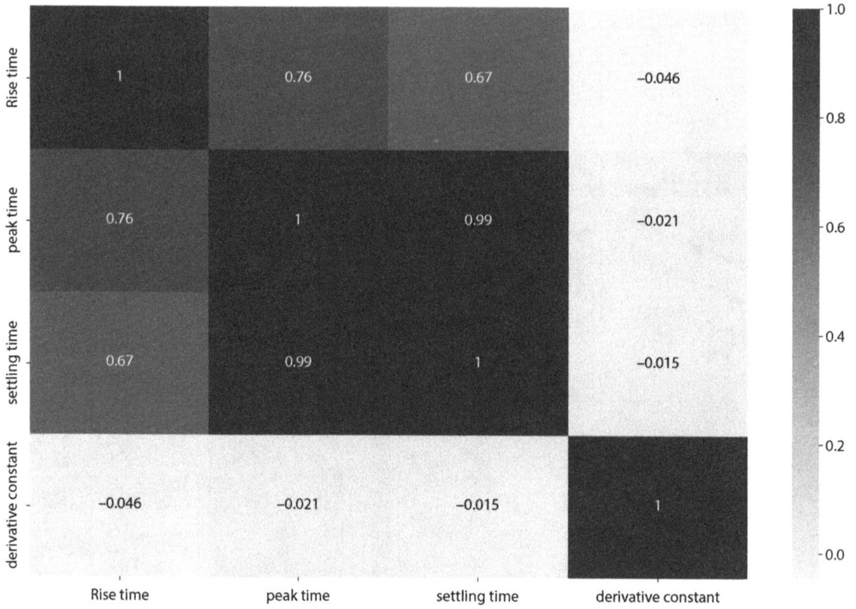

Figure 11.6 Heat map for derivate constant model.

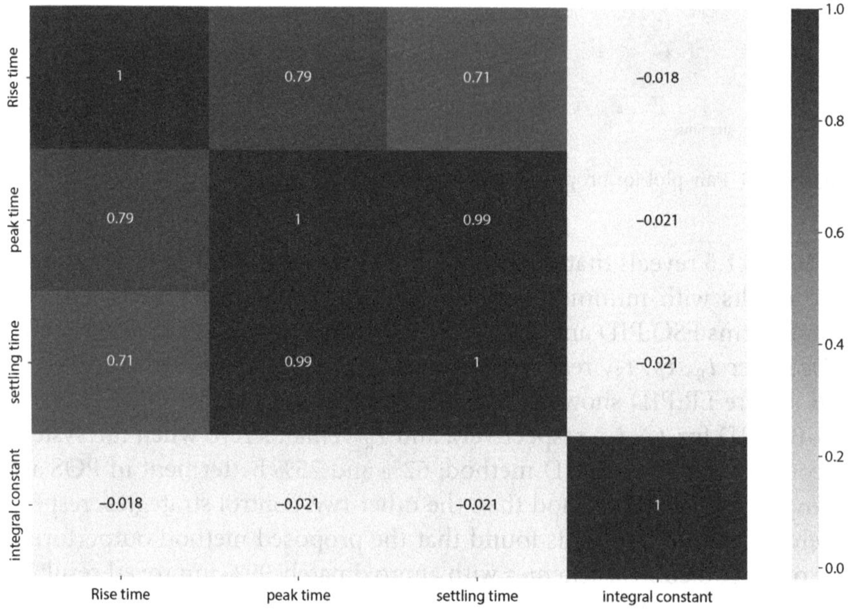

Figure 11.7 Heat map for integral constant model.

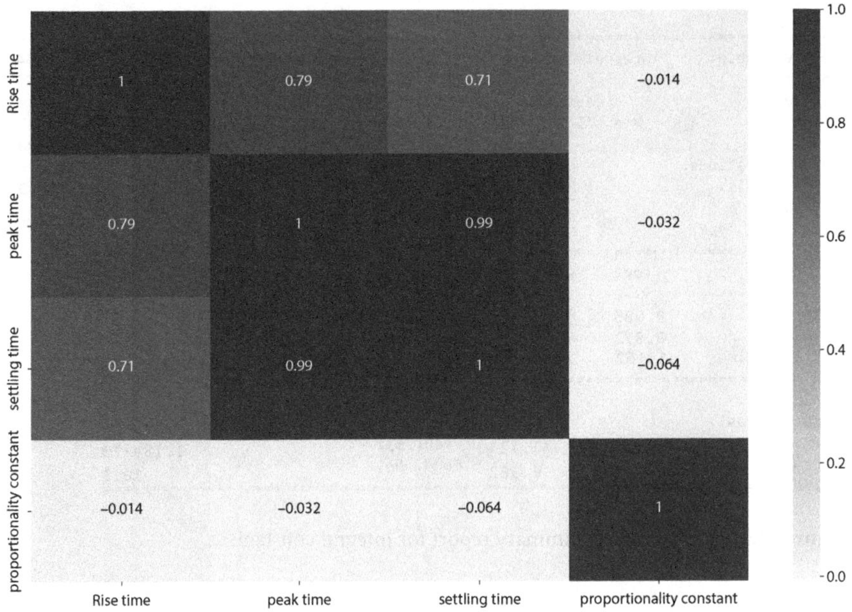

Figure 11.8 Heat map for proportionality constant model.

OLS Regression Results

Dep. Variable:	derivative constant	R-squared (uncentered):	0.864
Model:	OLS	Adj. R-squared (uncentered):	0.867
Method:	Least Squares	F-statistic:	428.6
Date:	Mon, 25 Mar 2024	Prob (F-statistic):	1.00e-157
Time:	14:39:03	Log-Likelihood:	13.255
No. Observations:	700	AIC:	-20.51
Df Residuals:	697	BIC:	-6.857
Df Model:	3		
Covariance Type:	nonrobust		

	coef	std err	t	P>|t|	[0.025	0.975]
Rise time	1.82	0.018	3.482	0.001	0.027	0.098
peak time	0.88	0.012	5.452	0.000	0.041	0.087
settling time	1.52	0.010	-3.295	0.001	-0.054	-0.014

Omnibus:	97.661	Durbin-Watson:	2.097
Prob(Omnibus):	0.000	Jarque-Bera (JB):	325.388
Skew:	1.130	Prob(JB):	2.20e-71
Kurtosis:	6.923	Cond. No.	10.6

Figure 11.9 Linear model summary report for derivative constant.

```
                              OLS Regression Results
=============================================================================================
Dep. Variable:       integral  constant  R-squared (uncentered):                        0.854
Model:                              OLS  Adj. R-squared (uncentered):                   0.897
Method:                   Least Squares  F-statistic:                                   107.9
Date:                  Mon, 25 Mar 2024  Prob (F-statistic):                         2.14e-57
Time:                          14:42:35  Log-Likelihood:                              -64.308
No. Observations:                   700  AIC:                                           134.6
Df Residuals:                       697  BIC:                                           148.3
Df Model:                             3
Covariance Type:              nonrobust
=======================================================================================
                  coef    std err          t        P>|t|       [0.025       0.975]
---------------------------------------------------------------------------------------
Rise time        0.086  0.017        6.277        0.000        0.074        0.142
peak time        0.872  0.014        3.468        0.001        0.022        0.078
settling time    1.152  0.013        3.124        0.002        0.015        0.065
=====================================================================================
Omnibus:                         97.054  Durbin-Watson:                         2.099
Prob(Omnibus):                    0.000  Jarque-Bera (JB):                    322.034
Skew:                             1.124  Prob(JB):                           1.18e-70
Kurtosis:                         6.902  Cond. No.                               10.3
=====================================================================================
```

Figure 11.10 Linear model summary report for integral constant.

```
                              OLS Regression Results
=============================================================================================
Dep. Variable:      proportionality constant  R-squared (uncentered):                   0.839
Model:                                   OLS  Adj. R-squared (uncentered):              0.836
Method:                        Least Squares  F-statistic:                              77.18
Date:                       Mon, 25 Mar 2024  Prob (F-statistic):                    3.13e-84
Time:                               12:29:30  Log-Likelihood:                          378.51
No. Observations:                        700  AIC:                                     -735.0
Df Residuals:                            697  BIC:                                     -691.7
Df Model:                                  3
Covariance Type:                   nonrobust
=================================================================================
                  coef    std err          t       P>|t|      [0.025      0.975]
---------------------------------------------------------------------------------
Rise time        0.784    0.014      2.958       0.003       0.014       0.071
peak time        1.126    0.030      7.772       0.000       0.174       0.293
settling time    0.071    0.021      9.397       0.000       0.160       0.244
==============================================================================
Omnibus:                       97.054   Durbin-Watson:                   2.099
Prob(Omnibus):                  0.000   Jarque-Bera (JB):              322.034
Skew:                           1.124   Prob(JB):                     1.18e-70
Kurtosis:                       6.902   Cond. No.                         10.3
==============================================================================
```

Figure 11.11 Linear model summary report for proportionality constant.

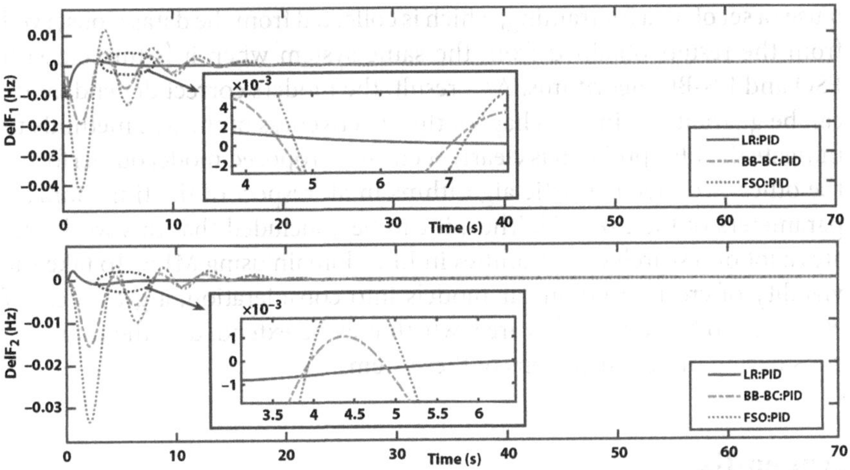

Figure 11.12 Simulation results of 2-AHPS using three different methods of tunning.

Table 11.5 Performance analysis of 2-AHPS with FSO:PID, BB-BC:PID, and LR:PID control.

Control methods	Signals	t_R	t_P	t_S	POS	PUS
FSO:PID	ΔF_1	3.82	4.15	22.15	0.013	−0.0407
	ΔF_2	4.64	5.81	21.87	0.008	−0.035
BB-BC:PID	ΔF_1	3.81	4.13	20.83	0.003	−0.019
	ΔF_2	4.63	5.77	20.76	0.004	−0.014
LR:PID	ΔF_1	1.16	1.32	5.18	0.0007	−0.01
	ΔF_2	0	0.07	4.07	0.003	−0.00012

11.6 Conclusion

A LR strategy based on gradient descent (GD) has been given in this chapter to model PID parameters. It makes an attempt to connect the transient specifications and PID tuning parameters. For analytical purposes, a straight line–based connection, or, in simple words, a linear relation between the controller specifications and the time domain parameters, is taken into account. This method's training strategy is supervised, meaning it uses a set of data for training, which is collected from the dataset observed from the results obtained from the same system when it is tunned with FSO and BB-BC algorithms. As a result, the model's correct dependability can be guaranteed. In this chapter, the effectiveness of the ML methods to mitigate the LFC problem is clearly seen. The proposed model outperforms the other two metaheuristic algorithms in all respect of the time domain parameters of the 2-AHPS. Thus, it can be concluded that this work creates a lot of research opportunities in LFC domain using MLE. To take the viability of creating nonlinear models into consideration, a great deal of effort has to be done in this area, which may be extended in the future by considering more dimensions of the system.

Appendix

a. For thermal power plant: $T_{G1} = 0.08,\ T_{T1} = 0.3,\ K_{G1} = 1,\ K_{T1} = 1$
b. For solar unit: $A = 0.08,\ B = 0.8,\ G = 1,\ F = 0.1$
c. For ocean thermal power plant: $K_{SG} = 1,\ T_{SG} = 0.08,\ T_t = 1.25$
d. For hydro power plant: $K_{GH} = T_{GH} = 85,\ T_{RS} = 0.513,\ T_{RH} = 5,\ T_w = 1$
e. For other parameters: $K_{PSi} = 120\frac{\text{Hz}}{\text{puMW}},\ T_{PSi} = 20\text{s},\ R_1 = R_2 = \frac{2.4\text{Hz}}{\text{pu}},$ $\beta_1 = \beta_2 = 0.425\frac{\text{puMW}}{\text{Hz}}$

References

1. Chaturvedi, S. and Kumar, N., Design and implementation of an optimized PID controller for the adaptive cruise control system. *IETE J. Res.*, 69, 10, 7084–7091, 2023.
2. Borase, R.P., Maghade, D.K., Sondkar, S.Y., Pawar, S.N., A review of PID control, tuning methods and applications. *Int. J. Dyn. Control*, 9, 818–827, 2021.
3. Samosir, A.S., Sutikno, T., Mardiyah, L., Simple formula for designing the PID controller of a DC-DC buck converter. *Int. J. Power Electron. Drive Syst.*, 14, 1, 327, 2023.
4. Bennett, S., A brief history of automatic control. *IEEE Control Syst. Mag.*, 16, 3, 17–25, 1996.
5. Minorsky, N., Directional stability of automatically steered bodies. *J. Am. Soc. Nav. Eng.*, 34, 2, 280–309, 1922.
6. Astrom, K.J. and Hagglund, T., Automatic tuning of PID regulators. *Instrum. Soc. Amer.*, 1988.

7. Ho, W.K., Gan, O.P., Tay, E.B., Ang, E.L., Performance and gain and phase margins of well-known PID tuning formulas. *IEEE Trans. Control Syst. Technol.*, 4, 4, 473–477, 1996.
8. Åström, K.J. and Hägglund, T., The future of PID control. *Control Eng. Pract.*, 9, 11, 1163–1175, 2001.
9. Cominos, P. and Munro, N., PID controllers: recent tuning methods and design to specification. *IEE Proceedings-Control Theory Appl.*, 149, 1, 46–53, 2002.
10. Toscano, R. and Lyonnet, P., A new heuristic approach for non-convex optimization problems. *Inf. Sci.*, 180, 10, 1955–1966, 2010.
11. Ntogramatzidis, L. and Ferrante, A., Exact tuning of PID controllers in control feedback design. *IET Control Theory Appl.*, 5, 4, 565–578, 2011.
12. Chakraborty, S., Mondal, A., Biswas, S., Roy, P.K., Design of FUZZY-3DOF-PID controller for an Ocean Thermal hybrid Automatic Generation Control system. *Sci. Iran.*, 2023.
13. Chakraborty, S., Mondal, A., Biswas, S., Design of Type-2 Fuzzy Controller for Hybrid Multi-Area Power System. *Fuzzy Log. Appl. Comput. Sci. Math.*, 107–124, 2023.
14. Chakraborty, S., Mondal, A., Biswas, S., Application of FUZZY-3DOF-PID controller for controlling FOPTD type communication delay based renewable three-area deregulated hybrid power system. *Evol. Intell.*, 17, 4, 2821–2841, 2024.
15. Suriyan, K. and Nagarajan, R., Particle Swarm Optimization in Biomedical Technologies: Innovations, Challenges, and Opportunities. *Emerging Technol. Health Literacy Med. Pract.*, 220–238, 2024.
16. Rad, A.B., Lo, W.L., Tsang, K.M., Self-tuning PID controller using Newton-Raphson search method. *IEEE Trans. Ind. Electron.*, 44, 5, 717–725, 1997.
17. Mitsukura, Y., Yamamoto, T., Kaneda, M., A genetic tuning algorithm of PID parameters, in: *1997 IEEE International Conference on Systems, Man, and Cybernetics. Computational Cybernetics and Simulation*, vol. 1, IEEE, pp. 923–928, 1997, October.
18. Zhao, J. and Xi, M., Self-Tuning of PID parameters based on adaptive genetic algorithm, in: *IOP conference series: materials science and engineering*, vol. 782, IOP Publishing, p. 042028, 2020, March.
19. Wang, Q.G., Lee, T.H., Fung, H.W., Bi, Q., Zhang, Y., PID tuning for improved performance. *IEEE Trans. Control Syst. Technol.*, 7, 4, 457–465, 1999.
20. Ding, Y., Ren, X., Zhang, X., Liu, X., Wang, X., Multi-Phase Focused PID Adaptive Tuning with Reinforcement Learning. *Electronics*, 12, 18, 3925, 2023.
21. Chowdhury, M.A., Al-Wahaibi, S.S., Lu, Q., Entropy-maximizing TD3-based reinforcement learning for adaptive PID control of dynamical systems. *Comput. Chem. Eng.*, 178, 108393, 2023.

22. James, G., Witten, D., Hastie, T., Tibshirani, R., Taylor, J., Linear regression, in: *An introduction to statistical learning: With applications in python*, pp. 69–134, Springer International Publishing, Cham, 2023.
23. Wang, X., Yan, L., Zhang, Q., Research on the application of gradient descent algorithm in machine learning, in: *2021 International Conference on Computer Network, Electronic and Automation (ICCNEA)*, IEEE, pp. 11–15, 2021, September.
24. Gupta, P. and Bagchi, A., Introduction to NumPy, in: *Essentials of Python for Artificial Intelligence and Machine Learning*, pp. 127–159, Springer Nature Switzerland, Cham, 2024.
25. Gupta, P. and Bagchi, A., Data Manipulation with Pandas, in: *Essentials of Python for Artificial Intelligence and Machine Learning*, pp. 197–235, Springer Nature Switzerland, Cham, 2024.
26. Guo, S.B., Du, S., Cai, K.Y., Cai, H.J., Huang, W.J., Tian, X.P., A scientometrics and visualization analysis of oxidative stress modulator Nrf2 in cancer profiles its characteristics and reveals its association with immune response. *Heliyon*, 9, 6, e17075, 2023.
27. Ioannidis, J.P., The proposal to lower P value thresholds to. 005. *Jama*, 319, 14, 1429–1430, 2018.

12

Implementing PID Controllers for Data-Driven Recognizing for a Nonlinear System

Susmit Chakraborty* **and Sagnik Agasti**

Department of Computer Science and Engineering (CS&DS), Brainware University, Barasat, West Bengal, India

Abstract

One of the core aspects within computer science is data-driven modeling (DDM), because it allows to analyze historical data and obtain predictions or engage in valuable insights regarding a vast range of types. A methodology referred to as data-centric modeling (DDM) utilizes the utilization of data to develop and improve models that may be applied to evaluate complex systems, predict outcomes, or lead decision-making processes. In fact, DDM has already become one of the most essential tools in finance, healthcare, and engineering fields as a result of ongoing increase in generation rates for larger volumes of information today. The implementation of Pyrenees, a prototype DDM system that translates together with some control actions (e.g., in commercial vehicles) using a PID controller to stabilize them in their legacy forms. This research aims at this through the utilization of several diverse datasets and computational algorithms, to elucidate how effective DDM can be on nonlinear control problems. Using tools such as Python and MATLAB, the study presents how these DDMs are implemented and evaluated. Essential evaluation metrics such as R^2 distance and root mean squared error serve to evaluate these models. It is compared to the existing PID optimization methods, i.e., particle swarm optimization and fire-bug swarm optimization technique, which are means of the Pitman–Isermann design.

Keywords**:** Root mean squared error (RMSE), R^2 value, PID controller, nonlinear control, linear regression (LR), data-driven modeling (DDM)

**Corresponding author*: susmit.eee@gmail.com

Arindam Mondal and Souvik Ganguli (eds.) Data-Driven Modeling, (257–272) © 2026 Scrivener Publishing LLC

12.1 Introduction

Machine learning (ML) constitutes a revolution in one of the subfields of artificial intelligence (AI), under which computers are to learn patterns and predict future events from given data [1]. At its roots, ML relies on statistical methods that permit computers to improve at performing a task without being explicitly programmed [2]. Data-driven modeling (DDM) is a family of statistical and ML techniques to create mathematical representations for the actual real-world processes *via* data [3]. As authors mentioned previously, DDM seeks to uncover new knowledge as insights, patterns, and linkages in data that might inform decision-making or better understanding. DDM based on ML is already being used in industries such as healthcare and banking to transform operations, resource allocation, etc., and help drive innovation [4]. In this review, authors investigate ML, which subsumes nonlinear governance and skills inspired by ML into the modern control theory framework to turn on their transformative power for future intelligent systems and automation with deeper implications in different areas. By making machines learn the data with algorithms such as supervised and unsupervised learning, ML is changing things in industries from healthcare to finance or autopilot by deriving insights based on optimizer roles for actions. ML algorithms are being proposed for climate analysis, despite their potential to understand the climate system, but their applications remain limited [5]. The use of AI and ML in spine diagnosis, highlighting strategies such as localization, image segmentation, and outcome prediction, is discussed in Galbusera *et al.* [6]. ML-based control integrates ML algorithms into control systems, optimizing real-time decisions and performance in robotics, autonomous vehicles, and industrial automation, enabling efficient and flexible control solutions. Wu *et al.* proposed an ML-based predictive approach using recurrent neural networks for handling process nonlinearity and uncertainty in chemical processes. This method ensures closed-loop stability, optimality, and smooth control operations, demonstrating its effectiveness in real-time control scenarios [7]. Zeng *et al.* introduce population extremum optimization based multivariable PID neural networks (PEO-MPIDNN), an adaptive populace extremal optimization technique, to address the challenge of initializing connection weight parameters in MPIDNNs for complex manipulation systems, demonstrating superior performance across various metrics [8]. Mo and Farid explore adaptive nonlinear methods for quad rotor flight control, addressing parametric uncertainties and coupled dynamics using fuzzy logic and neural network methods [9]. Wan *et al.* use a virtual linear data model and a nonlinear iterative learning control mechanism in their work. The study on Zr-4 alloy deformation using isothermal compressive tests on a Gleeble-3500 thermomechanical simulator showed strong agreement between measured and predicted values [10].

A hybrid particle swarm optimization assisted genetic algorithm (PSO-GA) training algorithm that uses ADAM optimization to train artificial neural networks enhances accuracy in medical diagnostic applications by 20% in average testing and 0.7% in experimental accuracy compared to traditional methods [11]. A new back-propagation neural network forecasting model using random forests to accurately forecast and analyze CO_2 emissions, addressing the global climate crisis, was developed by Wen and Yuan [12]. Woo *et al.* [13] introduce a deep reinforcement learning-based controller for unmanned surface vehicles utilizing an actor-critic framework and a Markov decision process model for autonomous path development. After a long study of the available literature, the authors claim ML and nonlinear control combine to enhance control strategies, providing flexible, efficient solutions in challenging environments and paving the way for smarter, more dynamic systems in research. In this chapter, the author implemented a data-driven training of a linear regression model (LRM) for controlling a nonlinear system such as second and third-order system. Time domain specifications such as delay time (DT), rise time (RT), peak time (PT), and settling time (ST) are the feature variables considered in this system. An LRM is developed and evaluated using the same time domain specifications as the controlled output.

12.2 System Model

The proposed system model contains an ML engine (MLE), which takes four time-domain specifications as the training variables, such as DT, RT, PT, and ST. The model works on the linear regression algorithm, where four features train the PID coefficients (proportional, integral, and derivative gain). A second-order model is considered here to have four coefficients: $A = 1$, $B = 13$, $E = 50$, and $D = 15$. The training was based on the previous dataset available after simulation using the same model with the FSO algorithm [14]. PID coefficients are tuned using MLE in real time. The output of the model is evaluated using the same four time-domain features mentioned above. A complete schematic of the system is depicted in Figure 12.1.

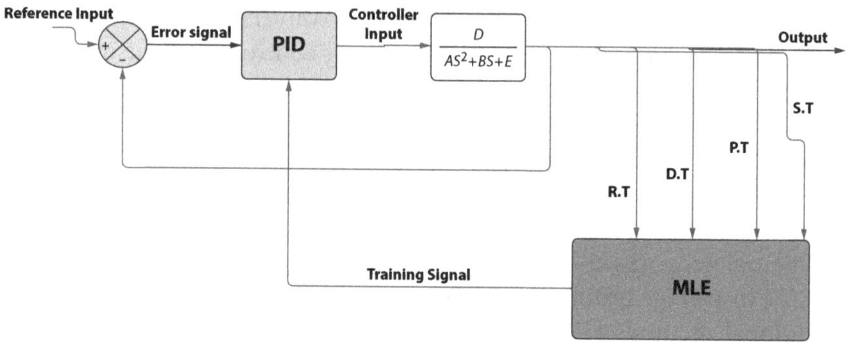

Figure 12.1 Schematic model of the proposed control system.

12.3 Nonlinear System

Consider an RLC series circuit as depicted in Figure 12.2.

Let $V_i(s)$ be the supply voltage, and $V_o(s)$ is the output voltage obtained across the capacitor as the system depicted in Figure 12.2.

KVL gives

$$v(s) = RI(s) + LCS(s) + \frac{I(s)}{cs} \tag{12.1}$$

$$v_i(s) = I(s)\left[R + LS + \frac{1}{CS}\right] \tag{12.2}$$

Similarly, the output voltage is

$$v_0(s) = \frac{I(s)}{cs} \tag{12.3}$$

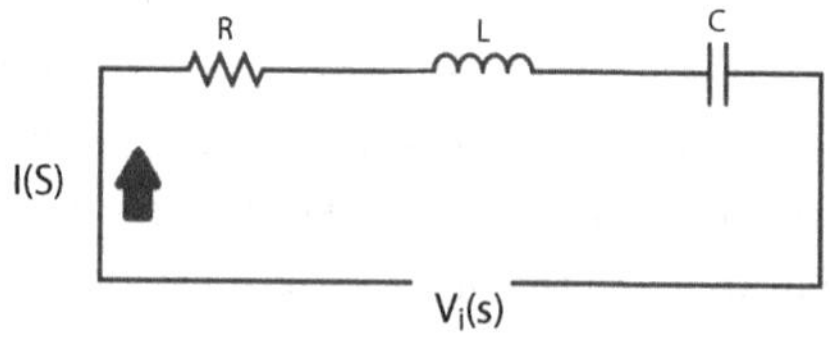

Figure 12.2 RLC series circuit.

Dividing Eqs. (12.3) and (12.2), Eq. (12.4) is obtained:

$$\frac{v_0(s)}{v_i(s)} = \frac{I(s)/cs}{\left(R + Ls + \frac{1}{cs}\right)I(S)} \tag{12.4}$$

$$\frac{v_0(s)}{v_i(s)} = \frac{\frac{1}{cs}}{R + LS + \frac{1}{cs}} \tag{12.5}$$

$$\frac{v_0(s)}{v_i(s)} = \frac{1}{RCS + LCS^2 + 1} \tag{12.6}$$

$$\frac{v_0(s)}{v_i(s)} = \frac{1/LC}{S^2 + \frac{R}{L}S + \frac{1}{LC}} \tag{12.7}$$

Eq. (12.7) is termed as the transfer function of the RLC series circuit. Eq. (12.7) can be reformed as Eq. (12.8).

$$\text{TF} = \frac{v_0(s)}{v_i(s)} = \frac{D}{AS^2 + BS + E} \tag{12.8}$$

where $A = 1,\ B = \frac{R}{L},\ E = \frac{1}{LC},\ D = \frac{1}{LC}$

Eq. (12.8) is a typical second-order function that is considered as the system to be controlled with the step input and LR-based ML control.

12.4 ML Engine

Linear regression [15] is a mathematical modeling technique that can be used to create a link between one or more feature variables and an output variable. This is a popular technique for data fitting. Three-time domain requirements, such as RT, DT, PT, and ST, are taken into account as the feature variables in this regression model. The target parameters that require optimization are K_p, K_i, and K_d in the PID. Three linear regression equations, denoted as hypotheses to obtain a concise model, are as Eqs. (12.9), (12.10), and (12.11).

$$K_p = A * R.T + B * P.T + C * S.T + D * D.T \tag{12.9}$$

$$K_i = E * R.T + F * P.T + G * S.T + H * D.T \tag{12.10}$$

$$K_d = I * R.T + J * P.T + K * S.T + L * D.T \tag{12.11}$$

where *A*, *B*, *C*, *D*, *E*, *F*, *G*, *H*, *I*, *J*, *K*, and *L* are the 12 coefficients of the four time-domain features that are used to forecast the four PID parameters in turn. When training the model, three MLEs that adhere to Eqs. (12.9), (12.10), and (12.11) are taken into consideration concurrently. The gradient decent (GD) method is the basis for how MLEs operate [16]. One training set of system output data, where the system is controlled by FSO-tuned PIDC, has been taken into consideration in order to train the linear model of the PID parameters. Tables 12.1, 12.2, and 12.3 present the training data used to predict PID parameters, namely, K_p,K_i, and K_d. Two other settings stay unchanged, whereas one is adjusted.

Table 12.1 Training dataset for K_p with $K_i = 0.010$ and $K_d = 0.677$.

Serial number	D.T	RT	PT	ST	K_p
1	1.048578	1.74763	5.74763	9.74763	1.947
2	0.373248	0.622079	6.622079	12.62208	0.822
3	0.926713	1.544522	5.544522	9.544522	0.638
4	0.761272	1.268786	7.268786	13.26879	0.637
.....	.....	.....	.....	.....	.....
.....	.....	.....	.....	.....	.....
998	2.090843	5.089084	7.089084	14.2341	2.339
999	2.093705	5.083705	7.703705	15.3281	2.339
1000	2.093562	5.084562	7.704562	14.9870	2.339

Table 12.2 Training dataset for K_i with $K_p = 0.732$ and $K_d = 0.677$.

Serial number	DT	RT	PT	ST	K_i
1	1.048578	1.74763	5.74763	9.74763	0.043
2	0.373248	0.622079	6.622079	12.62208	0.045
3	0.926713	1.544522	5.544522	9.544522	0.051
4	0.761272	1.268786	7.268786	13.26879	0.054
.....	.....	.....		.....	.....
.....	.....	.....		.....	.....
998	0.454635	2.775725	3.0126	4.775725	1.182
999	0.450398	2.450398	3.0223	4.450398	1.182
1000	0.41169	2.41169	3.0019	4.41169	1.182

Table 12.3 Training dataset for K_d with $K_p = 0.732$ and $K_i = 0.010$.

Serial number	DT	RT	PT	ST	K_d
1	1.048578	1.74763	5.74763	9.74763	0.634
2	0.373248	0.622079	6.622079	12.62208	0.609
3	0.926713	1.544522	5.544522	9.544522	0.584
4	0.761272	1.268786	7.268786	13.26879	0.641
.....	.....	.....	.....		.....
.....	.....	.....	.....		.....
998	0.67409	2.83082	4.837728	7.8724	0.882
999	0.277144	2.67409	4.67409	7.6521	0.896
1000	0.195088	2.277144	4.277144	7.5902	0.911

LRM is established in the Jupyter Notebook platform. The following programs are used for building the model.

```
from sklearn.linear_model
import LinearRegression
lm = LinearRegression()
lm.fit(X_train, y_train)
print(lm.summary())
```

The first line imports the "LinearRegression" module from the "sklearn. linear_model" package. The second line initializes the linear regression using the variable "lm." The "lm.fit()" method uses the training dataset shown in Tables 12.1, 12.2, and 12.3 to train the model. The final code retrieves the linear model's evaluation report. Using the GD approach, regression parameters are predicted according to Eq. (12.12).

$$\Delta C(t) = \frac{1}{2t}\sum\nolimits_{j=1,\ \ k\subseteq\{p,i,d\}}^{t}\left(C_k(t)^j - y_k(t)^j\right) \tag{12.12}$$

For the same two-order linear system, t is the number of training samples that are collected using FSO method and tuned PID parameters. $\Delta C(t)$ in Eq. (12.6) identifies the cost function for all four-parameter tuning. The PID parameter for the iteration sequence j is identified by $(C_k(t)^j)$ and $(y_k(t)^j)$, and here, the real parameter derived *via* various optimization methods is denoted by j.

12.5 Result Analysis

A second-order system representing a series RLC circuit is simulated using MATLAB using the MLE, which is formed by the training on the Jupyter Notebook platform. In this section, the results obtained in both phases, such as training in Jupyter Notebook and simulation in MATLAB, are analyzed. In the initial phase, three PID parameters are learned individually. The model begins by initializing modules such as numpy [17] and pandas [18], as well as importing the relevant CSV files. The next stage is to perform the statistical analysis as well as graphical observation using the following Python code:

```
df.head()
df.describe()
df.info()
```

The first code is used to check the data samples of the dataset named "df." The second code is used to obtain the statistical information of the dataset, such as the minimum, maximum, mean, and standard deviation values. A head view of all three datasets is depicted in Figure 12.3. Figure 12.4 shows three statistical descriptions of the datasets. Dataset information is illustrated in Figure 12.5.

	D.T	R.T	P.T	S.T	KP
0	1.048578	1.747630	5.747630	9.747630	1.947630
1	0.373248	0.622079	6.622079	12.622079	0.822079
2	0.926713	1.544522	5.544522	9.544522	1.744522
3	0.761272	1.268786	7.268786	13.268786	1.468786
4	0.778213	1.297022	5.297022	9.297022	1.497022

(a)

	D.T	R.T	P.T	S.T	KI
0	1.048578	1.747630	5.747630	9.747630	0.152710
1	0.373248	0.622079	6.622079	12.622079	0.012899
2	0.926713	1.544522	5.544522	9.544522	0.119277
3	0.761272	1.268786	7.268786	13.268786	0.053661
4	0.778213	1.297022	5.297022	9.297022	0.084113

(b)

	D.T	R.T	P.T	S.T	KD
0	1.048578	1.747630	5.747630	9.747630	1.967630
1	0.373248	0.622079	6.622079	12.622079	0.842079
2	0.926713	1.544522	5.544522	9.544522	1.764522
3	0.761272	1.268786	7.268786	13.268786	1.488786
4	0.778213	1.297022	5.297022	9.297022	1.517022

(c)

Figure 12.3 Head view of the datasets: (a) for K_p, (b) for K_i, (c) for K_d.

	D.T	R.T	P.T	S.T	KP
count	1000.000000	1000.000000	1000.000000	1000.000000	1000.000000
mean	0.763108	1.271847	6.279847	11.287847	1.471847
std	0.587268	0.978780	2.910936	5.091058	0.978780
min	0.006428	0.010713	2.012854	4.012854	0.210713
25%	0.283094	0.471824	2.994780	4.994780	0.671824
50%	0.577432	0.962387	6.196407	12.196407	1.162387
75%	1.130585	1.884308	8.508694	14.914574	2.084308
max	2.395456	3.992427	11.992427	19.992427	4.192427

(a)

	D.T	R.T	P.T	S.T	KI
count	1000.000000	1000.000000	1000.000000	1000.000000	1000.000000
mean	0.763108	1.271847	6.279847	11.287847	0.085623
std	0.587268	0.978780	2.910936	5.091058	0.090565
min	0.006428	0.010713	2.012854	4.012854	0.000003
25%	0.283094	0.471824	2.994780	4.994780	0.012941
50%	0.577432	0.962387	6.196407	12.196407	0.053980
75%	1.130585	1.884308	8.508694	14.914574	0.134341
max	2.395456	3.992427	11.992427	19.992427	0.398487

(b)

	D.T	R.T	P.T	S.T	KD
count	1000.000000	1000.000000	1000.000000	1000.000000	1000.000000
mean	0.763108	1.271847	6.279847	11.287847	1.491847
std	0.587268	0.978780	2.910936	5.091058	0.978780
min	0.006428	0.010713	2.012854	4.012854	0.230713
25%	0.283094	0.471824	2.994780	4.994780	0.691824
50%	0.577432	0.962387	6.196407	12.196407	1.182387
75%	1.130585	1.884308	8.508694	14.914574	2.104308
max	2.395456	3.992427	11.992427	19.992427	4.212427

(c)

Figure 12.4 Statistical observation of the datasets: (a) for K_p, (b) for K_i, (c) for K_d.

```
RangeIndex: 1000 entries, 0 to 999
Data columns (total 5 columns):
 #   Column  Non-Null Count  Dtype
---  ------  --------------  -----
 0   D.T     1000 non-null   float64
 1   R.T     1000 non-null   float64
 2   P.T     1000 non-null   float64
 3   S.T     1000 non-null   float64
 4   KP      1000 non-null   float64
dtypes: float64(5)
memory usage: 39.2 KB
```

(a)

```
RangeIndex: 1000 entries, 0 to 999
Data columns (total 5 columns):
 #   Column  Non-Null Count  Dtype
---  ------  --------------  -----
 0   D.T     1000 non-null   float64
 1   R.T     1000 non-null   float64
 2   P.T     1000 non-null   float64
 3   S.T     1000 non-null   float64
 4   KI      1000 non-null   float64
dtypes: float64(5)
memory usage: 39.2 KB
```

(b)

```
RangeIndex: 1000 entries, 0 to 999
Data columns (total 5 columns):
 #   Column  Non-Null Count  Dtype
---  ------  --------------  -----
 0   D.T     1000 non-null   float64
 1   R.T     1000 non-null   float64
 2   P.T     1000 non-null   float64
 3   S.T     1000 non-null   float64
 4   KD      1000 non-null   float64
dtypes: float64(5)
memory usage: 39.2 KB
```

(c)

Figure 12.5 Information of the datasets: (a) for K_p, (b) for K_i, (c) for K_d.

The following stage is standardizing the feature variables, which is accomplished using the "MinMaxScaler" module from "sklearn.preprocessing." In the following phase, correlations are discovered using the heat map approach [19]. Heat maps are visual analyses that deal with the correlation matrices between all variables in a dataset. Figure 12.6 illustrates that the parameters are highly correlated, and this observation is quite natural as the specifications are associated with each other for transient durations.

The "statsmodels.api.OLS" method is used to construct a matching linear model for all of the PID parameters straight from a standardized dataset. Three LRMs are finally evaluated using visual observation, such as a scatterplot between the actual result and predicted results for the corresponding PID parameters, and the scatterplots are depicted in Figure 12.7.

Figures 12.7(a), (b), and (c) illustrates the relation between the predicted coefficient values and the actual coefficient values of all three PID coefficients. Figures show that the model predicts very well for K_p and K_d, but slight error has been found in case of K_i, but the error is negligible. The

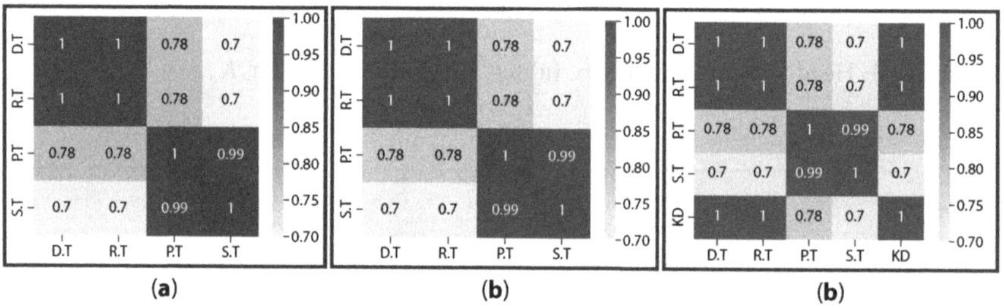

Figure 12.6 Heat maps of the datasets: (a) for K_p, (b) for K_i, (c) for K_d.

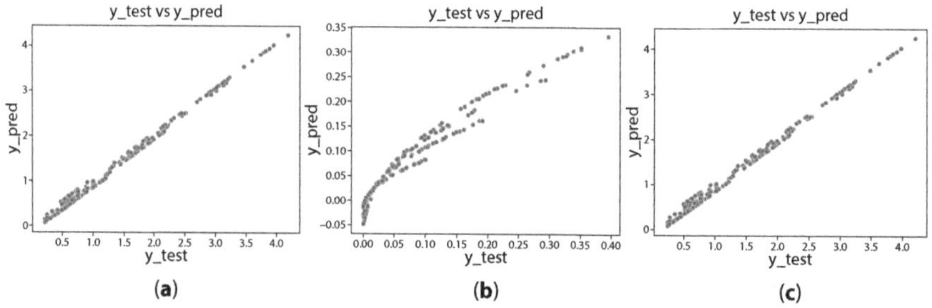

Figure 12.7 (a) Actual K_p versus predicted K_p, (b) actual K_i versus predicted K_i, (c) actual K_d versus predicted K_d.

models are further evaluated using root mean squared error (RMSE) [20] and R^2 matrices [21]. The mathematical definition of these two matrices is depicted in Eqs. (12.13) and (12.14), respectively.

$$\mathrm{RMSE} = \sqrt{\frac{1}{n}\sum_{j=1}^{n}(V_A - V_P)^2} \tag{12.13}$$

where n identifies total number of the data points considered to evaluate the LRM. V_A and V_P are the actual and predicted values of the coefficients, respectively.

$$R^2 = 1 - \frac{\mathrm{RSS}}{\mathrm{TSS}} \tag{12.14}$$

The statistical measure of the data's proximity to the fitted regression line is called R^2. It goes by the name of coefficient of determination as well. RSS and TSS stand for residual sum of squares and total sum of squares, respectively. The mathematical formulation of the RSS and TSS are obtained in Eqs. (12.15) and (12.16), respectively.

$$\mathrm{RSS} = \sum_{i=1}^{n}\left(y_i - f(x_i)\right)^2 \tag{12.15}$$

$$\mathrm{TSS} = \sum_{i=1}^{n}(y_i - \bar{y})^2 \tag{12.16}$$

where n is the number of data points considered, and y_i identifies the actual value of them. $f(x_i)$ represents the predicted value obtained from LRM, and $\bar{y}$ is the mean value of the actual data points. The evaluation matrix values, such as RMSE and R^2 values, are depicted in Table 12.4.

Table 12.4 Evaluation matrices values.

LRMs	**RMSE**	**R^2**
K_p model	0.03761	0.989212
K_i model	0.07452	0.872345
K_d model	0.03346	0.990949

Table 12.4 demonstrates how effectively the LRMs work, with RMSEs ranging only from 3.3% to 7.5% and very high R^2 values. High R^2 values indicate that the feature variables properly predict a very high proportion of the variation in the coefficients [22]. From Table 12.5, it can be stated that K_p, K_i, and K_d models are correctly predicted with 98.9%, 87.2%, and 99.1% data points, respectively. After successful training of the PIDCs, the coefficients are shown in Table 12.5.

Following the training phase, the chapter moves on to the simulation phase, when the model is tested against the same second-order system. MLE is used to optimize PID parameters in real-time simulations. MATLAB version 2020A replicates the MLE-aided system using an Intel Core i7 at 2.80 GHz CPU and 16 GB of RAM. Figure 12.8 displays the

Table 12.5 Linear regression coefficients.

A	B	C	D	E	F	G	H	I	J	K	L
1.377	2.263	3.817	1.665	0.829	2.512	1.290	2.811	2.261	0.991	3.981	0.777

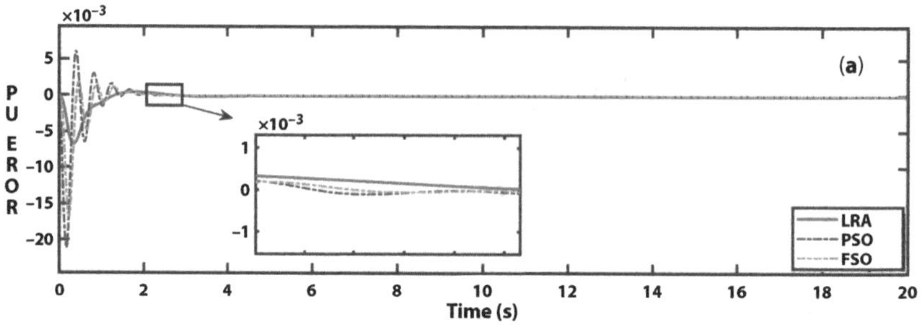

Figure 12.8 Simulation results of the second-order system using three different methods of tunning.

Table 12.6 Performance analysis of the second-order system with FSO:PID, PSO:PID, and LR:PID control.

Control methods	DT	RT	PT	ST
FSO:PID	3.82	4.15	22.15	0.013
BB-BC:PID	3.81	4.13	20.83	0.003
LR:PID	1.16	1.32	5.18	0.0007

system's per-unit faults when controlled by an FSO-tuned PID, a PSO-tuned PIDC, and an LR-tuned PIDC. It is evident that the LR-tuned PID surpasses the other two ways of controlling. Table 12.6 shows the specifics of the time domain output characteristics such as RT, DT, PT, and ST.

Table 12.6 shows that the suggested technique of control produces extremely accurate results with low frequency errors in both categories. LR:PID beats FSO:PID and PSO:PID by around 68% and 69% in terms of DT. For the other three specifications, such as RT, PT, and ST, LR:PID outperforms the other two control mechanisms by 98%, 80%, and 70%, respectively.

12.6 Conclusion

This chapter describes a linear regression (LR) approach that uses GD to model PID parameters. It tries to relate the transient specifications to the PID tuning parameters. For analytical considerations, we assume a linear connection between PID parameters and time domain parameters. This method's training strategy is supervised, which means it uses a set of data for training based on the results obtained from the same system when tweaked using the FSO algorithm. As a result, the model's correctness can be guaranteed. This chapter clearly displays the effectiveness of ML techniques in reducing the transiency of a second-order system. The proposed model outperforms the other two metaheuristic algorithms in terms of second-order temporal domain characteristics. Thus, it can be concluded that this study offers a multitude of research opportunities in the control area using MLE. To examine the feasibility of developing nonlinear models, major work must be done in this area, which may be expanded in the future to include more system aspects.

References

1. Alzubi, J., Nayyar, A., Kumar, A., Machine learning from theory to algorithms: an overview, in: *Journal of Physics: Conference series*, vol. 1142, p. 012012, IOP Publishing, 2018, November.
2. Michalski, R.S., Carbonell, J.G., Mitchell, T.M. (Eds.), *Machine learning: An artificial intelligence approach*, Springer Science & Business Media, New York, 2013.
3. Smith, S.T., The Role of Data-Driven Decision-Making in Organizational Transformation: A Case Study Analysis of Leadership and Organizational Actions Doctoral dissertation, Fordham University, 2023.

4. Costa, R.D., Hirata, C.M., Pugliese, V.U., A comparative study of Situation Awareness-Based Decision-Making model Reinforcement Learning Adaptive automation in evolving conditions. *IEEE Access*, 11, 16166–16182, 2023.
5. Huntingford, C., Jeffers, E.S., Bonsall, M.B., Christensen, H.M., Lees, T., Yang, H., Machine learning and artificial intelligence to aid climate change research and preparedness. *Environ. Res. Lett.*, 14, 12, 124007, 2019.
6. Galbusera, F., Casaroli, G., Bassani, T., Artificial intelligence and machine learning in spine research. *JOR Spine*, 2, 1, e1044, 2019.
7. Wu, Z., Rincon, D., Christofides, P.D., Real-time adaptive machine-learning-based predictive control of nonlinear processes. *Ind. Eng. Chem. Res.*, 59, 6, 2275–2290, 2019.
8. Zeng, G.Q., Xie, X.Q., Chen, M.R., Weng, J., Adaptive population extremal optimization-based PID neural network for multivariable nonlinear control systems. *Swarm Evol. Comput.*, 44, 320–334, 2019.
9. Mo, H. and Farid, G., Nonlinear and adaptive intelligent control techniques for quadrotor uav–a survey. *Asian J. Control*, 21, 2, 989–1008, 2019.
10. Wan, P., Zou, H., Wang, K., Zhao, Z., Research on hot deformation behavior of Zr-4 alloy based on PSO-BP artificial neural network. *J. Alloys Compd.*, 826, 154047, 2020.
11. Yadav, R.K., PSO-GA based hybrid with Adam Optimization for ANN training with application in Medical Diagnosis. *Cognit. Syst. Res.*, 64, 191–199, 2020.
12. Wen, L. and Yuan, X., Forecasting CO2 emissions in Chinas commercial department, through BP neural network based on random forest and PSO. *Sci. Total Environ.*, 718, 137194, 2020.
13. Woo, J., Yu, C., Kim, N., Deep reinforcement learning-based controller for path following of an unmanned surface vehicle. *Ocean Eng.*, 183, 155–166, 2019.
14. Chakraborty, S., Mondal, A., Biswas, S., Roy, P.K., Design of FUZZY-3DOF-PID controller for an Ocean Thermal hybrid Automatic Generation Control system. *Sci. Iran.*, 2023.
15. Maulud, D. and Abdulazeez, A.M., A review on linear regression comprehensive in machine learning. *J. Appl. Sci. Technol. Trends*, 1, 2, 140–147, 2020.
16. Badra, N., Haggag, S.A., Deifalla, A., Salem, N.M., Development of machine learning models for reliable prediction of the punching shear strength of FRP-reinforced concrete slabs without shear reinforcements. *Measurement*, 201, 111723, 2022.
17. Hazrat, R., The numpy Library, in: *A Course in Python: The Core of the Language*, pp. 183–209, Springer Nature Switzerland, Cham, 2024.
18. Sharma, S.K. and Paliwal, M., Overview of data mining with Python modules, in: *AIP Conference Proceedings*, vol. 2427, No. 1, AIP Publishing, 2023, February.
19. Gu, Z., Complex heatmap visualization. *Imeta*, 1, 3, e43, 2022.

20. Hodson, T.O., Root mean square error (RMSE) or mean absolute error (MAE): When to use them or not. *Geosci. Model Dev. Discuss.*, 2022, 1–10, 2022.
21. Onyutha, C., From R-squared to coefficient of model accuracy for assessing "goodness-of-fits". *Geosci. Model Dev. Discuss.*, 2020, 1–25, 2020.
22. Alghamdi, A.S. and Desuqi, R.K., A study of expected lifetime of XLPE insulation cables working at elevated temperatures by applying accelerated thermal ageing. *Heliyon*, 6, 1, 2020.

13

Temporal Resilience Redux: BiLSTM for Short-Term Load Forecasting in Deep Learning Domain

Ritu K. R.

Electrical and Electronics Engineering Department, UIT RGPV, Bhopal, India

Abstract

In the context of short-term load forecasting (STLF), the chapter explores complexities in sequential models with a particular emphasis on well-known style of bidirectional long short-term memory (BiLSTM). The intricate time-based dynamics present in load data are frequently too complicated for traditional forecasting methods, which makes the investigation of sophisticated neural network designs necessary. This chapter attempts to clarify BiLSTM concepts, structures, and uses in STLF by a thorough investigation. Reliable electrical load prediction plays an essential role in the safety and energy efficiency of the power system. To train LSTM networks to forecast electrical load, fictitious load data and historical environmental meteorological data are utilized. Based on historical energy consumption and meteorological data, the experimental findings demonstrate that the LSTM network model can produce rather accurate short-term power load predictions in the presence of copious amounts of high-quality data.

Keywords: Short-term load forecasting (STLF), bidirectional long short-term memory (BiLSTM), deep learning, electric load prediction, time series forecasting, energy

Email: rituuitrgpv@gmail.com

Arindam Mondal and Souvik Ganguli (eds.) Data-Driven Modeling, (273–294) © 2026 Scrivener Publishing LLC

13.1 Introduction

Forecasting electricity consumption is crucial for a variety of businesses. For instance, both optimum dispatching and power system stability depend on short-term load forecasting. Additionally, projection mistakes suggest lower profits in markets for power that are competitive [1]. Aside from preventing losses and electric energy waste, an electricity consumption prediction is helpful in the context of energy efficiency [2], as it may be used to identify abnormalities in end-user behavior or defective appliances [3]. The use of modern technology thus offers a wealth of opportunities.

For example, a 2022 study from the Santa Catarina State Federation of Industries [24] said that the CELESC distribution, transmission, and generation (Centrais Elétricas de Santa Catarina S.A.) projected that Brazil's annual waste of electric energy is around 43 TWh. It is estimated that the amount of garbage produced annually would cover the consumption of 20 million Brazilian households. Thus, developing electric power monitoring systems is essential for energy conservation. Planning, distribution, and consumption challenges with energy efficiency have been studied in relation to various artificial intelligence techniques [4]. Of particular interest is the application of deep neural network (NN) [5] for consumption prediction. These models may be applied to cloud or edge platforms in Internet of Things (IoT) systems [6]. They can also react fast after training and generalize over massive volumes of data (big data). In order to gather actual time-series statistics in an office setting utilizing an IoT system with edge computing, Lee *et al.* [25] developed prediction system for energy usage of long short-term memory (LSTM) deep neural network (DNN) [7]. Deep recurrent neural network (RNN) can be classified as one of the networks that include LSTMs.

Input–output mapping systems [8], which have applications in nonlinear prediction and speech processing, and associative memory are the two main uses of RNNs, which are systems having temporal processing for more than one feedback loop. Disappearing gradients in recurrent networks [8], however, indicate that deeper RNNs are not suitable for backpropagation training because of rapidly diminishing faults. Because long-term dependencies are difficult to comprehend because little changes made in the past by distant inputs might not have an effect, disappearing gradients impede or prohibit the network from learning. Another name for this issue is vital deep learning (DL) problem.

The LSTM network developed as a consequence to address problem due to vanishing gradient. This problem is resolved by LSTM due to its structure as it is the same for a standard RNN but uses memory blocks—basically, these blocks are recurrently connected subnets—instead of summing units in the hidden layer. Problems requiring long-term memory, such as protein secondary structure prediction and context-free languages [9], were solved using LSTM.

The development of forecasting solutions has benefited greatly from the various advantages provided by DL, which include greater generalization skills and the capacity to handle datasets of enormous amount, providing assistance with supervised as well as unsupervised learning strategies. The mapping functions between an initially labeled dataset's input and output variables are learned using algorithms in the supervised learning approach. The machine learning model may associate an activity class with the signal dataset through the use of supervised learning techniques. On the other hand, unsupervised learning algorithms may extract learning characteristics and recreate patterns from unlabeled datasets [10, 11]. Multiple linear processing layers and large-scale hierarchical data representation are what set apart supervised from unsupervised learning systems. Consequently, additional layers and more computational complexity might result in DL models with more complicated designs. DL algorithms can be used to evaluate and benefit from important properties of big data. Complex pattern extraction from datasets that are large, semantic indexing, data tagging, improvement of discrimination task, and fast retrieval of information can be done using these algorithms [12]. DL approaches such as gated recurrent units, stacked autoencoder coding, convolutional neural networks (CNNs), RNNs, and bidirectional LSTM (BiLSTM) networks are used in smart grids for load forecasting and monitoring applications [13–15].

13.2 Literature Review

The BiLSTM and LSTM models differ generally in the following ways: operators such as sum, multiplication, average, or concatenations are used for combining the output of both layers after the inverted sequence is added to the extra LSTM layer. In contrast, LSTM networks permit inputs in only one direction. Two flow directions provide for an improved learning experience.

According to Liang *et al.* [17], when the network reaches its bidirectional stage, inputs going in the positive direction are used to calculate LSTM-cell sequence's output in forward direction, whereas opposite direction inputs are used to calculate LSTM-cell sequence's output in backward direction. The LSTM-cell sequence output in forward direction will be computed using the positive path inputs, and the LSTM-cell sequence output in backward path is computed utilizing inputs in the inverted path. Concatenating outputs of the two and further utilizing SoftMax function to standardize their values to become probability distribution, which produces the desired outcome. The bidirectional RNNs (BRNNs) were presented by Schuster and Paliwal [18]. Essentially, they operate on the premise that, given data whose beginning and ending are known beforehand, two distinct networks may analyze the incoming data in opposing sequences, as in the case of the phoneme boundary estimate issue [19]. A single sequence is treated both in (forward state) traditional forward manner and from the end until the beginning, as shown in Figure 13.1. The traditional RNN's neurons are grouped into two groups within a BRNN structure: one group is for

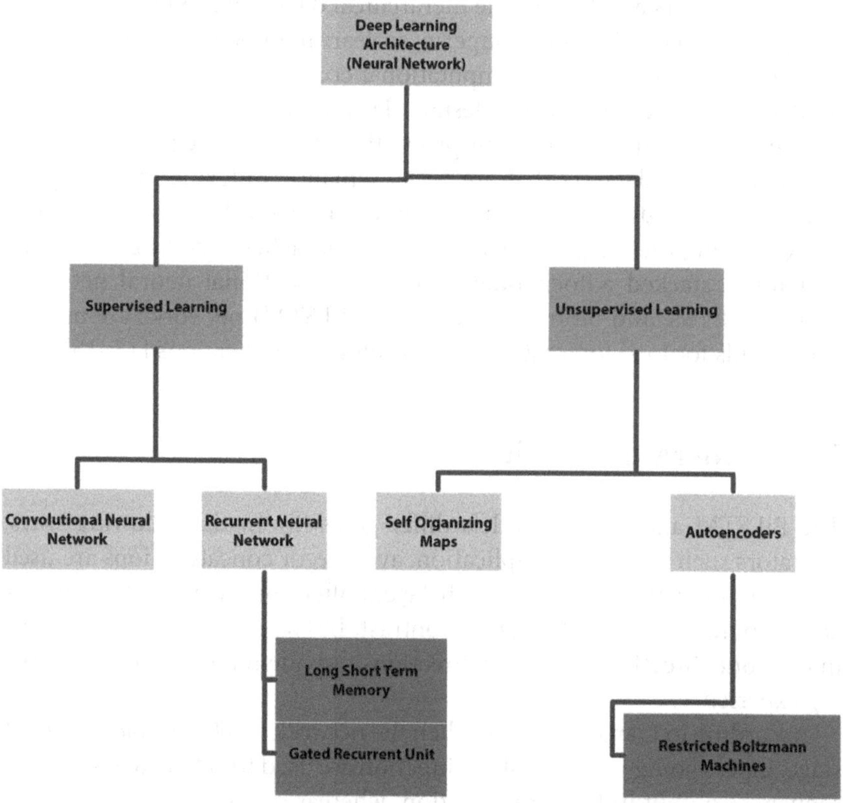

Figure 13.1 Type of deep learning architecture.

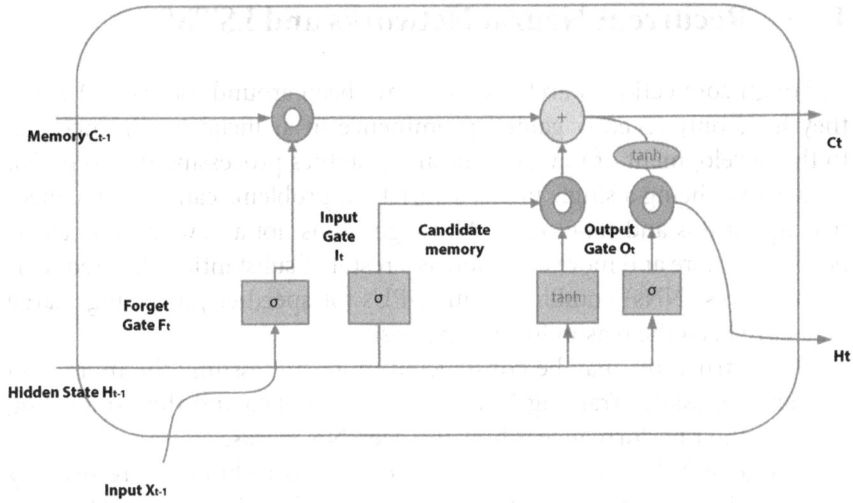

Figure 13.2 Architecture (LSTM unit).

forward states (positive time path), whereas the next group is for backward states (negative time path). The outcomes of either state have no bearing on the inverse direction's inputs.

Consequently, two directions of time may be used for input data from the future and the past. Combining LSTM structure with the BRNN idea led to the establishment of successful BiLSTM implementations [20–22]. According to Sharfuddin *et al.* [16], a BiLSTM is implemented using two LSTM layers. One of them will be in charge of previous states, whereas the other will control the forthcoming states, which is illustrated in Figure 13.2. The workings of the BiLSTM are covered in additional detail in Graves and Schmidhuber [23]. $S = \{yi,xi)\}N\ j = 1$ represents the set of N datasets. A three-dimensional path plus one-time clock comprise xi input for the sample. Depending on the tasks, different outcomes may be obtained.

The binary hit-miss value of *Yi*'s hit-miss classification work: Yi is the estimation of the subsequent point $xi + 1$ for the producing job. The notation below illustrates how the author additionally shows how a single BiLSTM layer may be used to concatenate both inverse sequence and direct sequence. Here, the weight is represented by W, the bias of a specific layer is characterized by b, and $g(\cdot)$ represents the activation function when all of the functions of a standard LSTM are represented by LSTM($\cdot$).

13.3 Recurrent Neural Networks and LSTM

Although connectionist architectures have been around for over 70 years, they have only recently gained prominence in artificial intelligence due to the development of new designs and graphics processing unit (GPUs). Rather than being a single tactic, a variety of problems can use DL collective algorithms and topologies. Although DL is not a new idea, its use is becoming more and more common as a result of substantially layered neural networks (NNs) combined with GPUs for speedier processing. Large data have been the reason for this expansion.

These structures may be constructed more successfully the more data that are accessible. Training NN using example data and then rewarding them on their performance is how the deep NN works.

A large and diverse range of architecture and techniques are used by DL. The six DL architecture that was developed in the previous 20 years is shown in Figure 13.1. Notably, LSTM and CNNs are the most broadly utilized techniques for a range of applications. They are also the top two techniques on our list.

Because the usual RNN has only one hidden state that is communicated over time, grasping from long-term dependencies is difficult. For addressing this problem, LSTM includes in itself the memory cells that can store long-term information. LSTMs include memory cells, which are long-term information storage units, to address this problem. Applications such as time-series forecasting, language translation, and speech recognition are well suited meant for LSTM networks because of the ability within them to master long-term dependency from sequential inputs. LSTMs can be used by other NN architectures, such as CNNs, to examine pictures and movies.

The output, input, and forget gates are controlled by the memory cell. Whatever data are inputted into, subtracted from, and outputted from the memory cell, these gates control those data. Whatever data are getting added in memory cell, the input gate controls it. The data that are removed from the memory cell will be regulated by the forget gate. The memory cells produce the data that are controlled by the output gate. That is why LSTM networks can learn long-term dependencies by giving them the right as it flows through the network to either accept or reject the information.

13.3.1 Architecture and Functioning of LSTM

Four NNs and a number of cells—memory building blocks—make up the LSTM architecture's chain structure; whereas cells hold data, the memories are manipulated by the gate. There are three gates in place.

Forget gate

It will remove the data that are no longer needed in the cell. The gate has two inputs, ht-1 (the output of the preceding cell) and xt (specific moment input), which is multiplied with weight matrices, and after this, addition of bias is done. The output in the form of a binary is obtained after being run by the activation function. When certain cell state is 0, the information would be lost, When the output is 1, this information is retained later for use. The equation for forget gate is as follows:

$$f_t = (W_f(h_{t-1}, x_t) + b_f) \tag{13.1}$$

here:

- W_f is the forget gates weight matrix.
- $[h_{t-1}, x_t]$ is concentration of current input, and previous hidden states are denoted here.
- b_f represents the bias of forget gate.
- σ is called sigmoid, the activation function.

Input gate

By inputting relevant data, the state of the cells of input gate is changed. The values to be remembered are filtered in a forget-gate-like fashion using the sigmoid function; here, it is initially utilized to manipulate information using ht-1 and xt as inputs. The previous hidden state ht−1ht−1 and the current input xtxt are passed through the tanh activation function to generate candidate values for the cell state, which lie in the range [−1,+1] [−1,+1]; this method yields an output that ranges in −1 to +1. Ultimately, by multiplying the vector values by the regulated values, the relevant information is retrieved. The input gate formula is:

$$i_t = (W_i(h_{t-1}, x_t) + b_i) \tag{13.2}$$

$$C_t = \tanh(W_c(h_{t-1}, x_t) + b_c) \tag{13.3}$$

We take the data we had earlier thought to ignore and multiply the previous condition by base. We then include it ∗ Ct. The candidates value update is represented here, with the edge updated amount taken into account:

$$C_t = (f_t \ C_{t-1}, x_t + i_{tC_t}) \tag{13.4}$$

where

- ʘ represents element-wise multiplication
- The activation function is tanh

Output gate

For showing the output, from the current cell state, the output gate takes the useful data. Initially, cell is subjected to the tanh function in order to construct a vector. After filtering the data using ht-1 and xt inputs for identifying the values that need to be remembered, the sigmoid function is utilized to alter the data. Ultimately, they undergo multiplication to transmit the controlled values and vector values as input and output to the subsequent cell. The output gate's formula is:

$$\mathrm{O_t = (b_o + W_o(h_{t-1}, x_t))} \tag{13.5}$$

13.3.2 LTSM versus RNN

Benefits and drawbacks of LSTM
Long short-term memory benefits

1. It is possible for LSTM networks to identify long-term dependencies. They have a memory cell that has a lengthy retention period for information.
2. Disappearing and bursting gradients are a problem with standard RNNs when models are trained over extended times. To tackle this problem, LSTM networks utilize a gating sequence that makes selected memories or forgets the data.
3. The model can identify and retain the important data even in circumstances when there is a huge lag between important events in the structure because of LSTM. For this reason, LSTMs are used in contexts such as computer translation where context information is essential.

LSTM drawbacks

1. The computational cost of LSTM networks is higher than that of simpler designs such as feed-forward NNs. This may restrict their capacity to scale in contexts with constraints or enormous datasets.
2. Because LSTM networks are computationally demanding, training them can take longer than training simpler models. Thus, in order to train LSTMs to high performance, more data and longer training cycles are frequently needed.
3. The processing of the phrases is done sequentially, word by word, making it difficult to parallelize.

A comparison of the LSTM and RNN models in various dimensions
LSTM is equipped with a specialized memory unit, which is used for capturing some long-term dependence in the consecutive data, which makes it useful at learning such relationships. In contrast, RNN lacks a dedicated memory unit, limiting its ability to handle long-term dependencies effectively.

Regarding directionality, LSTM can process sequential data in both backward and forward direction by giving it proper training, offering flexibility in learning patterns. In contrast, RNN is typically trained to process data in only one direction.

LSTM's complexity due to its gates and memory unit makes it more challenging to train compared to RNN, which is generally easier to train.

Both LSTM and RNN excel at learning sequential data, although LSTM's specialization in capturing long-term dependencies gives it an edge in certain tasks.

In terms of applications, LSTM and RNN find use in similar domains such as language processing, machine translation, and speech recognition. Additionally, LSTM is commonly applied in tasks such as text summarization and time-series forecasting, whereas RNN is also utilized in image and video processing.

13.4 Bidirectional LSTM

BiLSTM and RNNs can process sequential data in equally forward and backward paths. The ability to handle sequential input in only one direction sets BiLSTM apart from ordinary LSTMs and allows it to learn longer-range correlations in sequential data.

Two LSTM networks, one of which routes the input sequence forward and the other routes it backward, make up a BiLSTM. Next, the two LSTM networks' outputs are added to form the final output. It has been demonstrated that BiLSTM can produce cutting-edge outcomes on a range of tasks, such as text summarization, recognition of speech, and machine translation.

By stacking LSTMs, deep LSTM networks may be created that are capable of recognizing ever more intricate patterns within sequential data. Each LSTM layer records the incoming data's varying levels of abstraction and temporal dependency. The BiLSTM NN and the regular feed-forward mechanism NN are not the same. There are no connections between the interior nodes of any three layers. Multilayer stacked BiLSTM NN alternate prediction using BiLSTM. The introduction of a directed loop in the link between hidden layers, prior knowledge, and memorization and storage of the results in the memory unit can all serve to enhance an association between individual pieces of information in different time sequence. The current input when combined with previous output gives the NN's current output. The lack of a delay window width will cause problems with gradient expansion and disappearance as the time series' input data volume grows. The power load profile is affected by several elements such as humidity, temperature, and the way household electricity behaves. This problem is multidimensional and nonlinear. The accumulated error problem is resolved by the BiLSTM NN during the training phase. Additionally, DL-based bidirectional NN is combined for creating a BiLSTM multilayer NN. There are two components to the multilayer stacked BiLSTM: a forward and reverse structure.

The depth of the BiLSTM is increased by the multilayer stacks of BiLSTM neural. For improving the load forecasting precision, the input data can be learned for getting comprehensive comparison of the diverse characteristics of the data. Based on standard LSTM prototype, the BiLSTM NN will specifically advance the model's response for the sequence sorting problem by fully accounting for front and back association of the load data in time sequence. The input data sequence acts as the training sets from the forward layer throughout the procedure, whereas the inverse duplicate of the input data series is used by backward layer.

In order to prevent order information from being forgotten, bidirectional structure forecasted results are influenced with both the preceding and succeeding inputs. This raises the reliance between training data.

13.4.1 Bidirectional, Multilayer Stacked LSTM NN

As can be seen in Figure 13.3, forward layer saves the output of forward hidden layer at all movements after computing in the forward direction starting from 1 to *t*. Similarly to the backward layer, it retains the output of the hidden layer at all instances after it computes the reverse time series. Lastly, BiLSTM network output computation is performed. Figure 13.4 shows the architecture of the systems used in a multilayer stake BiLSTM.

The forward and reverse LSTM networks comprise two layers of the LSTM NN in the multilayer stacked design. By integrating the respective output results of forward and backward layer at all time points, the second layer of the forward and reverse LSTM gets first layers output result. The following represents the BiLSTM NN:

$$s_t = f(Ux_t + Ws_{t-1}) \tag{13.6}$$

$$s_t' = f(U'_{x_t +} W' \; s'_{t+1}) \tag{13.7}$$

$$o_t = g(V_{s\,+} V' \; s_t) \tag{13.8}$$

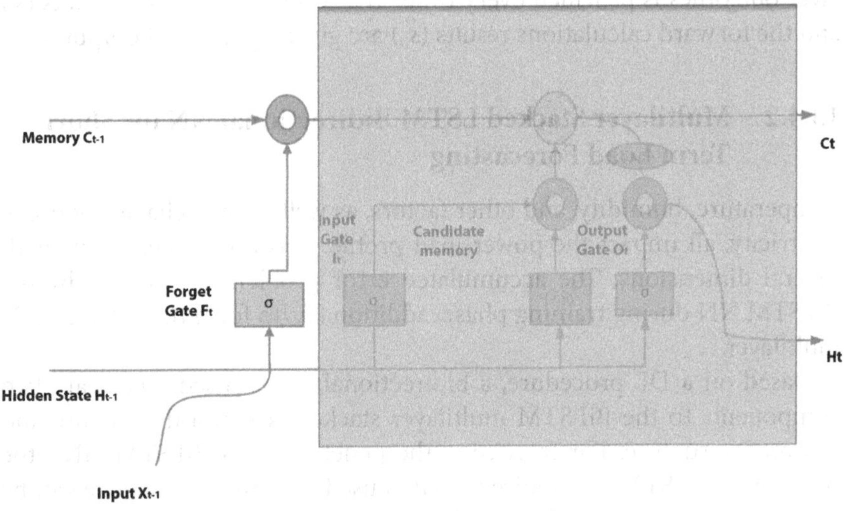

Figure 13.3 LSTM cells forget gate.

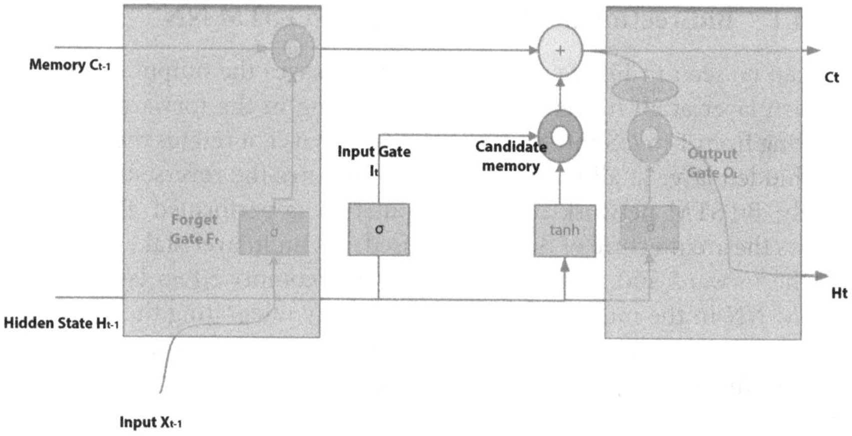

Figure 13.4 Input and candidate memory of an LSTM cell.

where W, V, and U represent the weight matrices that correspond to the appropriate reverse weight matrix, the hidden layer to the output layer, and the hidden layer to the input layer, respectively. Variables s_t, o_t, and s_t' are hidden layers: stable variables, output, and reverse hidden layers, respectively, at t time. The activation functions are f and g, and the input vector is x_t. Between the forward and backward layers, there is no shared knowledge on state weight matrix. The computation of the forward and backward layer outcomes is provided every time. The reverse calculation results (s_t) and the forward calculations results (s_t') are given by the final output (o_t).

13.4.2 Multilayer Stacked LSTM Bidirectional NN for Short-Term Load Forecasting

Temperature, humidity, and other factors, as well as the behavior of home electricity, all impact the power load profile. It is a nonlinear issue with several dimensions. The accumulated error problem is resolved by the BiLSTM NN during training phase, additionally, to form the BiLSTM NN multilayer.

Based on a DL procedure, a bidirectional NN is used. There are two components to the BiLSTM multilayer stacked: a forward structure and a reverse structure. For increasing the penetration of BiLSTM NNs, the multilayered LSTM NN bidirectional is used. The input sequence can be frequently learned in order to gain a thorough interpretation of the data properties and increase load forecasting accuracy.

13.4.3 Multilayer BiLSTM Stacked NN

Figure 13.4 shows the design architecture of multilayer BiLSTM stacked. The forward and reverse LSTM networks comprise LSTM NN, which is multilayer stacked of every two layers. The result output for the first layers of the reverse and forward LSTM is combined and sent to the second layer. Figure 13.4 depicts the construction of BiLSTM NN, which is multilayer. This NN model may be described as follows.

The forward and the backward outputs of every layer determine the results of the bidirectional multilayer stacked LSTM NN.

$$o_t = g(V^{(j)}.\, s_t^{(i)} + V^{(i)}.\, s_t^{(i)}) \tag{13.9}$$

$$s_t^{(i)} = f(U^{*(i)}.\, s_t^{'(-1)} + W^{(i)}.\, s_{t+1}^{'}) \tag{13.10}$$

$$s_t^{(1)} = f(U^{(1)}.\, x_t + W^{(1)}.\, s_{t-1}) \tag{13.11}$$

$$s_t^{'(1)} = f(U^{'(1)}.\, x_t + W^{'(1)}.\, s_{t-1}^{'}) \tag{13.12}$$

The ith hidden layer $t1$ and t have $s_t^{(i)}$ and $s_{t-1}^{(i)}$ as the state variables. The weight information is not shared by forward and reverse calculation. Input, output, and hidden layer in between weight matrix are given by $V^{(i)}$, $W^{(i)}$ and $U^{(i)}$ and $V^{'(i)}$, $W^{'(i)}$ and $U^{(i)'}$, which form the inverse weight matrix corresponding to the opposite calculation, respectively. i = 0, 1, 2 denotes output layer values, and i here is the number of the BiLSTM layers.

13.4.4 Load Forecasting of Multilayer Stacked BiLSTM

The power load statistical analysis, which forms the basis for augmented LSTM NN, may be obtained by training sample data restructuring. The next day's electrical usage is predicted by the BiLSTM network multilayer stacked (LSTM), which has been taught to do so. As shown in Figure 13.5, the following procedures make up the recommended model's prediction process. The outline of the recommended load forecasting approach is shown in Figure 13.5.

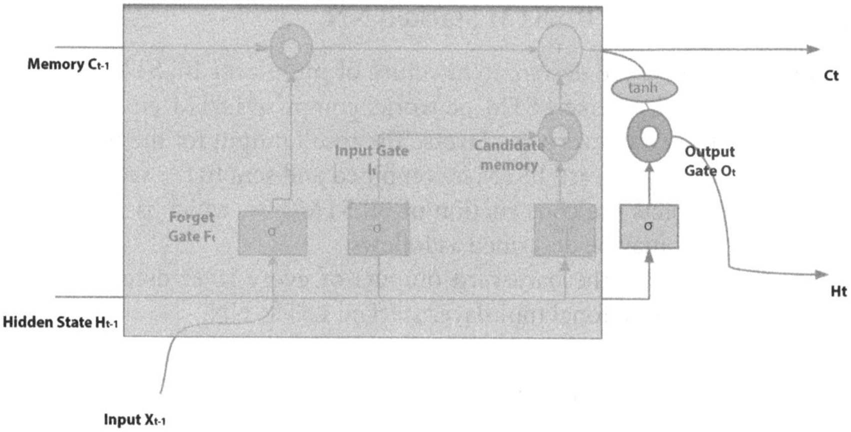

Figure 13.5 Output gate of an LSTM cell.

Step 1: Get the values ready in step 1. The historical data collected of the power load profile is preprocessed for removing abnormalities and errors before the training phase. However, original values are not standardized sufficiently to be used straight away. In order to normalize the original data structures, normalizing is a commonly used approach in system modeling. Normalization renders the initial input dimensionless, perhaps hastening the NN convergence. Following normalizing, [0, 1] must be the value of the original data. There are several methods for normalizing data, such as minimum–maximum scaling, decimal scaling, and Z score normalization. This study uses a linear normalizing method, which is stated as follows and is based on min–max scaling: (15)x = x min $x$max $x$min. Maximum and lowest values for the power load sample data are shown by the symbols $x$max and $x$min, whereas x represents the original sample numbers value, and x represents the standardized original value. Figure 13.6 illustrates the architecture of the stacked bidirectional LSTM neural network used for short-term load forecasting.
Step 2: Network instruction. Throughout the training process, the forward variables of the input data at time $t = 1$ and input at inverse state for time $t = T$ (where T is the training datasets last sampling period) are assigned a constant value of 0.5. Moreover, it is common practice to set both the derivative of initial value of the reverse state for time $t = 1$ and the input's forward value at $T = t$ to 0. It is anticipated that the most recent value would not significantly rely on earlier information.

The network training procedure consists of the following elements:

(1) **Forwarding information**: The anticipated outputs are computed using the time sequence $1 < t <= \text{T}$, which is used to

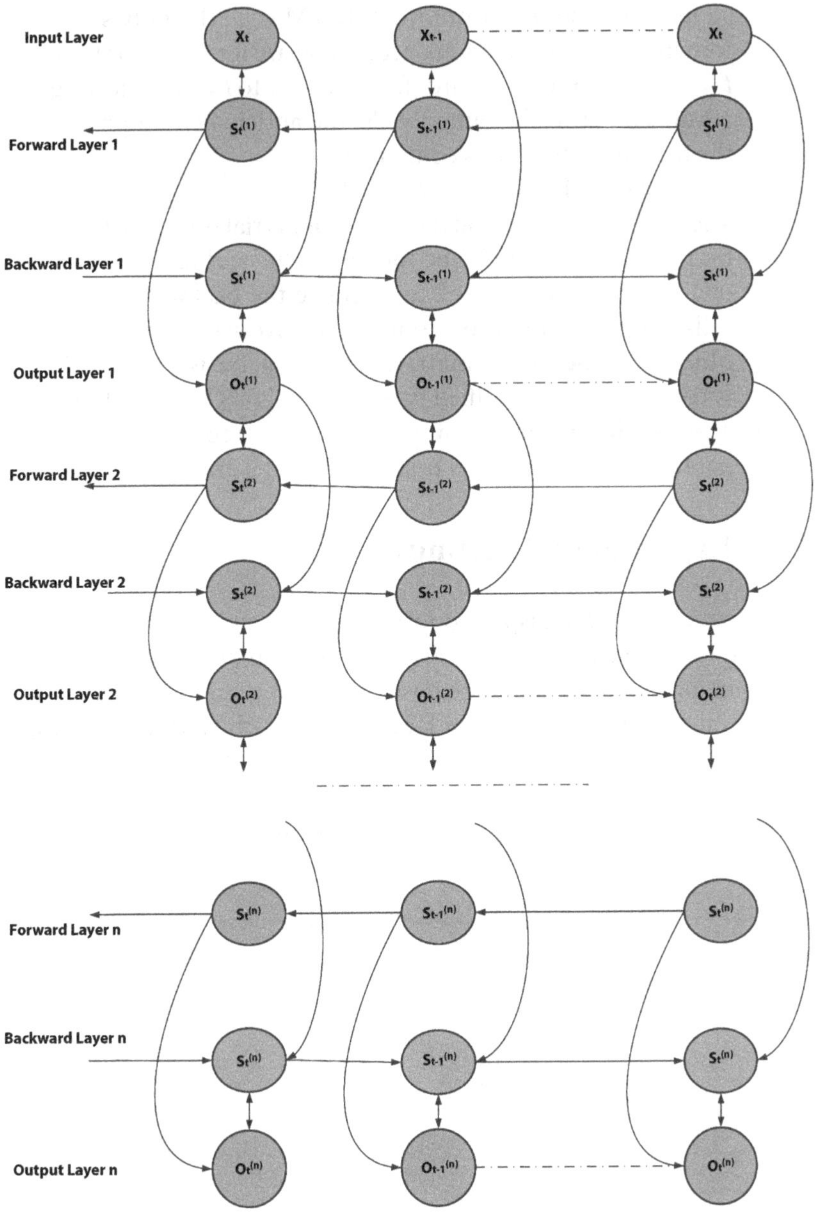

Figure 13.6 Bidirectional LSTM neural network (multilayer stacked).

supply training data from the BiLSTM cell. The only states for which forward ways are acceptable are forward (for time $t = 1$ to $t = T$) and backward (for time $t = T$ to $t = 1$). Following advancement in the output cells, the anticipated output for the nth layer ahead was computed.

(2) **Reverse transfer**: Using $1 < t <= T$.
The forward time period derivative of partial objective function will be computed. The forward value and reverse value of $1 < t \backslash= T$ will be used to calculate the backward LSTM cells. We compute the outcome of the inverted prediction.

(3) **Modifying the weight matrix**: In training, the weight matrix is computed and modified based on the NN's loss function.

(4) **The result's output**: Using bidirectional computing, the parameters of LSTM NN prediction model are computed.

13.5 Experimental Settings

Three inputs, which are displayed in Figure 13.7, and 700-point hypnotic data samples were used. It is displayed in a few samples. Figure 13.8 presents a part of the experimental dataset containing hourly values of temperature, humidity, and electrical load (kW), which were used as inputs

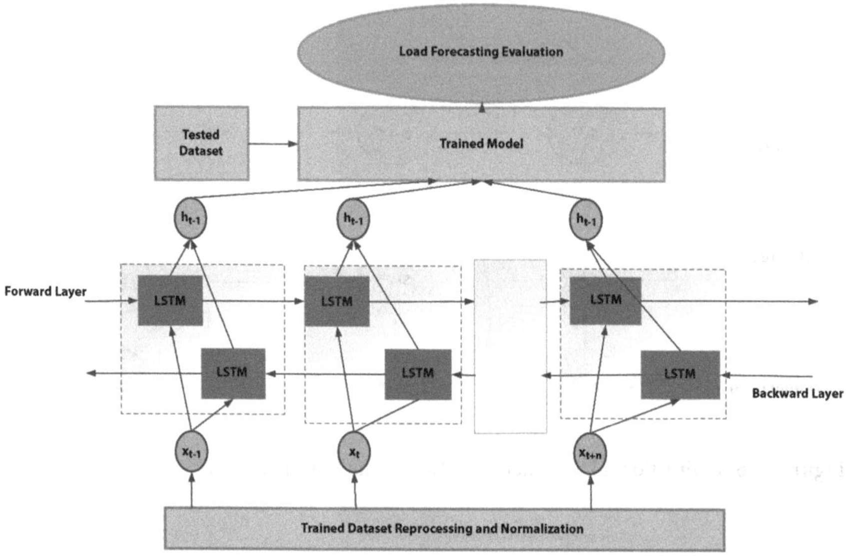

Figure 13.7 The load forecasting framework of the proposed method.

Hours	Temperature	Humidity	Load(kW)
1	13.5	77	124.1667
2	13.44167	78.08333	245.3333
3	13.38333	79.16667	366.25
4	13.325	80.25	483.4167
5	13.26667	81.33333	601.25
6	13.20833	82.41667	715.6667
7	13.15	83.5	830.1667
8	13.09167	84.58333	943.1667
9	13.03333	85.66667	1054.667
10	12.975	86.75	1164.75
11	12.91667	87.83333	1275.583
12	12.85833	88.91667	1384.917
13	12.8	90	1368.667
14	12.73333	89.83333	1354.417
15	12.66667	89.66667	1341
16	12.6	89.5	1330.833
17	12.53333	89.33333	1320.5
18	12.46667	89.16667	1312.75
19	12.4	89	1307.167
20	12.33333	88.83333	1303.917
21	12.26667	88.66667	1303.083
22	12.2	88.5	1304.833
23	12.13333	88.33333	1307.083
24	12.06667	88.16667	1312.583

Figure 13.8 Part of experimental data.

for model training and validation. The 400 epochs that we used contain three iterations per epoch and 1200 total iterations. Input layer has 3 * 700 neurons, the output layer holds one neuron, and hidden layer in the center contains one layer with 10 neurons. The error square was used as the loss function. The choice was made to use the Adam algorithm, a more sophisticated variation of random gradient descent. Through the computation of gradients' first and second moment estimations,

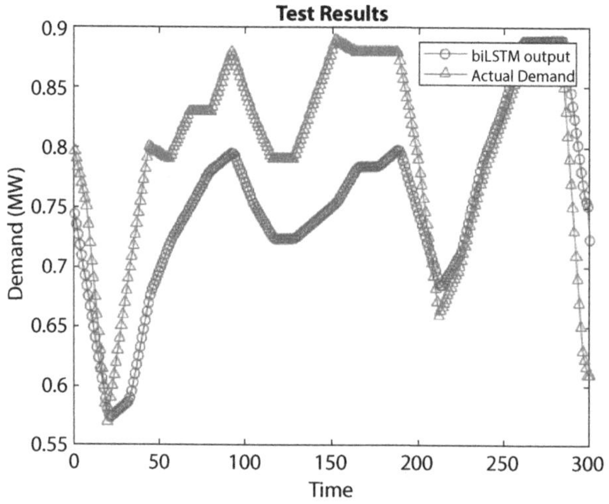

Figure 13.9 Forecasting using BiLSTM versus actual data.

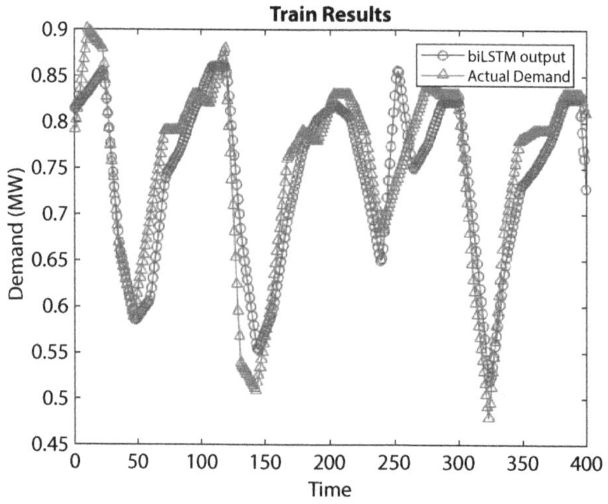

Figure 13.10 Training using BiLSTM versus actual data.

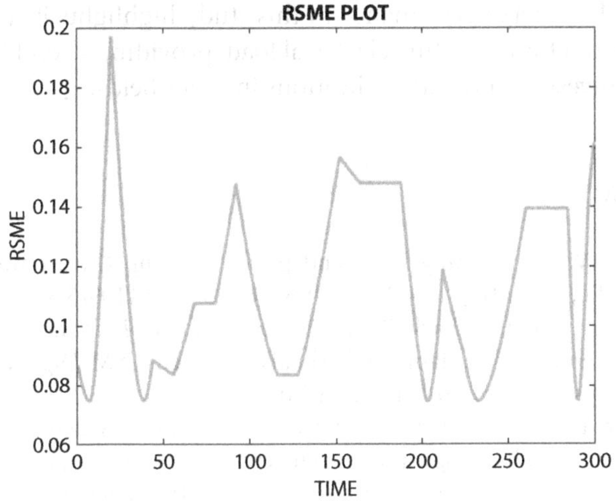

Figure 13.11 Root mean square error graph.

Adam may provide unique adaptive learning rates for different parameters, which can lead to improved results and expedite the process with good applicability. The starting rate of learning is 0.01. Figures 13.9 to 13.11 display the results of the test, train, and root mean square error plots, respectively.

13.6 Conclusion

Energy efficiency is currently a major issue from an environmental and economic standpoint. Testing new technologies for tracking and forecasting electric energy use is essential to address the pressing environmental and economic challenges of energy efficiency. In order to track and forecast electric energy use, new technologies need to be evaluated. To sum up, our study has shown that BiLSTM models perform better when it arises to short-term electrical demand forecasting. Despite the extended training durations needed, we achieved much better prediction accuracy by using only BiLSTM. The BiLSTM model showed strong performance and resilience when applied to various time-series data scales, such as home, building, city zone, and national levels. The results show that BiLSTM models are quite good at forecasting electrical energy use and can produce dependable and accurate predictions. This may be very important for lowering expenses, increasing efficiency, and optimizing energy management.

The BiLSTM model's performance in this study highlights its potential as an effective tool for predicting electrical load, providing a solid foundation for further investigation and applications in other fields.

References

1. Bunn, D.W., Forecasting loads and prices in competitive power markets. *Proc. IEEE*, 88, 2, 163–169, 2000. https://doi.org/10.1109/5.823996.
2. Martinez, D.M., Ebenhack, B.W., Wagner, T., *Energy Efficiency: Concepts and Calculations*, Amsterdam, Netherlands: Elsevier. USM Digital Commons, 2019, https://doi.org/10.1016/C2016-0-02161-7.
3. Himeur, Y., *et al.*, Artificial intelligence based anomaly detection of energy consumption in buildings: a review, current trends and new perspectives. *Appl. Energy*, 287, 116601, 2021. https://doi.org/10.1016/j.apenergy.2021.116601.
4. Ahmad, T., *et al.*, Energetics systems and artificial intelligence: applications of industry 4.0. *Energy Rep.*, 8, 334–361, 2022. https://doi.org/10.1016/j.egyr.2021.11.256.
5. Chollet, F., *Deep Learning with Python*, Shelter Island, NY, USA, 2018.
6. Serpanos, D. and Wolf, M., *Internet-of-Things (IoT) Systems*, Springer International Publishing, Cham, 2018, https://doi.org/10.1007/978-3-319-69715-4_5.
7. Hochreiter, S. and Schmidhuber, J., Long short-term memory. *Neural Comput.*, 9, 8, 1735–1780, 1997. https://doi.org/10.1162/neco.1997.9.8.1735.
8. Haykin, S., *Neural Networks and Learning Machines* (3rd ed.). Upper Saddle River, NJ, USA: Pearson Education (Prentice Hall), DAI, 2009.
9. Gers, F.A. and Schmidhuber, E., LSTM recurrent networks learn simple context-free and context-sensitive languages. *IEEE Trans. Neural Netw.*, 12, 6, 1333–1340, 2001. https://doi.org/10.1109/72.963769.
10. Hamdia, K.M., Zhuang, X., Rabczuk, T., An efficient optimization approach for designing machine learning models based on genetic algorithm. *Neural Comput. Appl.*, 33, 6, 1923–1933, 2021.
11. Alloghani, M., Al-Jumeily, D., Mustafina, J., Hussain, A., Aljaaf, A., A systematic review on supervised and unsupervised machine learning algorithms for data science, in: *Supervised and Unsupervised Learning for Data Science*, pp. 3–21, Springer Cham, Switzerland, 2020.
12. Emmert-Streib, F., Yang, Z., Feng, H., Tripathi, S., Dehmer, M., An introductory review of deep learning for prediction models with big data. *Front. Artif. Intell.*, 3, 4, 2020.
13. Mughees, N., Mohsin, S.A., Mughees, A., Mughees, A., Deep sequence to sequence Bi-LSTM neural networks for day-ahead peak load forecasting. *Expert Syst. Appl.*, 175, 114844, 2021. https://doi.org/10.1016/j.eswa.2021.114844.

14. Rai, A., Shrivastava, A., Jana, K.C., Arobust auto encoder-gated recurrent unit (AE-GRU) based deep learning approach for short term solar power forecasting. *Optik*, 252, 3, 168515, 2022.
15. Yang, Y., Zhong, J., Li, W., Gulliver, T.A., Li, S., Semisupervised multilabel deep learning based nonintrusive load monitoring in smart grids. *IEEE Trans. Ind. Inf.*, 16, 11, 6892–6902, 2019.
16. Sharfuddin, A.A., Tihami, M.N., Islam, M.S., A deep recurrent neural network with BLSTM model for sentiment classification, in: *Proceedings of the International Conference on Bangla Speech and Language Processing (ICBSLP)*, IEEE, pp. 1–4, 2018, https://doi.org/10.1109/ICBSLP.2018.8554396.
17. Liang, Y., Deng, J., Cui, B., Bidirectional LSTM: an innovative approach for phishing URL identification, in: *Innovative Mobile and Internet Services in Ubiquitous Computing: Proceedings of the 13th International Conference on Innovative Mobile and Internet Services in Ubiquitous Computing (IMIS-2019)*, Springer International Publishing, pp. 326–337, 2020, https://doi.org/10.1007/978-3-030-22263-5_32.
18. Schuster, M. and Paliwal, K.K., Bidirectional recurrent neural networks (Nov). *IEEE Trans. Signal Process.*, 45, 11, 2673–2681, 1997. https://doi.org/10.1109/78.650093.
19. Fukada, T., Schuster, M., Sagisaka, Y., Phoneme boundary estimation using bidirectional recurrent neural networks and its applications. *Syst. Comput. Jpn.*, 30, 4, 20–30, 1999.
20. https://doi.org/10.1002/(SICI)1520-684X(199904)30:4%3C20::AID-SCJ3%3E3.0.CO;2-E.
21. Graves, A., *et al.*, A novel connectionist system for unconstrained handwriting recognition. *IEEE Trans. Pattern Anal. Mach. Intell.*, 31, 5, 855–868, 2008. https://doi. org/10.1109/TPAMI.2008.137.
22. Graves, A. and Schmidhuber, J., Framewise phoneme classification with bidirectional LSTM and other neural network architectures. *Neural Netw.*, 18, 5–6, 602–610, 2005. https://doi.org/10.1016/j.neunet.2005.06.042.
23. Graves, A. and Schmidhuber, J., Offline handwriting recognition with multidimensional recurrent neural networks, in: *Advances in Neural Information Processing Systems 21*, pp. 545–552, MIT Press, Cambridge, MA, 2008.
24. FIESC. *Desperdício elétrico no Brasil equivale ao consumo de 20 milhões de residências.* Federação das Indústrias do Estado de Santa Catarina (FIESC), 2022. Available at: https://fiesc.com.br/pt-br/imprensa/desperdicio-eletrico-no-brasil-equivale-ao-consumo-de-20-milhoes-de-residencias (accessed December 2022). arxiv.org
25. Lee, S., Lee, T., Kim, S., Park, S., Energy consumption prediction system based on deep learning with edge computing. In: *2019 International Conference on Electronics, Information, and Communication (ELTECH)*, pp. 473–477, 2019. https://doi.org/10.1109/ELTECH.2019.8839589.

Index

Also of Interest

Check out these related titles from Scrivener Publishing

Quantum-Inspired Approaches for Intelligent Data Processing, Edited by Balamurugan Balusamy, Suman Avdhesh Yadav, S. Ramesh, and M. Vinoth Kumar, ISBN: 9781394336418. Stay ahead of the technological curve with this comprehensive, practical guide that showcases how the fusion of quantum principles and soft computing is delivering transformative solutions across finance, healthcare, and manufacturing.

Supervised and Unsupervised Data Engineering for Multimedia Data, Edited by Suman Kumar Swarnkar, J. P. Patra, Sapna Singh Kshatri, Yogesh Kumar Rathore, and Tien Anh Tran, ISBN: 9781119786344. Explore the cutting-edge realms of data engineering in multimedia with *Supervised and Unsupervised Data Engineering for Multimedia Data,* where expert contributors delve into innovative methodologies, offering invaluable insights to empower both novices and seasoned professionals in mastering the art of manipulating multimedia data with precision and efficiency.

Data Engineering and Data Science: Concepts and Applications, Edited by Kukatlapalli Pradeep Kumar, Aynur Unal, Vinay Jha Pillai, Hari Murthy, and M. Niranjanamurthy, ISBN: 9781119841876. Written and edited by one of the most prolific and well-known experts in the field and his team, this exciting new volume is the "one stop shop" for the concepts and applications of data science and engineering for data scientists across many industries.

Machine Learning and Data Science: Fundamentals and Applications, Edited by Prateek Agrawal, Charu Gupta, Anand Sharma, Vishu Madaan, and Nisheeth Joshi, ISBN: 9781119775614. Written and edited by a team of experts in the field, this collection of papers reflects the most up-to-date and comprehensive current state of machine learning and data science for industry, government, and academia.

DATA WRANGLING: Concepts, Applications, and Tools, Edited by M. Niranjanamurthy, Kavita Sheoran, Geetika Dhand, and Prabhjot Kaurk, ISBN: 9781119879688. Written and edited by some of the world's top experts in the field, this exciting new volume provides state-of-the-art research and latest technological breakthroughs in next-data wrangling, its theoretical concepts, practical applications, and tools for solving everyday problems.

ADVANCES IN DATA SCIENCE AND ANALYTICS, Edited by M. Niranjanamurthy, Hemant Kumar Gianey, and Amir H. Gandomi, ISBN: 9781119791881. Presenting the concepts and advances of data science and analytics, this volume, written and edited by a global team of experts, also goes into the practical applications that can be utilized across multiple disciplines and industries, for both the engineer and the student, focusing on machining learning, big data, business intelligence, and analytics.

CONVERGENCE OF DEEP LEARNING IN CYBER-IOT SYSTEMS AND SECURITY, Edited by Rajdeep Chakraborty, Anupam Ghosh, Jyotsna Kumar Mandal and S. Balamurugan, ISBN: 9781119857211. In-depth analysis of Deep Learning-based cyber-IoT systems and security which will be the industry leader for the next ten years.

MACHINE INTELLIGENCE, BIG DATA ANALYTICS, AND IOT IN IMAGE PROCESSING: Practical Applications, Edited by Ashok Kumar, Megha Bhushan, José A. Galindo, Lalit Garg and Yu-Chen Hu, ISBN: 9781119865049. Discusses both theoretical and practical aspects of how to harness advanced technologies to develop practical applications such as drone-based surveillance, smart transportation, healthcare, farming solutions, and robotics used in automation.

Printed in the USA/Agawam, MA
September 16, 2026

910661.084